BUILDING TRADITION

Copyright © 2018
Marie Rose Wong

ISBN: 978-1634059671

First [1] Edition

Publisher:

Chin Music Press
1501 Pike Place, Suite 329
Seattle, WA 98101
www.chinmusicpress.com

Book design:

Dan D Shafer

Library of Congress Cataloging-in-Publication Data

Names: Wong, Marie Rose, 1954 – author.

Title: Building tradition / by Marie Rose Wong.

Description: First edition. I Seattle, WA : Chin Music Press, 2018.
Includes bibliographical references and index.

Identifiers: LCCN 2018008197 I ISBN 9781634059671 (pbk. : alk. paper)

Subjects: LCSH: Architecture and society–Washington (State)–Seattle. I Single-room
occupancy hotels–Washington (State)–Seattle. I Asian Americans–Washington
(State)–Seattle–Social conditions. I International   District (Seattle, Wash.)–Buildings,
structures, etc. I Seattle (Wash.)–Buildings, structures, etc. I International District
(Seattle, Wash.)–Social conditions. I Seattle (Wash.)–Social conditions.

Classification: LCC NA2543.S6 W64 2018 I DDC 720.1/03--dc23
LC record available at https://lccn.loc.gov/2018008197

BUILDING TRADITION

Pan-Asian Seattle and Life
in the Residential Hotels

MARIE ROSE WONG

CHIN MUSIC
P R E S S

TABLE OF CONTENTS

To the "Main Street Gang," Joe Hamanaka,
Roy Hashimoto, Eddy Sano, and Tad Sato.
Thank you for making me #5.

PREFACE

In 1970, my father took my older brother Victor and me on another of his annual summer trips to the Chinese restaurants of Minnesota. Minneapolis was the first of our three-city stops from our home in Mason City, Iowa, and it was followed by visits to Rochester and Albert Lea, Minnesota. This was my first such trip with Dad as I was now 15 and considered old enough to go to the "big cities" and help him deliver vegetables and fruit to his restaurant friends in exchange for meat and poultry. This yearly journey happened every August at the time of Dad's garden harvest. He said that the vegetable delivery was the primary purpose of the week-long excursion, but my siblings and I knew that it was the camaraderie of conversation with restaurant workers and sharing the mutual experience as Chinese immigrants that made this trip so important to him. It was a way for this small and scattered community of Midwestern Chinese to socialize over the recent news of China, and share updates on people that they all knew. Occasionally, one of the restaurant cooks or workers would be referred to as a "cousin" but there was no explanation on how this connection was possible since it didn't appear that we shared any of the same relatives. Cultural connections created these near-familial ties.

    With each of these stops, we would carry the boxes of apples and pears, and galvanized buckets of vegetables into restaurant kitchens through alleyway doors. At every stop there was a restaurant cook on a break smoking a cigarette and resting on old delivery crates or whatever else was handy and available as a makeshift chair. The intonations of Cantonese pierced the air in these kitchens, echoing off the greasy surfaces of the refrigerators and the metal wall and ceiling panels. We spoke no Chinese so could only speculate on what was being said, with the exception of that initial greeting where nods and slaps on our shoulders indicated approval and good fortune that Dad had so many children: four sons and two daughters. I got special recognition that year as the "youngest of 'that Jimmy Wong's helpers.'" While Dad talked in the kitchen, we were waved toward the dining area, where we took a booth in the back and away from the paying customers. We were fed a meal without ever seeing a menu or making our own selections. I remember hearing Dad laugh from behind the swinging doors, something that I rarely heard him do at home.

I had lived my entire life in our small town. My familiarity with and expectations of cities had all been shaped by what I saw on 1960s television news and augmented with discussions in school. Reading about the grand buildings and opulent interiors of Washington, DC and Iowa's state capital didn't prepare me for what I found on this journey with Dad and Vic.

Motor hotels, or motels, had sprung up all over America by the early 1970s. They were easy to access from the highways, were clean and new, with ample places to park and the added convenience of chain restaurants that were very close by. But Dad preferred to stay in the heart of the city where he could wander the streets and visit other Chinese-operated businesses, like the Kwong Tung Noodle Factory, that were not part of the "business" purpose of these trips. We were there to assist in produce transactions and not provide unsolicited comments about where we would rather stay. His Chinese friends still lived in the skid row hotel buildings that were located in the peripheral fringes of the downtown cores. Dad knew these areas, proprietors, and the buildings very well.

We made our first delivery to the Fireside Ricebowl Restaurant in what was then a northern suburb of Minneapolis. After we finished lunch, we made our way to the first hotel where Dad wanted to stay; not one of the downtown, modern, high-rises but a simple brick mid-rise building that looked a lot like the warehouses in my hometown. We had barely parked the car when Dad shuffled off down one of the side streets. It was typical of him to walk away without a word of goodbye or any information on where he was going. In his old gray suit jacket, mismatched slacks, and loafer-like slipper shoes, no one would have guessed that he always carried $500 in a roll of bills that were bound with a rubber band. Before we had left home, he had given Vic instructions and cash to get us registered for a night at the hotel.

The hotel was on the busiest street I had ever seen in my life. It was filled with occupied cars, and people who were walking, running, and staggering. There were loud voices competing with louder music, car horns honking, and smoke that plumed around crowded doorways of select businesses. Some doors couldn't close from the number of people either trying to get in or out. As the commercial neon signs framed all of the events, the entire scene flashed like an exhibit of old nickelodeon movies at the Iowa State Fair.

My brother put his hand on my shoulder as we walked the long city block on our way to the hotel that was close to the train station parking lot where we left the car. As we approached the hotel entrance, a blackened glass door opened at one of the neighboring commercial storefronts. Out stepped a tall woman wearing stilettos. She was striking with her black hair that was partially managed with long "diamond" barrettes. The black stockings matched her hair and long eyelashes, and the pink powder painting her face nearly blended into her bright lipstick. The hem of her short turquoise dress was sagging a little but the garment glistened like her eye shadow. As we walked past her, I tugged at Vic's jacket and asked him where she might be going but he only pushed me through the hotel door and onto the first of a series of many stairs.

It was difficult to carry what little I had brought and remain steady as we walked up the steep and narrow staircase that had no railing. At the top of the stairs, there was a simple counter, a wire desk fan, and a registry of paper that looked a lot like the tablets we used in grade school. Behind the counter was a man dressed in a wrinkled short-sleeved shirt and slacks that seemed to merge into the smoky cloud of the unventilated area.

While Vic engaged in a conversation, I looked at the small space adjacent to the counter. There was a table that had served a dual purpose as a foot rest and library for the coverless copies of *Reader's Digest* that teetered on the surface edge. A couple of plastic chairs with blistering vinyl repair tape on the arms and backs were on either side of the table. Other than this and a rattling cigarette machine, there was nothing else to see. It was clean but spare. The desk clerk seemed to remember that our dad had stayed there before. Vic and I left our belongings with him and set out in search of Dad and of Chinese food for dinner.

There was always the possibility that we'd find him at the Kwong Tung Noodle Company as it was close to the hotel and was one of his favorite stops. The company occupied the street and mezzanine levels of a building that was shared with the Seville Hotel. The building was much like the one where we were staying but this hotel catered to an exclusively African American clientele. The commercial storefront of the noodle factory sold Chinese foods to neighborhood patrons and a small kitchen in the back provided meals for the employees of the store and the factory workers upstairs. Since Dad knew the owner, we were included in the receipt of a free meal. The mezzanine level had a small office at the far side of the front entrance and one large room that spanned the depth of the building.

The Kwong Tung made Chinese fried crispy noodles that were delivered to various Chinese restaurants in the city and likely to other destinations and the employees were a mix of Caucasian and Chinese workers. According to my brother, in the mid-1960s the company had a small restaurant and was primarily a one-person manufacturing operation. But the Kwong Tung was more than a company or restaurant. It was a gathering point for residents of the neighboring hotels as it created an arena for conversation.

In five years, the company operation had grown, a sure sign that "the Chinese boys were good in business" according to my dad. When Vic and I arrived at the Kwong Tung, a small group of less than a dozen Chinese women were sitting on either side of a flour-dusted conveyor belt. The women deftly scooped the crispy noodles up from the creaking belt and quickly placed them into ten-pound cardboard boxes. At the end of the conveyor, the boxes were whisked away and stacked awaiting shipping and delivery. "Has anyone seen Jimmy Wong?" my brother asked loudly. "Just here...gone!" was the reply. Vic went to the mezzanine window, brushed the combination of flour silt and grease from the glass and pointed his finger to indicate that Dad was a block away and on his way to somewhere else. How could a man who walked so slowly be so difficult to keep up with?

Vic and I left the Kwong Tung and found some dinner in a café between our hotel and the noodle factory. We had spent the afternoon following Dad but never meeting up with him. When we returned to the hotel we found him already snoring in the small room with a single closed window that had been sealed with a few coats of paint. There were three beds there, a double that Dad had already taken and one rollaway each for Vic and me. The room inventory included a small washstand used as a table, no lamp, and some hooks on the wall for clothing. There was no other furniture, and no bathroom or water supply of any kind in the room. Those needs were met down the hall in a communal bathroom that looked a bit like a smaller and danker version of the gym showers at school. I was scared to go down the hall by myself and too embarrassed to ask my brother to take me. I remember what a restless sleep I had that night with no television to watch and nothing else to do but lay on my back, listen to sounds of walking and talking in the hallway, and count the cracks on the ceiling on either side of the dangling bare light bulb . This only light source was located dead center but the missing paint chips made the square ceiling look off balance. As I fell asleep, I found myself wishing that morning would come quickly so that we could leave this place and that Dad would let us stay in a motor lodge when we got to the Rochester stop. I didn't know why our dad chose this hotel and I was really missing home.

  In that first and in subsequent years, the routine was the same in each of the restaurants, hotels, and the cities I visited with Dad. My mother never liked my dad's choice of where we stayed and it was years before I found out that this bias came from her own early experiences when she and Dad had lived in a similar hotel building for three years in Des Moines, Iowa. They had been married less than two years and my sister, Moy, was a baby at the time. As a mixed-race couple, my mother and father were turned away from leasing a number of apartments. From her 1942 letters to a friend, she wrote that "with all of the apartments in the city, none were available to us so we were still living above the King Ying Low restaurant...in a room that was far too small and with everything we owned being stacked along the walls with a narrow path to a dresser and high chair...the soot from the chimney came through the windows and left a film of grime on everything that couldn't be cleaned." With no locks on the door, a man who had too much to drink came into their small single room in the middle of the night when my dad was working the graveyard shift as a restaurant cook. It was a harmless encounter and the man left after my mother asked, "What do you want?" She didn't understand the buildings any more than I did.

  My early city experience of staying in this "odd" hotel and light indus-trial district of Minneapolis resurfaced as a meaningful memory and a personal and professional quest some twenty-five years later. In 1997, as a new assistant professor of urban planning, I had the opportunity to participate as one of the assistant guides for a tour of Seattle's Chinatown-International District. That fall, the National Conference on American Planning History was in Seattle and touring historic neighborhoods was part of the agenda. One of the first stops was the Panama Hotel, a 1910 single-room occupancy (SRO) residential hotel. The exterior of the Panama looked like the hotels of my youth. The only difference was that the businesses and its built history had a direct link with Japanese America.

At the time of the conference, I had lived in Seattle for ten years and had been a practicing urban planner for seventeen years. As a newly-minted academic, I was pleased to have the chance to share the neighborhood that I had come to think of as home. I knew the district through experience with community committee work with the nonprofit agencies, and from shopping, socializing, and enjoying the wide array of Asian American food from any one of the 90 independently-owned and operated restaurants. The majority of my friends either worked or lived in that neighborhood. This is where I spent my time and I was personally vested in this community.

As we passed by the old Republic Hotel, I overheard a discussion that expressed disappointment in the district. "It didn't look like San Francisco's Chinatown...there was no gateway, no 'Asian' ornamentation or colors, no Chinese-looking architecture...the area wasn't even 'officially' called Chinatown." It wasn't "obvious" that the district was Asian American at all. With the exception of two buildings with non-structurally authentic upturned roof eave awnings, almost every other building in the district consisted of turn-of-the-20th-century brick buildings that you could find in the majority of American city centers.

At first, I wanted to defend the district's appearance and as a neighborhood where Asian American youth, elders, and new immigrants still lived and worked. I began to wonder if scholars, tourists, or residents of Seattle understood the Asian American connections with the residential hotels that were such a big part of cultural identity in this south downtown neighborhood of the city. Why was it so easy to dismiss the structures that anchored the livelihood of this ethnic community that began in 1850? The Asian American district with spare facades and interiors of the residential hotel buildings warranted a closer and deeper examination.

It has been over two decades since the end of that conference and the beginning of this project. It has been a personal and professional challenge, mission, and journey of my heart that has helped me understand my father and the history of pan-Asian Seattle through the lens of residential hotel living.

Since that time, I have engaged in hundreds of hours of conversations and interviews with community elders who lived in and operated residential hotels and businesses that helped support the people of this neighborhood. Speaking with the second generation of Asian Americans has been a precious spiritual gift and treasured all the more since many of the elders have passed away since this research began. They openly shared their documents, diaries, photographs, and stories. These and thousands of primary resources and archival documents have been collected and interpreted to tell this history of pan-Asian Seattle, life in the residential hotels, and the early evolution of the district's development.

In the course of understanding these structures and Asian American settlement, and how home, family, community, and "place" have been and are defined, I have come away with much more than this research. I have experienced deeper and more meaningful relationships to many of the Chinese, Japanese, and Filipino American people who have graciously given their time to educate me on the past and provide perspective on the district's future. As interviewees, they patiently answered my questions, and corrected and expanded both my research and my life. The greatest blessing has been the extension of immeasurable personal kindnesses and being adopted and invited to participate as a "family member" at picnics, reunions, and holiday celebrations. It is in this spirit that I discovered a profound connection of a community tradition of belonging that goes far beyond what can readily be seen when looking at the brick building facades in the Chinatown-International District.

The area has had so many labels over the decades in order to identify its location in the south central downtown, with "Chinatown" being the kindest. Even this label has been too frequently tinged with the negative connotation as a neighborhood ghetto. It has always been populated by an interspersed pattern of immigrants and Americans of Asian, Scandinavian, Italian, and German decent along with African and Native Americans, and all of them joined by the common bonds of being part of the city's urban poor.

The cover of this book is of special significance as the screened image is of the East Kong Yick building, one of two such flagship buildings of the Chinatown core. Built as an SRO residential hotel, it was intended to provide for the needs of a population of transient, immigrant Chinese laborers. Having been restored and used for a different function, it still stands as a reminder of early Chinese settlement and the hundreds of occupants who stayed and socialized there. The corporation that built this building and its twin, the West

Kong Yick building, still exists and is one of the oldest and longest-standing licensed corporations in the State of Washington. In 2010 and as part of the centennial recognition of the corporation, former Secretary of State Sam Reed noted that of the 3,200 corporations that were filed in 1910, the Kong Yick company was one of only sixty-five that were still in existence. In 2012, after years of research on this project, I was asked to serve on the board of directors of the Kong Yick Investment Company and in 2015 I became the president of the board. It is an honor to share in this legacy of the district with six other board members whose roots extend back to the first Chinese pioneers who settled in the Pacific Northwest.

My father knew something that he did not or could not explain and that I could not understand as a child but that I would come to learn through time, experience, research, and empathy. In his choice of an SRO to accommodate my brothers and me on our travels, he knew that "families" were often created out of groups of strangers who stayed in seemingly spare residential hotels. It was and is far more than the accommodations and surface decorations that made and make these places home.

INTRODUCTION

Three lone remnants of Seattle's original Chinatown still stand in an area that is west and two blocks away from the current pan-Asian community. These buildings were single-room-occupancy (SRO) residential hotels that were commissioned by Chinese immigrant pioneers Chun Ching Hock and Chin Gee Hee. Built simultaneously, they were the first brick buildings constructed in the lower downtown immediately following Seattle's 1889 fire that devastated the core of the city. Known as the Lexington, Phoenix, and Chin Gee Hee Buildings, they contained ground-level commercial retail stores and restaurants, and services that included employment agencies, an herbalist, a doctor, and a barber. The upper floors were sparely furnished, single-room rentals that served as a home base for their fellow countrymen while they learned the hardships of what it meant to be a Chinese American. Today, the original, splendid brick design of these buildings is barely recognizable as a result of a 1927 major public works program.

These and other subsequently constructed SRO hotels were and are places of cultural memory that reflect an urban and architectural history that is rich with the complexity of economic class, race, gender, and multicultural occupancy.[1] While these hotels have not held a glamorous design reputation in architectural form and are frequently classified as vernacular buildings, they should not be mistakenly seen as structures that are "simple" or "plain" or without intentional design.[2] The Lexington, like many residential hotels that were built throughout the lower downtown, exemplified spatial identity of the Chinese,

Japanese, and Filipino American communities despite the absence of any clear geographic boundaries that demarcated the respective territories of these ethnic groups. The residential hotels of pan-Asian Seattle are core landmarks of community and a means to understand "place" identity in an intricately layered, multi-ethnic neighborhood.[3] In great part the simple, prescriptive design of a commonly recognized turn-of-the century building became an icon of cultural identity and an expression of "architecture as built sociology."[4]

There is also a very practical and driving economic force of the SROs to "place-making" from both a historic and contemporary urban perspective that reflects the role that consumerism played in the design of these structures.[5] Buildings became recognizable to the public for their lodging function. The construction of SRO hotels was driven by resident need and demand and at the same time created a neighborhood of "place identity" for Asian Americans who lived in and operated them. From the perspective of the greater community, the SROs were identified with ethnic communities and the urban poor. In this way, structures and social community created simultaneously developing and shared identities in the urban landscape.[6]

The identity of an SRO is one that is more generally understood than specifically defined by most city planning departments. The term "SRO" is one that is coined as a commonly understood concept, much like the word "duplex," but it is not a term that is typically found in city building codes. Along with the absence of a specific definition that describes the typology of these structures, there is the additional complication of whether these buildings are considered to be temporary lodging, such as a motel, or if they can be considered as a long-term or more permanent residential facility, such as an apartment. In city codes, the presence of a kitchen or private bathroom has helped determine whether the unit was to be used as a place for "dwelling" or for "sleeping." This is a very fine distinction that is open to further questions, particularly when apartment-sized stoves or hot plates are added by the residents for their own convenience, economy, or necessity.

As a building, the SRO hotel holds a special place as a housing option that sprang up throughout American downtown areas in the late nineteenth century and continued to evolve into the economic building boom of the early twentieth century. Some of these modest hotels have survived in towns and cities across the United States through historic recognition, preservation designation, and often from simple neglect that bypasses property redevelopment.

In other areas, residential hotels and supporting neighborhood commercial districts have been razed or altered for capital, renewal, or land redevelopment projects to "higher and better" uses.

In 2001, Seattle's Nisqually Earthquake tested the land use classification and retention of SRO buildings when some of the privately-owned damaged hotels were denied Federal Emergency Management Agency (FEMA) restorative funding because they were not considered to be permanent housing stock, but rather as commercial businesses.[7] Consequently, the residents of these buildings were viewed as temporary lodgers and yet a number of them had lived in these hotels for periods spanning between seven to forty years. In the absence of a decision on whether these buildings were and are commercial or residential, the confusion of how to classify these structures is passed on to the residents who live in them. Like the buildings themselves, the tenants often fall prey to anonymity or neglect by the world outside of the residential hotels and efforts to reach them may be abandoned for any number of reasons that include language, as well as economic and class barriers. For decades, the collection of US Census information in Asian American enclaves has been questionable with misreporting of names and suspected omission of residents in those buildings that were not easily accessible or were deemed undesirable places to enter.[8]

After over a century of residential use, the people who live in the SRO residential hotels are still considered to be transients, just as they had been identified in the late 1800s when questions regarding the moral health of individuals living in close quarters spawned so much interest from social reformers. The people are typically lower-income; a status that is equated to a condition that bears a strong social stigma. Poverty has come to be viewed as a crime in itself. Even more sobering are the many labels that are attached to the residents and buildings, the majority of which portray a picture of loneliness, drunkenness, decadence, and depravity. The SRO people bear the same stigma that the Asian American communities have had since their initial settlements.

Seattle's waves of Asian immigration began with significant arrivals of Chinese in the 1870s followed by Japanese in the 1880s and Filipinos in the 1920s, all of which coincide with the development height of SRO hotel construction. The difference in their arrival timeframes could have kept the communities in separate geographies or neighborhoods, but this was not the case. While other cities, such as San Francisco and Los Angeles, developed urban patterns of individual and more clearly defined ethnic communities of Chinatown, Japantown, and some with a Manilatown, Seattle's south downtown neighborhood has always been the home to all three of these groups.[9]

As Seattle was growing as a major port city, the Chinese, Japanese, and Filipino American community was also being shaped by the passage of federal and local legislation. In the national arena, all three of these groups were prey to discriminatory federal immigration laws that marked efforts to keep their labor out of the United States during periods of cyclical national economic depression, and property ownership out of the hands of Asian immigrants. The series of these laws, beginning with Chinese Exclusion (1882), followed by the Alien Land Laws (1913, 1921), Immigration Law of 1924, and the Tydings-McDuffie Act (1934), were each tailored to a specific group of Asians that directly affected the respective demography and development of the social community, and that in turn shaped the needs of the physical community in spatial location, building design, and types of businesses.[10]

At no time was the presence of the pan-Asian population ever free from a myriad of regulations. It was a legacy that passed from one group to another as laws and public sentiment saw each successive Asian American group gain or fall out of favor. In the end, the legal measures that continued to evolve excluded them from participation in specific aspects of the "American Dream" in citizenship and private property ownership.

The pan-Asian area could be identified by their businesses and homes, but their tenure on the land that they occupied was anything but secure for them. Land ownership was inextricably linked with legislative and court decisions on color, assimilation, country of origin, and the issue of defining "race" that was central to determining the right to become a naturalized citizen. For the Chinese, the debate was introduced following the Civil War with the ratification of the 14th Amendment to the Constitution in 1870, which included a right of naturalization for "persons of African descent," but was not extended to the Chinese. Explicitly stated, land ownership was forbidden to Chinese immigrants because of their ineligibility for citizenship. The 14th Amendment was applied a second time to Filipino immigrants as they entered the United States as US Nationals following the Spanish–American War and as the Philippines began its decades-long protectorate status. While they were allowed to immigrate with US passports, legal rights for Filipino Nationals stopped short of the opportunities afforded citizens, including property ownership.

The same connection of citizenship with property ownership occurred with the passage of the Alien Land Law in California in 1913 with an extension that prohibited majority control of stock in a company that would potentially try to own land. In 1920 the law was expanded to prohibit the transferring of land to noncitizens, which prevented anyone from making such purchases on behalf of immigrant Japanese. Washington followed suit, as did eight other states, and passed their respective version of the law in 1921 with an extension of restrictions in 1922 that prohibited leasing, renting, and sharecropping of land.[11] The effect of the law that prohibited leasing was most keenly felt by those Japanese agricultural operations that were unable to extend the three-year maximum time frame for leased land and who depended on selling produce to Japanese-operated businesses in urban Seattle. For some Japanese, if only for a short time, there was a possibility of purchasing property in the name of their American-born children, but transferring land to alien parents would not be possible. The state reserved the power to claim any property that was procured in an illegal fashion. It is a certainty that some property was purchased through the second generation, *Nisei* children, though the exact number of such transactions along with the court cases challenging these purchases is unknown.

As Chinese Exclusion Law effectively reduced immigration and the size of the community, the numbers of Washington Japanese immigrants were increasing in both rural and urban areas between 1910 and 1930. One estimate for 1917 was that 70 percent of vegetable production in and around Seattle was being done by the Japanese, even with the high leasing rental fees and unreasonable terms.[12] The Japanese American community was showing a strong urban presence in business ventures that included groceries, laundries, dry cleaning, sundry shops, restaurants, and most notably in their operation of residential hotels.

The nature of a transient lifestyle that followed the fishing season to Alaska, and harvesting of agricultural crops kept Filipinos migrating up and down the West Coast in the agricultural belts of the San Joaquin Delta in California, Willamette Valley in Oregon, and the Yakima Valley in Washington. Like the Asian laborers before them, "home" was made in the rooms of the residential hotels. Few fully-developed, independent enclaves of Filipino businesses formed in American cities, but pockets of identity from labor contracting and other business enterprises appeared scattered throughout urban cores and amid the already established neighborhood of Seattle's Chinese and Japanese Americans.

One of the earliest recorded documents showing Asian American Seattle is from 1890 when the Immigration and Naturalization Service devised a map that was used as part of the local interrogation process for Chinese immigration. Like all US immigration stations, officials in Seattle used landmarks and locations in the city to help verify personal identity and the right to land for incoming Chinese immigrants. While the number of Chinese businesses was still very modest, the map recognized how scattered these and their residences were and that any property from the waterfront eastward to 6th Street, and from Mill Street (now Yesler Way) south to King Street encompassed what could be considered the "Chinese District."

Firsthand knowledge of the city and the ability to answer questions correctly about building interiors, exteriors, and their location was often the deciding factor on admittance or deportation. A common question for an immigrant Chinese claiming Seattle as their home was their knowledge of the location of the Wa Chong Company and ability to identify the physical layout of "Chinatown" through location of its streets and transportation facilities, its mercantile stores as landmarks , and the specific features of the residential hotels. Questions never surfaced that asked about the community boundaries of Chinatown. At various times throughout the history of this community, there have also been residents that have represented a smaller number of Scandinavian, Italian, and Native and African Americans but who did not gain a separate or specialized identity classification within the neighborhood.[13] Other ethnic groups that include more recent Asian and African immigrants keep the neighborhood populated and new businesses evolving. With each successive addition, these ethnic groups have lived and worked with and among one another in a shared location that has grown, intermingled, and shifted.[14]

The occupancy of so many ethnic people has always put the neighborhood in somewhat of a crisis as to what the district's name should be and still be able to give recognition to each group that has contributed to its history, growth, and development. For the first half of the twentieth century, part of the current pan-Asian neighborhood was recognized as Chinatown and part as Japantown, but the identity of these "places" was intuitive, internally understood by the residents, and based on the respective histories and stories that had been passed down to successive generations. As in the past, the depicted boundaries

MAP I-1: *Immigration Interrogation Map [Chin Kung Shun, RS 1672; Chinese Exclusion Act Case Files, Seattle District; RG 85; The National Archives at Seattle]*

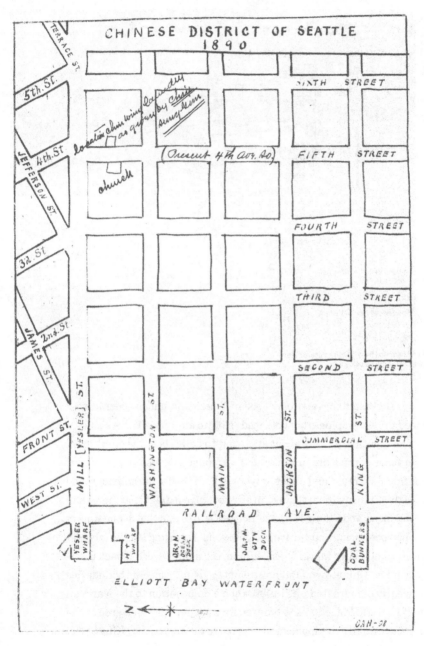

MAP I-2: *Chinatown-International District Boundaries [Author]*

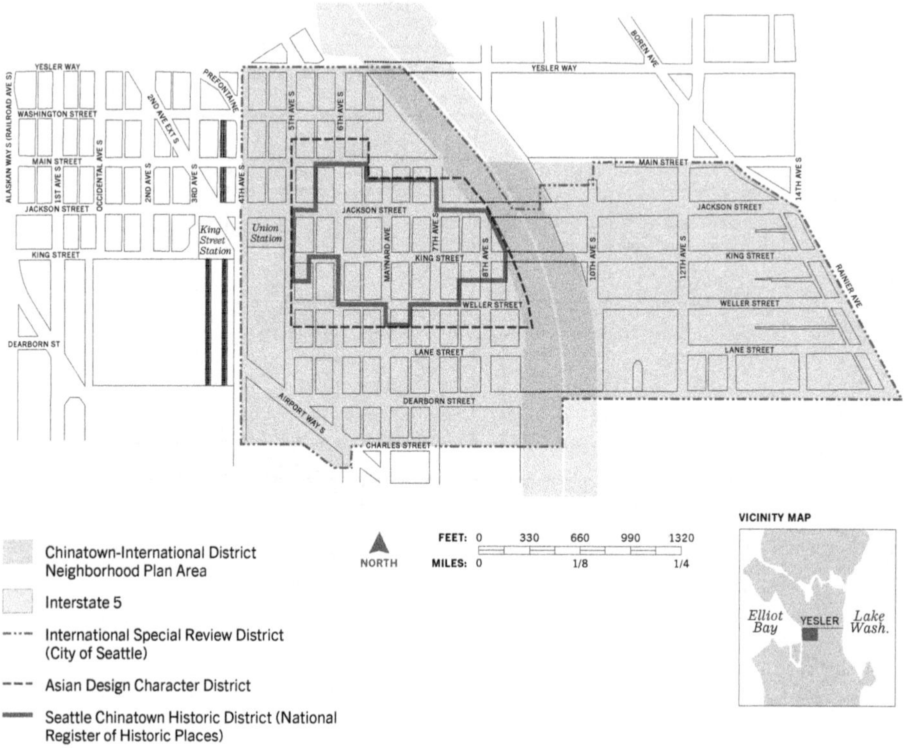

Chinatown-International District
Neighborhood Plan Area

Interstate 5

International Special Review District
(City of Seattle)

Asian Design Character District

Seattle Chinatown Historic District (National
Register of Historic Places)

FEET: 0   330   660   990   1320
NORTH   MILES: 0   1/8   1/4

VICINITY MAP

Elliot Bay   YESLER   Lake Wash.

on city maps suggested the territory of Asian Americans, but no specific lines apportioned the geographies that belonged solely to any one of these groups.

The identity of the district and what to call it became significant during the years of the Korean War and in response to a resurgence of anti-Asian sentiments. In 1951 and under Mayor William Devin, the neighborhood was coined the "International Center" in an effort to recognize that more than Chinese, Japanese, and Filipinos had settled in the area and that at one time or another it had been a multicultural district beyond Asian and Pacific Islander roots. In 1972 and under Mayor Wes Uhlman, the name reverted back to the more descriptive "Chinatown." But no attempt to identify specific boundaries was ever clearly demarcated until 1986 when a nomination to the National Register of Historic Places was submitted for a seventeen-block area of the neighborhood. Initially, the application referred to the area as the "King Street

Historic District" that encompassed old Chinatown. Community complaints that the title of the application did not accurately recognize the neighborhood's varied Asian roots led to a name change and ultimate approval of the district as the "Seattle Chinatown Historic District." Yet on closer examination of the neighborhood's past, many of the buildings of the "Chinatown District" are clearly and historically associated with the development of Japanese or Filipino Seattle, which puts the title of the National Register designation into question.

In 1988, City Ordinance 119297 was passed that amended and expanded the state-mandated Seattle Comprehensive Plan to incorporate neighborhood plans throughout the city and the "Chinatown-International District (C-ID) Strategic Plan" was developed. But the adoption of the neighborhood plan's title did not establish that this was the "official" title of the district, "nor was this direction expressed in the strategic planning document."[15] Even without being official, the "C-ID" label continued under the mayoral office of Paul Schell in 1998.

In the absence of a name that satisfied the area's multi-ethnic identity and in efforts to remain "politically correct" without any show of favoritism, the district unofficially reverted to using a more generic "International District" or "ID" in 2007. It has been argued that the attempts to find the perfect unifying municipal name for the district have had, in many ways, the opposite effect. Such a label has stripped the district of a more descriptive phrase that gives a clear mental picture of Asian American identity. The word "International" simply has too many possibilities.

There are elders of the Chinese community and descendents of those early Chinese settlers who are clearly dissatisfied with the loss of identity in the acronym "ID," as they deem it to be disrespectful of that first Chinese immigrant community that came to Seattle in the 1860s. In 1983, Paul Woo, President of the Chong Wa Benevolent Association, was quoted as saying that "of the area that has become known as the International District, there is a part of that area that always has been and always will remain Chinatown. Without Chinatown there is no International District."[16]

Reinforcement that this was indeed Chinatown in the minds of the descendents of the original Chinese immigrant settlers came in 2008 when the community dedicated the Chinatown Gateway at the intersection of 5th Avenue South and South King Street. It was a celebration of a structure that was fifty years in the making as long-time resident and community leader Tuck Eng and the members of the Historic Chinatown Gate Foundation garnered financial and community support and finally the city's approval to build it.[17] The new Chinatown Gateway marked an entrance to the Chinese community, but it was more symbolic than an actual location that marked the official geography of a Chinatown boundary.

So much of Japantown is gone from years of renewal, redevelopment, and neglect that began in earnest with the WWII period of community evacuation and incarceration that the reports of Japantown's boundaries and location have been as unclear as that of the extent of Chinatown. The recollections by the *Nisei* of the remnants of Japanese businesses near the node of South Main Street and 6th Avenue South, and a significant core of community anchors, such as the Japanese Language School at 14th and Weller, have helped to keep the *"Nihonmachi"* geography alive.[18] Even with the absence of physical structures, the area is still acknowledged by people in and out of the area as the place where a booming Japantown once stood. City sustainable landscape projects, such as the Maynard Avenue South Green Street Project , have reinforced a commitment to retain and celebrate both place memory and the tangible evidence of what still remains.[19] There is very little documentation on how expansive Nihonmachi was or awareness of how much has really been lost of this Seattle community. Instead, more emphasis is placed on the location that was the node or core of Japantown.

The present Filipino community, as well as the *Manongs* as the first generation of immigrants from the Philippines who settled in the C-ID in the 1920s, refer to the general locations of the district as Japantown or Chinatown. The label of "Manilatown" was reserved for cities with communities that showed a concentration of Filipino businesses, such as those found in San Francisco, Sacramento, or Stockton. Historically, the Filipinos living in or referring to the C-ID never thought of any part of the district as "Manilatown." This latter term was coined well after the presence of Filipinos first appeared in America and during the time of the 1970s Asian American Movement and the associated development of Asian American Studies as an academic discipline.

This book is a regional history of Seattle's early Chinese, Japanese, and Filipino American community and is written from the perspective of an urban planner and historian. With so much uncertainty on borders, boundaries, and elements that identify the C-ID community, this book provides an account of the multi-layered settlement process of Seattle's Asian American historic core through urban planning and development history, and the construction of the city's single-room occupancy residential hotels. It is not a book on critical race theory or one that is written from the lens of transnational or post-colonial studies, but rather serves to augment and inform such approaches as scholars continue to seek interpretations and understanding of the pan-Asian American experience.[20]

This study is based, in great part, on over fourteen years of sifting through thousands of primary research materials that include state, county, and city archival documents, such as corporate records, memoranda, and ordinances; personal and business correspondence and ledgers; court records, hearings, assessor's data, and public testimonies; family diaries; city infrastructure and title records; and articles from newspapers and journals. The richest of these research materials and the soul of this work came from extensive conversations and over one hundred interviews with former and current C-ID residents who were and are second-generation Asian Americans and who served as the bridge for and voice of their immigrant parents. Without exception, it was the expressed wish of contributors that they not be portrayed as victims but as individuals who built homes, a community, and this city. This is their story of strength, tenacity, and fortitude. Their reflections provide richness to the framework of policies and legislation.

Together the documents and recollections provide the foundation for understanding the evolving settlement patterns of these three social communities and where their lives intersected with the development of an American building type that provided both home and economic livelihood. In this way Asian American Seattle was defined as much by economic class as by issues of race. Specifically, this story examines how the community was defined by and through the architecture of the single-room occupancy (SRO) residential hotels that were constructed in tandem with the population growth of Asian American Seattle. SRO hotels dominated the urban landscape of the district along with associated urban planning and policy development that directly contributed to building, shaping, and connecting the residents to this diverse neighborhood.[21]

The term "community" is most typically defined by a number of academic disciplines as being an interactive product of social and physical components that include people and the built world, but there is also the "spirit" of community that unites the two and provides an additional dimension of "place" and community identity.[22] "Spirit" is influenced by culture and culture influences how the community and "place" are defined. For Chinese, Japanese, and

Filipino Americans, life was lived within a communal setting of relationships where the individual was secondary to the security of the community. The personal costs of being in America without being considered an American were very high prices that the Asian immigrants paid with grace. The immigrant generation of these groups placed great hope in fairness, dignity, and success that would surely be realized for their American-born children. The connection of history and tradition to the present was as significant as the connection of the individual to the common good. While many avenues for civic input were inhibited or prohibited, the Asian American communities in Seattle developed and relied upon community engagement within their close, and sometimes closed, social circles. It was a means of surviving so much hostility and they did so with courage and dignity.

The history of Seattle's Asian America is one where the function of community is the epitome of what French historian and political scientist Alexis de Tocqueville admired so much about community engagement in his 1830s visit to America, and a modification of which recent writings on social capital celebrate.[23] It was and is recognized that the "forming of associations" and civic engagement are measures of the strength and success of the greater community and of "place making." It is also a testament to the character of the individuals within the community.

This book contributes to both the existing literature on SRO hotels and broadens our understanding of design expression and community development as it relates to Asian American settlement.[24] Two works have been particularly influential in writing this history. Kazuo Ito's book, entitled *Issei: A History of Japanese Immigrants in North America,* was written about Japanese American settlement in the Pacific Northwest. It is not widely known in the history, design, or city planning professions, but it is well noted in the ethnic community with almost every Japanese American household owning a copy. In 1965, Ito, a Japanese journalist, made his first visit to America to begin collecting information about the Japanese immigrant experience and the formation of the Japantowns of Seattle, Spokane, Tacoma, and Vancouver, British Columbia. He used documents from the Japanese Foreign Ministry and personal accounts and interviews to reconstruct a history of the communities and capture the voices of the immigrant first generation or *Issei.* Written in Japanese, the thousand-page book was later translated into English in 1972 by Shinichiro Nakamura and Jean S. Gerard. Included in the text is a small chapter about the

"Cheap Hotels and Flop-houses" and other major businesses that helped shape the commercial economy of the neighborhood.

A second meaningful work was published in 1986 by architectural and cultural historian Paul Groth. It addressed the range of multi-family living units that was and is part of our central cities in *Living Downtown: The History of Residential Hotels in the United States*. This is a seminal work that included single-room occupancy residential housing, and reiterated the need for and the shortage of "literature [that described] the building types or the social history woven into the available range of single room housing."[25] In over three decades since that acknowledgement, there continues to be a modest body of literature that has been written about the single-room occupancy (SRO) residential hotel as an American building type or its connection to place-making and culture.

This book is divided into six chapters. **Chapter 1** provides a description of Seattle's early platting and development as a city, the arrival and growth of the Asian American community and their intersection with the city's geography, buildings, and construction. Amid legal sanctions each group in turn found their livelihood and identity in their own supportive "non-clave" system.[26] The profile of the first settlements of Chinatown and Japantown are set within the early and pre-industrialized development of Seattle and as the city was growing and attempting to establish a strong national and international identity.

Chapter 2 introduces the dichotomy of civic embarrassment and pride. The City of Seattle was making determinations on a redline district and the politics of dealing with prostitution and vice within a growing urban population while engaging in large scale redevelopment projects that created a new geography and development potential for property north and south of Yesler Way that divided the north and south downtown areas.[27] The vice district and capital improvement projects had direct bearing on settlement and the day-to-day life for Chinese, Japanese, and Filipino immigrants within the city. Seattle's planning for a world's fair paralleled the recognition that the booster spirit could create beauty and economic gain amid political acceptance that designation of a vice district was also necessary for planning the city.

Chapter 3 provides a discussion of the typology of single-room occupancy residential hotels and the conflicts that have existed in defining the qualities and characteristics of lodging that would earn the title of "hotel." The stories of two of the primary entrepreneurs and land developers who were instrumental in building residential hotels are included in this chapter. Former

Klondike gold miner William Chappell was a developer of bawdy houses and prostitution hotels. Chinese immigrant Goon Dip spearheaded the construction of SROs that would serve an immigrant community of Chinese, Japanese, and Filipinos in what became the core of the relocated Chinatown of Seattle at the turn of the twentieth century. The construction of these and other small developer hotels were the dominant building type south of Yesler Way and in an area that was known as being "below the line" of propriety and morality.

Chapter 4 profiles the architect-designed residential hotels and the means by which the pan-Asian population of Seattle was involved in property and business ownership even as the laws worked to prevent their citizenship and consequent property ownership. This chapter also provides perspective on the businesses and services that supported the neighborhood of SRO hotel residents and the vice activities that shared the neighborhood. Portions of hundreds of interviews taken during the course of this research are included in Chapters 4 and 5, providing a rich perspective on community life and the people who lived and worked in the residential hotel buildings.

In Chapter 5 Seattle's neighborhood of Asian Americans is discussed as a district that was shared by a multi-ethnic and diverse population and in a neighborhood where the common bond was sharing a lower economic class distinction. Families, transient laborers, short- and long-term single residents, inebriates, gamblers, and prostitutes added to the pastiche of the Asian American neighborhood. All of these people were in some way affected by the organizational structures that created sophisticated systems of hotel operation in the Asian American community amid a sense of family, personal responsibility, and transplanted traditions from home countries. Maps in this chapter are original artwork developed from translated Japanese hotel directories, Sanborn Fire Insurance Maps, and Polk City Directories.

Chapter 6 provides an examination of local legislation in ordinances and fire codes that challenged the viability of the SRO as a part of Seattle's downtown low-income housing stock and as a new economic threat to the Asian American community.

Concluding commentary in the Epilogue reviews policies, programs, and development that have worked toward and against the rebirth of the Chinatown-International District and the SRO residential hotels.

ENDNOTES

1   Dolores Hayden, *The Power of Place: Urban Land-scapes as Public History* (Cambridge: MIT Press, 1995), p. 46.

2   Notable exceptions of early books addressing SRO hotels include Robert Hamburger, *All the Lonely People: Life in a Single Room Occupancy Hotel* (New York: Ticknor and Fields, 1983), and Charles Hoch and Robert A. Slayton, *New Homeless and Old* (Philadelphia: Temple University Press, 1989).

3   Dan Abramson, Lynne Manzo and Jeffrey Hou, "From Ethnic Enclave to Multi-Ethnic Translocal Community: Contested Identities and Urban Design in Seattle's Chinatown-International District," *Journal of Architectural and Planning Research*, 23:4 (Winter, 2006), pp. 341–360.

4   Dolores Hayden, "The Meaning of Place in Art and Architecture," *Design Quarterly*, No. 122 (1983), pp. 18–20. In 2008, the *Amerasia Journal* dedicated an issue to the question of "How Do Asian Americans Create Places?" In it, scholars acknowledged an increasing need to examine Asian America in terms of *foregrounding* spatial dimensions in order to understand "how Asian Pacific Americans use space/place, how experience is embedded in place, and how space holds memories that implicate people and events."

5   John Chase, "Consumerism in American Architecture," *Journal of Architectural Education*, Vol. 44, No. 4 (Aug., 1991), pp. 211–224. http://www.jstor.org/stable/1425143, accessed 27/01/2013. Chase distinguishes consumerist architecture from traditional vernacular architecture in that the former "induces consumption" (p. 211) while the latter is, among other possibilities, a cultural building practice. In the case of the residential hotels, they were both.

6   Jan Lin: *The Power of Urban Ethnic Places: Cultural Heritage and Community Life* (New York: Routledge, 2011), p. 243. In a contemporary sense, understanding and acknowledging these ethnic sites can meaningfully contribute to local preservation efforts in an age of urban sustainability, promote local history, and serve as a mechanism to encourage tourism and enhance economies.

7   Federal Emergency Management Agency (FEMA) money was made available to those hotels that were under the control of non-profit organizations such as the Seattle Public Development Authority.

8   In 2010, the postal service and City of San Francisco entered into litigation over non-delivery of mail to individuals living in Chinatown's SROs; an action that is both illegal and socially marginalizing.

9   "Manilatown" is but one accepted designation that is used to identify an historic (extinct or extant) or more recently settled enclave, area, population concentration, neighborhood, or district of Filipino Americans. There are other titles that are given to describe these areas, some of which have been officially designated by municipal ordinance. Much of selecting a title to reflect the Filipino community depends on the city that had or has these areas and the input of the local community that recognizes the heritage and place of origin of the first Filipino immigrants who settled there. Stockton, California refers to the Filipino American settlement area as "Little Manila" with a city resolution officially designating the "Little Manila Historical Site" in 2000; the first such designation in the US. In August 2002, the City of Los Angeles officially designated one of the first and enduring areas of Filipino American settlement as "Historic Filipinotown" (sometimes referred to as "Hi Fi"). In San Francisco, the historic Filipino settlement that was an area centered around the Kearny Street corridor and adjacent to Chinatown has been referred to as "Manilatown" and also "Filipino Town" with a more recently established Filipino community in the South of Market (SoMa) neighborhood and officially designated as the "SoMa Pilipinas Filipino Cultural Heritage District" in 2002. In September 2017, Seattle Resolution 31769 included "Filipino Town" as an integral part of the C-ID neighborhood. The resolution adopted the nomenclature that was used in the nomination of the historic pan-Asian core to the National Register of Historic Places in 1986.

10 The Immigration Act of 1924 established a national origins quota system that limited immigration numbers to 2% of the foreign-born nationalities who were in the United States in 1890 and with preference provisions given to arrivals

from Western European countries. The 1890 cutoff date was significant as the total number of immigrants from Southern and Eastern European countries (such as Italy, Greece, Bulgaria, Poland, and Russia) would be based on smaller numbers of arrivals that took place before the major waves of immigration from these countries. With Chinese Exclusion law in place and growing dissatisfaction with the Gentlemen's Agreement by exclusionists, the 1924 law would have the same effect as Chinese Exclusion in prohibiting the entry of Japanese into the US. Clause (13C) of the Act stated that immigration for permanent residence would not be allowed for aliens ineligible for citizenship. While it did not specifically say "Japanese," the intention of the law was clear since naturalization to Asian immigrants was prohibited. Sixty Eighth Congress. SESS.I. Ch. 185, 190. 1924."An act to limit the migration of aliens into the United States" (approved May 26, 1924). The Statutes at Large of the United States of America, from December, 1923 to March, 1925. Vol. XLII, Part 1, pp. 153–169 (Washington, DC: Government Printing Office, 1925).

11 Washington's Territorial Legislature passed an Alien Land Law in 1853 that barred non-citizens from owning property. Any lease agreements or purchase arrangements that were made prior to passage of the 1921 law were held as valid transactions. The Alien Land Law was not repealed in Washington until 1966.

12 Sydney Strong and U.G. Murphy, "Report of the Committee on Orientals" (Seattle, Seattle Ministerial Federation, 1917), p. 4.

13 I am grateful to Professor Gary Kinté Perry, Sociology and Global African Studies at Seattle University, for his invaluable assistance in clarifying the "racial formation of B/blackness" with use of the terms "Black/black American" and "African American." Both terms are used throughout this manuscript with recognition that the current literature acknowledges that a preferred racial terminology remains a point of debate. Whenever possible, the selection of the term that is used reflects historically relevant language and/or as the preferred reference of the population.

14 These dates account for significant numbers of these immigrant groups, though it should be noted that the Territorial Census indicates one Japanese female in Washington Territory in

1880 and a small number of Filipino immigrants who were in Washington State as early as 1910, according to the US Census.

15 Official Correspondence of Hazel Bhang Barnett, Deputy Director, Department of Neighborhoods, City of Seattle, dated 18 August 2009.

16 "Chinatown Right Name," *Seattle Post-Intelligencer*, 11 March 1983, p. A10, col. 2.

17 Unlike San Francisco, the City of Seattle made the decision not to fund any maintenance of the Gateway. This is the long-term responsibility of the foundation.

18 Sometimes the area is also referred to as "Japantown."

19 In 1992, one block of Maynard Avenue South between Main and Jackson Streets was designated as a Green Street or an urban landscape area. As such, it is intended to provide pedestrians with a walkway that includes a linear open space or park-like experience. The design of this street included community involvement meetings with Interim Community Development Association. The street serves as a landscaped open space connection between the Danny Woo Community Garden to the north and Hing Hay Park to the south. Design elements of the Maynard Avenue Green Street include a water feature that captures rooftop storm water runoff, plantings, signage, benches, and public art.

20 Scholarship in Asian American Studies includes a wide range of complex perspectives and subject matter that embrace interdisciplinary work and extends to theoretical perspectives including critical race, transnational, and post-colonial theories. For recent research and writing in these areas, the reader is encouraged to see Mary Ting Yi Lui, *The Chinatown Trunk Mystery: Murder, Miscegenation, and Other Dangerous Encounters in Turn-of-the-Century New York City* (Princeton, NJ: Princeton University Press, 2005); Scott Kurashige, *The Shifting Grounds of Race: Black and Japanese Americans in the Making of a Multiethnic Los Angeles* (Princeton, NJ: Princeton University Press, 2008); Kornel Chang, *Pacific Connections: The Making of the US-Canadian Borderlands* (Berkeley: University of California Press, 2012); and Shelley Sang-Hee Lee, *Claiming the*

Oriental Gateway: Prewar Seattle and Japanese America (Philadelphia: Temple University Press, 2012).

21 Hayden refers to this as "place memory" that "triggers social memory through the urban landscape" that reveals common connections to a shared public past, p. 46.

22 Some of the more noted and classic definitions of "community" that are people- and place-focused include those that are presented by Herbert Gans, *The Urban Villagers* (New York: Free Press, 1982); Charles Abrams, *Language of Cities: A Glossary of Terms* (New York: Viking Press, 1971); Del Upton, *America's Architectural Roots, Ethnic Groups that Built America* (New York: John Wiley & Sons, 1986); and Edward Relph, *The Modern Urban Landscape* (Baltimore: Johns Hopkins University Press, 1973).

23 Robert D. Putnam, *Bowling Alone* (New York: Simon and Schuster, 1973), p. 17. Putnam notes that the segregation that occurred based on race, gender, and social class skewed representation in civic engagement.

24 Dell Upton and John Michael Vlach, eds., *Common Places: Readings in American Vernacular Architecture* (Athens: University of Georgia Press, 1986), xvi–xvii and as quoted in Paul Groth, "Making New Connections in Vernacular Architecture," *Journal of the Society of Architectural Historians*, 58.3, (Sept. 1999), pp. 444–451. http://www.jstor.org/stable/991538. Accessed 27 January 2013.

25 Paul Groth, "Marketplace Vernacular Design: The Case of Downtown Rooming Houses," in *Perspectives in Vernacular Architecture, II*, Camille Wells, ed. (Columbia: University of Missouri Press, 1986), p. 180. Groth assumes the challenge of the shortage of research on hotel housing in his book *Living Downtown: The History of Residential Hotels in the United States* (Berkeley: University of California Press, 1994).

26 "Non-clave" refers to the cohesion of a community that is based on social structure and shared goals and identity as opposed to geographic location alone, such is produced in an enclave or ghetto. For a full description, see Marie Rose Wong, *Sweet Cakes, Long Journey: The Chinatowns of Portland Oregon.* (Seattle and London: University of Washington Press, 2004, 2011), p. 267.

27 According to the *Encyclopedia of Prostitution and Sex Work*, Melissa Ditmore, ed., (Westport: Greenwood Press, 2006), the term "sex worker" is the current and more inclusive term to describe a commercial profession that includes prostitution without implying societal disvalue of the individual practitioner. For the purpose of this work, the word "prostitute" or "prostitution" refers to the historic language used in civil and municipal codes at the time.

Asian American Seattle and the Laws of Land

Platting the City of Seattle began shortly after the 1853 arrival of the Denny Party, a group of settlers that included the families of Arthur Denny, Asa Mercer, Carson Boren, and Charles C. Terry. With the specific intention of developing a town site, the Denny Party seized the opportunity to acquire land through the Donation Land Claim Act of 1850. Section 4 of the Act promoted homestead settlement in the Pacific Northwest by offering an opportunity for land ownership and the profit that could be made from property with a modest investment of time. The Act linked the importance of nationality, race, and citizenship to property ownership. In part, it "granted to every white settler...being a citizen of the United States, or having made a declaration...of his intention to become a citizen...the quantity of one half section...of land...."[1]

The first two plats of Seattle were filed on 23 May 1853. Arthur Denny and Carson D. Boren established a grid pattern on land that ran parallel to the shoreline of Elliott Bay, and David Swinson "Doc" Maynard aligned a second and separate grid pattern that was designed to a true north–south orientation. The east-to-west road known as Mill Street acted as a "seam" that joined the two plats, but the resulting connections of north–south-running streets did not always find a ready or easy alignment.[2] It was the unofficial but acknowledged boundary that divided the commercial, business, and financial center that was developing to the north from the south downtown. Far more wooden-framed buildings were constructed and the city had laid almost three times the number of wooden-planked sidewalks in the area north of the Mill Street "dividing line."[3]

The real significance of these two separately-filed grid plans went beyond the street alignments and directional orientation in that each of these plats was thought of differently when it came to the development type, identity, and reputation of Seattle's central city real estate, and the economic class and race of people who lived and worked there. Whether related to the legend and reputation of Maynard as a man who had a high tolerance for a bawdy lifestyle and vice within the City, or from the evolving laws and lawlessness in the first century of Seattle's history, Maynard's Plat was referred to in polite society as that area "below the line" and the line was Mill Street.

In 1870 and in one of the earliest city directories for Washington Territory, the area south of Mill Street was recognized as the "Lava Beds...a slang term applied to the saw-dust fill...[and the] wild and unimproved land."[4] The geographic area that was created by Mill Street to the north, 14th Avenue South to the east, Dearborn Avenue to the south, and 1st Avenue South as the western boundary was shared by gamblers, thieves, drunkards, transients, sex workers, and Asian Americans who thought of the area as home.

Seattle had established a strong urban presence from building industries that capitalized on the natural resources of the Pacific Northwest. The development of the cannery industry, coal mining, farming, and lumber mills helped build and sustain the economy of the city and the state. The location of the city, port, and railroad transportation systems enabled the movement of goods that met product demands in the national and international markets, and this opportunity encouraged people to come and seek work and personal fortunes in Seattle.[5] Among these Pacific Northwest immigrants were the Chinese, Japanese, and Filipinos who came in steady and overlapping waves. Asian American settlement began with one Chinese person that was recorded in both the 1850 and 1860 Washington Territorial Census and prior to the incorporation of the City of Seattle on 2 December 1869.

With a modest beginning as a settlement site supported by Henry Yesler's 1853 Sawmill, Seattle quickly became the largest city in Washington Territory. In the 1870s and with a population of about 1,200, Polk's *Oregon and Washington Gazetteer* reported that the city was already well-established with city utilities, newspapers, coal mine development, and transportation and

29

MAP 1-1: *Maynard's Plat, 1853 [Records of King County, Washington Territory, Volume A, page 6, King County Assessor's Office]*

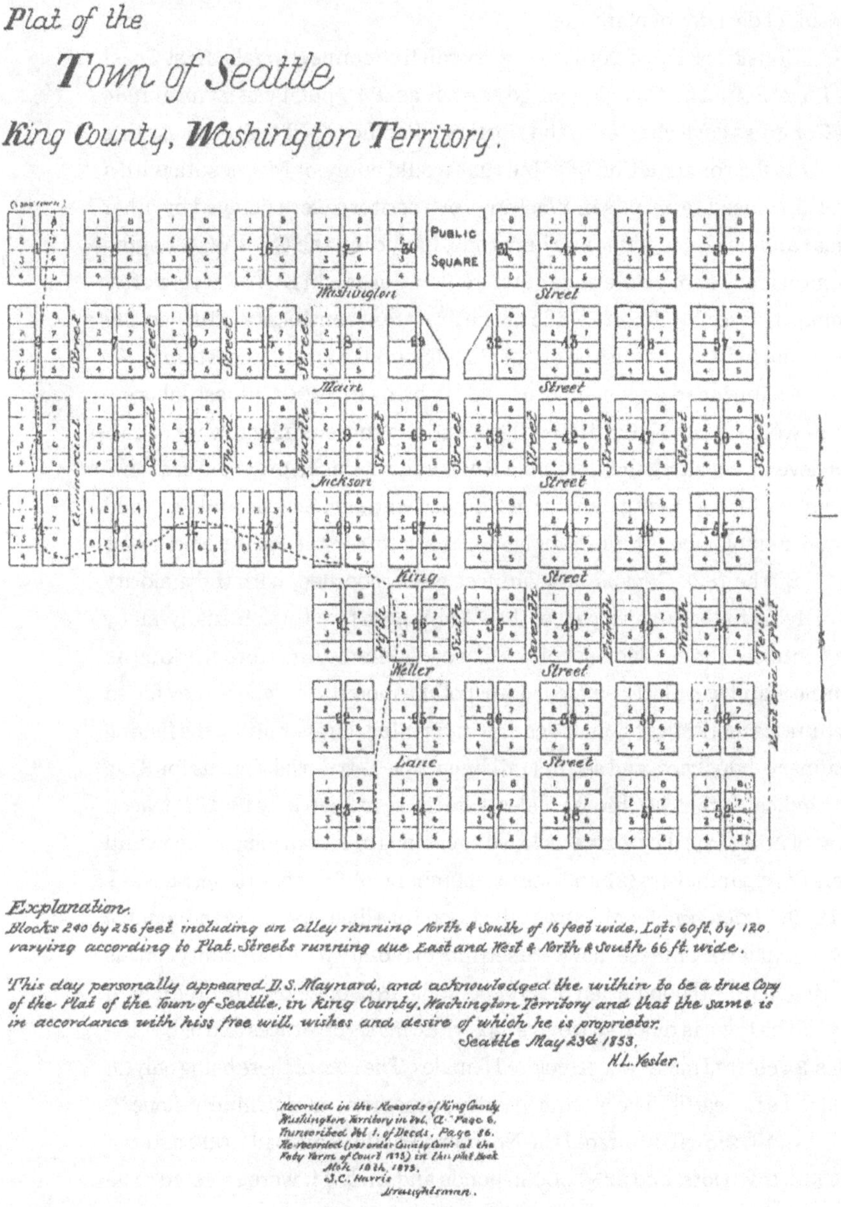

Plat of the

Town of Seattle

King County, Washington Territory.

Explanation.
Blocks 240 by 256 feet including an alley running North & South of 16 feet wide. Lots 60 ft. by 120 varying according to Plat. Streets running due East and West & North & South 66 ft. wide.

This day personally appeared D.S. Maynard, and acknowledged the within to be a true Copy of the Plat of the Town of Seattle, in King County, Washington Territory and that the same is in accordance with hiss free will, wishes and desire of which he is proprietor.
Seattle May 23d 1853.
H.L. Yesler.

Recorded in the Records of King County
Washington Territory in Vol. "A" Page 6.
Transcribed Vol. 1. of Deeds. Page 86.
Re-recorded (per order County Com'r at the
Forty Terms of Court 1875) in this plat book
Note 18th, 1875.
J.C. Harris
Draughtsman.

communication advancements that included graded streets, steamship lines, a telegraph system, and the construction of railroads in Washington Territory as a result of decades of planning.

Consideration of a cross-country rail line connecting the East Coast to the Puget Sound had been proposed as early as 1845, but it wasn't until 1864 when Congress gave charter to the Northern Pacific (N-P) Railroad. By this time, plans for construction of a line that would connect Minnesota with a not-yet-disclosed terminus in Washington Territory were delayed by other political and national economic demands, including the Civil War. Laying portions of track at opposite ends of the N-P line began in 1870, the year after the completion of the Union Pacific as the first transcontinental railroad, but the terminal location of the line on the Puget Sound was still uncertain.[6]

An initial arrangement was made to bring in 7,000 Chinese laborers to begin work on the N-P rail line. This and the increasing number of canneries developing along the Columbia River and in Alaska provided seasonal employment for a growing number of Chinese workers. Seattle and Portland were major employment centers for labor contractors in the Pacific Northwest.

By the 1870 Census, 234 Chinese were recorded, with the majority of them living in the eastern part of the Washington territory.[7] Initially, many of the Chinese who settled east of the Cascade Mountains were working as gold miners and were later employed west of the mountains where they found opportunities working as domestics and in farming, lumber mills, the fishing and cannery industries, and setting rail lines. The Territorial Census for King County indicated that 32 Chinese males were living in Seattle by 1871.[8] Between the ages of 20 and 39, they were employed as cooks (10), laundrymen (8), sawmill workers (7), cigar makers (2), and one tea merchant.[9] A few years later, Seattle's *Daily Pacific Tribune* noted the strong likelihood of a discrepancy in the count of the total number of Chinese that were settling in the city with the county census indicating "a [total] population of 2614 persons, 1512 of whom are credited to Seattle.... The town is reported to have 842 white males of all ages and 636 white females; 24 colored males and 10 colored females. The idea of there being only 34 colored folks in Seattle! There are at least five times that many Chinese alone."[10]

In 1872, Seattle offered the Northern Pacific Railroad 3,000 acres of land, 7,500 town lots, and $250,000 in bonds and cash if it were selected to be the terminal city of a rail line that would traverse the Western United States from Minnesota. But Seattle lost the bid for selection when a final decision

Hop Sing Laundry, 1874. One of the earliest images showing the Chinese business community in what became the core of Seattle's early Chinatown. This location was to the northeast of the early Wa Chong business that was at 15 Mill Street and west of Commercial Avenue. [Courtesy The Seattle Public Library, spl_shp_23074]

was rendered in 1893 that selected Tacoma, a less-populated city thirty miles to the south.

In a series of independent ventures that took the focus away from the N-P terminal loss, Seattleites focused on the business of funding and constructing their own local spur railroad lines and expanding ports on the waterfront to take advantage of growing commodity markets. Lumber from the Pacific Northwest was in demand in rapidly growing cities such as San Francisco, and as the prominent city of the Territory, Seattle was a supplier of goods, services, and labor for the growing cannery industry in Alaska.

By 1876 and as the Chinese were becoming more noticeable, editorials were drawing public attention to what they viewed as an alarming increase in the number of Chinese in Seattle. The *Seattle Business Directory* indicated that there were "250 Chinamen in [the] City" and twelve Chinese businesses, the majority of which were clustered around Washington Street between 2nd and 3rd Avenue South.[11] The *Daily Intelligencer* offered this opinion in an 1876 editorial entitled "Too Many Celestials."

...so large a number of Chinamen are flocking to our city that we are receiving more than our share of this undesired class of emigrants...about twenty Chinamen arrived. They marched up Mill Street in single file, with their bamboo sticks across their shoulders, and attracted a great deal of attention. [They]...came from Portland, and were among many who recently arrived at San Francisco from China.... What is to be done with so many Chinamen?...this large influx of labor alarm[s] the laboring classes.... We would be better without them...the law of finance has its application to peoples as well as currencies, and that is, in the labor market an inferior race will drive out a superior one. If Chinese immigration continues...their disguised slavery...will take the place of free white labor in all the trades and lines of production and manufactures.... Chinese labor is, becoming more unpopular every day.[12]

Although they were clearly unwanted, it was believed that the labor market and hiring practices would ultimately serve to discourage their settlement. Comparatively speaking, figures for 1878 indicated 210 Chinese in Seattle that accounted for less than 4.5% of the total 4,681 population of the City.[13] In fact, capitalists who were building Seattle kept employing the Chinese as railroad spur lines continued to expand in the Pacific Northwest. Seattle was identified as not only the largest but "the leading city of the territory."[14] In 1880, the Seattle & Walla Walla was purchased and reorganized as the Columbia & Puget Sound Railroad by Oregon rail magnate Henry Villard. Villard constructed another spur line that connected present-day Auburn with Seattle and spent the next decade in a flurry of activity that included hiring 6,000 Chinese to complete a line that would connect Portland with California by the end of 1883.[15]

CHINATOWN AND THE WA CHONG COMPANY

Chun Ching Hock arrived in the United States in 1863 when he was 18. Born in Long May Village, Sunning District, China, Chun travelled from San Francisco to Portland and arrived in Seattle to begin his career as a wholesale and retail merchant, labor contractor, and ultimately a property owner. The personal needs of the Chinese railroad and cannery laborers were provided by a few scattered businesses near the tideflats at Commercial and Mill Streets. Two of the earliest businesses at this location included a cigar manufacturing company that was

MAP 1-2: *Wa Chong Store, Seattle – 1870 [Author]*

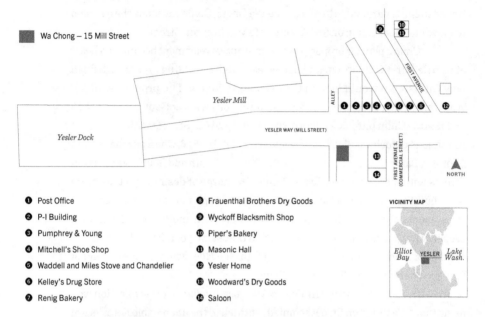

■ Wa Chong — 15 Mill Street

Yesler Mill

Yesler Dock

YESLER WAY (MILL STREET)

NORTH

❶ Post Office
❷ P-I Building
❸ Pumphrey & Young
❹ Mitchell's Shoe Shop
❺ Waddell and Miles Stove and Chandelier
❻ Kelley's Drug Store
❼ Renig Bakery
❽ Frauenthal Brothers Dry Goods
❾ Wyckoff Blacksmith Shop
❿ Piper's Bakery
⓫ Masonic Hall
⓬ Yesler Home
⓭ Woodward's Dry Goods
⓮ Saloon

VICINITY MAP

Elliot Bay   YESLER   Lake Wash.

operated by Chinese as early as 1866 and a mercantile store that was begun by Chun in 1869 on property that had been leased to him by Henry Yesler and across from the sawmill.[16] Chun's store offered an array of services and merchandise and was called the Wa Chong.[17] It was the beginning of his long-term commitment as a leading merchant and a founder of the Chinese settlement in Seattle. Of tremendous importance, the Wa Chong Company was also the beginning of corporate identity that would allow the purchase of land by aliens ineligible for citizenship, a tactic that would benefit Asian immigrants from China, Japan, and the Philippines.

Chun's first recorded property purchase was in April 1871 when he relocated the Wa Chong store to the NE corner of 3rd Avenue South and South Main Street and out of the tideflat area. The 1871 Seattle Directory recorded four additional Chinese businesses in the Wa Chong vicinity, all of which were "China Wash-houses."[18] By 1872, the number of washhouses increased to seven with six other businesses that included two chop houses, one drug store, and three cigar manufacturing businesses.[19] The *Weekly Intelligencer* noted the construction of buildings in the area that included a new Chinese store on Second Avenue measuring twenty feet wide and forty feet deep.[20] As these new businesses continued to cluster around Mill Street, the Wa Chong Company made the decision to move one block north on 3rd Avenue and Washington Street.[21]

Chun's plan for property ownership and development became the heart of Seattle's first Chinatown and helped establish a building type that defined how Chinatown would look in the decades to follow. The properties along Washington Street became the focus of numerous transactions between 1876 and 1890 as Chun purchased lots between 2nd and 6th Streets with the largest contiguous parcels on Block 16 of Maynard's Plat. In 1876, Chun purchased lots 3 and 4 of Block 16 at the NE corner of 2nd Avenue South and South Washington Streets with local architect Isaac Palmer in charge of designing a two-story brick building for the Wa Chong expansion.[22] Chun's portfolio included total investments of over $8,000 in Seattle real estate with another $4,000 in rural property purchases in Kitsap County.[23] In that same year, he took in a junior partner of fellow Chinese immigrant, Chin Gee Hee, who was the second of four such partnerships for the Wa Chong.[24]

In an 1877 editorial in *The Seattle Post-Intelligencer* recognition was made that "Washington Street seem[ed] entitled to the unenviable notoriety of Dupont Street in San Francisco, that of being the Chinese headquarters...with twenty-seven Chinese houses in less than half a block [with] one or two very fine stores [with] the Wa Chong being the principal one."[25]

In spite of the earlier predictions that local hiring practices would keep Chinese employment and their immigration numbers in control, the core of a strong Chinatown was developing in the lower downtown as these businesses began to prosper. Chin Gee Hee hired Seattle architect William Boone in 1883 to design the Wa Chong building at the 2nd Avenue and Washington Street location. McDonald and Reitz were general contractors in charge of providing materials and directing the construction that included a Chinese crew to dig the building foundation. As the building was under construction, the *Seattle Post-Intelligencer* noted that "The new Wa Chong brick building [would] decidedly top over any of the other houses of the neighborhood...[and while it] will not be as good a building as a number of others in town, it will be a vast deal better than a large majority, and will serve as an incentive to other builders...to put up houses better than those of a Chinaman...."[26]

By 1884, there were 400 Chinese living in Seattle and the district had expanded to include eighteen commercial businesses, fifteen Chinese dwellings, ten Chinese wash houses, and Chun Ching Hock's residential buildings that had been rebuilt on the NE corner of 2nd and Washington Streets.[27] The node of this second Chinese District consisted primarily of a collection of frame buildings that were constructed on pilings or stilts in areas prone to flooding and on land that was owned or leased by the Chinese. At the time, it was reported that "there were twenty-seven Chinese houses in about half of a block."[28]

In an editorial about Seattle's growing Chinatown, *The Seattle Post-Intelligencer* commented that the property between Commercial and Washington Streets had become home to the Chinese and "other obnoxious classes, which seriously detracted from the value of property."[29] The area was viewed as a barrier between the downtown financial district and residences up the hill and farther east along Washington Street. Chinatown was spreading with the editor warning of an extension that could cover blocks as far south as Jackson and east to 5th Avenue unless "preventive measures were adopted" to stop leasing property to the Chinese.[30] The following month, the City Stable property at the NW corner of 2nd and Main was rented to Chinese under a ten-year lease. The wooden frame building was converted to a lodging house that expanded Chinese-occupied property along Main Street to 4th Avenue South on both sides of the street. The public inquiry questioning the legality of an ordinance to prohibit leasing property to Chinese was decided on 11 April 1884.[31] Seattle City Attorney Richard Osborn reported to the city council that the city had no right to pass such a law. Any attempt would violate an owner's right to sell or lease their property and would amount to "seizure of land without due process of law and be in violation of both the US Constitution, and the Burlingame-Seward Treaty between the US and China."[32] No mention was made of the more recent Chinese Exclusion Law that would have had the legal power to prevent the Chinese from property ownership. At the end of that year the King County Assessor's Office included the Wa Chong Company as one of the wealthiest property owners, with holdings amounting to $21,270. Of the sixty-two corporations and individuals listed, the Wa Chong was the only Chinese company that was included for its financial performance.

ANTI-CHINESE AGITATION AND THE SINGLE ROOM OCCUPANCY RESIDENTIAL HOTELS

As Seattle's Chinatown was growing, so was the faction of national and local anti-Chinese agitation.[33] An anti-Chinese congress with delegates from throughout the territory met in Seattle on 25 September 1885. With committees in the major cities of Seattle, Tacoma, and Olympia, the congress intended to remove the Chinese by 1 November. At the same time, a group of Seattle's and the territory's governing elite, including Territorial Governor Watson C. Squire, Assistant United States Attorney C.H. Hanford, and Judges Roger S. Greene, James T. Ronald, and Thomas Burke, were organizing their own coalition of Seattleites who were committed to retaining law and order in the city.

The issue of circumventing mob demands and violence became all the more critical when Tacoma's anti-Chinese forces expelled seven hundred Chinese and looted and burned the city's Chinatown on 3 November 1885. The two hundred and fifty deputies that were sworn in by the Pierce County sheriff were no match to the overwhelming sentiment of Tacoma's residents who favored quick and immediate expulsion of the city's Chinese.

Aware of the anti-Chinese movement in the territory, Chin Gee Hee sent a telegram to the Chinese Consul General's office in San Francisco: "Chinese residents of Tacoma forcibly driven out yesterday. From two to three hundred Chinese now in Seattle in imminent danger. Local authorities will but not strong enough to protect us. We ask you to secure protection for us."[34] Replies on 5 and 9 November by Consul General Ow Yang Ming indicated that help was forthcoming with instruction to "Tell the Chinese to remain in Washington Territory."[35]

As expulsion plans were underway and as Chin monitored conditions, Seattle followed other West Coast cities in passing a residential ordinance on 24 November 1885 that was similar to those in San Francisco (1871) and Portland (1873) in addressing living conditions and minimum spatial requirements. The Seattle ordinance regulated hotels, lodging houses, tenements, and sleeping apartments by requiring that "each would provide 512 cubic feet of space for each person lodging or occupying such room or apartment" and that any violation of such was a misdemeanor and subject to a one hundred dollar fine.[36] It was the responsibility of the Chief of Police, all officers, and the health officer to enforce the law and any suspected residential violation was subject to inspection at any time. It was common knowledge that the lodging houses and residential hotels in the Chinese District were crowded with Chinese who sought to reduce rents and save what earnings they made as laborers by having multiple occupants who shared the cost of a room. San Francisco and Portland enforced their respective ordinances with officers who checked the accommodations in Chinatown to ensure that the minimum required livable space per occupant was being met. Any violation resulted in a jail term with a possible fine. Seattle's rooming ordinance went beyond the prescribed fine when a group of exclusionists caused the first and only anti-Chinese demonstration, riot, and attempted expulsion of the entire Chinatown community.[37]

Positions on the Chinese presence in Seattle were mixed. There were those who employed Chinese as house servants, including Mayor Henry Yesler, and those Chinese who were labor contractors and wealthy merchants in the city, such as Chin Gee Hee and Chun Ching Hock, with laborers that were employed by the businesses in Chinatown. While there were some who expressed sympathy toward Chinese labor, there was a rising faction of King County and Seattle employers who were no longer hiring the Chinese to work in the mills or factories. It was believed that this peaceful measure alone would ultimately eliminate them from the city for lack of employment. But the time to test the idea that the Chinese would willingly leave the City never occurred.

Seattle's anti-Chinese riot began on Saturday, 6 February 1886 when a group of "concerned" citizens met to discuss the blatant violation of the city's cubic air ordinance in the Chinese District. Early the next day, the group decided that this would not be handled as a simple misdemeanor, but act as the platform for a radical and decisive action to expel Chinese from Seattle.

At 7:00 Sunday morning, 7 February 1886, anti-Chinese vigilantes aided by Seattle Police and Acting Chief-of-Police W. M. Murphy went into the 2nd Avenue and Washington Chinese quarters on the pretext of conducting an inspection of lodging houses under the authority of the city's cubic air ordinance.[38] In a clean sweep through the densely crowded Chinese-occupied buildings, they were instructed to leave the city. With a series of multiple wagon trips, the vigilante mob gathered about 350 Chinese and their belongings, placing them at the dock at the foot of Main Street. The intention was to load the Chinese on the *Steamer Queen of the Pacific* that was en route to California from Port Townsend, Washington. Until that could be accomplished, all of the "trembling and crying" Chinese were placed under guard by mob members.[39]

At the time of the incident, Territorial Governor Watson C. Squire and his wife, Ida Remington Squire, were visiting Seattle at the invitation of Mayor Yesler. The Squires were staying in the Occidental Hotel, a luxury accommodation that was located on a triangular-shaped block between 2nd and Front Streets and James and Mill Streets just one block north of the Chinese District and in full view of the Chinese expulsion and the ensuing riot. As the removal of Chinatown residents continued, Governor Squire issued a proclamation in response to a plea for protection from Seattle Mayor Yesler "warning all persons to desist from breach of the peace...[and ordering] the military companies...to immediately place themselves under arms...in maintaining the law."[40]

With a defiant crowd of onlookers, the Home Guards were placed in Chinatown along with territorial militia Company D, one of two companies of the Seattle Rifles. Under Captain George Kinnear of the Home Guards and Captain Joseph Green of the Seattle Rifles, orders were dispensed to protect the city from violence. With little training, each member of the Guards was armed with a gun and given orders to use them only in self-defense. According to *The Post-Intelligencer,*

> The [Home Guards and Seattle Rifles] did not leave their homes and risk their lives to protect the Chinamen because they loved them, or because they were not anxious for them to leave the city and country. ... It was not a question of friendship for or hostility to Chinese labor, but a question of supporting the laws or of seeing them disregarded. ... The fight was made for America—not for China. It was...a struggle to uphold the law—not a struggle made in the interest of the Chinese.[41]

Boarding the Chinese on the *Steamer Queen* was in full progress with the $7.00 per person fares collected from the citizens supporting the expulsion. Even so, only 100 of the Chinese at the dock were allowed to board without exceeding the ship's passenger capacity. The expulsion plan was altered to wait for subsequent steamers that would remove the remaining Chinese who were being detained in a nearby warehouse.

Squire had joined Judges Burke and Greene early in the morning of 8 February 1886, presumably to collaborate on a plan that would keep the Chinese and the city safe. By that afternoon, Squire had written Washington, DC, notifying President Cleveland of the Chinese dilemma in Seattle and requesting the dispatch of federal troops for help. By 4:00 p.m., Squire declared martial law in Seattle, a portion of which read, "Whereas, An insurrection exists...by which the lives, liberty and property of citizens of the territory are endangered; and.... The necessity for martial law within the city exists...it is deemed proper that all needful measures should be taken for the protection of such citizens and sojourners...."[42] All businesses selling liquor were issued orders to close at 7:00 p.m. along with a call for volunteers who could join in peacekeeping. No person would be allowed to wander the streets during curfew without expressed written permission from A.E. Alden, the Provost Marshal, giving the beleaguered militia and guards a chance to prevent any unruly crowds from gathering that might duplicate Tacoma's violence.

Before the *Steamer Queen* was able to sail, Judge Greene issued a writ of habeas corpus to the ship's Captain Jack Alexander. The writ dictated that the Chinese aboard ship be brought to the court house by 8:00 a.m. the following morning so that it could be determined if they were leaving Seattle voluntarily.

A squad of the Home Guards, aided by the University Cadets and both companies of the territorial militia, lined the entrance to the dock as they carried out their orders to escort the ship-boarded Chinese to the courthouse for the hearing. In her account of the incident, Ida Remington Squire recalled a conversation with General John Gibbon of the Infantry noting "how brave the cadets were—how firm they stood against the mob—[with] every boy's face white as death...."[43]

With the mob numbers increasing, Kinnear recalled that members of the Home Guard were also targeted by death threats for aiding the Chinese and that some of the crowd included the Tacoma anti-Chinese vigilantes.[44] Of the 100 Chinese that were taken to the courthouse, all but fifteen opted to leave Seattle.[45] Those who stayed were escorted to the dock to collect their belongings and return to Chinatown.

As the *Steamer Queen* sailed and the remaining few Chinese were escorted along Main Street, the first gunfire was exchanged; it killed one person and injured four, three of whom were rioters. According to Squire's report, "... the rioters sprang at the Guards and seized a number of their guns...the guards were...facing the docks, where...dense mobs were in the streets to the North... the street was packed full of raving, howling, angry men, threatening revenge on those...interfering with their lawlessness."[46]

By the late afternoon of Wednesday, 10th February, federal troops from the 14th Infantry stationed at Vancouver finally arrived in Seattle by the *Steamer Emma Hayward*. Their rerouting and late arrival was due to a rail fire that had been set just south of Tacoma station; presumed to have been set by activists who wanted to see Seattle's Chinese removed from Washington. By the evening of the 10th, control of Seattle's peacekeeping mission had been turned over to the three hundred men of the 14th Infantry.

While angry sentiments simmered in the following weeks, the focus was on those individuals who had interfered with the expulsion rather than on the Chinese. Threats to peacekeepers included burning buildings and private property. In the week following the riot, J.M. Colman, the foreman of the grand jury who was investigating Chinese murders in neighboring Squak Valley, was killed. Nine men were turned over to United States Commissioner Eben Smith on charges of conspiracy and as the leaders of the Seattle expulsion project, but their trials reached a decision of acquittal as had been the case in the Tacoma Chinese expulsion.[47] In her final diary entry of the Chinese riots on 14 February 1886, **Ida Squire** reflected on the events of the week following the riot.

> ...the [*George W.*] *Elder* [sailed] with 120 Chinese on board—who were anxious to go... there were one hundred and eighty very anxious for tickets, but the *Elder* could only take 120. Our people...collect[ed] the money to pay the passage, the agitators keeping entirely in the background.... The Chinamen went...without escort...it seems ominous the way they are let alone by the mob.... A case of arms was discovered to-day [sic]— secreted and ammunition [sic]—what does that mean? ...we hear of secret meetings. The Anti-Chinese Congress held a meeting at Portland—passed resolutions.[48]

No mass riot against the Chinese or immediate inspection of Chinatown for compliance with the city's cubic air ordinance occurred in Seattle again, but the population of the Seattle Chinatown core was dramatically reduced to about 340.[49] Nine Chinese businesses reported damage from the riots, including the Wa Chong Company.[50] The following month, *Harper's Weekly* noted that:

> The experience of Seattle has caused...other towns in Washington Territory and in Oregon to make preparations against attempts at violence.... [S]ince the disgraceful butchery of Chinese in Wyoming several months ago the anti-Chinese feeling in the extreme North-

west has become more violent and more nearly universal. An "Anti-Chinese Congress" has been held at Portland, which adopted a resolution calling upon the people in every town in the Northwest "peaceably to assemble and politely request the Mongolian race to remove"—a resolution that is a trifle less polite than it seems to be, since it follows a declaration that the Chinese are "immoral and degraded and a constant menace to free institutions, to the home, and the family." The experience of Seattle therefore, may at any time be repeated at other towns.[51]

The warning was heeded in neighboring Portland as Mayor John Gates denounced public agitators and union representatives who would bring violence to the city as they had in Seattle under the guise of inspecting the density of lodging hotel residents. Gates took out an advertisement in *Harper's Weekly* affirming that no such violence would be tolerated in Portland.[52]

Territorial Governor Squire affirmed his belief that there was a need for the Chinese Exclusion Law that had passed in 1882 after witnessing what he called "the intense feeling of antagonism seated in the breasts of the great body of our laboring people in reference to the Chinese."[53] In his 1 October 1886 report to the federal government on conditions regarding the Chinese in the Pacific Northwest, Squire concluded that while some Chinese, such as Chun Ching Hock, were honorable businessmen, this did not appease general sentiments about the population.

...the people of the Pacific coast, with very few exceptions, possess a spirit of hostility toward the Chinese residents, and a large proportion of our citizens...are inclined to be lenient to those who engage in acts hostile to the Chinese and this fact makes it extremely difficult to secure convictions of this class of offenders against the law. This feeling has been greatly aggravated by the fact that large numbers of Chinese have continued to cross the border from British Columbia in defiance of the [Exclusion] law...[54]

At the time of the anti-Chinese riots, King County figures for the Washington Territorial Census indicated that there were 635 Chinese in Seattle in 1885 with a dramatic decrease to 135 in 1887; a number that reflected the decline of the community with a total that had not been as low since 1873.[55] The Seattle Chinese community had increased to 359 by the time of the 1890 US Census and by 1900, their numbers had marginally increased with an additional 79 in the city. The state population of Chinese declined in the post-Exclusion years as the administrative mechanics of enforcing federal immigration law became more finely tuned, understood, and implemented; a phenomenon that was duplicated in Chinese communities in both Oregon and California.

THE GREAT SEATTLE FIRE AND THE BUILDING BOOM OF RESIDENTIAL HOTELS

In the midst of a national economic depression and the Territory's bid for statehood, Seattle suffered a devastating loss of its downtown from a fire. On 6 June 1889, sixty-five blocks or 116 acres of frame and brick buildings were destroyed that included those in the Chinese District. The total loss of property was estimated in excess of $12,000,000.[56]

The thirteen-year partnership of Chin Gee Hee with Chun Ching Hock and the Wa Chong Company was also coming to an end. Speculations on the dissolution ranged from a contentious disagreement to each man wanting to pursue a different business proportion of mercantile focus to labor contracting. Other reports included Chin's ambitions for a Chinese consular seat that would diminish the amount of time that he would have to run the Wa Chong. Whatever the motivation, the dissolution was an amicable and legal one with the division of properties that had been purchased on behalf of the company in the Chinatown node. On 7 October 1889, both men agreed to sign quit claim deeds to legally divide two adjacent company properties at the NE corner of the 2nd Avenue South and South Washington Street intersection.[57] No other cash was exchanged as each man took clear title of their respective properties. The distribution of lots 3 and 4 of Block 14 included a covenant agreement that any future construction on either site would include a mutually designed and agreed upon fire and party wall and a suitable building height.

On the one-year anniversary of the fire, the *Seattle Post-Intelligencer* ran a full-page review of its aftermath and the rebuilding progress in the burned downtown district.

> The fire wiped out of existence practically the whole business district of the city.... Not a building remained standing...which formed...the very heart of the city...[yet]...within the year 130 buildings have been constructed of brick, stone and iron, ranging in height from three to eight stories...when all...are completed their total cost will reach...$6,682,700.

MAP 1-3: *Early Chinatown Property Ownership – 1871–1889 (pre-fire) [Author]*

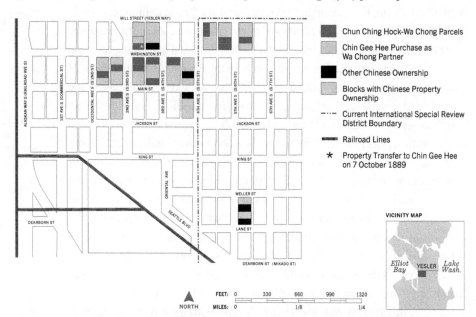

Within the same time there has been…335 frame and corrugated iron buildings [constructed] at a cost of $1,266,400 [and] 60 wharves with a frontage of more than two miles, with coal bunkers, warehouses [and] street improvements.[58]

   Among the structures that were included in the listing of new construction projects were two buildings reestablishing the Chinese core at the northeast corner of the 2nd Avenue South and South Washington Street intersection. Both buildings and land were adjoining and owned outright by Chun Ching Hock; one of which was the Phoenix Hotel located on the corner and the other immediately to the north called the Lexington Hotel or "CCH Block," named after its owner and recognized as being "one of the handsomest in the city."[59]

   Designed by Seattle building contractor, David Dow, the Phoenix Hotel was the first masonry SRO residential hotel to be owned by a Chinese. It was the beginning of Chinese corporations that would focus on the construction of this unique American building type.[60] Like many in the building professions, Dow was able to capitalize on the massive reconstruction that was taking place in the city. In the coming years, his close professional and personal relationship with Chun Ching Hock brought him additional Wa Chong commissions that included between 20 to 30 buildings and houses along with an additional major SRO residential hotel commission in 1911.[61] Dow designed the foundations and the circular and semi-circular windows of both the Phoenix Hotel and the CCH Block. The latter building took advantage of the eastward rising slope of the parcels with construction of the buildings set into the block's hillside so that four stories were visible from the 2nd Street front façade with three stories visible at the back of the building facing the alley. As the foundation was being dug, a natural spring was tapped, which led to the addition of a windmill atop the structure that was used to supply water to the building rather than pay the city for the utility.[62] The CCH Block contained the relocated Wa Chong Store as one of the three commercial bays on the ground floor. The sixty-room Lexington residential hotel was owned and operated by Chun. He donated two office spaces on the third floor of the building; one of which was the Gee How Oak Tin Family Association and the second as a larger community hall on the second floor that, according to reports, was capable of holding three hundred people.[63]

A third noted building for that first post-fire year was one that was owned by Chin Gee Hee and located adjacent to and immediately to the east of the Phoenix Hotel on Washington Street.[64] The new building reflected Chin's share of the investment holdings earned from his partnership association with the Wa Chong Company. Chin Gee Hee's brick-and-stone building housed his new business, the Quong Tuck Company. Like the CCH Block and Phoenix Hotel buildings, it was a mixed-use commercial and SRO residential building. While a party wall was not constructed per the partnership dissolution agreement, an access alley was included in the design that allowed for windows and additional door access to both the Chin and Chun buildings.

The two brick-and-stone SROs of Chun Ching Hock each cost $18,000 and fully occupied the lots with 60′ building frontages. Chin Gee Hee's 43′ x 60′ SRO added a $14,000 building to the Chinatown core. The three structures combined created a continuous façade of Chinese businesses for the better part of two block faces. All three SRO hotel buildings followed the typology of at-grade-level commercial bays and spare rooms on subsequent floors that were intended for a transient population of Chinese immigrants.

The size and important function of these two businesses were recognized by the peer community as the beginning of the "Chinese Headquarters"

Lexington & Phoenix Hotels. [Courtesy University of Washington Libraries, Special Collections, UW4491]

as early as 1890.[65] These buildings created a more concentrated pattern of commercial and residential development and advanced beyond the early frame, sparingly ornamented, and scattered collection of Chinese buildings that had been near the tideflats. Nine other Chinese-operated businesses were added to this Chinese District by 1890, all of which were laundries and only one of which was located north of Yesler Way. The most notable frame construction fronted the alley between Yesler Way and Washington Street between 3rd and 4th Avenue South. Its third floor included a temple room and, like the buildings of Chun and Chin, it held lodging house rooms on the second and successive floors.[66]

Labor contracting, residential accommodations, and commercial services were a good business combination and it was a formula that Chun Ching Hock understood well as he focused on building a Chinatown and financial empire for the Wa Chong Company through real estate. His post-fire construction successes were directly related to what he had learned in his two decades of Seattle residency. As early as 1870, Chun was buying and selling rural property, urban parcels, and commodities. Under the corporate identity of the Wa Chong Company, he purchased land parcels, houses, and commercial structures throughout the Puget Sound with a majority of his real estate in downtown Seattle. The greatest activity in transactions took place after the construction of the Lexington and Phoenix hotel buildings and in the first decade of the 20th century as the retail and wholesale financial power of Wa Chong grew. Permits were taken out for the construction of hotel buildings and renovation of single-family housing to lodging houses for properties that were concentrated in an area between 3rd and 6th Avenues South along Washington and Main Streets. Four such housing projects provided living quarters for 85 Chinese cannery workers who had relocated from Portland.[67]

The early establishment of Japanese businesses was beginning to appear in and among the buildings of Chinatown in that first year of post-fire rebuilding. In 1886, there were no more than 9 Japanese living in Seattle, but by 1890, there were 125 Japanese in the city or about 35% of the total 360 who were reported as living in the state.[68] In the decade following the fire and as the population of Japanese was growing in the city, the Chinese and Japanese businesses continued to intermix in a more scattered pattern of adjacent businesses and modest wooden frame dwellings; sometimes creating small business nodes by each of these groups. Seattleites recognized the concentration of Asians living south of Yesler Way and identified Chinatown, but any specific enclave boundary for Japanese was not identified as such.

> On Washington between Second and Third Avenues South, there [was] more life and greater crowds than in any other part of what is termed Chinatown. The trouble with... [Chinatown] in this city is that the Chinese occupy three or four different localities, all concentrated enough to be properly termed Chinatown. The second district commences on the north side of Washington Street between Front and Fifth Avenue South. The third district is located on Fourth Avenue South between Washington and Main Streets [but] the principal feature of this district is the big Wa Chong building.[69]

While the fire ravaged so much of the central city, it did nothing to damage the reputation of Seattle as a prosperous place to live and work. There were employment opportunities for clearing away debris from the fire and engaging in any profession that contributed to physically or economically rebuilding a modern city. According to the *Seattle Post-Intelligencer*, the fire made a clean sweep of the lesser structures of the city and enabled improvements that would have otherwise taken several decades to be removed and with rebuilding done "on such a scale that the city outshined all her rivals and established her supremacy...."[70] Between 1880 and 1890, Seattle's population grew over a thousand fold as it went from 3,533 to 42,837.[71] The city was examining the building potential of the tideflats, and engaging in issuing permits for the feverish rebuilding of the south downtown, including new buildings to replace the Chinatown District, bordellos, gambling establishments, and the "female boarding houses" that had been lost in the fire. In that decade, the Chinese of Seattle had barely gained an additional eighty permanent residents while neighboring Portland outnumbered the Seattle Chinese by 18:1.

The coming decade brought prosperity, population growth, and more land speculation ventures. In conjunction with the great fire clean-up and rebuilding of the city, discussions by Eugene Semple and the Harbor Line Commission were underway as to how to reclaim the nearly two thousand acres of the Elliott Bay tideflats, some of which were adjacent to the city's tenderloin. Cutting a canal to Lake Washington through Beacon Hill would redirect the drainage of the area and the dirt from the hillside would be used to fill the tideflats. The reclaimed land could then be developed for industrial uses, rail line expansions, and urban growth south of Yesler Way. In 1891 and 1893, the State Legislature passed two acts that allowed people who made improvements to tideflat land to purchase the property from the City and authorized excavated waterways material to be used as fill. The sale of reclaimed properties paid for excavation that was undertaken by the Seattle & Lake Washington Waterways Company. By the turn of the twentieth century, over 1,400 acres of land was reclaimed for the construction of street and sewer lines and the associated activities of platting and building construction.

Seattle's local economy and population spiked when the steamer *Portland* docked in the city in 1897 with news of riches and a cargo of over $800,000 in Yukon gold. In 1898, Seattle's economic rise was instantaneous when it became a port city that was the supply gateway to the Klondike Territory of the Canadian Yukon. The city's Alaska Bureau kept pace with the latest news and updates from returning miners and provided recommendations on what to purchase. Seattle outfitted outbound prospectors with every piece of equipment, including dogs and sleds that would be needed for the estimated eight to twelve months that would be spent in the Yukon. While Juneau had what the miners needed, Seattle had a greater variety of merchandise with competitive prices between the local stores.

By 1900 the city had nearly doubled in size, reaching a population of 80,671 that included 438 Chinese and 2,990 Japanese.[72] The number of Chinese was modest when considering the slow and steady relative population increase in the forty years since their first arrival to the city and indicative of the determination of this ethnic community to remain in Seattle under the restrictions of Chinese Exclusion Law and efforts toward their expulsion.

UNION INTERESTS AND ASIAN LABORERS

Even with the passage of Chinese Exclusion Law, organized labor did not stop directing attention to the elimination of Chinese. In March 1891, the Laundry Workers Assembly of the Knights of Labor and local laundry proprietors petitioned the city council to deny permits for Chinese laundry businesses, citing that while white laundry employers put money into the community, the Chinese spent nothing but rather sent their wages back to China.[73] A second claim indicated that Chinese laundries were not complying with city sanitation regulations, though no proof of such a claim was ever verified. If the estimated 300 Chinese who were engaged in laundry work in Seattle were to lose their licenses, the work could be given to white workers. In a public circular the organization stated that:

> We, the white laundry workers employed in the white laundries of this city, desire to call the attention of all persons who patronize Chinese laundries in Seattle to the fact that you are co-operating with the Chinamen to deprive us of the opportunity to earn a livelihood. …Encouraged by the patronage…in the laundry business, he is now engaging in other branches of industry…. How soon it may be when he invades your business…if you are a wage earner and giving your washing to a Chinese laundryman, do not be surprised if you see the white laundries of this city closed.[74]

It was a commonly presented argument by organized labor in communities up and down the coast that American businesses and the economy would suffer as long as there was no means of preventing the Chinese from entering businesses that would be financially competitive.

By 1900, Seattle had become a stopover point for Chinese laborers from San Francisco, Portland, and smaller communities in Washington State as they awaited passage to employment opportunities farther north. Nearly every steamer leaving Seattle was crowded with Chinese passengers bound for the canneries in Blaine and Bellingham. With each shipload carrying about 150 laborers, it was estimated that about 2,000 would arrive in the course of a month to be employed in the manufacturing of salmon cans that were needed prior to the beginning of the fishing season.[75]

The effects of Chinese Exclusion Law, and a population of elderly bachelor males returning to China was being felt in Seattle's Chinatown. The *Seattle Post-Intelligencer* noted that the political platform that California labor had decreed twenty years earlier, that "The Chinese Must Go," was becoming a reality.[76] Indeed, the Chinese were leaving with an estimate that eighty of every one hundred Chinese bound for China were not returning; a migration that was the greatest since their arrival.[77] Instead, immigration and labor needs were being filled by Japanese immigrants. Seattle's Chinatown was changing.

In two successive interviews, Chin Gee Hee spoke of the difficulties in finding enough contract labor for Seattle's white society that wanted Chinese servants and cannery workers, and lamented on the changed character of the 2nd and Washington Chinatown.

> Chinamen are going back to China very fast. Ten years more and there will be no more Chinese labor. I have very hard work to get enough to run my cannery and I pay them $2 to $3 a day or $1.50 and board. . . . Chinamen always stay where they are sure of pay. There is no Chinatown anymore. I can remember when there was a theater here filled every day at $1 a head. I can remember when there were plenty of Chinese ladies. Now there are only a half dozen or so, wives of merchants. Chinese come here in season, work in the canneries, earn their money and go away and take it with them. Seattle has no Chinatown, no more, no more.[78]

It is likely that Chin's comment was a reflection of the near-stagnant number of Chinese as a result of Exclusion law and a shift in hiring practices. Between 1890 and 1900 the numbers of Japanese immigrants to the city dramatically soared from 125 to almost 3,000.[79] This increase of Japanese in Seattle generated a number of supportive businesses throughout Seattle's downtown and specifically in the area south of Yesler Way where they were interspersed and adjacent to the Chinese district. In addition to the Japanese-operated businesses they were employed as contract laborers in the canneries, lumber mills, rail lines, and in construction-related industries. Labor contractors were showing preference to hiring young, single, strong, and inexpensive Japanese males to replace an aging population of Chinese laborers.[80] While canneries and lumber mills were paying $2.00 per day to white workers, the Japanese were working for $1.25 per day, of which ten cents went to the labor contractor.

Japanese labor contractors typically operated lodging houses as well. Like the Chinese hotels, the boarding houses that filled with Japanese laborers were found to be in violation of the 1885 cubic air ordinance that had been renewed in 1887 with a slight penalty modification of a fifty-dollar misdemeanor fine. In 1900, thirty Japanese laborers were arrested for violating the code and occupying condemned buildings south of Yesler Way. With the aid of a court interpreter, the case was dismissed when it was discovered that the laborers were unaware of the meaning of the condemnation order at the time they rented the frame buildings from white property owners. No charges were filed against the owners.

As Japanese workers became increasingly noticeable in city industries, labor found another reason to rally support for some form of restriction of another Asian American group. The city's first brick makers' union was organized in 1900, primarily to protest the hiring of Japanese at the Gribble, Duhamel & McGrath kiln. The firm paid white workers $2.10 per day, and like cannery and lumber work, the Japanese were paid less at $1.25 per day. The firm guaranteed that no Japanese would be hired unless it was unable to hire enough white workers. Union organizers had no solution to fill vacant positions at the foundry and did not address a pending possibility of factory closure for a lack of laborers. Hiring was restricted to union members, which precluded Japanese laborers who were ineligible to join according to the union bylaws.

The labor report for 1901 salaries in the Puget Sound indicated that despite labor union protests, Chinese and Japanese continued to work in the canneries.[81] Outcries for labor reform from the media were not altering hiring practices in the Pacific Northwest canneries.

Pine City Hotel at 314-5th Avenue South included the Togo Employment Contractor. [Courtesy Seattle Betsuin Buddhist Temple Archives]

Grocery Store in the Pine City Hotel. [Courtesy Seattle Betsuin Buddhist Temple Archives]

...2,708 Chinese and Japs were employed...and their earnings for the season averaged $200 in round numbers, while the earnings of the 1,145 whites employed in the canneries averaged $300. There is no good reason why this valuable food product should not be prepared exclusively by white people, untainted by the loathsome diseases common to the dirty Oriental slave, who lives like a maggot. A national, as well as a state pure food law, should be adopted to regulate the labeling of cans so that consumers may know the food put up by Chinese and that put up by white men.[82]

Seattle, like many other American cities, was experiencing unprecedented growth and development from immigration and migration, evolving economic development, and a progressive local political system that had been fifty years in the making. As had happened before national recession and the Panic of 1893, the growth of the city came too quickly and as the population swelled, necessary services and construction tried to keep pace.

Money, people, and prosperity poured into the city in earnest for the next two decades from Alaska trade and grand civic ventures such as the Alaska-Yukon-Pacific Exposition that honored the financial connection with Seattle. In 1910, it was reported that the merchants of Seattle practically controlled the trade of Alaska and the Yukon Territory with a value that had reached about $22,000,000 by 1909.[83] The population multiplied nearly 300% between 1900 and 1910 to a total of over 237,000 people, of whom less than 3% were Asian.[84]

VICE "BELOW THE LINE"

As the city grew, its reputation was becoming tainted as portions of the downtown became known for pleasure establishments where liquor, gambling, opium, and prostitution could be easily obtained. These vices were part of the businesses that were located in and among the lodging house and single-room occupancy residential hotel buildings of the Chinese District with a multi-ethnic clientele. Illicit activities were common in the downtown and a part of everyday living. The process of police raids, arrests, fines, and releases was a frequent cyclical activity.

The pre-fire prostitution houses and cribs in the area surrounding the Chinese businesses were expanding south of Yesler Way and covering an area from 1st Avenue to 6th Avenue South and in the area north of the tideflats. Newspapers and Seattleites referred to the area closest to the waterfront as the

"Tenderloin," in reference to a similar prostitution district in San Francisco. By 1888 and in just four years there were an increasing number of saloons and "female boarding houses" that shared the four-block Chinese District with some prostitution rooms located in floors above the Chinese stores. "Cribs" were small windowless prostituting areas that typically subdivided small hotel rooms into spaces that were only large enough for a bed. As the lowest form of prostitution facilities, sex workers who plied the cribs were also in violation of the city's cubic air ordinance. While newspapers recorded arrests, fines were minimal and typically between five and ten dollars without further charges and not enough to discourage the spread of prostitution within the Chinese core.

> From Washington to Main Street was a nest of saloons and cheap lodging-houses, and tough cribs occup[ying] a large part of the block to Jackson Street. On the west side [of South Third Street] stood a one-story grocery…a row of Chinese joints in little shacks and a saloon on the Washington Street corner [with] Robert Abrams' livery stable occupying the rear of the corner lot. Up Washington Street to Fourth beyond the alley in the rear of Wa Chong's store was a row of cribs and disreputable houses. Another nest of cribs extended across to Jackson Street.[85]

In 1891 and as the crib houses expanded, the area to the east of the Tenderloin was coined as "Whitechapel" by local newspapers, a term that was borrowed from a London district where murdering of sex workers had taken place from 1888–1891. In both London and Seattle, Whitechapel became a district that captured the interests of social reformers considering means to redeem the area for appropriate urban uses.

Prostitution was condemned by various segments of the population in Seattle and most specifically by the area's churches. As the Seattle Ministerial Federation was considering the challenges of eradicating prostitution, a number of the opium dens were becoming a second focus in the buildings between 5th and 6th Avenues on Washington Street.

Gambling and opium-smoking establishments were located in rooms behind or above first floor commercial retail storefronts or in the basements of Chinese-occupied buildings and amid the legitimate business operations of Chinatown. Investment in a vice den required very little for its operation; a "gate keeper" who recognized the regular customers and thick doors that connected convoluted passage ways that protected the patrons from raids and arrests. In an 1894 description of razing the Gee Lee building at 311 Jackson Street, construction workers confirmed the suspicions that the building had been used as a gambling establishment and opium hotel.

> At the side of the building was…a small door, which gave entrance to a narrow staircase of twenty steps. [On the east side of the hall] each room was supplied with barred windows and the doors with bar locks. The beds had been removed but [with]…the smell of opium there could be no mistaking the use to which the apartments had been put. One flight above was the gambling room, the floor of which was covered with cards an inch deep…. The heavy iron bars showed the caution used by the Chinamen to guard against unexpected visits of the police.[86]

City building inspections, as well as immigration interrogations to verify a person's legal right for admission into the US typically went into great detail about the uses in a building and whether any part of the structure was used for a gambling establishment, with witnesses called to corroborate stories. One such case involved the Tuck Tung Company, a sundry shop across the street from Chin Gee Hee's mercantile store. Chin Wing, one of the business partners of the Tuck Tung, was interrogated by immigration officials on his return from China. Chin denied that any gambling or lottery operation was part of the company and that other than a lodging house hotel on the second and third floors and a mezzanine-level restaurant that was sublet for $40 per month, there were no other businesses.

The testimony of witness **Charles A. Bailey**, a general construction foreman with the Seattle-Tacoma Power Company, indicated otherwise. In the course of his job, Bailey had spent considerable time in the buildings of Chinatown and as a labor contract employer of Chinese workers. Providing a description and a sketch of the gambling operation, Bailey detailed the business of marking tickets and selling them to players.

> The [Tuck Tung] store is located [at 213 Washington] in a three story brick building, adjoining the alley between 2nd and 3rd Avenues…[with] a lodging house above. The store is about 24 x 50 feet, the space used for merchandise being about fifteen feet back from the front door. There is a counter on the right as you enter, with a few shelves along the wall behind the same. There is no counter or shelves on the left…there is a

[mezzanine] reached by a flight of stairs...that cover[s] the entire portion of the store
except the portion in the front designated "store proper".... The space being used for
the gambling is not shut off from the store, though there is a door some three and a
half feet wide which...has never been closed when I was there. The lottery table can
be seen...from the counter. From what I have seen...I believe that...gambling [is] the
principal part of their money.[87]

Subsequent investigation and interior photographs of the store became
a part of the interrogation file that verified Bailey's description.[88] The final
report of immigrant inspector **Edward Wells** to A.H. Geffeney, Immigrant
Inspector-in-Charge , concluded that testimony indicated that there was no
solid evidence that Chin was a US citizen and that his status as a merchant
partner was also questionable. There was no doubt that the Tuck Tung Company
was involved in gambling.

While Chin Wing disclaims any connection on the part of the...Tuck Tung Company
[in] gambling...I visited the store...to inspect the surroundings. At the time a Chinese
lottery was in operation at the table...some twenty players being seated. In the center
of this store room is...a gambling table...occupying a space...of about 12 feet by 14
feet...between [the table] and the counter of the store is a partition partly of lattice work,
and in which there is a doorway about 3 ½ or 4 feet wide...the only mode of entrance...
[and] open at all times.... In the rear of the office and the gambling room is a kitchen
occupying a space of about 20 feet by 24 feet.... The cooking that is done in this kitchen
provides meals for a restaurant that is conducted in the gallery above the gambling room
and the kitchen..... Aside from the results of my own observation, ...there could be but
one conclusion as to the real nature of the business of the firm of Tuck Tung Company.[89]

All of the gambling halls were reportedly operated by a few local men
who had the large capital needed to pay off an occasional winning patron and
officers of the police force who would allow games to continue by looking the
other way. Employees of the halls earned from $5.00 to $15 per day, with the
higher sums going to dealers and operators who could continue to win money
for the house. Lottery games were plentiful with a small risk of arrest, but their
potential profits were far less than the gambling halls. Within a few blocks of the
courthouse was the core of the 2nd Avenue South and South Washington Street
Chinese District and the central marking headquarters for the lotteries where

Tuck Tung & Company Interior 1. [Courtesy Chin Kung Shun, RS 1672; Chinese Exclusion Act Case Files, Seattle District; RG 85; The National Archives at Seattle]

numbers and tickets would be selected. Ticket marking places were located in numerous establishments, including restaurants, barber shops, groceries, or mercantile shops, and where the operators would receive a share of the profits for managing ticket sales. In 1896, the Ti Loy Lottery was operating as the Chinese Charitable Association, so that it could claim itself in an exempt status from Washington State laws that allowed lottery games if they were conducted for charitable purposes. There was always a lottery game running somewhere in Chinatown.

Opium was not a substance that was deemed illegal in the United States until 1909, but the city considered possession of it a misdemeanor. The majority of opium came from Victoria, British Columbia, or Hong Kong and when legally imported it was a commodity that carried a customs stamp that verified payment of the federal import tax. In one invoice to the Yee Hing Company, Wa Chong filled an order for "ten pounds of opium [and] one English and Chinese Dictionary."[90] US Customs officials seized opium as an illegal substance if it was smuggled into the country without paying the tax and would then make it subject to public auction.[91] In one incident in 1892, officers led a sting operation at 512 Washington Street for retrieval of a rumored 375 pounds of opium that was going to be sold at a market value of $3,000. With a bogus payment of plumbing washers that were painted to look like $20 gold pieces, officers found that only eight pounds were opium and the rest of the five-tael cans were filled with a mixture of molasses and tar that resembled the color and weight of opium.[92]

Opium dens, like laundry businesses, required a small outlay of capital, spare and simple furnishings of wooden boards for beds and wooden blocks for pillows, and a rudimentary ability in the English language. While these establishments might be easily found, it was impossible to accurately assess a count of the number of people who patronized such establishments since beds were shared through rotation of patrons. While West Coast Chinese and Chinatowns continued to be associated with opium dens, the reputation outpaced the reality. As a substance, opium was an ingredient that was found in many medications that were readily available to the general public, which should have taken the focus and problem of opiate addiction into American homes.[93] But the sensation of the drug stories remained synonymous with descriptions of Chinatown. Those dens that were more elaborate combined drugs with prostitution cribs.

The most important need of any gambling, prostitution, or opium business was the ability of the operator and the building to protect the patrons. Barred windows and bolted heavy doors, places to hide, circuitous hallways and passages, and quick means of egress were essential structural retrofits. While a number of raids were regularly reported in Chinatown, few arrests were made. As *The Seattle Post-Intelligencer* noted:

> Detectives…[raided] a Chinese gambling house, under Geo Lee's place at Fourth Avenue South and Washington Street, and captured a lot of odds and ends of apparatus and gambling devices. There is no doubt in the minds of the officers that the games had been running full blast immediately before their arrival…. The ringing of an electric bell was heard as soon as the building was reached, and when the room where the games had been running was located, not a Chinaman was to be found…. The police state that every time a game is pulled the entire arrangement of doors and partitions is changed.

No matter how familiar the police may make themselves with a building where Chinese games are conducted it is sure to be changed on the occasion of another visit. The delay last night was owing to a new series of blind passages.[94]

Reporters focused on the negative stereotypical image of Chinatown and presented a hopeless resignation that vice would continue regardless of the size of the ethnic community.

...it is doubtful that the "dope dragon"...would ever have built a lair in this fair land had there never been a Chinatown. While Chinatown in Seattle is small...it remains a fact that the canker...does more to poison the body polite of this city than all other vice together. Chinatown has probably less than 500 bona fide residents...but even where the few are gathered...there will be their customs and their habits. The Chinese is an inveterate gambler...willing to risk his little and...all on the buttons in the fan tan bowl, the turn of a domino or a die, or the drawing of a card. Frequent raids by the police and subsequent heavy fines have broken up open gambling among the Chinese...but they gamble in secret just as much as ever and fan tan flourishes in every secret meeting room .... Try hard as they do, the police in New York,...San Francisco, or...Seattle cannot eradicate the evil...It is the same with the lottery. But what can you do about it? The other night, after forcing their way through three heavy bolted and barred doors, the detectives finally reached a little room...for a lottery. But it was empty of Chinese. There was the table, chairs...ink pads...brushes, the wicker and the railing.... It's easier to catch a weasel asleep than a Chinese gambling....[95]

The first decade of the 1900s brought unparalleled changes and development opportunities in Seattle as a result of public works projects. The small Chinese and Japanese American communities would be directly affected by urban changes. The 1890 scattered and intermingled pattern of land settlement for Asian Americans around the node of the 2nd and Washington Street Chinese District continued to have a tenuous foothold even as the Asian American communities began to migrate to a new location. In the face of escalating land values, the core of Chinese and Japanese businesses and homes would be forced to move along with those uses that had earned and would retain their reputation for corruption.

ENDNOTES

1   The Donation Land Claim Act (Ch. 76, 9 Stat.496, 27 September 1850) was enacted by Congress and directed to settlement in Oregon Territory that included land in Oregon, Washington, and Idaho. The Act expired on 1 December 1855 with two interim amendments in 1853 and 1854 that reduced the size of land claims in half.

2   The street was renamed Yesler Way on 8 December 1888.

3   *Choir's History, Business Directory and Immigrants' Guide Book to and throughout Washington Territory and Vicinity, 1878.* University of Washington, Special Collections. http://content.lib.washington.edu/u?/pioneerlife, 1133, p. 23. Accessed 4 January 2013. Wooden-framed buildings north of Mill Street totaled 131 in contrast to the 85 constructed in the south portion, with the City building 6,618 feet of sidewalk as opposed to the 17,390 linear feet of lumber walkways in the north downtown.

4   Ibid. City directories were intended to provide a detailed view of development, land use, population, commercial development, and public services in order to inform visitors and people who were considering relocation to the area.

5   Shelley San-Hee Lee, *Claiming the Oriental Gateway: Prewar Seattle and Japanese America.* (Philadelphia: Temple University Press, 2010). See Lee's work that includes a discussion of multicultural settlement in Seattle and urban growth for its specific focus on the international connections between the Pacific Rim countries and the Pacific Northwest.

6   The line heading west began in Duluth, Minnesota and the eastern line originated in Kalama, Washington Territory, approximately 140 miles to the south of Seattle.

7   Marjorie Rhodes, Transcriber. *1870 US Census and 1871 Territorial Census for King County, Washington Territory with 1871 Seattle Business Directory for The Weekly Post-Intelligencer*, 25 December 1871.

8   Ibid.

9   Ibid.

10   *Daily Pacific Tribune*, 18 September 1877, p. 2, col. 1.

11   Kirk C. Ward, *1876 Seattle Business Directory.* Seattle Public Library, p. 88, 90. Of the businesses listed, nine were laundries. The remaining three businesses were listed under "Groceries and Provisions." The total population of Seattle at the time was listed as 3700 with a "floating population of 300."

12   "Too Many Celestials," *The Daily Intelligencer*, 18 August 1876, p. 3, col.1.

13   M. Choir, *Choir's History, Business Directory and Immigrants' Guide Book to and throughout Washington Territory and Vicinity*, 1878. University of Washington Special Collections, Ref F891/C54, p. 23.

14   R.L Polk & Co., *Polk's Oregon and Washington Gazetteer*, 1901–1902, 637.

15   The first spur rail line, the Seattle & Walla Walla Railroad, connected the Elliott Bay waterfront to a coal deposit located five miles to the southeast of the city. James M. Colman, who had taken charge of building this rail line, hired Chin Gee Hee to provide the labor for an extension of rail lines that would access coal deposits in nearby Newcastle and Black Diamond.

16   Some articles in the local newspapers referred to Chun Ching Hock as Ching Chong Hock. Prior to coming to Seattle, Chun's second partner, Chin Gee Hee, had spent almost ten years as a miner in California.

17   Wa Chong translated was a prophesy for "a prosperous China." The spelling of the store's name has been referred to under a number of variations that include Wa Chong & Co, Wah Chung, and Wah Chong. Stock certificates in the company indicate the correct spelling was Wa Chong.

18   "Seattle Directory," *Weekly Intelligencer*, 25 December 1871, p. 1, cols 4–6.

19 "The City of Seattle," *Weekly Intelligencer*, 30 December 1872, p. 2, col. 1.

20 *Weekly Intelligencer*, 19 September 1872. p.3, col. 2. Second Avenue was renamed Occidental Avenue in 1895.

21 The reference to 3rd Street refers to what that street was called at the time Chun Ching Hock established his store at that location. By 1895, a number of the north-south oriented streets had changed names and all of those that were previously known as "Streets" were now "Avenues." There were also changes to the east-west streets of Mill Street, which became Yesler Way, and Mikado Street that became Dearborn Street. For its location using current street names, Chun's store would have been at 2nd Avenue and Washington.

22 The streets that are identified in this narrative refer to the current street names and locations.

23 *The Seattle Post-Intelligencer*, 2 November 1876, p. 2, col. 2.

24 Chun's first junior partner was added to the Wa Chong when he first leased property from Henry Yesler. There is no recorded name of this initial partner and it was of short duration due to his death. Chin Gee Hee was a partner from 1876–1889, Chin Quong as a third partner from 1884–1904, and finally Woo Gen as the fourth and final partner from 1891–1927. Woo managed Chun's business affairs during the times when Chun was on extended stays in China from 1905–1924.

25 *The Seattle Post-Intelligencer*, 7 September 1876, p 2, col. 1.

26 *Seattle Post-Intelligencer*, 27 September 1883, p. 2, col. 3. In addition to downtown building construction, the Chinese were also active in submitting public works contracting bids for work commissioned by the city. The Quong Coon Lung firm submitted the lowest bid of $9,000 in a proposal for grading Front Street. Work on the project by the Chinese laborers stopped in September 1876 and all of the workers were replaced by whites the following month, but the reason for this is unknown.

27 This population figure was recorded in *The City Directory of Seattle, 1884–85*. Seattle: The Industrial World, 1884. This dwelling count only includes those parcels specifically identified as "dwellings" on 1884 Sanborn Maps. It is reasonable to assume a typical pattern and common in Chinese American communities that the stores and businesses also provided housing either behind the storefronts or on floors above at-grade commercial.

28 Clarence B. Bagley, *History of Seattle from the Earliest Settlement to the Present Time* (Chicago: S.J. Clarke Company, 1916), 173.

29 *The Seattle Post-Intelligencer*, 15 March 1884, p, 2, col. 1.

30 Ibid.

31 *The Seattle Post-Intelligencer*, 13 April 1884, p. 2, col. 1. http://clerk.seattle.gov/~F_archives/subjectfiles/1801_12/SEACPM18840411.pdf, page 455. Accessed 28 August 2016.

32 Ibid.

33 The US Congress was under the assumption that passage of a restrictive Chinese immigration law would satisfy the demands of anti-Chinese exclusionists, prevent jobs from going to Chinese laborers, and curtail the violence that was erupting in communities with Chinese workers. Rioting and expulsion in mining areas of Idaho (1866–1868) and in urban areas of Los Angeles (1870), and Denver (1880) encouraged legislative action. Restricting the immigration of Chinese was accomplished through adoption of national legislation that began with the Chinese Exclusion Law of 1882. The law focused on preventing the immigration of Chinese skilled and unskilled laborers but allowed a few exceptions for occupations and vocations that would be harmless and would not be a drain on the US economy and might in fact help support local economic development. Exemptions were extended for those Chinese entering the United States as scholars, diplomats, and merchants. Those Chinese already in the United States could apply for a re-entry certificate that would allow them to go to China and return to the US. The act also formally and explicitly prohibited the naturalization of Chinese. In the following years, Exclusion law was renewed, amended, and expanded. The Scott Act (1884) made re-entry certificates null and void

and resulted in prohibiting an estimated 20,000 Chinese from returning to the United States. The law was extended and expanded again in 1892 under the Geary Act by requiring that all Chinese pay three dollars to obtain and carry a Certificate of Residency that would prove their legitimate right to be in the US. While the certificate was mandatory, the enforcement of who needed to register for one varied by city. Of the larger port cities, Seattle was the only one that required this of merchants as well as laborers. Eventually the law barred the wives of Chinese laborers (1884) and merchants (1904) from entering. While the 1882 Exclusion Law was to be in effect for a ten-year period, the regular renewals ultimately led to an indefinite extension of the law until its repeal in 1943.

34 Willard Jue Papers, 1880–1905. University of Washington Special Collections. Collection 5191-001. Telegram 4 November 1885.

35 Ibid.

36 Seattle, Ordinance 694 (24 November 1885). San Francisco law dictated a required 500 cubic feet of air and Portland required 550 cubic feet. Seattle's 512 cubic feet would have corresponded with a small lodging house room dimension of 8' x 8' x 8'.

37 There was an incident of vandalism at the Chinese-run cigar factory at Commercial and Mill Street in December 1866 when an object that the newspaper described as a "missile" was thrown through a window, hitting a lantern and causing a fire in the building space. No arrests were made. "A Malicious Act," *Puget Sound Weekly*, 31 December, 1866, p. 1, col. 3.

38 No figure has been given on the number of police who were involved in assisting with the expulsion. Kinnear's memoirs indicate that it was "nearly all of the police force," p. 6.

39 Watson C. Squire Papers, University of Washington Special Collections, 1838–1926. Accession #4004-001. Letter of Ida Remington Squire dated 7 February 1886.

40 Watson C. Squire Papers, University of Washington Special Collections, 1838–1926.

41 *The Post-Intelligencer* as cited in Frederic Grant, p. 206.

42 Squire Papers.

43 Ibid.

44 Kinnear, p. 8.

45 This figure is provided in the memoir of Ida Remington Squire and in the recollections of Captain George Kinnear. Frederic Grant's 1891 account of the expulsion indicates that "sixteen of eighty-nine" (total Chinese) indicated a desire to stay. p. 198.

46 Squire Papers.

47 The nine men held for trial included C.H. Metcalfe, Louis R. Kidd, J.J. Quinn, M. McMillan, D.T. Cooper, J.T. Winscott, Michael Cunningham, Junius Rochester, and John Keane.

48 Squire Papers. The diary entry indicates a number of Chinese that was 20 people higher than other accounts, including Kinnear's estimate.

49 The total number of Chinese left in the city is based on 1885 Census counts that were taken for King County. Chinese in Ward 1 of Seattle totaled 524 as of April 1885. The 320 person figure used here takes into account a loss of 85 Chinese who left on the *Steamer Queen* and 120 Chinese who left on the *Steamer Elder*. An additional 21 Chinese from Snohomish were added to Seattle's Chinatown under protective cover during the week of the riots. See 1885 King County Census in Washington Territorial Census Rolls (Olympia, Washington State Archives) microfilm Reel 5, p. 201.

50 Williard G. Jue, "Chin Gee Hee, Chinese Pioneer Entrepreneur in Seattle and Toishan," *The Annals of the Chinese Historical Society of the Pacific Northwest*, 1983, p. 31–38.

51 *Harper's Weekly*, 6 March 1886, p. 155, col. 2.

52 Ibid., p. 142, col. 1.

53 "Squire on Chinese," *Seattle Post-Intelligencer*, 2 May 1892, p. 9, col. 2.

54 Ibid. In a number of articles about Chun Ching Hock, his name became synonymous with "Wa Chong," the name of his store.

55 1887 King County Census, Washington Territorial Census rolls, Reel 5.

56 "Walls of New Seattle," *Seattle Post-Intelligencer*, 6 June 1900, p. 8, col. 1.

57 The reader is reminded that the present-day 2nd Avenue South that is used in this narrative was 3rd Street at the time of the property division by Chun and Chin. Wooden-framed tenement buildings had been on the two parcels prior to the Seattle fire.

58 Ibid.

59 *Post-Intelligencer*, 11 August 1890, p. 5, col. 1. In 1892, Chun Ching Hock altered the Phoenix Hotel by adding an ornamental iron front to part of the façade. In September, 1890, the Wa Chong Company carried an interest-free $6,000 mortgage on the brick building located at the SW corner of 3rd Avenue South and South Washington Street and across the street from the Chinatown SRO residential hotels. The loan was given to Seattle madam Lou Grant. Grant had purchased the property two weeks earlier with a first mortgage to the German Savings and Loan Society of San Francisco for $12,000. The loan from Chun was paid in full in June 1894.

60 Dow had arrived in Seattle in 1868, around the time that Chun Ching Hock established the first Wa Chong store on Mill Street.

61 National Archives Seattle, RS 31/695, Chun Ching Hock.

62 The windmill was torn down around 1900.

63 "A Highbinder Court," *Seattle Post-Intelligencer*, 2 May 1892, p. 8, col. 1. Chun was a member of this family association.

64 In 1896, Chin Gee Hee was appointed the first Vice Consul in the Pacific Northwest. The Chinese of Portland were amazed that someone from Seattle was selected, particularly given the small size of the Chinese population in Seattle when compared with Portland. At the time, Seattle had 438 Chinese residents compared to Portland's 4,990. When asked how this selection could have happened, Chin told them that the Seattle Chinaman was like the Seattle white man—he hustled. "First Vice Consul," *Seattle Post-Intelligencer*, 29 October 1896, p. 3, col. 3.

65 "Old and New City," *Seattle Post-Intelligencer*, 6 June 1891, p. 10, col. 7. Business offices of the Wa Chong store expanded a third time to Main Street between 3rd and 4th Avenue South that also housed the Chinese Mission and a school that taught Christianity and courses in English. The Wa Chong expanded operations again to 217 South 5th Avenue by 1893 and by 1902 offices and a store were located around the corner to 406–408 Main Street. The latter address contained a joss house and the building was surrounded on all sides of the half-block by Japanese lodging houses. The sixth and final move of a Wa Chong mercantile business occurred when the business relocated to the East building of the Kong Yick Investment Company at 7th Avenue South and South King Street.

66 Temples were included as rooms in a building or as separate structures that were called a "joss house." On 4 October 1897, the building housing the joss house was destroyed by a fire.

67 *Seattle Star*, 24 October 1901, p. 3, col. 3.

68 "Report of the Committee on Orientals," The Seattle Ministerial Federation. 1917, p. 1.

69 "Their Happiest Day," *Seattle Post-Intelligencer*, 2 February 1897, p. 8, col. 1. The article described the celebration of Chinese New Year in Seattle and the location of Chinese in the city.

70 "Old and New City," *Seattle Post-Intelligencer*, 6 June 1891, p. 10, col. 1.

71 US Census.

72 Ibid.

73 "Against Chinese Laundries," *Seattle Post-Intelligencer*, 3 April 1891, p. 8, col. 1.

74 "The Whites Shall Wash," *Seattle Post-Intelligencer*, 10 April 1891, p. 8, col. 1.

75 "Chinese for Canneries," *Seattle Post-Intelligencer*, 4 April 1900, p, 10, col. 3.

76 "By and by, No More Chinese," *Seattle Post-Intelligencer*, 13 December 1899, p. 1, col. 2.

77 Ibid.

78 In an interview from "Simply Chinatown," *Seattle Post-Intelligencer*, 16 April 1899, p. 8, col 4.

79 US Census and City of Seattle, Office of Policy Planning. There were a number of catalysts that encouraged emigration from Japan. The 1868 Meiji Restoration had introduced governmental programs and changes that were intended to industrialize and modernize Japan; the economic effects of which were keenly felt in the 1880s. The cost of modernization resulted in a taxation system that placed a tremendous burden on farmers that was further exacerbated by an economic depression. The combined financial crisis forced numerous agricultural land sales and widespread unemployment from the inability of farmers to make the tax payments. Notable emigration of Japanese begins in the 1880s when the Japanese government loosened its long-time policy restrictions on foreign travel for its citizens and allowed laborers to seek employment with Hawaiian plantations. Employment on the United States mainland offered Japanese workers similar opportunities to earn a living. Historian, Ronald Takaki notes that 200,000 Japanese emigrated to Hawaii and the US mainland between 1885 and 1924. For further reading see Ronald Takaki, *Strangers from a Different Shore: A History of Asian Americans* (New York: Back Bay Books, 1998) and Sucheng Chan, "European and Asian Immigration into the United States in Comparative Perspective" in *Immigration Reconsidered: History, Sociology and Politics*, ed. Virginia Yans-McLaughlin. (New York: Oxford University Press, 1990), 37–75.

80 The Seattle & International Railroad hired Japanese rather than Chinese or white laborers in 1897 to build segments of the rail line in Arlington, Washington.

81 *Seattle Mail & Herald*, 22 March 1902, p. 5, col. 2.

82 Ibid.

83 R.L. Polk & Co., *Polk's Oregon and Washington Gazetteer*, 1909–1910, p. 999. In an earlier book of 1901–1902, Polk noted that gold receipts had totaled over $40,000,000 in Seattle's Assay Office from the beginning of 1900 through January 1901.

84 Ibid.

85 "Old and New City," *Seattle Post-Intelligencer*, 6 June 1891, p. 10, col. 7.

86 "Secret Halls and Rooms," *Seattle Post-Intelligencer*, 19 April 1894, p. 8, col. 4.

87 National Archives, Seattle RS 1609, Box 41, Chin Wing.

88 Interior photographs of businesses were rarely taken in immigration interrogation hearings or investigations.

89 National Archives, Seattle RS 1609, Box 41, Chin Wing.

90 Willard Jue Papers, 1880–1905. University of Washington Special Collections. Accession 5191-2. 12 November 1880.

91 A typical size was a five-tael can that would contain about half a pound of opium.

92 "Chinese Gambling House Raided," *Seattle Post-Intelligencer*," 9 July 1896, p. 8, col. 3.

93 Barbara Hodgson, *Opium* (London: Souvenir Books, 2000), p. 106. Hodgson indicates that advertisements and patent medicine applications reveal that at least 200 contained opium as an ingredient.

94 "Chinese Gambling House Raided," *Seattle Post-Intelligencer*," 9 July 1896, p. 8, col. 3

95 "Wrapped in the Coils of Yen Shee, Tales of Chinatown," *Seattle Post-Intelligencer*, 16 April 1899, p. 8, col. 2.

Prosperity "Below the Line"

BUILDINGS, BOARDING, AND BORDELLOS

Seattle entered into a period of grand schemes and aggressive developments in the first decade of the 1900s. There did not seem to be any obstacle or project too great or expensive to be tackled by engineers and developers who had visions for the downtown areas north of the central business core and south of Yesler Way. These endeavors included a major project for the south downtown tideflats made possible by an 1893 act of the State Legislature that allowed private individuals or companies to fill in tideflat lands for developable property. The tideflat fill project and construction of railway terminals and tunnels was referred to by *The Coast* journal as "a period of grades and regrades, of vanishing hills and of skyscrapers [and] the climax [of] the beautiful Alaska-Yukon-Pacific Exposition," altering more than two thousand acres of land in Western Washington.[1] It included a large section of property south and east of Seattle's Tenderloin and the 3rd Avenue and Washington Street Chinese and Jackson Street Japanese Districts.[2] So many capital building projects began to erode the settlement of Chinese and Japanese businesses and the old converted wooden-framed single-family lodging houses that they operated. Creating

MAP 2-1: *Chinese and Japanese Businesses – 1901 [Author]*

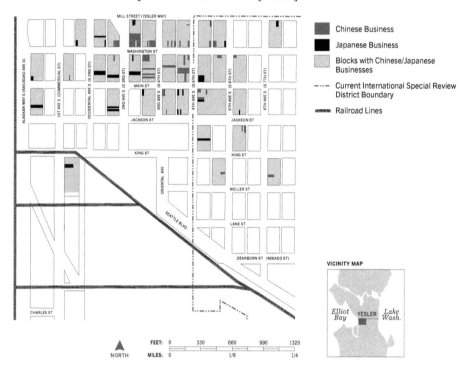

an improved geography for the city opened new opportunities for real estate development. It included a shift and resettlement of both ethnic communities at a time when downtown residential hotel structures were becoming a new building type to add to the commercial wealth of the city. The proposed projects were favorably viewed by Seattle's citizenry, particularly since improvements would eradicate many properties that carried a negative social stigma from both vice activities and the boardinghouse and commercial businesses of the Asian American settlement.[3]

From the early years of Seattle's lumber industry and Henry Yesler's Mill, various titles identified portions of the south downtown area. These included "Down on the Sawdust" in the 1870s, "Whitechapel" and "Blackchapel" in the 1880s, the "dead line" in the 1890s, and the "Red Light," "Restricted District," or "Tenderloin" in the early 1900s.[4] Like pieces of a puzzle, vice areas intertwined with one another and the Asian immigrant settlement. The alleys, streets, land uses, and clientele who frequented the neighborhood and buildings united all these pieces into a whole.

The first "official" Tenderloin was bordered by an imaginary line sixty feet south of Yesler Way to include the blocks north of Jackson Street with an eastern boundary of Third Avenue and a western boundary of the alley between First Avenue South and Occidental Avenue. The vice that took place in this area violated the city's early ordinances against such, but Seattle assumed a position that any city had to reserve some part of town for activities that were going to occur regardless of the law. It was feared that enforcing prohibition of all vice might encourage patrons to spend their money on illicit activities in other neighboring cities. Money wouldn't stay in downtown Seattle. It was explained that "the cleanest cities on earth [were those] which ha[d] a "Restricted District" for the prostitutes."[5]

The "Restricted District" had been established by default during the administration of Mayor James T. Ronald (1892–94) and remained south of Yesler Way even after Ronald's attempts to eliminate immoral activities had failed. While the label of "Restricted District" was misleading, it was defined as an area to which all morally offensive uses would be allowed to take place. According to one editor of *The Sunday Times*, this district was occupied by "French, Spanish, English, Italians, and hordes of Orientals, either slow shambling Japanese or the quicker Chinaman with his swinging gait...and women of the underworld [in] their second story rooms in...tumbledown shacks."[6]

"Whitechapel" and "Blackchapel" were differentiated as the two bordello areas that were socially distinguished by the color of the sex workers who occupied the single-room cribs in the wooden-framed buildings that were constructed on piers over the tideflats. Judge Ronald sadly noted that

> ...common prostitute[s]...as a part of that human wreckage found in seaport cities....
> must live in cheap tenements and minister to any comer, and in any form, in any way,
> after any mode or custom, and at any price. So long as they...pay to the owners the rent-
> al—exorbitant considering the crib—they [are] permitted to occupy the place, but when
> misfortune or lost health or any other circumstances...make it impossible for them...to ply
> their vocation, they [are] cast out to drift with the other flotsam and jetsam of humanity....
> Whitechapel [is] peopled by women of all nations who [are] white, while the denizens of
> Blackchapel [sic] consist of black or brown or yellow from whatever part of the earth....[7]

Geographically, these two areas were divided by the Seattle Gas and Electric Company plant on Jackson between 4th and 5th Avenues.[8] It was the same dividing line that was used to identify one of the boundaries of the city's Japanese District. Unscrupulous landlords continued to rent spaces in old and decaying structures; some of which had been previously condemned by the city's health department. In 1900, thirty Japanese immigrant workers were arrested for occupying rooms in a number of Blackchapel buildings and in violation of a condemnation order. With the aid of an interpreter, the workers explained their belief that the rent payment was legal and entitled them to occupancy. The judge ordered their release but no charges were brought against the property owners.[9]

The first two decades of the 1900s saw a strong crusade of the middle class who were scrutinizing the red-light district businesses and vice operations that were appearing to take over properties that Seattleites wanted to see used for ethical businesses. Much of the debate was directed against the open policy of vice and what seemed like city hall's acceptance of moral ruin from the existence of activities in the designated Restricted District. Church ministers and congregations directed their grievances at whoever was in the position as Seattle mayor.

Under the administration of Mayor Thomas J. Humes (1897–1904), the city was rife with every form of gambling, crime, corruption, and vice that a growing city could offer. This open policy of acceptance was compared to "compromising with criminals" and efforts were being made by church groups, including the Plymouth Congregational, First Baptist, and First and Cumberland Presbyterian Churches, to vote Humes out of office in favor of electing democrat George Cotterill.[10] Sermons and special meetings continued to be called to discuss how Seattle could be converted to a clean city. *The Seattle Times* reported what they saw as a "tremendous civic crisis."

> The city is dominated by thugs to an alarming degree.... Gambling [is] encouraged by a system of nominal fines. Nearly every saloon has its family entrance...the brothel. These are indications of the condition under a "wide-open" policy. [Mayor Thomas Humes] says it makes business, brings tenants, brings customers, brings capital...Shame on a city that makes money out of monthly fines from prostitution. Gambling is absolutely prohibited by the State law. A city ordinance provides that [saloons] shall be closed from midnight until 5 o'clock the next morning...yet [they] are allowed to run night and day and on Sunday without the least interference on the part of the mayor....[11]

As city-wide discussions were focusing on vice and the upcoming reelection of Mayor Humes, efforts to close the worst of the prostitution houses focused on any means available, including seizing business records of gambling operations and prosecuting any establishments that were selling liquor to minors.

In March 1902, J.W. Goodwin ran against incumbent Mayor Humes. *The Seattle Times* editor-in-chief **Alden J. Blethen** stated that while the responsibility to clean up the city lay in the Mayor's office, there was little chance of that happening.

> ...the practical matter [is] that such an undertaking cannot be accomplished this side of the millennium. Gambling and social evil exist in every urban community on earth and have existed ever since the history of human depravity began...it fills the foulest pages in the history of the city—it is known to every intelligent person on the Pacific Coast that since November 1897, the vicious elements have controlled the government of the City of Seattle; have outlined its policies and directed its course....Every city has its "white chapel," or "blackchapel," or "tenderloin," or a "deadline" of some sort—not through choice, but through necessity.... The very defeat of Humes will be a reform. It will be a notice to the "sports" that they must get "under cover" and that the "pimps," "thugs," "pickpockets," "the women in saloons," and those who are soliciting on the streets must leave the city....[12]

In spite of the campaigning and rhetoric, Thomas Humes won a third term in March 1902. In the coming years, there was only measured improvement on the part of Seattle's mayors at controlling vice or preventing the kickbacks that filtered through the police department in return for the privilege of staying in business.

Urban development and a rise in the number of company offices and factories south of Yesler Way dictated one move of the Restricted District in 1902 under Police Chief John Sullivan. Sullivan associated the vice and prostitution with Asian immigrants who lived and ran businesses in that area, aggregating them as "various grades of degradation [and a] class who live in the night."[13] He believed that the economic success of the industrial area depended on relocation of the vice district and while he promised to do so within a year's time, Sullivan doubted that such a move would totally improve the area as long as Asian immigrants lived there. "Today these buildings are the haunts of the vicious. Tomorrow they will be the marts of commerce and the dive and the brothel will have been forgotten....With the number of buildings already in the possession of Chinese and Japanese merchants, it is not likely that this district will be a first grade district for retail trade."[14]

Positions in favor of retaining a Restricted District considered such an area a matter of free enterprise and an expression of individual civil liberty. Proponents presented a case that cautioned against any sudden measures for complete removal of such a zone without a plan for their immediate replacement in the city. Others argued for the immediate and complete eradication of the vice district in order to preserve the moral character of the community and city. It was clear that any decisions to eliminate, move, or retain an area of questionable moral character was not going to be easy and that the city administration was caught in the middle of the morals debate . The business community purported a compromise where "the immoral and vicious elements and resorts be driven further southward into a more secluded portion of the city...where their viciousness and immorality will not be flaunted daily in the face of innocent and unwilling...good citizens."[15] Prostitution and vice could be taking place covertly throughout the downtown, but in the Restricted District, billboard advertisements and electrically lit signs were allowed to advertise immoral activities. The effect of vice on Asian Americans who were living amid these activities was not part of the voiced concern in protecting Seattle's decent citizens.

In many ways, the decision-making process to determine boundaries of the future Tenderloin was as unclear as when the area was first established. Public opinion on who should have the right to make the final location decision was divided between vesting the full power with the mayor or city council. City administrators and police were certain that eliminating vice from the existing Tenderloin buildings was going to allow wholesale business houses to flourish. Police Chief Sullivan attempted to uphold Superior Court Judge Bell's promise to close the parlor houses in upper downtown and those that were centered on Washington Street between 2nd and 3rd Avenues before the end of the year. These uses had to be moved farther south and out of the north downtown where municipal dollars were being expended for newly laid brick paving in hopes of attracting a better class of people and commercial uses.

The new boundaries created a similarly sized district that was farther to the east and south and in a location that was projected to be within the

Lila Young's House, a noted house of ill-repute from 1905–1911 is seen in the blade sign above the corner entry to the Liberty Bar. Both uses were in William Chappell's U-I Hotel at the SE corner of 6th Avenue South and South King Street. [Courtesy Washington State Historical Society at WashingtonHistory.org, Asahel Curtis Collection, 1943.42.5216]

Jackson Street Regrade area. The new Restricted District was demarcated as South Jackson Street, Maynard Avenue South, South Dearborn Street, and 5th Avenue South and it would retain the corruption that had existed when the area was designated as Blackchapel. The substantive difference was an increase in its size.

The relocation of bawdy houses to the South Jackson Street area augmented the more discreet female boarding houses that had already settled on 5th and 6th Avenues South and that joined the few neighboring Chinese laundries and Japanese-operated hotels and businesses that were on those blocks. The decaying old frame buildings would be replaced by new structures devoted to immorality and the commercial businesses that would help support them. As planned, the new Restricted District would be more isolated from the downtown; located east of the noxious fumes and odors of the Seattle Gas and Light Works and tucked between the tideflats and a near impassable hillside to the east.

MAP 2-2: *Restricted District Boundaries [Author]*

1892/1894 Boundary Area

1902–1908 Boundary Area

Future Interstate 5 Alignment

---- Current International Special Review
District Boundary

Mayor Humes' office released an official announcement of the new location of the Restricted District. In an interview with the *Seattle Times*, Humes acknowledged the practical limitations of city hall. "Men will gamble if they want to...the Seattle Tenderloin has been on a sort of a wild-eyed jag of late, and while I am sorry...I'm not in the reformatory business. If the...so-called legitimate gambling houses, ever do operate again...will they be compelled to go to the southern part of the city, known as the old black Chapel [sic] district? I am no prophet...Do I look as though I had just stepped from the pages of Bible history?"[16]

The announcement of the relocation spurred rental price increases and speculative development by Blackchapel property owners who looked at new construction possibilities and the remodeling of existing buildings to house relocated gambling facilities and prostitution hotels. At the same time the new Restricted District location was announced, the Great Northern Railroad was negotiating for a franchise in that general location that would enable them to construct a tunnel for train tracks that would travel under the downtown buildings.[17] The gambling joints, bordellos, and variety theatres were quickly ordered to move.

As part of the Jackson Street regrade, new building construction for expanded illicit facilities was likely. At the beginning of November 1902, a new crib house opened on the east side of the 6th Avenue corridor and south of King Street, just outside of the official Blackchapel boundaries. Called the new Midway Hotel, it occupied a quarter of a block and operated ground floor cribs that violated city law, which prohibited these uses as at-grade commercial spaces even in the restricted zone.

The hotel buildings in the first Restricted District that had once hosted prostitution remained standing, but their uses were converted to legitimate hotel patronage or light manufacturing. As two of the most notorious brothels, the Paris and Cosmopolitan House hotels at the intersection of 2nd Avenue South and South Main Street were now respectable buildings. The operators of these hotels ultimately moved their businesses and the names of their hotels to the second Restricted District.

According to city ordinance, the internal design of hotels that were used as parlor houses in the new Restricted District could not include any staircase that would directly connect a saloon to upstairs rooms. All areas of private tables that contained curtains or doors that would prevent an open view of activities were now forbidden in all saloons. But the rules were not being observed as the construction of the Dreamland Hotel was underway. While prostitution was the central focus of relocation to the new Restricted District, all sorts of gambling could still be found anywhere south of Jackson Street.

By May 1903, Sullivan was actively making good on the promise to clean out the vice in the first Restricted District with almost all of the parlor houses being relocated, including the larger ones that were run by Madams May Roberts, Lila Young, and Lettie Raymond. Sullivan acknowledged that it was an impossibility to rid the city of all prostitution, but that there was great utility in regulating vice to relocate in the new Restricted District. If nothing else, activities would be easier to monitor, and other neighborhoods would be protected from having bordellos. In a press conference, Sullivan explained that "When you close up all houses of prostitution, you drive immoral women to all parts of the city. They will secure rooms in residences throughout the city, [and] will be found in every lodging house...to the cheaper class of hotels...

Such a condition as this...can only be remedied by close confinement of all of this class of people to a district with clearly defined boundary lines."[18] The new Restricted District was a destination location and was not en route to anywhere else in the city. There was no mention of the rising numbers of Chinese and Japanese who were settling in and operating legitimate businesses in the city's relocated red-light district.

While there were Japanese stores and lodging facilities interspersed in the Chinese core of 2nd and Washington, there was also a multiethnic community living amid the Japanese businesses that were located two blocks further to the east and south and tucked amid the steep grades south of Yesler Way. In 1903 as the move of the Restricted District was underway, **Nagai Kafū**, an author from Japan, described his visit to Seattle and specifically his stay in a "filthy, wooden hotel" in what he identified as the Japanese District.[19] Kafū provided colorful descriptions of the people who patronized the businesses that defined the area on his eastward trek along Jackson Street that began at 4th Avenue South.[20]

> [The] melancholy surroundings [remind] one of a person down on his luck...the worst section of town. [These] filthy wooden houses were the haunts of Chinese and Japanese people...and populated by Caucasian laborers out of work and...blacks who suffered from poverty and oppression.... Pungent smells that filled the air...distinct odor of sweat and alcohol...a constant parade of heavy shoes, abusive language, dirty, torn shirts, ragged pants and caps, laborers passed like dark shadows...wherever I looked, all I could see were signs in Japanese.[21]

In mid-January 1905, there was speculation that city hall was going to move the Restricted District a third time, but the questions of when and where were unclear. Major transportation projects that included intra-city railways meant that legitimate businesses and factories could be built adjacent to the stations, but not as long as the existing vice businesses in the red-light area were in full view of residents and people visiting the city. With the impending completion of Union Depot, the city would need to "be made respectable so that... palatial trains...bearing passengers...[would] not be shocked by stepping from the sleepers to the bad lands."[22]

If the rumors of a move were true, real estate in the third Tenderloin could garner as handsome a profit as had been done from the first relocation.

Jackson Street looking east from 5th Avenue, ca 1907. [Courtesy Paul Dorpat]

The Seattle Times noted that early investors stood to gain a fortune as soon as there was any confirmation.[23] Real estate speculators waited for an answer, but the relocation of the Restricted District was postponed due to another mayoral election and Seattle boosters who were focusing efforts on launching a world's fair exposition in the city.

When William Hickman Moore became mayor in 1906, he made the public announcement that "the red light district would not be moved from its present location during his term in office."[24] Any position to relocate immorality on properties to the east of King Street Station was not going to proceed while there were so many other civic improvement projects to address. Moore directed the police force to uphold state law that dictated that saloons be closed on Sundays and that, at least officially, gambling houses would be closed. The red-light district of the city remained intact and licenses issued to saloon establishments increased regardless of Moore's campaign promises to clamp down on vice.

With the relocation of the Restricted District on hold, the booster "spirit of community" was pervasive as Seattleites adjusted to the chaos and daily inconveniences of urban redevelopment while fervently supporting an agenda of mega-scale projects. Seattleites were willing to put up with whatever inconveniences would occur to build a beautiful, affluent, and more functional city. So much of the attention and goals of civic projects revolved around financial gain that could be accomplished through improving and expanding land opportunities for development, furthering transportation systems that had already begun in the lower downtown and waterfront, and expanding the Northwest economy through international trade relations. Major capital and public works projects were simultaneously being planned and executed, prompting the Asian American community to respond in kind as occupancy in their lower downtown neighborhood was threatened with the presentation of so many redevelopment plans. As the dramatic land use changes progressed, the businesses of the Asian American core began to look at the reality of displacement and the opportunity that reclaimed tideflat and regrade land might offer.

Local media kept reflecting on Seattle's history and recognizing that significant changes were looming in the "troubled" areas south of Yesler Way. In a 1906 exposé, one reporter recalled his 1890 visit and compared it to the changes that were transforming the city.

> Insurmountable hills and sloughs of water [are becoming] wonders in steel and stone and mortar. There is no city...so fascinating for capitalists or [one that] invites such quick interest in projected or suggested investment as Seattle. There is no place toward which so many railroad lines strive like mad Titans as Seattle....She knows no defeat... her citizens are united. Enthusiasm is catching; enterprise is contagious; the "Seattle spirit" is infectious.[25]

In 1909, *The Coast* journal dedicated an entire issue on major projects that had transformed the city, "reclaiming vast areas from the desert waste [and] providing the home seeker and homebuilder with an opportunity [to become] a producer and a possessor."[26]

REALIZING THE RAILS

The rail lines brought tremendous central city development, but it was also done at a cost to the core of the Asian American district. There was little doubt that Seattle's rail opportunities were helping to build the city and economy,

but there was debate on the best way to handle the numerous rail tracks that
were inundating the downtown and waterfront as property owners, developers,
and city officials were considering proposals on how to alleviate some of the
congestion that they caused.

In 1885, H.H. Dearborn and Company held a majority of land holdings
south of Yesler Way. The company invited letters of support from the general
public, railroad officials, and manufacturers to advance what they considered
"one of the most important and beneficial public improvements that could be
undertaken in the city."[27] The value of property east of 8th Avenue South and
south of King Street was projected to be worth five times its current value if
improvements would be made to rail line locations, filling the city's tideflats,
and improving the difficult-to-maneuver street grades.

In 1893 and under public criticism for his decision, City Engineer
Reginald Thomson refused to agree to a franchise that was requested by the
Great Northern Railroad that would allow the construction of a rail line through
the downtown. Thomson argued that the approval of such would only serve
to separate the waterfront from downtown development and that a system
of at-grade lines would limit the possibilities of surface improvements in the
business district. While Thomson advocated a tunnel system that would put
south-to-north rail lines below the city, the proposal was initially ignored.
The Northern Pacific was opting out of their agreement to share the Columbia
Street Depot facilities with the Seattle, Lake Shore, and Eastern railroads.
Representatives of the Northern Pacific made an announcement that a new
terminal of their own would ultimately be built in the city. Filling the tideflats
and the regrade of Beacon Hill was progressing even as the debate over rail line
and depot location found new urgency.

An agreement was reached for land procurement and construction of
a terminal for the Northern Pacific in 1900. Construction of underground and
unimpeded rail lines would be less likely to interfere with regrade opportunities. An application for a franchise was made for the construction of a tunnel
from the proposed new station and rail yard south of Yesler Way and through
the entire downtown northward to Virginia Street and running beneath 3rd
and 4th Avenues.[28]

In March 1902, the Great Northern began the task of planning for the
southern tunnel entry point as the city assembled properties under eminent
domain for the needed right-of-way. The most affected part of the rail plan

was for blocks 18 and 19 of Maynard's Plat that were located between South Washington and Jackson Streets and 3rd and 4th Avenues South that served as part of Seattle's Japanese community and the core area of Chinatown. The proposal threatened demolition of a four-story residential hotel of Chun Ching Hock along with the Gom Hong Restaurant, Sun Lion's tailoring, the Wah Yuen Company, Dr. J. Watanabee , the Shing Chong Company, Washington Rice Milling Company, the Hop Sam Company, M. Sato & Company, a Japanese fruit and confectionary house, a Japanese tailor and several other Chinese and Japanese mercantile establishments. *The Seattle Post-Intelligencer* reported that "the proposed tracks [would] run directly across the present Chinatown" and that the "only building of any consequence [to be removed] was the four-story brick of the Wa Chong Company which [stood] immediately in the track of the proposed right of way."[29]

Merchants like Chun Ching Hock were considered to be important to the commercial economy of Seattle, but at the time that the tunnel was being considered, Chinatown overall was still viewed as an unknown "city within a city," a separate world of "highbinders, gamblers, merchants and thieves."[30] Less than a month before a decision was rendered on the tunnel location, the *Seattle Post-Intelligencer* ran an exposé that portrayed Chinatown as morally depraved. With an alignment decision so close at hand, the article's intimation left little doubt that very little would be sacrificed if the Asian American community were razed.

> Go into almost any of the Chinese stores...on Washington Street between Second Avenue South and Fifth Avenue South and you can see the operations of the several lottery companies in full blast...the players mostly white men, in these public places, come and go with unceasing regularity and the stream of small silver that flows across the table into the till of the marker is constant and unbroken up to the hour set for the drawing. These are laborers, merchants, small tradesmen, an occasional youth not yet out of his teens, a goodly array of those loathsome creatures who live upon the earnings of fallen women, thieves, professional "bums" and opium, morphine and cocaine "fiends".... It is not a pretty sight, nor one calculated to better the morals of anyone, man or boy. But such as it is, it is Chinatown and a feature of the quarter, unlovely though it be.[31]

While the tunnel proposal had no adverse effect on the CCH Block, the Phoenix Hotel, or on the Chin Gee Hee building, it did affect other land holdings and buildings of the Wa Chong Company that were used for storage and sales. The Company sold one six-story property at 4th Avenue South and Washington Street for $50,000 within a month of the Union Pacific's franchise application. In anticipation of the loss of Chinatown, the Wa Chong Company purchased property for construction of a new mercantile building further to the east and in the Japanese district on Main Streets between 5th and 6th Avenues South. Procuring other holdings was proving difficult as real estate costs in the area were escalating. Unable to buy affordable property, Woo Gen, the new partner and manager of the Wa Chong, opted to construct two three-story buildings on land that was under a twenty-year lease.

On 5 January 1903, City Ordinance 9116 was passed, granting construction and operation of rail tracks and the tunnel to the Seattle and Montana Railroad Company and the Northern Pacific Railway Company. Section 2 of the ordinance stated that the southern entry point of the tunnel would "be situated at such place within the limits of the east half of block 18, D.S. Maynard's Plat of the Town of Seattle, lying between Washington Street, Fourth Avenue South, Main Street and the alley running through the center of said block...."[32] The language of the ordinance and the location ultimately made the acquisition of Chun Ching Hock's property unnecessary, but it was too late to save one of the Wa Chong stores and a residential hotel building from demolition that was completed on 1 June 1903.

Plans to construct the King Street Station (then Union Depot), a passenger station that would serve the Great Northern and Northern Pacific rail lines, began in 1904. Located at the southwest corner of South Jackson Street and 3rd Avenue South, the new station was completed in 1906. The Oregon–Washington railway and Union Pacific Railroad looked at the opportunity of purchasing more land that would be an ideal site for a second passenger terminal building. In 1907, Edward H. Harriman of the Union Pacific chose a location one block east of the King Street Station that would be the home of Union Station. With other major municipal projects that included a regrading of the south downtown and filling the tideflats, the City of Seattle granted the right to construct the new rail station on March 1908 with an agreement that surrounding streets would be improved and widened.[33] The new terminal would replace a tar roofing industrial plant and coal gas plant and storage tanks facility, Chinese laundries, and Chinese and Japanese lodging houses on the block immediately to the north on Jackson.[34]

ROADS, TIDEFLATS, AND REGRADES

Like the rail and tunnel projects, local streets were being developed every-where and in what one journal referred to as "the city gone mad on the subject of street improvements."[35] In an 1895 city ordinance, 230 street alignments, some of which were under multiple names, were renamed for consistency and to simplify their identity and location within the city. The Dearborn Street alignment that was to ultimately contribute to the southern boundary of the Asian American district included renaming a five-block long stretch of road known as "Mikado Street" and a section of the South 3rd Street alignment that led into Chinatown as "Oriental Avenue."

Land cuts and fills were occurring everywhere with as much as 25% of new project grading and paving being paid by the taxpayers. This and reve-nues from saloon taxation were attributed as the two top revenue sources that gave the city a large cash surplus of over $54.5 million in the 1903 municipal budget. The public was supportive and excited about building a bigger, prosper-ous, and progressive city, but the looming question in the years to come would need to address how Seattle's polite and moral society could continue to allow the city improvements to be built on monies collected from the city's saloons and vice.

Seattle consisted of islands of development that were isolated from one another because of impassable hillsides, ravines, or tidal areas.[36] The vision of a city that would be responsive to transportation access needs and industrial land development and expansion were realized under City Engineer Reginald H. Thomson and former Territorial Governor Eugene Semple directing the Seattle & Lake Washington Waterways Company.[37] These men literally moved mountains of soil irrespective of the city's hilly topography in order to attain their goals of an accessible Seattle.

The tideflats south of the first Tenderloin were eyed as a nuisance to development since they were covered with one to twelve feet of water at any one time, a condition that worsened during the rainy winter months. It prevented the expansion of industrial development that was beginning to settle in that area of the city. The tideflats were identified as the "only level tract of land within the city and close to the business portion available for the location of railway depots and terminal facilities, mercantile warehouses and

SOUTH WELLER STREET

5TH AVENUE SOUTH (FUTURE ALIGNMENT)

SOUTH DEARBORN STREET (FUTURE ALIGNMENT)

Residential hotels along the tideflat area that was filled from the Jackson Regrade project. Photo shows the back facades of Eagle House Hotel, Hotel Fremont, and the Hotel Wayne (left to right) that were all built on piers. All three were Japanese-operated hotels. The entry to these hotels fronted 6th Avenue South. [Courtesy Washington State Historical Society at WashingtonHistory. org, Asahel Curtis Collection, 1943.42.10258]

manufacturing plants."[38] Piers provided the structural foundation system for buildings that were constructed close to the tideflats, many of which were residential hotel buildings.[39] The solution to problems with water-inundated lands and impassable hills rested in a proposal to construct a canal that would connect Lake Washington with Elliott Bay and use the eastern sloping hillside of Beacon Hill to fill in the adjacent tideflats.

Between July 1895 and May 1896, the Seattle & Lake Washington Waterways Company began the South Canal connection by sluicing the Beacon hillside and filling almost 100 acres of the tideflat lands. On completion, the 5,802,000 cubic yards of soil created an estimated 175 acres of developable land at a cost of slightly less than $3,000 per acre. It was a sum that was still far less than the cost of building wharves in order to accommodate development.[40]

The loan for the $500,000 financial undertaking was guaranteed repayment through the sale of properties that would be made possible from the reclaimed tideflat lands. Semple was convinced that the company would recover many times the amount of the loan from the increased value of buildable parcels. The H.H. Dearborn Company regularly ran advertisements for the sale of 150 total lots that would be recovered south of King Street once the tideflats were filled. Developing industrial property that had ready access to the waterfront would be a guarantee of increasing trade with the Orient and the West Coast, according to *The Seattle Post-Intelligencer*.[41]

The planning phase for a massive regrade project leveling out the hills south of Yesler Way was also beginning in earnest. The potential benefit of transportation and public works projects grabbed the attention of Seattleites with reports that recognized what the improvements would mean to the prosperity of the City in expanding commercial business and industrial markets on level land. The proposed cut and fill of the regrade and tideflat projects were touted as being "among the greatest and most beneficial engineering works of the age and the wonder of the world [in making] Seattle an ideal commercial city."[42]

The challenge of both projects was considerable as grades and impediments of accessing properties to the east and southeast of the Tenderloin were severe. In one example, the 1889 planking and grading of the west to east Mikado Street were 7' where it crossed 8th Avenue South and rising to 168' at the west side of the 12th Street intersection. Thomson's vision championed the dominance of urban planning as being a function and responsibility of city government. Private enterprise and the railroads were acknowledged participants in building a strong city, but decision-making power rested with the municipality. A plan to regrade large sections of Seattle's downtown had two issues for property owners: one was how the elevation changes in public rights-of-way would be evaluated for their effect on private property values and a second concern was how private property parcels and existing buildings would physically meet the new topography.

Thomson's regrading campaign had to address an 1892 State Supreme Court decision that offered "municipal consideration" to property owners. The Court determined that adjacent property owners had to give consent to proposed street improvements, including any cuts and fills that might affect their property, and that waivers to any claims of damage or loss of property values must be signed prior to work commencing.[43] The court further stated that Seattle's long-standing practice of establishing the grade of a street by connecting sections based on cross-street elevations could no longer be done without regard for its effect on private property. The burden of proof was on the property owner to show damage and, if substantiated, the city would be responsible for compensation that would be paid in advance of the work. *The Seattle Post-Intelligencer* reported that the work

> ...revolutionize[d] the methods of street grading in Seattle. Grades are no longer to be in straight lines from one cross street to another....In all other cases the street will follow the inclinations of the ground...the greater the hollow or rise, the greater the necessity for adhering to it... cities...have no power to condemn land or to damage it without the consent of the owner....[44]

Neither the litigation process nor the number of property owners who would be affected by the regrade dissuaded Thomson's plans to unite sections of the city with broad and traversable streets that would create development opportunities.[45]

Thomson's regrade plan greatly benefitted from an October 1905 property owner petition to the Board of Public Works. Under the terms of the city charter, local improvements could be initiated through petition by property owners that included the nature of the improvement, street names, and a fee to the city.[46]The petition was granted the following month with estimates of frontage improvements in excess of 51,566 feet and at a cost of $450,000. There were four separate regrade project areas south of Yesler Way that included 5th Avenue South, 12th Avenue South, South Jackson Street, and South Dearborn Street that collectively became known as the Jackson Street Regrade project.

On 14 December 1905, City Ordinance 13102 established that property condemnation proceedings could begin. Trials by jury over property compensation disputes commenced in September 1906 in the Superior Court of King County. The Supreme Court for the State of Washington affirmed the validity of the Jackson Street Regrade condemnation proceedings in October 1907. As individual property owners brought suit against the city for inadequate compensation, local assessment districts were being created by the city to pay the cost of the improvements. Juries were instructed to evaluate individual cases on the damages that would be suffered by the proposed regrade less any benefits that would be realized. Damages included the degree of loss to any building and other effects on the land.[47] Benefits to properties were assessed at $6.00 per frontage foot. In January 1908 a court judgment determined a total payment of $132,309 for 552 property owners. The Washington Iron Works Company was awarded $40,000 in damages, the largest sum that had ever been awarded in a property condemnation suit. Some of the larger amounts that were paid went to public entities such as the Northern Pacific Railroad ($14,500) and the Seattle School District #1 ($10,000). As the largest private-property owner of land south of Yesler Way, William Chappell received $14,500 for what the *Seattle Times* called "injury to his dive property."[48] Of the total award, only $652 was paid out to Japanese businesses that were located in areas south of Washington Street, with $1.00 as the judgment for the Japanese Baptist Church.[49]

In March 1907 and as property proceedings progressed, the City's Board of Public Works advertised to receive project grading bids. Seattle awarded the contract to Lewis and Wiley, the only firm that responded to the requests for proposal. The contract gave the firm thirty months for completion, beginning in April 1907 and with completion by October 1909. The total area was defined by South Main Street to the north, 12th Avenue South to the east, Addition Street as the southernmost boundary and Seattle Boulevard/4th Avenue South as the western boundary. The total area included changes to 5.8 miles of streets, 125 acres of land, and removal of 3,400,000 cubic yards of earth south of Yesler Way.

Advocates of the Jackson Street Regrade project commented that there "never was...a regrade in the history of the city that was more important than this" and they anticipated that single-family homes would be built in the area when the regrade was completed.[50] The project began at the intersection of Lane Street and 8th Avenue South on 1 May 1907. Sluice mining operators who gained their experience from Alaska mining operations ran the machinery that removed and relocated soil. The operation employed one foreman in charge of earth above grade and a second who supervised below-grade operations. Above-grade supervision monitored earth and building removal, the latter of which included moving structures to another site or demolishing them. Moving existing housing was a lucrative business where a "three-story frame building, 60 x 120 feet in plan, [could] be raised 40 feet and blocked for about $2,000."[51] The below-grade supervisor was in charge of filling operations and had to monitor settling and stability of the wet soil and raising some buildings so that earth could be placed beneath them.

Regrading private property was done simultaneously with work on the city roads. The cost of ten cents per cubic yard charged to the owner was deemed minimal in lieu of the greater value that would result from having more accessible and higher-quality development property.[52] It was believed that vice in the Restricted District would ultimately disappear once modern buildings and housing were constructed that would bring a better class of clientele to the neighborhood.

Areas where soil was cut or removed from around the buildings required the construction of a new first floor if the building was to remain. Commercial storefronts that had been the first-floor businesses prior to the regrade now became the second story. One such building was the Fujii Hotel. As one of fifty-three Japanese-operated hotels in Seattle at the time of the Jackson Street Regrade, the Fujii was also one of the three oldest Japanese-operated hotels in the city. When Japanese immigrant Chojiro Fujii purchased and renamed the Rainier Hotel at the northwest corner of Maynard Avenue South and South King Street in 1899, it was considered to be the only luxury boarding house hotel for Japanese immigrant patrons; costing fifteen cents for a one night stay. It was the largest of the three oldest Japanese-operated hotels, with nine rooms that each had eighty board-slab beds that were located on the second floor above at-grade level commercial storefronts. It was considered an innovative design, specifically since the other two 1899 hotels—the Nakanishi and Yamamoto—provided sleeping accommodations in their basement spaces.[53] The new first floor of the Fujii Hotel enabled an expansion of commercial businesses with the addition of a grocery and liquor store on the South King Street and Maynard Avenue South corner and a stepped addition to the hotel that responded to the new land grade.

The Japanese Baptist Church, located at 6th Avenue South and South Jackson Street opted to sell the property they had owned since 1901 for $14,000 and relocate two blocks north to 6th and Washington near the heart of Nihonmachi and just beyond the regrade's northern boundary. The building that they had occupied was a featured advertisement for the L.B. Gullett Company as an example of how a building could be saved from the dramatic topographical changes caused by the regrade. When the regrade was completed, a new first floor was built beneath the wooden-framed former church structure with a connection to the brick residential hotel that was built on the parcel to the west. The new connection provided seven storefronts and a central entrance to

Above: Fujii Hotel, before the Regrade. [Courtesy Minoru Fujii Family]

Below: Fujii Hotel, after the Regrade. [Courtesy King County Assessor's Office, Property Record Cards, 1937–1973, Puget Sound Branch, Washington State Archives]

Above: Future Havana Hotel, seen elevated in preparation for the regrade, 5 February 1910. In the background to the right are two other buildings that are also elevated. [Courtesy Washington State Historical Society at WashingtonHistory.org, Asahel Curtis Collection, 1943.42.17319]

Below: Havana Hotel [courtesy King County Assessor's Office, Property Record Cards, 1937-1973, Puget Sound Branch, Washington State Archives]

the forty upper-story rooms of the Havana Hotel, one of the district's growing numbers of single-room occupancy residential hotels in the regrade area.[54]

Work on the regrade project was ongoing with 24-hour, six days a week scheduling with an average of 111 men working on-site every month. Amid the regrade work, the normal operations of the city's rail transportation continued and businesses remained open. Of the 56 blocks affected by grade changes, 29 were excavated and 27 were filled with the removed earth. Waste material was emptied into the tideflat area north of Connecticut Street.[55] Grade changes to the area's streets were dramatic, with South Jackson Street reduced from 15.16% to a 5.04% grade after an 85' cut was completed at the 9th Avenue intersection. The additional 30' widening of Jackson

L.B. Gullett Company Building Movers Advertisement

Street created even more fill dirt for the tideflat area.[56] With the completion of the 12th Avenue Bridge as part of the regrade project, South Jackson Street acted as a conduit to connect Beacon Hill to the downtown and waterfront.

City-owned property comprised over 1,810,000 cubic yards of excavation with an additional excess of 1,458,000 accounting for private property excavation. Mud slides, overflowing and disrupted sewer lines, and sanitary fill added to the cost estimate and extended the completion date of the project. With the majority of the work completed in December 1909, the Board of Public Works accepted the project as finished on 8 March 1910, six months beyond the initial contract deadline.

With buildings moved, altered, or demolished, and streets that were improved and accessible, the vacant properties in the Jackson Street Regrade District were ripe for development. In the area between South Jackson Street, 12th Avenue South, South Dearborn Street, and 5th Avenue South, 374 frame structures had been relocated or razed for new development "below the line." Of forty-four US cities that had been surveyed by the *American Contractors,*

MAP 2-3: *Jackson Street Regrade Cut and Fill [Author]*

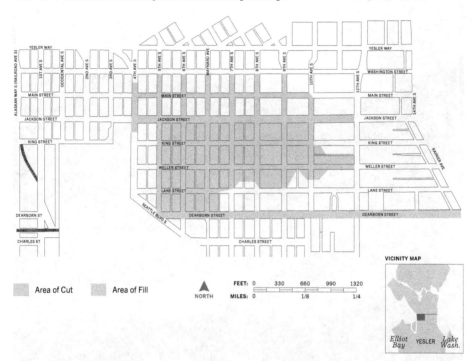

Area of Cut   Area of Fill

NORTH

FEET: 0   330   660   990   1320
MILES: 0   1/8   1/4

VICINITY MAP

Elliot Bay   YESLER   *Lake Wash.*

The Hotel Beacon (center) on South Weller Street was one of the first SROs built in the newly regraded area, ca 1913. [Courtesy Jerry Arai]

Jackson Street Regrade at 8th Avenue and South Weller Street, 1908. [Courtesy The Seattle Public Library, shp_spl_5588]

building operations in Seattle were noted as having declined by over 24% between 1909 and 1910. Yet, no mention had been made of the regrade as a reason for the decline or the prime development lots that were now in demand. *The Seattle Times* reported that "every prominent real estate office in Seattle was canvassed daily for business frontage or improved apartment property... with few genuine bargains...."[57]

The first Chinese District and the interspersed pattern of Japanese retail stores were losing control of the core properties and businesses that they had owned and occupied for decades. In 1906, the two-block area bounded by Yesler Way, Main Street, Fourth and Fifth Avenues South had fifty-seven retail businesses and nearly all of them were either Chinese or Japanese. A move to another location was imminent if the two ethnic communities were going to remain in Seattle. The *Seattle Times* concluded that the most logical place for relocation would be the new development area created by the regrade.

Chinatown cannot be moved north across Yesler Way, west into the new wholesale district, or south into the railroad properties, and therefore east is the logical position for the new Chinatown. It is believed this site may be in the section of four blocks bounded by Yesler Way, Main Street, Fifth Avenue South, and Maynard Avenue. Three or four brick blocks are already planned for this district. The Japanese Bank, now at the corner of Fifth Avenue South and Main Street, is seeking new quarters, and may take one of these proposed buildings.[58]

With the regrade completed and the opening of Union Depot in 1911, factories, businesses, and an expanded commercial and industrial fringe were replacing the land to the south that had once been marshy tideflats. The Asian American community that had been north of the completed station began to shift.

ALASKA-YUKON-PACIFIC EXPOSITION AND PAN-ASIAN SEATTLE

While it wasn't America's first World's Fair city, the 1893 World's Columbian Exposition in Chicago proved that developing a successful international fair could act as a major catalyst for city planning and design.[59] A city that was selected for such an event would reap the benefits of tourism and financial gain. Over 27.5 million visitors saw the World's Columbian Exposition with a financial return of almost $33 million in gross revenues and a $2.25 million return for exposition investors.[60] Money that was indirectly spent on area transportation, food, and hotels for visitors would be an additional gain for private businesses. World's Fairs also brought near limitless opportunity for property redevelopment. The Chicago Exposition had converted a marshy area into a wonderland of Beaux Arts buildings. It had introduced a new idea of the city center that could be created as a cohesive single district from artful placement of municipal buildings. For American cities and municipal governments, it was a venue to answer a call for civic reform and orderly design. As cities became larger and more populated, issues of providing quality environments that addressed health, function, sanitation, housing, transportation, and urban poverty were critical topics. It was the advent of the City Beautiful movement, where function, aesthetics, and financial gain could be accomplished with careful planning, community support, and strong leadership.

In 1904, with the regrade, railway, and tideflat projects underway, city boosters made another civic commitment as they submitted a proposal for Seattle to be the site of a world's fair. There was some speculation about whether Seattle would be able to accommodate the projected number of visitors for the fair if the existing city housing stock could not respond to the more immediate needs of the growing population. Planning, existing municipal projects, and administrative problems delayed the anticipated 1906 date with a new grand opening of the fair planned for 1 June 1909. Unlike other world's fairs, Seattle's would be different in two important aspects. The theme or focus would not be in celebration of a single event commemorating the past as had been done in previous fairs but would have a central theme to celebrate the future and regional resources. Secondly, products from Asia would receive a comprehensive display that had not been done at any other US fair. This event would promote the economies of Alaska, the Yukon, and the Pacific Northwest and publicize the trade that existed with Asian countries. With the goal and theme of building economic alliances with Asia and creating an inclusive regional fair, it was called the Alaska-Yukon-Pacific Exposition (AYPE).

Emphasis on the connection with Asia was done in spite of the knowledge that the United States had but a small share of the world market trade with Asia.[61] City boosters knew that the Chinese and Japanese of Seattle had already shown an active and strong commitment to retaining social ties and developing import and export trade with their native countries. *The Seattle Mail and Herald* predicted that the fair would "increase the commerce of the Pacific by teaching the merchants and manufacturers of the Orient and Occident the needs of the people of their respective markets, and how to secure and hold the business."[62]

A fair that would draw crowds from across the US and showcase Asian connections had the potential to change the trade balance to further develop commercial trade for the United States. Ironically, while acknowledging the importance of international trade and its potential meaning worldwide, there was little if any discussion that connected the impact of federal and local laws that were discriminating against the very Asian American groups whose home countries were the focus of building trade relations.

The fair site was chosen on 285 acres of the University of Washington campus in spite of some expressed concerns that this location was too far from the core of the downtown and that access to the train stations and accommodations were located five miles to the south. While other fairs had constructed a majority of temporary structures that would be dismantled or rebuilt for permanence after a fair was over, the AYPE planning committee opted for permanent structures that would be financed by other countries or states. After the fair, the larger permanent exhibit halls and buildings could be donated as educational facilities for the university, which provided a double benefit for any monies that were appropriated for the fair by the state.[63] It was estimated that the cost of the fair would be $10,000,000, with three-fourths of the money anticipated to come from state and foreign country participants, exhibitors, and concessionaires.

Frank L. Merrick, who was in charge of AYPE publicity and marketing, noted that while the entire city was addressing land improvements and road changes, there was still work that needed to be done in Seattle in order to accommodate visitors during the Exposition. The demolition of old buildings and construction of new ones would continue and while there were some hotels being built, many more would be necessary. Any person contemplating development was urged to get started immediately in order to cash in on the anticipated revenues. According to Merrick, Seattle would be the "queen city... the hostess to many hundreds of thousands of visitors during the exposition, and...the personification of the City Beautiful."[64]

In Spring 1909, passenger managers from James J. Hill's Northern Pacific and the Union Pacific along with those of every other rail line that connected Seattle met and assessed the end-of-the line issues of traffic management and solving problems of how to accommodate regular passengers and those only coming for the fair. T.S. Eustis, passenger manager for the Chicago, Burlington and Quincy Railroad, remarked that "there had never been such a demand with any event as there was now in the Northwest," and while there was every indication that the fair would be a success, Seattle would not likely be able to handle what was about to happen with transportation needs or the hotel accommodations for individuals who would stay after the fair was over.[65]

Portland's 1905 Lewis and Clark Exposition had given the public a preview of what the Northwest had to offer, and now it was Seattle's turn to emphasize the economic power, Pacific Rim connection, and quality of life in Washington. Cities throughout the state looked at the fair as an economic "spillover" opportunity where the entire State of Washington would "sizzle with business activity even after the A-Y-P exposition [and] fill up...with new people the year following the exposition than in any previous year since statehood."[66]

Hill also looked at potential revenues and permanent population as "it was settlers and not sightseers that would show that the Northwest was not just a good place to visit, but a great place to live."[67]

While economic gain was paramount in the minds of Seattle boosters, it was not the overriding concern of Seattle's Asian Americans. Such an event carried the potential to place the ethnic community in a better political and social light, both nationally and internationally. Leaders of the Chinese and Japanese communities clearly understood that their successful involvement and support for the Seattle fair presented an opportunity for them to be culturally understood by the greater community as Americans of Asian heritage.

As the pan-Asian community entered the planning phase of the fair, Asian America was under the cloud of a collection of federal immigration laws and a political arrangement that included the Gentlemen's Agreement, which included new restrictions for Japanese immigration.[68] By the 1 June 1909 opening day of the fair, the Chinese Exclusion law had been in effect for 27 years, with an 1892 renewal and no projected term limit of the law. In 1906, while planning for the Seattle Exposition was underway, Victor Metcalfe, Secretary of the Department of Commerce and Labor, was recommending changes to the exclusion law that included omitting the rule which provided for the admission of persons who would be participating in exhibitions that were authorized by Congress.

While other participating countries paid exhibit construction fees, the Chinese Government made the decision not to provide any funding for building structures for the AYPE. Prior Chinese governmental support to help the Chinese in America as they fought the constitutionality of the Geary Act had proven to be ineffective in 1892, and general sentiment was that the Chinese in America were on their own for fair participation. China's internal political situation and impending changes under the Nationalist Party were at the forefront. As Honorary Consul for Seattle and one of the city's prominent and successful Chinese businessman, Goon Dip saw the fair as a political opportunity and one in which the Chinese might be viewed more favorably and by a large segment of the American population. Even without the financial backing from China, the Chinese American merchants of the West Coast were engaged in planning exhibits and financing a magnificent display.

In addition to exhibits from European countries, the Foreign Exhibits Palace building would house displays from Formosa, Korea, and Thailand. The

United States would pay for the construction of separate building exhibits for Hawaii and the Philippines while China and Japan were to have separate buildings and exhibits whose costs would not be covered.[69]

For the Chinese, the opportunity for participation in the fair held diplomatic possibilities, a fact exemplified by the comments of Seattle Chinese entrepreneurs Ng Hock Moy, Consul Goon Dip, and Chinese American-born scholar and merchant Lew Geate Kay.[70]The work of these three fair proponents organized the construction of a three-building Chinese Village as an exhibit on the "Pay Streak" that was the primary road of the fair. The celebration of China Day on 13 September 1909 was part of the fair's agenda. The Chinese were not interested in simply participating; they were going to engage in an elaborate production and display of the Chinese community in a way that had never been done before. They had the financial means, political savvy, and community support that were necessary to accomplish a grand scale project. Goon Dip served as the overall chair for Chinese participation in the fair with Lew G. Kay as his assistant who was in charge of the China Day Parade. Ng managed the construction and entertainment of the Chinese Village that consisted of the market or bazaar, a Chinese Temple, and a restaurant and tearoom that hosted the China Day banquet as concessionaire for the fair.

In November 1908, the AYPE board approved Ng's plan for construc-tion of a Chinese Village in what would be a replication of a city street scene in China. His idea was "to make the most complete Chinese exhibit ever attempted at an exposition...[and] to bring over a large number of [his] countrymen" to work on the fair.[71] On 7 December 1908, he left Seattle for a five-month trip to China to select and collect materials for construction of the village and to find Chinese talent, primarily from Shanghai, Canton, and Hong Kong, that would exemplify various aspects of Chinese art, entertainment, food, and culture.

As one of the wealthiest Chinese merchants, Ng recognized the sig-nificance of the import and export trade between Seattle and China and the financial backing that Seattle Chinese had made to various industries that were developing in China that included railroads, sawmills, and shipbuilding. He arranged for the performance by the Tin Yung Qui Troupe, a five-member ensemble of acrobats, jugglers, and magicians.[72] As one of the most distinguished performing groups, they had received critical acclaim and $5,000 for a single performance for the Dowager Empress, a fact that raised the cost of their performance in Seattle. Each performance was different, which encouraged crowds of returning patrons.

The Chinese Village cost $25,000 to construct, including over $15,000 for the cost of building the theatre, temple, and exhibits. The Village had the ideal location near the south main entrance and with a 75′ Pay Streak frontage. Members of Seattle's Chinese community contributed an additional $5,000 for China Day, a special one-day extravaganza whose highlight was a downtown parade. Planning for China Day was touted for its uniqueness, with *The Seattle Times* reporting that "no similar pageant [had] ever been presented outside San Francisco, or New York and [that] the Seattle Chinese, working with the greatest enthusiasm and lending every support to their diplomatic head, Consul Goon Dip who is at the head of the China Day Ceremonies...[it] promise[s] to present a show that one cannot afford to miss."[73]

The morning parade began in Chinatown at 3rd Avenue South and Washington Street and proceeded to the north downtown commercial core. It ended at 6th Avenue and South Pine Street where crowds boarded street cars bound for the special events at the Chinese Village that included a second after-noon parade which wound through the Pay Streak of the fairgrounds. The China Day Parade was spectacular, with bands, traditional costumes, thirty autos, and ten floral floats that included advertisements for local Chinatown businesses. The procession was led by Goon Dip and J.E. Chilberg, AYPE president, who rode in the consulate's personal automobile. Between parades a special luncheon was served at Ng's restaurant for both Seattle and fair dignitaries that included Mayor Miller, Chilberg, AYPE entertainment committee members, and leading members of the Chinese community. As grandson **Richard Lew Kay** recalled:

> The 150′ dragon that was in the parade was one that my grandfather, Goon Dip, had bor-
> rowed from Marysville, California. The parade went from old Chinatown up 2nd Avenue
> to Pike. It took over fifty people just to carry the dragon. There were Chinese marching
> and on horseback who were dressed in ancient warrior costumes. All the Chinese con-
> tributed money so that the Chinese community could participate in the two parades.... [74]

While the costumes were traditional Chinese, the Seattle Chinese Americans presented a program that was very Westernized that included singing patriotic American songs. Many of the children who participated were from Portland, with Rose Moy Ling featured as a piano soloist. Lew G. Kay

Chinese Village at the AYPE. [Courtesy The Wing Luke Asian Museum, 1992.069]

Kwong Wa Chong Company float. [Courtesy Richard Lew Kay]

Moy Back Hin. Moy (far left) served as the honorary consul representative in Portland beginning in 1905 and until his death in 1935. In the early years of Goon Dip's arrival to America, he worked for Moy who tutored him on becoming a successful businessman. Their association and friendship lasted for their lifetime and long after Goon's relocation to Seattle. In this photo, Moy is seen with his family members. [Courtesy Richard Lew Kay]

Dragon for the AYP Exposition Parade. [Courtesy Richard Lew Kay]

seized the opportunity to include a political statement in his address to the crowd, thanking America for using the Boxer Indemnity for bringing young Chinese to study at American universities. The day's events were capped by a tremendous double display of fireworks sponsored by the Chinese community and a second exhibition by the Los Angeles Fireworks Company.

At the close of the fair on 16 October 1909, the Chinese Village had made slightly over $16,500, which was about $9,000 less than the total cost of building the exhibit and providing the talent.[75] Before the fair had opened and during the initial stages of planning, Ng had anticipated that this would likely be the case, but then, the intention of the Chinese committee was not motivated by profit but as a display of community solidarity and diplomacy.[76] The Seattle Chinese had indeed "worked with quiet effectiveness and with only about 900 Chinese in Seattle they had organized the largest Chinese celebration that had ever taken or would take place in the city."[77]

The Japanese in America were all settling into the provisions of the Gentlemen's Agreement as plans were underway for the construction of a Japan Village for the AYPE fair. In 1909, 6,124, or about 2.5% of Seattle's total population, were Japanese, outnumbering the Chinese population by about 7:1.[78] The direct and indirect effects of Chinese Exclusion and an aging population of Chinese were decreasing the size of the community while the number of Japanese families in Seattle was on the rise from the provision of the Gentlemen's Agreement that allowed the immigration of parents, wives, and children to Japanese laborers already in the United States.

In February 1909, members of the Washington State House and Senate were each grappling with issues on the treatment of Japanese visitors to the AYPE and those Japanese living in America. Both the House and Senate had voted to assure Washington, DC, and the Japanese government that no bond requirement would be made regarding Japanese who would come to the US to visit the AYPE as long as they gave an assurance that they would make a timely return back to Japan. As introduced by State Representative Lester Edge of Spokane, a measure was being considered that would forbid the employment of Japanese in Washington State to work on public-works projects unless they were going to declare intention to become naturalized citizens, which was impossible under the provision of the Gentlemen's Agreement. Senators James Ghent of King County, John Campbell of Snohomish County, and Representative James Weir of the 44th District favored passage of such a bill as this would ensure that citizens would be employed over foreigners. Campbell argued that if the bill would keep "Japs and Chinese off of public work, he'd support it."[79] The principal argument in favor of indefinite postponement was that the cost of public-works projects would overburden taxpayers. With the second reading of the bill, and following a heated debate on whether such an employment restriction position should be indefinitely postponed until after the fair, it was decided in a 62 to 27 vote to pursue its passage. That same month, T. Takesawa, commissioner for Japanese for the AYPE, had arrived from Japan and declared that whatever anti-race sentiments existed toward the Japanese in America would not impede plans for the largest exhibit ever done by Japanese abroad.

Japanese involvement in special events for the fair was twofold: the 4 June celebration of Japanese Navy Day with the arrival of the ships *Aso* and *Soya* shortly after opening day of the fair, and Japan Day on 4 September. Unlike China, the Japanese government provided financial support for the accompanying Japanese exhibit with a ¥200,000 contribution, the equivalent of $119,300 in funding for the construction of a Japan Village that was located at the center of the exposition site with exhibits representing almost all prefectures.

Japan's naval training squadron, led by Admiral Hokojiro Ijichi, arrived in San Francisco and travelled to the Tacoma port before arriving in Seattle for Japanese Navy Day at the fair. While anti-Japanese sentiments continued in employment sectors, the Japanese fleet had received a hearty welcoming reception from all three cities with the *Olympia Record* reporting that "care should be exercised that there be no demonstration of anti-Japanese sentiment by individuals, no insults to the men of the squadron or anything to mar the welcome.... Let the state's welcome to the Japanese at its chief ports be of a character to further cement the friendly relations between the nations."[80]

Announcement and invitation to the 21 July 1909 dedication and opening reception of the Japanese building were issued by Hajime Ota, Imperial Japanese Commissioner-General to the exposition, and Taichi Takesawa, Director of Exhibits.[81] Festivities for the formal presentation of the building to fair commissioners included an exclusive luncheon of Japanese dishes for Seattle's most prominent citizens and fair officials, a music program and dance in the evening, and gifts to the guests. The design of the Japan building replicated a tenth-century Japanese residence on the exterior with interior decorations of mixed floral arrangement including wisteria as Japan's national flower, and hundreds of glass ornaments on the building interior.

Streets of Tokio, AYP Exposition. [Courtesy The Wing Luke Museum, 1999.098.055]

As festivities of the fair and visitors to the Japan Village continued, Seattle's Japanese community organizers continued the course of planning events for the Japan Day celebration that was scheduled for Saturday,
4 September. The local planning committee consisted of Charles Tetsuo
Takahashi, a prominent banker and acting committee chairman, Y. Kuskibiki
as vice-chairman and head of the exploitation department, with committee
members Tetsuya Arai and H.H. Okuda. Arai was the only Asian American on
the AYPE planning committee and responsible for selecting the date for the
special one-day celebration on behalf of the interests of the greater Northwest
Japanese community. The date was chosen in order to accommodate the schedule of visiting Consul-General Chozo Koike from New York, and visitors who
were to arrive on the *S.S. Minnesota* from Tokyo that included members of
the Imperial Board of Education, the Japanese press, and forty-two of Japan's
leading businessmen and manufacturing moguls.[82]

The latter group of distinguished guests was acting as an honorary
commercial commission on behalf of the industrial centers of Yokohama, Tokyo,
and Osaka. Their visit centered on interest and support of local Japanese at
the AYPE, but also to tour industries and factories of 42 major US cities in a

three-month scheduled visit. [83] The Seattle Manufacturers Association and local chamber of commerce hosted a day-long visit to various area industries on 3 September with each manufacturing site being shown by factory presidents.[84]

As the Japanese Commercial Commissioners toured the factories, the local Japanese community was finishing the months-long preparation for Japan Day. With advanced notice of the agenda, *The Seattle Times* reported that Japan Day was anticipated to be the

> most elaborate parade and fireworks in [the] fair's history [with] four thousand Japanese... taking part.... Fourteen floats...designed at a cost of several thousand dollars...from [one] float there will be scattered thousands of Japanese pennies....Along with the thousands of Japanese residents of Seattle and vicinity, the sons of Nippon are coming from all along the Pacific Coast and throughout the Northwest to take part in the parade and in the day's celebration. From Eastern cities, even...Montreal and New York, and on out along the line, Japanese are coming to Seattle.[85]

To maximize the opportunity for Seattle's Nikkei to attend Japan Day, every Japanese business in Seattle agreed to close. A $10,000 contribution from members of Seattle's Japanese community was donated to cover the costs for this single event. Like China Day, the festivities began with a downtown parade in the morning and were followed by events on the fairground. Beginning in Pioneer Square, the route went north along First Avenue at Yesler Way, turning on Virginia and heading south along 2nd Avenue and terminating at Yesler Way and 3rd Avenue just north of Chinatown.

Japanese businesses were decorated with US and Japanese flags, bands played national anthems of both countries, and the visiting commissioners rode in a fifty-automobile procession, with each car decorated in the national colors and flags of both. A second parade was at the fairgrounds and equaled the spectacular display that had occurred downtown. The *Bellingham Herald* recalled that "fifty Samurai in ancient armor [sic] were followed by 100 flower girls in native dress...200 merchants in native costume and...500 Japanese representing the various trades and professions of Japan.... Two beautiful girls riding on a temple float and representing the goddess of wealth and beauty threw thirty thousand Japanese coins to the crowds as they passed."[86]

Upon entry through the east gate of the fairgrounds, each visitor received a flag of Japan. Ten thousand flags were available for disbursement,

and 1,000 had a lucky number imprint that entitled the visitor to a corresponding numbered prize that was redeemable in the exhibit building.[87] With
50,000 Japanese lanterns decorating the Pay Streak and placed throughout
the fairground streets and buildings, the vision was meant to transform the
fairgrounds into a Japanese town, an image that would enhance the parade
as it progressed along the Pay Streak. One of the main features of the parade
was a $1,000 float that re-enacted the signing of the Treaty of Kanagawa (now
Yokohama), the first treaty between the United States and Japan, with figurines
representing Commodore Perry and statesman Prince Kamon. The capstone
of the day was a dinner at the National Building, honoring the commissioners
from Japan with an entertainment program in the Auditorium, followed by a
night fireworks display.

In addition to the bands, dignitaries, Seattle police, and samurai on
horseback, the Seattle Japanese community exhibited a depth of solidarity in
that they not only financially supported the parade, but were also participants in
the procession. Floats celebrated Japanese tradition and culture with historic
and folklore characters, sailors, and warriors, but they also exemplified the life of
Japanese in America with floats depicting the Japanese American newspapers
in Seattle, Japanese barbers and billiard hall operators in the city, and Japanese
American farming and crop production in Washington State. Marching through
the Pay Streak and intermittent with the bands and commissioner cars were
the merchants and workers of Nihonmachi: tailors, fruit and vegetable stand
operators, restaurant owners, waiters and dishwashers, artisans, steamship
employees, and the owners of and workers in the Japanese boarding houses and
residential hotels. At the end of Japan Day, it was estimated that all of Seattle's
4,000 Japanese were in attendance, along with 3,000 more that represented the
areas surrounding the city and rural communities, and 2,000 parade watchers.
By every account, Japan Day was a success and credited to the Nihonmachi
community. According to *The Seattle Times:*

> It was a proud day for the Japanese of two hemispheres—an occasion for mutual
> congratulation and rejoicing on the part of the distinguished members of the Imperial
> Japanese Commission now honoring Seattle and the exposition with their official visit...
> the up-and-coming sons of the Mikado who now make this city and this Coast their home.
> Japan Day...was by far the greatest demonstration of the land of the chrysanthemum yet
> made on the Western continent. In many ways it emphasized the present and constantly

growing intimate trade relations between the two great countries bordering the extreme confines of the broad Pacific. Japanese government officials who have traveled all over the world say that there has never been such an assembling of their people outside Japan.[88]

Like China Day, Japan Day netted about $16,000 at the close of the Exposition. Seattle's Chinese and Japanese communities were both well-represented and proactive in their respective exhibit planning at the fair, but attendees were presented a skewed image of Filipinos in the United States.

The War Department had sponsored construction of similar Filipino community exhibits at prior fair events, including the Louisiana Purchase Exposition in St. Louis in 1904 and at the Lewis & Clark Centennial in Portland in 1905. The people of the AYPE Igorrote Village were viewed more like a sideshow and referred to as "half-naked savage(s) of the tropics."[89] The AYPE displayed the Bontoc people, who were from the mountainous region of Luzon Island in the Philippines, much like the Barnum and Bailey circus had done with the display of Chinese in traditional dress as part of their sideshow attractions of the 1870s.[90]

The replicated village of small huts was located at the head of the south Pay Streak. The native dress, songs, dance, weaving, and language of the mountain people drew in massive crowds, who were clearly fascinated with what they saw. Wearing the scant clothing native to their culture and region brought protests by the local Women's Christian Temperance Union (WCTU) on the grounds of moral indecency. They made a request for review of the appropriateness of the exhibit to Seattle Reverend Mark Matthews. Additional protests were voiced by the Filipinos of Seattle, who took exception to both the exhibition of the Bontoc and the misrepresentation of the Filipino immigrant population. Both the popular press and official guide book noted the "tattooed barbaric beauties and cutest of children" and that Igorrote Village needed no promotion to draw patrons as it was "the most extensive, interesting, and amusing exhibit at the exposition."[91]

The Philippine Island display contained "obsolete Spanish stocks and other historic paraphernalia...magnificent pieces of workmanship of the manufacturers of woods as they were made upon the Islands" and an exhibit that *The Coast* journal further characterized as depicting the years of "Spanish misrule [where] a great work has been accomplished....[T]he Yankee school-marm and her brother...have wrought almost miracles in educating the raw material which fell into their hands. Best of all is the wholesome and hearty public spirit and patriotism that is exhibited by the little ones who are pupils in the schools there and in a few years will be the public men and women of that part of the United States"[92]

In addition to the AYPE, 1909 marked the first significant wave of Filipino immigration into America as *Pensionados*; young men who were selected by the US government to access post-secondary educational opportunities. These students represented the brightest and best Filipino scholars. The fact that the United States recognized Filipinos' potential as scholars and professionals in the Philippines made the construction of the Igorrote Village exhibit of the AYPE even more of a shocking dichotomy. The exhibit portrayed a distorted identity of Filipino Nationals to fair goers, who assumed that the display of the indigenous Bontoc tribe was representative of the Philippines and the general Filipino population. American visitors were fascinated by the people and re-created native village with part of the curiosity being motivated by the recently acquired Protectorate status of the Philippines by the United States.

Aside from the Igorrote Village exhibit, the Philippine Constabulary Band, an 84-piece musical ensemble from the Philippines, had a two-week engagement at the fair that began in mid-September in the same week as the China Day celebration. The media had nicknamed the performers "Taft's Own Band" in recognition that they had initially been organized by President Taft when he held the earlier post of territorial governor to the Philippines.[93] The fair was near the end of the band's seven-month tour of the US. With two daily performances, the band served as official musical escort to the president on his visit to the fair and the official Taft Day of the AYPE. Delighted with their performance at the AYPE, Taft stated that their presence in the United States did more to dispel the ignorance concerning the Filipino than any form of favorable legislation for them.[94]

At a total cost of $10,000,000 and with 90% of the $350,000 bond paid by mid-September, the fair's executive committee anticipated that the last two weeks of the exposition would cover the rest of the bond and return a net profit, particularly with the guaranteed presence of President Taft and the performances by the Philippine Constabulary Band. By all accounts the AYPE was a commercial success, with an average daily attendance of 27,000 people.

As the fair closed, the interest in Seattle was growing exponentially, and property values, investments, and development opportunities were at the

A scene from Igorrote Village, showing men and children with Masonic Lodge Members. [Courtesy MOHAI, Frank H. Nowell Alaska-Yukon-Pacific Exposition Photographs, 1990.73.144]

forefront of conversation with real estate companies, private owners, and the press. As James J. Hill had predicted, the increase of Seattle's resident population from 1900 to 1910 almost tripled to a phenomenal 237,194. *The Coast* reported that "real estate values had risen so rapidly that strangers unfamiliar with the circumstances have regarded the advances with suspicion....Unless one understands the causes from the inside, such as radical changes in the physical character of a district wrought by a giant regrade...and the coincident of half a dozen transcontinental railway systems racing for entrance into Seattle at the same time, he must be justified if he is skeptical."[95]

The combination of developable land, the exposure from the Alaska-Yukon-Pacific Exposition, and accessibility from comprehensive and completed rail lines that could serve an incoming and curious population of visitors and would-be Seattleites was a formula for a boom in the city's manufacturing and industrial growth and the consequent need for housing a broad spectrum of workers to Seattle.

Under the leadership of Asian American Seattle, both the Chinese and Japanese Village buildings were planned in a way that would be visually satisfying to the public's expectation of Asia and Asian America in that they were designed to be reminiscent of traditional Oriental temple buildings. They employed the illusion of the classic and characteristic architectural motif of rooflines, upturned eaves, and screens that were not in keeping with authentic structural members of temples, such as the Chinese Village pavilion or the Temple of the Goddess Kishibojin at Hamamura Japan that was used as the prototype for the Japanese Village.[96] The fair perpetuated an image of Asian America through use of a satisfying familiar design concept. The AYPE event and the newly graded land of the south downtown coincided with the timing of the building of Seattle's new core for Chinatown and Nihonmachi. The Asian motifs of buildings that were selected by and represented Asian American Seattle at the AYP Exposition were not mimicked or duplicated for their community. The architectural design and construction of pan-Asian Seattle was the single-room occupancy residential hotel.

ENDNOTES

1   Edmond S. Meany, "Historical Sketch of Seattle," *The Coast*, October, 1909, Vol. XIX, No. 4, p. 226.

2   The term "Tenderloin" refers to the vice district of a city.

3   Matthew Klingle: *Emerald City: An Environmental History of Seattle* (New Haven: Yale University Press, 2007), p. 96.

4   Greg Lange, Senior Archivist, Puget Sound Regional Archives. Conversation 3 September 2010.

5   "Hypocrisy as Usual," *Patriarch*, 25 June 1910, p. 1, col. 3.

6   "The Removal of the Tenderloin," *The Sunday Times*, 11 May 1902, p. 1, cols. 1–6.

7   Mildred Tanner Andrews, ed. *Judge J.T. Ronald: Reflections Along the Wayside of Life* (Shoreline, WA: Shoreline Historical Museum, 2003), 128–129.

8   Judge Ronald coined the terms and description for these two areas.

9   Ronald's past efforts to eradicate Black Chapel surfaced again in 1900 when City Health Officer Dr. McKechnie vowed to rid the area of "unhealthy" buildings and practices within the buildings that were contributing to unhealthiness.

10 "Clean People of Seattle in Revolt," *The Seattle Daily Times*, 5 March 1900, p. 1, col. 7. Humes defeated Cotterill and was re-elected as mayor on 6 March 1900.

11 Ibid.

12 "Mr. Godwin's Letter," *The Seattle Daily Times*, 1 March 1902, p. 6, col. 1, 2.

13 "Moving the Deadline," *The Seattle Mail and Herald*, 5 April 1902, p. 4, col. 1.

14 Ibid.

15 "The Removal of the Tenderloin."

16 "Stands by Sullivan," *The Daily Times*, 2 December 1902, p. 7, col. 4–6.

17 Some of the property for the southern mouth of the tunnel had been purchased in early 1902 from local land mogul William Chappell.

18 "Chief of Police Defines His Course," *The Seattle Daily Times*, 3 April 1903, p. 1, col. 3, p. 2, col. 1.

19 Stephen W. Kohl, ed, and translator "An Early Account of Japanese Life in the Pacific Northwest," *Pacific Northwest Quarterly*, April 1979, Vol. 70, No. 2, p.60. Accessed 29 May 2013. http://www.jstor.org/stble/40489823. Kohl's translation is based on Nagai Kafū: *America Monogatari* (American Tales), 1908. Kohl notes that Kafū was the author's pen name and that his real name was Nagai Sōkichi.

20 Ibid. Kafū specifically identifies the beginning of the Japanese District at a point where a "foul-smelling" and "large black gas tank" was located. Sanborn Fire Insurance Maps note this as the Seattle Gas and Electric Company Plant that was located at Jackson Street and 4th Avenue South.

21 Kohl, p. 61–62.

22 "New District is Talked of Again," *The Seattle Daily Times*, 9 February 1905, p. 4, col. 4.

23 Ibid.

24 *The Seattle Times*, 21 April 1907, p. 29, col. 4.

25 Ernest Crutcher, "Yesterday, Today and Tomorrow," *The Seattle Mail and Herald*, 21 May 1906, Vol. IX, #27, p. 5, col. 3.

26 "Announcement," *The Coast*, August 1909, Vol. XVIII, p. 66, 71.

27 "Underground Railroad Tracks: A Feasibility Plan to Provide for the Requirements of the City," *Seattle Post-Intelligencer*, 1 January 1895, p. 10, col. 4.

28 Negotiations were done with James J. Hill, with the interests of the Great Northern represented through attorney Thomas Burke, representatives of the Northern Pacific, and city engineer, Reginald Thomson.

29 "Tunnel Under Business Section," *Seattle Post-Intelligencer*, 23 March 1902, p. 3, cols. 1, 2. The Snowshoe and Peerless saloons would also be removed.

30 "Seattle's China Town As It Is," *Seattle Post-Intelligencer*, 14 December 1902, p. 43, col. 7.

31 Ibid.

32 Seattle, City Ordinance 9116 (5 January 1903).

33 While it was hoped that the Union Pacific Station would be finished in time for the 1909 Alaska-Yukon-Pacific Exposition as Seattle World's Fair, the passenger terminal did not open until 20 May 1911.

34 Seattle, City Ordinance 9116 (5 January 1903).

35 E. Hofer, "The Problems of Seattle," *Pacific Monthly*, June/July 1904, Vol. 11, p. 116.

36 Early regrading projects began in 1876 with the First Avenue project from Pike to James Streets. While discussions were ongoing on street improvements, substantial grading changes in the upper downtown didn't occur until after the 1889 fire. Yesler Way was regraded and widened to 84' in order to create a street system that was manageable for horse and wagon. Streets throughout the city were being raised and lowered with fire debris to fill gullies and the tideflats. From Third Avenue South through the core of Chinatown, Yesler Way's grade was elevated one foot with a grade increase of 35' that went three blocks to the south at Jackson Street.

37 Semple served as the governor of Washington from 1887–1889. Thomson was appointed as City Engineer three times with the first service in 1882–1886, followed by reappointment in 1892–1911, and finally 1930–1931.

38 "Seattle's Tide Flats: A Vast Improvement
Enterprise to Be Commenced Soon," *Seattle
Post-Intelligencer*, 1 January 1895, p. 25, col. 6.

39 Railroad lines in the city and along the waterfront
were limited to lands that avoided the tideflats
or used trestle systems to skirt the worst of the
water. Beacon Hill was an impediment as it separated the coal and timber resources east of Lake
Washington from convenient and ready shipping
from Elliott Bay.

40 Myra Phelps, *Public Works in Seattle: A Narrative
History The Engineering Department 1875–1975*
(Seattle: Kingsport Press, 1978), 62.

41 "Who Says Boodle?" *Seattle Post-Intelligencer*,
22 January 1900, p. 9, cols. 1–4.

42 "Seattle's Tide Flats," *Seattle Post-Intelligencer*,
1 January 1895, p. 25, col. 6.

43 Seattle Municipal Archives, Record Series 4404-
01, Box 1 Folder 1, 1890.

44 "Street Grade Law," *Seattle Post-Intelligencer*,
18 October 1892, p. 5, cols. 3, 4.

45 The Denny Street project on the north side of
the downtown was the first such major regrade
that began in the city with the first construction
contract awarded in 1898.

46 Seattle, City Ordinance 13309 (9 February 1906).

47 Superior Court of King County, Washington,
Civil Case #50960, Condemnation for Jackson
Regrade, 10 December 1906.

48 "Regrade Work to Start Soon," *The Seattle Daily
Times*, 28, October 1906, p. 2, col. 3.

49 Properties that were occupied by the Chinese
and Japanese north of Washington Street were
located outside of the Jackson Street Regrade.

50 "Advocates Regrade of Twelfth Avenue," *Seattle
Post-Intelligencer*, 4 April 1909, p. 1, col. 3.

51 "The Seattle Regrade, with Particular Reference
to the Jackson Street Section," *Engineering News:
a Journal of Civil, Mechanical, Mining and Electrical Engineering*, 12 November, 1908, Vol. 60,
No. 20, p. 511.

52 Fees were payable in cash or in installments of up
to ten years.

53 The Nakanishi Hotel at 206 Jackson Street had
seven rooms with fifty beds and the Yamamoto
Hotel on Jackson Street between Third and
Fourth Avenues had 5 rooms and 50 beds. The
beds were arranged in bunk fashion. In July 1913,
the Seattle City Council made the decision that
sleeping rooms located in basements that were
located 2/3 below grade needed to have windows
that were at least 1/10 the dimension of the total
basement floor area. Basements that were used
for lodging purposes had to provide a window for
every room that was incorporated in an outside
wall of the building or to a wall leading to a court-
yard.

54 One of the most substantial buildings to be razed,
and occupying the equivalent of an entire city
block in the regrade area, was the Academy of
the Holy Names, a Catholic girls' school that sat
imposingly on a hilltop at the southeast corner
of South Jackson Street and 7th Avenue South.
The area that had been home to the Academy
remained vacant until 1916 when a residential
hotel was built by the Bing Kung Tong. It was
one of the last hotel buildings that would be
constructed south of Yesler Way.

55 Phelps, p. 22.

56 Streets between Yesler Way and Jackson Street
were largely left undisturbed, and grades at 10th
Avenue South remained at 36%. Streets south of
Jackson all underwent some changes, ultimately
being in a grade range of .07% to 7.25%. Dearborn Street's grade was reduced from 19% to 3%
with a 112' cut at 12th Avenue South.

57 "First Class Lots in Demand," *Seattle Times*,
24 January 1909, p. 7, col. 2.

58 "Old Chinatown is to be Wiped Out," *Seattle Times*,
2 March 1906, p. 1, col. 2.

59 The first US exposition was the Centennial
Exposition in Philadelphia that ran from May to
November 1876.

60 Alexander Garvin, *The American City: What Works,
What Doesn't* (New York: McGraw Hill, 1996), 76.

61   The Department of Commerce and Labor recognized that of the $3.7 billion of annual import and export activity of countries bordering the Pacific Ocean, 4/5 of the trade with Asian countries was between Asia and Europe, a phenomenon that the government attributed to as a better knowledge of trade conditions.

62   "Alaska-Yukon Pacific Exposition," *The Seattle Mail and Herald*, 17 November 1906, Vol. 9, #52, p. 4.

63   Seven major buildings were donated to the University of Washington following the close of the fair. These included the Auditorium, Fine Arts, Machinery, Washington, Arctic Brotherhood, Forestry, and Women's buildings.

64   "Says City Should be Bright for Fair," *Seattle Post-Intelligencer*, 29 July 1906, p. 11.

65   Ibid.

66   "State Growth Follows A.Y.P.," *Morning Olympian*, 7 January 1909, p. 1, col. 3.

67   "What the AYP Fair Means to the Pacific Northwest," *Oregonian*, 16 May 1909, Section 5, p. 4

68   Japan and the United States entered into an informal agreement in 1907–08 that would stop the immigration of Japanese skilled and unskilled laborers coming into the country and enable the US to deny secondary immigration of Japanese seeking to enter from neighboring Canada and Mexico. In return for Japan's cooperation, President Theodore Roosevelt guaranteed that San Francisco's School Board decision that was segregating Japanese school children would be rescinded. Roosevelt sought to appease both the Japanese Government and a growing faction of Japanese Exclusionists in California. Called the Gentlemen's Agreement, the political arrangement did not have the same effect as Chinese Exclusion law in that it included exceptions for provisions of entry that were given to wives, children, and parents of Japanese laborers already in the US, an action that helped balance the gender disparity of a primarily male population and enable the birth of second-generation Japanese Americans. The Gentlemen's Agreement was superseded with the Immigration Act of 1924, which stopped all Japanese immigration.

69   The commitment to pay for exhibition buildings for Hawaii and the Philippines directly related to imperialist control of these islands. See Kornel Chang, *Pacific Connections: The Making of the US-Canadian Borderlands* (Berkeley: University of California Press, 2012). Independent nations were expected to cover their own costs for participation in the fair.

70   Ng was more popularly known as Ah King. Seattleites, in both the white and Chinese communities, thought of him as the unofficial mayor of Chinatown. *The Seattle Times* made reference to him as "Mayor of the Local Mongolian Colony." Shortly following the closing of the fair, Ng was summoned to help mediate the end of tong wars in San Francisco and Oakland. The conference of Chinese delegates took place in Portland, Oregon, in December 1909. In an interview with *The Seattle Times*, Ng related that "Seattle Chinese are interested [in settling tong disputes] only in so far as they propose to protect the good name of the race…all Chinese in America are deeply concerned to make the best impression upon the American people as is possible and we cannot hope to do this if we are going to permit the lawless ones among us to do as they are doing in California. The ordinary peace laws of America will never stop the wicked ones among my people from fighting, but Chinese have customs of their own, which generally prove effective." "Dire Threat made to Stop Tong War," *The Seattle Times*, 19 December 1909, p. 10, col. 2.

71   "Chinese Temple to Grace 1909 Exposition Grounds," *The Seattle Sunday Times*, 15 November 1908, p. 20, col. 3.

72   The troupe consisted of five performers, one of whom was a woman, and their manager. Their fair performance was so successful that they were contracted to play in some East Coast vaudeville theatres following the AYPE. According to immigration rules, their US stay would only be allowed until 10 February 1910.

73   "Chinese to Have Their Own Day," *The Seattle Sunday Times*, 12 September 1909, p. 3, col. 5.

74   Conversation with Richard Lew Kay, son of Lew G. Kay and grandson of Goon Dip, 17 September 2009.

75 Patricia Hackett Nicola, "Day of the Dragon: The Chinese Community's Participation in the Alaska-Yukon-Pacific-Exposition," *Columbia*, 24, 2, Summer 2010, p. 14–17. Hackett notes that the total revenues from the China Village were $21,451 with $4,863 of that amount going to the AYPE revenues as the cost for participation.

76 Presentation by Howard King, grandson of Ah King at the "Asian-Pacific Perspectives at the AYPE" symposium. Seattle, Washington, 13 September 2009.

77 Ibid.

78 City of Seattle, Office of Policy Planning: Population Trends by Race in the Seattle Area 1900–1976 (February 1977).

79 "Jap Question Before House," *Morning Olympian*, 11 February 1909, p. 4, cols 4, 5. The issue of Asian American labor on public works contracts had been one of concern since at least 1876 when Quong Coon Lung submitted the lowest and winning bid of $9,000 for grading Seattle's Front Street. The city council and local newspapers received a number of complaints regarding their hire. Without comment or explanation, the Chinese company withdrew its bid on 30 September 1876. Three days later, the work had commenced with a crew of sixty white workers.

80 *Olympia Record*, 24 May 1909, p. 2, col. 3.

81 The original anticipated date of the opening was 15 July.

82 The ship was scheduled to dock in Seattle on 2 September 1909.

83 Special invitation for the tour of US cities and industries had been extended by local chambers of commerce along with the Board Commissioners of the fair. Roger S. Greene of the US Consular Service was detailed to accompany the envoy via special rail service to all of the US cities. The goal of the visit was making economic connections and ascertaining what potential exports and imports could be developed for trade between the two countries. Tacoma, Spokane, and Seattle were on the agenda for Washington State visits, with Seattle being the first city.The route of the trade visit included, in order: Seattle, Tacoma, Portland, Spokane; St. Paul, Minneapolis, and Duluth, Minnesota; Butte, Montana; Anaconda, Fargo, and Grand Forks, North Dakota; Madison and Milwaukee, Wisconsin; Chicago, Illinois; Grand Rapids and Detroit, Michigan; Toledo and Cleveland, Ohio; Buffalo, Rochester, Syracuse, New York City, and Albany, New York; Newark and Paterson, New Jersey; Philadelphia and Pittsburgh, Pennsylvania; New Haven, Connecticut; Providence, Rhode Island; Boston, Massachusetts; Washington, DC; Baltimore, Maryland; Indianapolis, Indiana; St. Louis and Kansas City, Missouri; Omaha, Nebraska; Denver, Colorado; Albuquerque, New Mexico; Los Angeles, San Diego, Oakland, Redlands, and San Francisco, California. The entourage left the US for Japan from San Francisco on 23 November 1909.

84 Visits in Washington included the Seattle Brewing and Malting Company, Washington Shoe Manufacturing Company, Moran's Shipyard, and the Pacific Coast Condensed Milk Company in Kent with an additional industrial visit to the Albers Brothers Milling Company in Portland, Oregon.

85 "Nippon's Day to be Big Event," *The Seattle Times*, 3 September 1909, p. 1, col. 1.

86 "Japs Give Fair Oriental Hue," *Bellingham Herald*, 4 September 1909, p. 1, col. 2.

87 Ibid. Prizes included tea, pottery, art, embroidery, pearl jewelry, and a rare tea set.

88 "Japan's Day Marks New Era," *The Seattle Times*, 4 September 1909, p. 1, col. 3; p. 2, col. 2.

89 "The Alaska-Yukon-Pacific Exposition," *The Coast*, September 1909, Vol. XVIII, No. 3, p. 174.

90 Ibid.

91 *Official Guide to the Alaska-Yukon-Pacific Exposition- Seattle, Washington, June 1– October 16, 1909*, p. 44. *The Seattle Sunday Times*, 11 July 1909, p. 29.

92 The A.-Y.-P. Exposition is a Success," *The Coast*, August 1909, Vol. 18, #2, p. 77.

93 The band played at Taft's inaugural parade in Washington, DC on 4 March in 1909.

94 "Philippine band at Fair for Two Weeks," *The Seattle Sunday Times*, 12 September 1909, p. 18, col. 4. Like Igorrote Village, the Constabulary Band was a part of the 1904 Louisiana Purchase Exposition. The Philippine band made multiple performances and received both surprised reactions and critical acclaim when they defeated John Philip Sousa's Band, the English Grenadier's Guard, and the Royal Italian and Mexican National Bands in the St. Louis fair's international band contest.

95 "Seattle Real Estate Values and Investments," *The Coast*, September 1909, Vol. XVIII, No. 3, p. 155.

96 "Chinese Temple to Grace Exposition Grounds," *The Seattle Sunday Times*, 15 November 1908, p. 20., col. 2.

The Business of Building Residential Hotels

DEFINING SINGLE-ROOM HOUSING

From the mid-1850s into the 20th century, American cities were experiencing unprecedented growth made possible by technological advancements in manufacturing, the rise of industrial developments, and the expansion of transportation systems. The combination was transforming the physical appearance of downtown centers and offering an economic livelihood for anyone who was willing to work or live in a diverse urban core.

Inventions such as the Otis elevator in the 1850s and the ability to use innovations such as steel frame for building construction enabled the city to dramatically expand usable space vertically as lower-rise wooden-frame buildings began to give way to taller and more lucrative construction projects. While the elevator helped create the tall office buildings, it was an invention that also enhanced hotel design and its associated appeal to potential residents. The elevator was one amenity that helped classify the type and quality of a hotel from a cheap sleeping-room building to one that was a luxury accommodation.

Tall office buildings reflected growing commerce in central business districts with the surrounding fringe areas of the downtown used for low-rise commercial services and lodging facilities for workers.[1] The development of railroad stations and the influx of visitors and travelers exacerbated an already existing demand for housing in Seattle and other cities that were experiencing rising populations. The lives of business entrepreneurs and moguls, visitors, land speculators and developers, workers and transient laborers created the human mosaic of the city, but their social lives rarely intersected with one another as each economic class found accommodations and social acceptance in their respective places of work and residence.

Since the Civil War, traveling associated with various sectors of transient and temporary employment had been increasing and becoming commonplace.[2] Transportation modes and means linked metropolitan centers to agricultural and industrial belts beyond the city limits and changed the demographics of central cities where the population could shrink and swell depending on employment opportunities in and outside urban cores. Central-city accommodations for a single laboring work force in nineteenth-century America consisted of living in single rooms that were made available for rental in a number of building types. These included boardinghouses and lodging houses that were, for the most part, adapted from single-family detached housing units or in generic loft buildings whose interior rooms and hallways could be altered to respond to any market-based user preference.[3] The boardinghouses that provided meals on the premises as part of the night's rental fee and within a socially interactive setting were reported as a residential type that "[had] passed out of existence in the modern city" by the mid-1920s.[4] In its place were structures that were specifically designed to function as lodging facilities and referred to as a rooming houses, depot hotels, or single-room occupancy (SRO) residential hotels.

The rising number of people who were seeking hotel living was a markedly different trend from the late-1850s, when hotel living in general was said to be on the decline with the rising interest in domesticity. *Harper's Weekly* noted that this social characteristic was "dealing a death blow to the old system of family life in hotels."[5] During these earlier years, public commentary indicated that hotel living was thought to be an unhealthy environment for both women and children; a pervasive sentiment during the Victorian influence on housing and design that, among other things, eliminated temptation of immoral behavior by separating rooms according to their function.[6]

The creation of the "railroad depot hotel," or SRO lodging facilities, met the demand for housing the city's laboring-class, poor, transient, and

immigrant populations. The economic and social standing of the patrons ultimately shaped the design and amenities of the building and differentiated them
from upper-class hotels. The appeal of the SRO hotels was in their immediate
accessibility to railroad stations and inner-city transit and their flexibility for
short- or long-term stays at a very modest price. A lease was neither necessary
nor desirable for a patron who might want to move at a moment's notice to take
a job elsewhere or to relocate to another SRO hotel if a more attractive room
became available. The scale of "attraction" could be as simple as providing the
resident with a sink in their room, a desk in addition to the bed, a wardrobe closet
in place of hooks on the wall, or having more bathing facilities on each floor.
The more upscale lodging hotels might have a sink with hot and cold running
water in the room, a desirable amenity that was advertised in city directories
or on advertisement signs painted on buildings to attract potential patrons.[7]

Unlike the more centrally located luxury hotels that presented an
environment of "grandeur, comfort, and service" with posh furnishings, formal guest services and amenities such as valets, maids, desk clerks, and private bathing and dining room facilities, a typical lodging house design was a
sparsely-furnished room without a kitchen in or available to residents of the
building.[8] Small rooms of 6′ x 8′ to 10′ x 12′ were typical sizes of Seattle's SRO
hotels; a dimension that was just adequate enough to meet the needs of a bed
and maybe a small desk or bureau for a single person.[9] Small rooms intended
for one person characterized the design and their identity as "single-room-occupancy residential" hotels. Many variations existed in the material used in
the construction, height, the layout or incorporation of window light wells, the
façade, and floor plans of these buildings. The most common characteristic that
distinguished these hotels was the combination of a small room for sleeping and
shared dormitory-style bathing facilities located down the hall.[10] The number of
baths and toilets depended on the design and construction cost that was at the
discretion of the building owner. By 1910, a typical ratio of plumbing facilities
to the number of rooms per floor could be 1:12 or higher.[11]

Early hotel design often relied on pot belly stoves to provide heat in
common public areas with no such amenity in patron rooms. Harnessing steam
from basement boilers in order to provide radiator heat to individual rooms
became part of upper-class hotel design in the late 1840s, with such a luxury
creating yet another division in ranking the quality of the spare residential
hotels. By the mid-1850s, heat from a central boiler allowed for auxiliary uses

of the basement, such as incorporating laundry facilities that were used to wash and dry hotel linens in-house as opposed to sending them out to a commercial service.

Anyone could be a guest in an SRO hotel and for perhaps only a night, your room would be home. The spare economy of the room shaped the demography of the hotel patrons and attracted a host of unskilled and transient laborers, immigrant populations, and those individuals who could easily come and go in response to whatever work opportunity was presented both in and out of the city. The residents were generally thought of by mainstream society as people who were "down on their luck" or people who were, in some way, deemed socially unacceptable.

The SRO was a unique building type that was affordable to build, quick to construct, and capable of bringing a good economic return. This new addition to the downtown building and housing stock made a sudden and dramatic change to the urban landscape. The building maximized development potential and profit by covering one hundred percent of the building lot. In downtown neighborhoods where SROs were predominant, the hotels would create the look of a continuous building façade along the block face of the street and one where individual buildings were only discernible by variations in façades, materials, or designs. By city building codes, light wells were included as part of the building design to prevent cavernous, dark interior rooms and to solve the lack of side façade windows that could occur from the construction of a building on an immediately adjacent parcel. These light wells, along with transom windows above room doors, provided light and air to the rooms and shaped the corridors and stairwells of the floor plan.

For the owners of SRO hotel buildings, the economic return was dependent on the total number of rooms and the corresponding number of paying residents, along with the rental fees collected for the at-grade commercial bays that were part of the building design. The commercial services in these bays and within the neighborhood catered to and were supported by the area residents and the hotel patron community. Commercial uses, such as restaurants, grocers, bars, drug stores, sundry shops, laundries, barbers, and bathhouses, and other necessary and affordable services, provided arenas for social interaction. The idea that a single person could live beyond the confines of a nuclear family and establish a one-room "home" challenged social reformer viewpoints. Family and home could encompass the unrelated people in the building and the community-at-large. While intended for short stays, it was common for long-term occupancy to occur, particularly for those transient laborers who would use their rooms to store personal belongings as they travelled to seasonal or temporary work in canneries, in mines, on farms, or with the railroads. There was security in knowing there was a place that held your possessions and comfort in knowing you could return to your "home."

In the absence of a national standard, each American city relied on its own definition of "hotel" through municipal codes. In 1909, the City of Seattle Building Ordinance defined a hotel as "a building or part thereof intended, designed, or used for lodging purposes and having more than twenty sleeping rooms for guests."[12] It was the number of sleeping rooms in the building that differentiated a "hotel" from either a "boardinghouse" or "lodging house" in that the code indicated that these latter two residential types contained between five and twenty rooms, a much smaller number than the residential hotel buildings that had been constructed in the building boom years between 1910 and 1925.[13] By 1912, the city code included the word "transient" to describe the guest. Ultimately for Seattle, an SRO came to be known as a building type that was "understood," but without any specific definition in the city building code. Whether to include the word "hotel" in the name of the establishment continued to be an issue that was at the discretion of the building or business owner and to the chagrin of the National Hotel Association.[14]

Without a more precise definition that would categorize hotels, and amid growing suspicion about the legitimacy of activities that were taking place within these buildings, the residents assumed the same characterization as the hotels, and most especially so with the SROs. In the tradition established by social reformers and opinions that connected tenement living of the mid-1800s with social demise, sociologists of the 1920s did not profile lodging-house living favorably. Living in a hotel was depicted as remote and socially detached from other patrons of the establishment and where residents lived in the absence of interpersonal and meaningful relationships. In a *Monthly Labor Review* article, hotel living was seen as

> ...the evil-effects of [an] isolated, anonymous life, with its thwarting of normal emotional impulses, upon the character of the individual. Suicide is frequent, social and civic responsibility unknown. The person tends to act without reference to social definition. Behavior is individualized—impulsive rather than social.[15]

In 1922 and with so many buildings being referred to as "hotels" within urban downtown cores, *Hotel Monthly* magazine sought national clarification for the meaning of the word itself. With a careful dissemination of the evolution and differences between taverns and inns, boardinghouses, apartment houses, and transient and luxury hotels, the journal sought to legitimize this building type to reflect the social propriety of those who would stay in a building that was intended for temporary lodging. Without some sort of accepted legal standard, it was unlikely that the building type or people who frequented them would have any kind of clear identity. Among its objections, the journal asserted that:

> The word "hotel" is in many respects, the most abused in the English language…. In its legitimate sense it has a true meaning…. It is not intended as a permanent home or residence for any except the proprietor's family and his servants. The word "hotel"…is placed over the doors of houses of many sorts, offering accommodations either restricted, or exclusive, or for lodging only, or for permanent home, as the family hotel and apartment hotel. Many structures with the word "hotel" over the door are houses of ill-fame and where such is the case the word "hotel" suffers its worst abuse. There should be a law making this a disgrace to the town in which they operate…[and] a criminal offense; for such houses are not only a disgrace to the town in which they operate, but an insult to every respectable traveler beguiled within the portals by the name over the door…. The word hotel, in its abused sense, has kept the legitimate hotel business from tabulation in the United States census. There should be some line of demarcation by which the government…could have a census of the legitimate hotels. Under existing conditions, however, this is impossible. The great need is to have a uniform law defining a hotel….[16]

While the call for a "uniform law" was not forthcoming, the Hotel Association of New York City attempted to perform a count of what they considered to be "legitimate" hotels in the United States in 1922. They eliminated any building that was considered to be a "rooming house or houses of ill repute."[17]

It was unclear whether residential hotel buildings were included in any of the national data counts that assessed housing starts as new construction nor was it evident whether the people who lived in them were considered to be any kind of addition to the numbers that reflected urban populations.[18] While SROs were in most American cities, the Bureau of the Census kept no statistical count of the number of people who lived in the building type and there was no indication of common criteria as to how each city was defining the word "hotel" as either a building type or for residential use.[19]

In 1928, Washington State defined a "hotel," but definitely not to the recommended standard that *Hotel Monthly* magazine had wanted to see six years earlier. For the State, a hotel was "any building or dwelling which contained five bedrooms to be rented out to transient guests...by the day or the week."[20] There were still no national statistics on the rising SRO hotel population, but a 1928 study of hotel residents of 437 of Seattle's upper-class and transient residential hotels indicated

> ...seasonal fluctuations...[with] two and one-half times as many couples without children as couples with children.... The guest is only a number and is characteristically detached from the place in which he sleeps. In some cases this anonymity and impersonality encourages a restless, lonesome, unhappy state of mind. In other cases it encourages an escape from the restraints of more intimate groups, such as the small town or the ghetto.... The individual who lives continually in hotels tends to become either blasé or urbane. The hotel child...is usually over stimulated.... The individual may gradually accustom himself to "living in public, eating in public, and all but sleeping in public"... [and] may become so accustomed to [this] environment that he may feel that his "real home" is a hotel.[21]

SROS AND THE MEN OF PAN-ASIAN SEATTLE

The successive waves of Chinese, Japanese, and Filipino immigrants who were locating and relocating into West Coast cities paralleled the development and increasing numbers of SRO hotel buildings being constructed in downtown neighborhoods. Largely viewed as inassimilable to the greater population, their presence in neighborhoods of residential hotels emphasized the unacceptability of these buildings and further negated any possibility that these places were decent or respectable. The buildings created an identity specific to Seattle's Chinatown and Japantown that was made all the more culturally complicated within an ethnically diverse community of low-income residents that included the Chinese, Japanese, and Filipino Americans, and Italians, Norwegians, and African Americans. The residential hotels were home to members of these groups, whether married or single. A majority of these buildings housed a mixed-race population, and only a few hotels would house a specific race. Polite society developed an understanding of the hotels, their residents, and a life that was associated with skid row living.[22]

While numbers on the male to female gender ratio for Seattle's Chinese, Japanese, and Filipino communities are unavailable from 1880 to 1920, there are indications of the severity of gender disparities in the Washington State Census figures for these three groups, and reasonable assumptions that can be made on the number of families that would be possible and the types of living accommodations that were needed by these Seattle Asian American communities. The state figures indicate that in all of these communities, men far outnumbered females and that the number of traditional family units would have been small in the years leading up to 1910. The need for and construction of SRO hotels met the population demographics of pan-Asian Seattle.

In 1880 the ratio of Chinese males to females was at its worst at 126:1. In the decades to follow, this ratio slowly improved, partly from years of decline or modest growth in the population of Chinese males and partly from the steady growth of the number of Chinese females. In 1910, only about one-third of the state's total of 2,709 Chinese lived in Seattle; a figure that increased in 1920 to 1,351 or 57% of Washington's Chinese population.

The first significant wave of Japanese Washingtonians was recorded in 1900 with a male-to-female ratio of 29:1 that improved to almost 7:1 by 1910 and with less than a 2:1 disparity by 1920.[23] Over 45% of the state's Japanese population for this latter year was living in Seattle. The birth of the Nisei took place over a 25-year period that essentially placed a "generation gap" between the community's oldest and youngest of this second generation.

Washington's Filipino community began to become noticeable in 1920 with a male-to-female ratio of 21:1 that worsened to over 31:1 by the time of the 1930 US Census. Reaching a 2:1 ratio did not happen until 1950 for the Chinese and 1960 for the Filipinos of Washington, which in both cases can be attributed to early patterns of immigration and ultimately to the restrictive immigration laws that prohibited free immigration of females.

What is strikingly noticeable is that the total population of Japanese in Seattle greatly outnumbered the Chinese or Filipino Americans in the city from 1900 until 1960 and that the male-to-female ratio disparity of Japanese Americans in Washington had dramatically improved within a twenty-year

TABLE 3-1: *Asian American Population In Seattle*

		1880†	1890	1900	1910	1920	1930	1940	1950	1960	1970
Chinese	Male	—	—	—	—	—	969	1,287	1,733	2,367	3,277
	Female	—	—	—	—	—	378	494	917	1,709	2,984
	Total	—	359	438	924	1,351	1,347	1,781	2,650	4,076	6,261
Japanese	Male	—	—	—	—	—	4,741	3,746	3,066	4,649	4,662
	Female	—	—	—	—	—	3,707	3,229	2,712	1,234	5,324
	Total	—	125	2,990	6,127	7,874	8,448	6,975	5,778	5,883	9,986
Filipino‡	Male	—	—	—	—	—	1,563	1,213	—	4,702	3,370
	Female	—	—	—	—	—	51	179	—	2,521	2,460
	Total	—	—	—	—	458	1614	1,392	2,357	7,223	5,830

Sources:

† No counts of Chinese or Japanese were provided for Seattle in the 1880 Census

‡ Population of Filipinos as a separate racial group first appeared in the 1920 Census though in 1910, Filipinos were acknowledged as being included in "Other" as a racial classification.

1870: US Census Office: Table III: Population of Civil Divisions Less than Counties

1880: US Census Office: Table XIX: Sex of the Colored, Chinese and Japanese, and Civilized Indian Population, with General Nativity: 1880

1890: US Census Office: Table 19: Population by Sex, General Nativity and Color, of Places Having 2,500 Inhabitants or More

1900–1970: City of Seattle, Office of Policy Planning: Population Trends by Race in the Seattle Area 1900–1976 (February 1977)

1900–1920: US Bureau of the Census: Table 18: Indian, Chinese and Japanese Population for Cities having in 1920, 25,000 Inhabitants or More

1930–1940: US Bureau of the Census: Table A-36: Race by Nativity and Sex for the City of Seattle; Table A-37: Potential Voting Population by Citizenship, Race, Nativity and Sex for the City of Seattle

1950: US Bureau of the Census: Table 47: Indians, Japanese, and Chinese by Sex, for Selected Counties and Cities

1960–1970: US Bureau of the Census: Table 23: Race by Sex for Areas and Places

TABLE 3-2: *Washington State Asian American Population*

		1870	1880	1890	1900	1910	1920	1930	1940	1950	1960	1970
Chinese	Male	—	3,161	3,210	3,550	2,519	2,088	1,723	1,749	2,288	3,229	4,801
	Female	—	25	50	79	190	275	472	596	1,120	2,262	4,400
	Total	234	3,185	3,260	3,629	2709	2,363	2,195	2,345	3,408	5,491	9,201
Japanese	Male	—	0	—	5,432	11,241	11,322	10,200	8,033	5,163	7,882	8,912
	Female	—	1	—	185	1,688	6,065	7,637	6,532	4,531	8,770	11,423
	Total	—	1	360	5,617	12,929	17,387	17,837	14,565	9,694	16,652	20,335
Filipino	Male	—	—	—	3	17	915	3,374	1,958	3,271	4,585	6,520
	Female	—	—	—	—	0	43	106	264	1,003	2,525	4,942
	Total	—	—	—	3	17	958	3,480	2,222	4,274	7,110	11,462

Sources:

1870: US Census Office: Table 16: Chinese Population

1880: US Census Office: Table XIX: Sex of the Colored, Chinese and Japanese, and Civilized Indian Population, with General Nativity

1890: US Census Office: Table 14: Chinese, Japanese, and Civilized Indian Population, By States and Territories: 1860–1890

1900: US Census Office: Table 17: Population, Race by Sex

1910–1930: US Bureau of the Census: Table 2: Color, Nativity, and Sex for the State, Urban and Rural

1930–1940: US Bureau of the Census: Table A-37: Potential Voting Population by Citizenship, Race, Nativity and Sex for the City of Seattle: 1940 and 1930.

1940–1950: US Bureau of the Census: Table 14: Race by Sex, for the State, Urban and Rural

1960–1970: US Bureau of the Census: Table 17: Race by Sex

period from 1900 to 1920. The cause of the increase of females in the Japanese American community is directly attributable to a provision in the Gentleman's Agreement that allowed the immigration of wives of Japanese men who were already in the United States. About half of all Japanese Washingtonians lived in Seattle between 1900 and 1920 and during the peak development years for the construction of the city's residential hotels.

For Asian Americans, the SRO residential hotels reflected the accommodations that were needed for a society that was skewed to more males than females. Federal immigration law prohibited the immigration of Chinese women under Chinese Exclusion Law (1884, 1926), of Japanese women and men under the Immigration Act of 1924, and immigration of Filipino women and men in 1934 with passage of the Tydings-McDuffie Act, which granted the Philippines its independence from US control. While gender figures were not recorded for the City of Seattle until 1930, figures for the State of Washington indicate a male-to-female ratio of 13:1 for Chinese, 7:1 for Japanese and 17:1 for Filipinos in 1910, when SRO hotel construction was beginning in the newly regraded area south of Yesler Way.

The 1930 Census for Seattle indicates that the number of males to females was 3:1 for Chinese and 30:1 for Filipinos with the Japanese American community reaching a near 1:1 ratio.[24] In the early years of settlement for all of these groups, the gender disparity, social stigma, and shunning of intermarriage prevented both marriage and opportunities for a family life. In the absence of the latter, hotel living and a wide range of available neighborhood commodities offered commercial substitutes for the comforts of a single-family home and the companionship of a wife.

A sleeping room could be rented for between $.10 and $.50 a night or with special rates of $8.00 to $10.00 per month, and depending on the preferences of the business owner, it was often paid in advance.[25] Less than a dozen residential hotels south of Yesler Way offered rooms for a price as high as $2.00 per night.[26] Competition for the higher economic and social trade was done through advertisement of amenities, and these rooms commanded the higher room rate. The Milwaukee Hotel advertised its accommodations with "telephones in every room at 50 cents a room for shared bath and $1.50 for a private bath."[27] Bath facilities were located down the hall and all of the necessities and services of grocers, drug stores, clothing and sundries, laundries and dye-works, cafés and restaurants for daily living, and assorted opportunities for gambling, drinking, and companionship were located both in and behind the commercial bays of a hotel and the low-rise commercial buildings down the street.

Nationally, the bachelor society of Chinese immigrants made their homes in the lodging houses and residential hotels of American Chinatowns out of convenience and necessity. The spare and utilitarian accommodations were typically rented by a number of men in order to reduce the per-person cost of accommodations.[28] It was the most effective way for an immigrant Chinese to be able to save money from meager labor wages that could then be sent to China to help the family that was left behind or to perhaps, one day, have a family in America.

The over-capacity occupancy of even the cheapest rooms was often the subject and cause of city ordinances that forbade multiple persons per room; a code that was passed under the auspice of protecting public health. In reality, this type of multiple-occupancy was a common Chinatown phenomenon. Whether Chinatown was cordoned off and ghettoized in the city, as was the case in San Francisco, or left to develop its own urban pattern, as was true of Portland and to an extent, Seattle, the residential hotels were the only "home" that was possible or necessary for a primarily male population.

A number, if not all, of the hotels provided a place for a system of social support that included any service or vice that would be needed for single Chinese men who needed a respite from the day's labor or escape from the realization that they could not have a family life under the federal immigration laws. Rooms for gambling, drinking, drugs, and ample opportunities for "female companionship" could be as easily found in the hotels and neighborhood commercial businesses as could any commodity. Hotels, whether luxury or lodging houses, provided privacy for illicit activities and sexualized spaces, though the focus of reformers tended to target only those buildings, owners, and occupants of the SROs.[29] Vice and the demography of transient men created a symbiotic neighborhood relationship.

Chinese Family or District Associations and Tongs that provided social service support, dispute resolution, or paid protection were located in many of the hotel buildings, typically taking an auspicious location for meeting hall rooms on the upper floors. Their importance and prominence was easily identifiable by the street passersby and from architectural features of projecting or recessed balconies that altered an unadorned building façade. Balconies on all of the Chinese hotel buildings were a transplanted element from urban structures in China. As a design feature, a balcony offered additional

Norway/New American Hotel. [Courtesy King County Assessor's Office, Property Record Cards, 1937–1973, Puget Sound Branch, Washington State Archives]

space for living and for viewing the activities and celebrations that took place on the street below. For residential hotels, a balcony could be incorporated in the original plan or added after a building was occupied by the Chinese; either way, it was a visible indication that the building "belonged" to them in ownership or operation.

While the single rooms of a hotel were humble designs, the association rooms were not. Kitchen facilities for meetings and celebratory banquets, altars, and art that included paintings of ancestral founders along with the finest affordable imported mahogany and rosewood furnishings adorned the spaces for board members. The more affluent the association, the grander and more elaborate the furnishings with inlaid mother-of-pearl or other precious stones.

Interior of the Bing Kung Tong, located in the New American Hotel [Author]

THE EMPIRE OF WILLIAM CHAPPELL

Born in 1867 in Kankakee, Illinois, William Chappell was an adventurer and an astute, if not a notorious, businessman and developer of SRO residential hotels in Seattle. He was described as

> ...a man of large affairs and notably keen discernment and command[ing] an unbounded measure of respect and admiration. He was a man of marked executive ability who found deep enjoyment in business and ever remained its master, never allowing it to master him. He always had some plan in the making and his labors were manifestly resultant. He possessed in large measure that quality which has been termed "the commercial sense"...[30]

Most accurately, he was both respected and despised and a subject of fascination to Seattleites who were interested in the activities of a very rich man.

William Chappell, ca 1910. [*Seattle and Environs, 1852–1924*. Seattle: Pioneer Historical Publishing Co., 1924]

While in his early twenties, Chappell had relocated from his Illinois home to Duluth, Minnesota, where he worked as a hotel proprietor while becoming involved with the timber industry; this move began a lifelong involvement in construction and real estate speculation. When he heard about the Klondike Gold Strike, Chappell joined the earliest of the 1897 fortune seekers in Alaska's Bonanza Creek area.[31] Chappell initially had two partners, and each of the three men drew straws to determine who would get one of the three claims that they collectively filed. Chappell succeeded in selecting the one claim that contained his second financial fortune.

As a miner, Chappell purchased supplies in Seattle and this gave him his initial familiarity with the city. He returned to Seattle in 1899, just as the city was underway with its plan to fill the tideflats and begin discussions of regrading land for downtown development. Chappell was interested in investing in Seattle's booming real estate market. With $750,000 capital in hand from his mining venture, he considered the city's public-works projects and engaged in what he saw as the making of his third fortune from land speculation and Seattle real estate development.

Chappell believed that properties south of Yesler Way would one day become the city's financial center and be worth a fortune to those who were smart enough to procure and hold on to their land. Parcels would dramatically escalate in value, particularly from land that was slated to be cleared, leveled, and readied for large-scale new rather than infill development. In the meantime, existing buildings and property could be put to good use and collect handsome returns with little financial investment.[32]

With confirmation that the Tenderloin would remain as part of the south downtown, Chappell engaged in property purchases and construction plans. Originally, Chappell's 1901 land purchase at 6th Avenue and King Street for $70,000 was deemed folly, given that this same parcel had sold the year before for $28,000. But local newspaper reports on Seattle real estate began to acknowledge that Chappell's land purchases were capitalizing on the changes to the Restricted District. He became known as the "luckiest of [property] owners" as he accumulated parcels in the Restricted District.[33]

Seattle Ordinance 4953 required that all persons, firms or corporations file an annual report to the city that would outline specific information and terms of franchises that had been granted from the city.[34] Among other things, a franchise would allow a property owner to place heat, water, and electrical lines for a building beneath and within the boundaries of city rights-of-way that included streets, alleys, and sidewalks.[35]

Chappell began to comprehensively plan the development and utility franchise connection of his properties. In February 1902, he entered into an agreement with the City of Seattle that in exchange for his waiving any and all damages to his properties from the Jackson Street regrade, he would be allowed to erect a two-story frame building that would be supported by piers.[36] This bargain allowed Chappell to construct a new building as an exception to city ordinance that required all buildings to be placed on solid wall foundations. Any city regrading would need to work around and with Chappell's construction project. The resulting two-story single-room-occupancy residential hotel, known as the St. Paul House, was the first for Chappell, with twenty-five rooms on the second floor, a saloon and barber shop at-grade, and a burlesque theater in the basement.

In August 1902, Chappell applied for and was granted a franchise district permit that allowed him to construct and operate a utilities system that would provide hot and cold water as well as steam heat to buildings that

St. Paul and Diamond Hotels; both owned by William Chappell. [Courtesy Shigeko Uno and Tomio Moriguchi]

were within a specified area. The franchise allowed Chappell to lay pipes under and within city rights-of-way and above the tideflat areas of Elliott Bay for a thirty-year period.[37] With his franchise district established, plans were drawn to place and operate six- and eight-inch steam and hot water pipelines below grade. This ambitious utility system ran along the two north-to-south alleys between 5th Avenue South and Maynard Avenue South and from the north side of Jackson Street to the south side of Weller Street.

Two months later, Chappell was granted another permit to connect lots 2, 3, and 4 of Block 34 to an electric lighting and power plant that would be constructed at the Southwest corner of Block 35 on lots 3 and 4. This time, franchise term limits to operate the plant would last until such a time as municipal services would be extended to the properties. At the time, the City of Seattle had no foreseeable plans for municipal utilities for that part of town.

With a corporate name that camouflaged his sole control of development, Chappell started the Rainier Heat and Power Company in 1902. Of the 15,000 shares that were part of the corporation, 14,896 belonged to him. The corporation would serve his plans for developing a neighborhood of residential hotels and commercial businesses. He would sell power plant utilities to other owners in the district who did not want to wait for the extension of city services to their properties, and to anyone who rented space in a Chappell building. The plant and three steam boilers plunged three stories below grade. The structure was a triangular-shaped brick-and-cement power plant that was constructed for $10,000. Above ground a small building was surrounded by a board and wire fence and only visible to passers-by from the smokestacks that rose into the air.

Tunnels and an additional access point allowed for repair and periodic inspections by city engineers. Aside from the main entry was a second one that was accessed through the alley between Jackson and Main Streets on a lot that was owned by Chappell. The power plant pipes that connected his properties created an expanse of underground caverns that were frequently occupied by Seattle's homeless men who sought shelter and warmth from the steam heat lines. In a 1906 routine inspection by city Franchise Inspector Walter S. Wheeler and Fire Marshal Gardner Kellogg, it was discovered that a few of these underground pockets were also being used for fireworks storage by Chinese businesses whose building basements were able to access the underground pipe area. In later years, these cavernous spaces created a greater and unsubstantiated legend that an identical subterranean Chinatown existed below the streets of Seattle. Sensationalized stories reported numerous passageways that connected buildings beneath alleys and streets and with rooms for illegal activities that included opium dens and refuge areas for Chinese who were being smuggled into the city. The legend in coming decades remained strong and far larger than fact with no actual proof that any Chinese ever lived or traversed an environment beneath the public streets of Chinatown.

While the power lines were being built in advance of the Jackson Street Regrade, Chappell expanded his land holdings by purchasing additional parcels on the St. Paul House block and the blocks to the north and east of the Rainier Heat and Power Company plant. Between 1901 and 1906, Chappell purchased 41 lots south of Yesler Way, half of which were located in the area that was occupied by Chinese and Japanese businesses. With only three of the lots vacant, the remainder of his wooden-frame buildings were occupied with an eclectic mix of businesses that included theatres and arcades, a shoe and shirt warehouse and factory, barbershops, a blacksmith, a tinsmith, billiard halls, and numerous saloons. Chappell acted as landlord for Japanese-operated

Rainier Heat and Power Company Power Plant exhaust stacks just beyond the Waste Laundry. [Courtesy Shigeko Uno and Tomio Moriguchi]

businesses that included laundries, restaurants, and lodging house hotels, along with one Chinese boarding house. With the purchase of an additional eight properties, only two of Chappell's blocks were located outside of the area that was directly affected by Thomson's regrade project. Of all property owners in the Jackson and 12th Avenue regrade area, Chappell held the greatest number of parcels under a single ownership.[38]

In 1902, Chappell hired architect Max Umbrecht to design the three-story, fifteen-room wooden-framed St. Nicholas Hotel near the southwest corner of King Street and 6th Avenue and adjacent to his other hotel buildings that included the Russell, Hamilton, UI, and New Paris Hotels on the eastern half of that same block.[39] Continuing his monopoly of property ownership in that area, Chappell purchased the eastern four-lot block face of 6th Avenue South between Jackson and King streets in 1905 for $50,000. These lots contained a number of simple wooden-framed houses, some of which were being occupied by Japanese laborers. Chappell purchased the Welcome Hotel, an 1880 three-story wooden-frame lodging house that was on 6th and Jackson and one of the oldest hotels in the area.[40] The lot on the northeast corner of South Jackson Street and Maynard Avenue South was purchased for $25,000 in 1906 and left vacant until 1917 when Chappell moved the supervisory leasing activities to a new office and commercial retail building that became the headquarters of the Rainier Heat and Power Company.

The press was fascinated with the boldness of Chappell's undertakings; and vacillated between applauding his opulent lifestyle on Queen Anne Hill and condemning the source of his growing income.[41] He was coined as having some of the "lowest dives" in Seattle that included hotel buildings with gambling and liquor establishments, pool halls, shooting galleries, arcades, and some of the lowest houses of prostitution.[42]

As the first Tenderloin was being ordered to move immediately, Chappell seized the opportunity to expand his property empire and hired fifty carpenters to quickly construct buildings for rental properties. Land costs rose dramatically once the announcement of the Tenderloin relocation was made public, and the value of Chappell's properties in the second Tenderloin skyrocketed. *The Seattle Sunday Times* reported that "some of the property... increased in value more than one hundred per cent since the announcement [with]...some of the lots in the district chang[ing] hands three or four times, each time bringing a higher price than before...."[43]

Between 1902 and 1909, Chappell built, bought, and leased the spaces of his mixed-use residential hotel buildings that included the Welcome Hotel (ca. 1895), which later expanded to include the Welcome Hotel Annex; the New Paris Hotel (1902); St. Paul House (1902); St. Nicholas Hotel (1903); and the Dreamland Hotel (1909), all of which were used in part as bordellos and cribs. Property for the frame construction of the St. Paul House on 5th Avenue between Jackson and King streets and the St. Nicholas Hotel on 6th Avenue South and King Street had been purchased and totally rented out for multiple-year leases before either of these residential hotels had begun construction. On its completion in early 1902, the New Paris Hotel had been fully rented with the basement space used for gambling, three saloons at-grade, and the upper two floors of thirty rooms rented out for cribs at $300 a month.

Seattle was gaining a strong national reputation for tolerance when it came to recognition of the thriving Tenderloin district and the open advertisement of businesses that centered on vice. Out-of-town visitors were adding the

MAP 3-1: *William Chappell Prostitution Hotels – ca. 1918 [Author]*

--- Chappell Franchise District

▨ Future Interstate 5 Alignment

---- Current International Special Review
District Boundary

❶ St. Paul House

❷ Diamond Hotel

❸ Welcome Hotel

❹ Welcome Hotel Annex

❺ Dreamland Hotel

❻ St. Nicholas Hotel

❼ Russell Hotel

❽ Hamilton Hotel

❾ U.I. Hotel

❿ New Paris Hotel

FEET: 0   330   660   990   1320

MILES: 0   1/8   1/4

NORTH

VICINITY MAP

Elliot Bay   YESLER   Lake Wash.

Tenderloin as one of the "must see" locations. On a routine visit by aldermen
and police detectives from other cities, the New Paris Hotel and Standard
gambling house were two sites on the tour that were selected as examples of
the worst that Seattle had to offer.

Outside Seattle's jurisdiction, the Immigration and Naturalization
Service had engaged in a two-year investigation and report on white slavery, and locations where prostitution was occurring in American cities. For
Washington State, it included Spokane, Bellingham, Everett, Walla Walla,
Hoquiam, Aberdeen, and Seattle. A correspondence outlining the investigation
found that "Seattle, owing to its close proximity to such Canadian border towns
as Vancouver, and Victoria, offers exceptionally good facilities for the operations of importing, and distributing women for the purposes of Prostitution."[44]

The report indicated that there were 193 total "resorts," or those places that were identified as destinations for acts of prostitution after a meeting in another location, typically a street, saloon, restaurant, or dance hall. The "resorts" that were under surveillance included lodging houses, hotels, and apartment hotels. Of this total, thirty-six were identified as being south of Yesler Way with "twenty of the rooming houses operated by Japanese proprietors."[45]

According to city ordinance, the internal design of hotels that were used as parlor houses in the Restricted District were forbidden to include any staircase that would directly connect a saloon to upstairs rooms. Private tables that contained curtains or doors that would prevent an open view of activities were forbidden in all saloons. But the rules were not being observed as the construction of the Dreamland Hotel was underway. From the exterior facades, the design of Chappell's Dreamland Hotel looked like any other residential hotel in the district, but it was the interior floor plan that revealed the special nature of the building. Entrance to the hotel portion of the building was through the first floor pool room and saloon. Unlike any other SRO, the majority of the sixty-eight rooms were double-loaded along the corridors with each room having a large window that faced the interior hallways. A patron of the bordello could then walk through the hall, look through the open curtains and "shop for" and select a sex worker that was available for business.

Beginning in 1903 and over the coming decade, Chappell would be arrested and released on bail a number of times for allowing gambling and prostitution to take place in the New Paris and his other properties. The fact that the hotels were in the business of pleasure-seeking was not the issue since they were in an area that the city had designated for red-light activities. The issue was that Chappell was not paying his fair share of 20% of the monthly receipts to the police, a sum that could go into patrolling the area and ignoring vice.

Local courts gave police the legal power to act in whatever way they deemed necessary when it came to the operation of dance halls that fronted saloon operations. The Arcade Dance Hall, located in the basement of the St. Paul House, was closed in 1910 for serving near-beer that was shown to have an alcohol content of almost 4 percent. Operated as a "box house," the Midway Saloon included private cubicles that could be closed off from spectators with privacy curtains. Fifty-five of the total sixty-six houses of prostitution in the city were located south Yesler Way.[46] There were also smaller prostitution businesses that were located in Chappell's framed houses and false-front storefronts

Paris Hotel, located at 523-6th Avenue South. Before (upper) and after (lower) the Jackson Street Regrade. Businesses included a grocery and ice cream parlor, and the Hinode-Yu Japanese bath house. [Courtesy Shigeko Uno and Tomio Moriguchi]

that held much cheaper crib businesses in rooms that were only large enough
to contain a bed. Considered to be the lowest order of prostitution houses, they
were referred to as "French resorts" or "parlor houses." The Cosmos and the
Red Light hotels each had twenty-five rooms, and the sixty-room Tokio Hotel
were all crib businesses that were leased in Chappell's buildings on 6th Avenue
South between King and Weller streets.[47] All of these businesses combined
were part of what was known as Chappell's "million-dollar enterprise" and all
of them were built in a shared geography that included the heart of Seattle's
established and growing district of Chinese and Japanese businesses.

Leasing the SRO buildings could be done in any number of ways. An
individual could rent the entire building and sublet the commercial storefronts
and upper-level hotel spaces or all of the spaces could be handled as separate
leasing contracts. The majority of the commercial storefronts in Chappell's
SRO bordello hotels were operated by legitimate Japanese American businesses
regardless of the leasing arrangement.

Police reports indicated the regularity of extortion, robberies, murders
and suicides that were considered auxiliary to the existence of cribs and bordellos. The city had instated a monthly license or fine of $5.00 for the practice
of prostitution. The police courts and city attorney were reluctant to prosecute
sex workers who robbed their clients during a business transaction, stating that
"the monthly fine or license paid by [a] woman for the privilege of practicing
prostitution also gave her permission to steal with impunity."[48]

As the chief of police under Mayor Moore, Charles "Wappy"
Wappenstein came to the job with a disregarded record of being dismissed as
a Seattle police detective on previous charges of bribery and exacting police
protection. Without going so far as to close immoral businesses, Wappenstein
declared that all owners of buildings that housed such businesses in the
restricted zone should be subject to monthly fees for the privilege of staying
open. For Wappenstein, it was not an issue of morality, but a simple business
transaction. As long as criminal activity was attracted to the restricted zone
and more police were needed to maintain law and order, the payment for additional enforcement could be collected from property owners running vice
operations in the residential hotels. The proposed law suggested collection of
a fine not to exceed $100 from each building and a penalty of 30 days in jail for
the owner who didn't pay the fee. Given that the city had quarantined vice and
criminal activities south of Yesler Way, it was a dichotomy to penalize property

MAP 3-2: *William Chappell Properties – ca. 1920 [Author]*

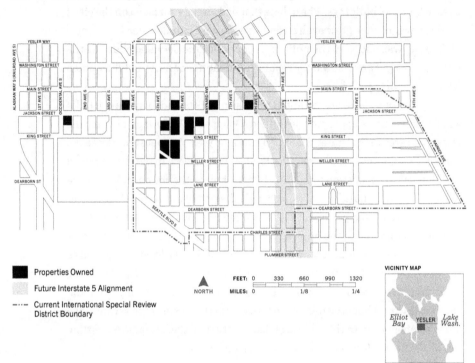

Properties Owned

Future Interstate 5 Alignment

Current International Special Review
District Boundary

FEET: 0   330   660   990   1320

MILES: 0   1/8   1/4

NORTH

VICINITY MAP

Elliot Bay   YESLER   Lake Wash.

owners for engaging in businesses that the city had essentially allowed there. The proposed fee would have been a substantial portion of the average $250 per month rental fee that Chappell was collecting for his buildings. For the next few years, Attorney Arthur Griffin spent a great deal of time posting bail and defending Chappell and his property interests as he worked around the system to maintain his client's "bawdy house" businesses without paying the city for the privilege.

Chappell's buildings included 31 of the 36 prostitution houses in the city's "restricted zone" in 1906 along with numerous saloons and gambling establishments that were located behind the commercial storefronts of the residential hotel buildings. He based his lease agreements with tenants on the use of the building rather than the square footage and in some instances refused to rent spaces for legitimate purposes unless this was part of a "front" for the true nature of the business. As Chappell built his real estate portfolio of SROs he also encouraged combining saloons and dance halls as commercial uses in his hotel buildings. The debate that had already surfaced on the city's morality war on vice grew even stronger in the next four decades as the topic of dancing was added to the political, economic, and social agenda. As the red-light district grew, so did the reputation of the dance halls and the women who worked in them.

In 1906, Seattle attempted to close all of the red-light dance halls when Police Chief Wappenstein identified "Chappell's Tenderloin" as being the worst such area in the United States.[49] That same year, Wappenstein closed the Strand, Casino, and Gaiety dance halls, all of which were in buildings owned by Chappell. Wappenstein found that like the hotels, the actions taking place within the dance halls were "exceedingly disgusting in nature"; neverthe-less, they netted Chappell about $2,000 per month in addition to the $1,000 in utilities that he sold to the proprietors of these businesses.[50] The New Paris Hotel, known as the largest "bawdy house south of the line" and recognized as the worst prostitution crib in the restricted district, was also closed pending investigation of a number of robberies. Wappenstein stationed officers at the New Paris throughout the night to make certain that none of the seventy-five sex workers housed in the building tried to return to their rooms. According to *The Seattle Daily Times,* the New Paris Hotel was a

> ...den of iniquity run by Lizzett Smith, a negress [sic] who rents the building from Millionaire William Chappell. For more than two years its rooms and its halls have been the scenes of robberies almost nightly. The lowest of the low women of all nationalities are housed under its roof and the woman who runs it is regarded as extremely dangerous.... The police...say that not more than 25 per cent of the robberies that occur there are ever reported to the police for the victims would rather lose the money than have their names involved in the investigation. Men have been knocked down, drugged and robbed....[51]

Within two days, two more of Chappell's crib house residential hotels, the St. Paul House and the Diamond Hotel, were closed along with a Chinese lottery and gambling house on 2nd Avenue and Washington Street in Chinatown.

The Chinese lottery was closed following Chief Wappenstein's inves-tigation and discovery that it was a continuously operating day-and-night business. Wappenstein lamented that no sergeant or patrolman had reported any gaming activity at the Washington address, a violation of City Ordinance 1090. The ordinance dictated that it was a misdemeanor if a police officer failed to "watch for, search out and promptly arrest, or cause to be arrested, all persons whom they have reasonable cause to believe [were] offenders," punishable by a minimum $25 fine and removal from service.[52] Wappenstein relied on information about gambling activity from his own paid informants. The closing of the hotel and raid on the Chinatown business produced nothing more than bundles of tickets and a box that was used for drawing a winner; no patrons were found the evening of the search. Infuriated with the lack of enforcement from the patrolman assigned to the Washington Street beat, Wappenstein dismissed Officer Guy Carlton for breaking police regulations, the ordinance, and pawning his city-owned revolver for a $10 chance to participate in the game.

Chappell was arrested again on 18 July 1906, making it the sixth time in a ten-day period that he was jailed for operating buildings for prostitution and gambling in the restricted district.[53] The arrest and morals charges were extended to Eugene Levy, owner of the Midway Hotel, Frank Buty, who owned the Idaho House hotel, and Adam Orth for ownership of a small wooden-framed crib building on King Street known as "Little Casino." Bail was set at $1,200 for Chappell and $600 for Levy and Buty, who were considered minor players in the prostitution racket. Chappell's other hotels and buildings were allowed to remain open pending trial or if all of the men agreed to a regular monthly fee payable to the city treasurer in order to keep the buildings in "good standing" for operation. Since Chappell owned the majority of the vice businesses, the press, property owners, and police were waiting to see if he would agree to what amounted to a monthly tax on an allowable land use.

As Chappell's court date neared, the newspapers reported his control over people, activities, and properties.

> Entire blocks of cheaply constructed frame buildings, the upper stories of which are rented exclusively by men and women who make a living from the shame of unfortunate females, are rented at exorbitant prices by Chappell, contrary to both the state and city laws and the moral law. Saloons, dance halls, drug stores, variety theatres, shooting galleries, restaurants, fruit stands, etc., pay monthly tribute to the man who is growing richer because he has invested his money in a section of the city set apart for vice of all forms. [His properties] house women of all nationalities.... For the past three years

Chappell has owned and rented these dives and for the privilege the city of Seattle has not been paid a penny. ... Chappell put up cheap frame buildings...that have been filled without interruption...[and] are said to bring rates higher than good property on First and Second Avenues. ... Today he is rated by those who know him to be worth close to $2,000,000, more than 50 per cent of which has been made from renting buildings for immoral purposes in the past three years and a half.[54]

On 1 August 1906, the city attorney and council, with the enforcement of Chief Wappenstein, imposed a monthly fine that equaled 20% of the rents that were collected for every building that housed illegal activities. Attorney and State Senator Ralph Nichols managed and supervised the Chappell properties and assured the payment of the fines.[55] Imposition of this fee and enforcing the personal fines of $5.00 per sex worker were finally going to meet the financial demands assumed by the city for the additional officers that were needed to monitor criminal activity. All of the accused property owners agreed to the fines rather than continue lengthy and costly legal proceedings. Buty and Orth agreed to pay the fines that amounted to $24 and $40, respectively. Keane paid $70 while Eugene Levy paid $140 per month to keep the Midway open. Chappell's monthly fines were in excess of $580 per month and the largest share of the $6,000 total monthly revenue that the city was now going to collect for illegal uses of property. The St. Paul House and New Paris brought in the highest fees totaling $140.[56] The Diamond House, St. Paul, and the New Paris hotels were allowed to reopen for business.

In 1908, two fires occurring a month apart caused over $60,000 worth of damage to newly-framed hotel buildings and businesses that were being constructed on both sides of 6th Avenue at Weller Street. The first and smaller fire severely damaged the Dreamland Hotel shortly after its grand opening. The July 1908 blaze devastated numerous Japanese-owned storefront businesses, destroying eight lodging house hotels that were on a single block and leaving nearly 200 minority-occupied hotel residents homeless. The blaze would have been far worse and Chappell would have lost his nearby hotels had it not been for the proximity of the hydraulic equipment that was being used for the Jackson Street regrade. Men who were sluicing the hillsides aided firemen by turning the saltwater hose on the burning buildings. The following month, an August fire originating in the Kurosai Restaurant of the Dreamland property cost another $1,000 in damage to the building with about $450 in lost furnishings.

Dreamland Hotel. Businesses in the Dreamland building included a barbershop, Japanese restaurant, noodle house, shoe repair and a Salvation Army Mission. [Courtesy Shigeko Uno and Tomio Moriguchi]

The Japanese storefront businesses were completely lost as was everything in the Kurosai Restaurant.[57]

     With his vacant properties along South Jackson Street, Chappell turned his vision to developing a legitimate venture. The discussion on removal or relocation of the restricted district was heightening as regrade and transit projects were nearing completion and as neighboring citizen groups looked to city hall for removal of red-light uses. In June 1908, the Rainier Heights Improvement Club and residents from Seattle's Second Ward to the east of the downtown area challenged the mayor's office to make good on the campaign promises that called for the removal of red-light uses. Objections to the current location focused on the fact that the cribs and gambling halls were directly and clearly visible from the Jackson Street cable line as residents went between their homes and the south downtown businesses. The mayor's office was unsuccessful in appeasing neighbors with the announcement that Chappell's plans for new "legitimate use" buildings on Jackson Street between 6th and Maynard avenues and the erection of advertising billboards would block the view of the vice district as people traveled east and west of the lower downtown. With the threat of litigation to abolish the district in total and fear that such an action could disperse sex workers throughout the downtown, Mayor John Miller issued a statement on 29 August 1908 that the Restricted District would be moved and that all crib houses in the current district would be permanently closed by 1 September.

With advance notice and options to purchase property in the new Restricted zone, Chappell continued his monopoly of bawdy house properties. The proximity of both rail stations offered an opportunity to capitalize on tourists, visitors, and business people who were coming into Seattle while the buildings in the City's second Restricted District were being converted into more suitable uses. The electric signs that were offering vice and "personal services" were ordered to be removed. The official boundary of the new tenderloin would be cut to one-third the present size and consist of two blocks between 7th and 9th avenues and Plummer and Norman streets farther to the south and away from the central core of what was developing as a community with a high concentration of Asian Americans. Unofficially, prostitution as a business enterprise was not going to be leaving the residential hotels.

In early Spring 1910, the city's focus was on the mayoral race between Republican Hiram C. Gill and Democratic Mayor William H. Moore.[58] Political posturing days before the election centered on which of the two candidates would be successful in addressing the need to clean up the lower downtown. Moore's past record weakened his bid for mayor as it was pointed out that his prior promises to reduce saloons by denying business licenses had not been met. It was also revealed that William Chappell had been and was a major contributor to Moore's re-election with a $10,000 donation to his campaign. Gill won the election.

Gill's political platform promised that rather than having "social evil" and corruption available throughout the downtown, the Restricted District area would contain all the city's vice activities. It was believed that any announcement of immediate closure would scatter some of the estimated 100 women of the crib houses into a broader area of the downtown and as far north as Pike Street. By the fall of 1910, it was clear that the term "vice" was used to identify specific Tenderloin hotel buildings and not one that was necessarily associated with the sex workers themselves. With numerous robberies reported in the Tenderloin area's La France House, Sixth Avenue House, and Chappell's

Tokio House and Diamond Hotel, all of the establishments were ordered closed pending investigation, but the sex workers were allowed to relocate to other neighboring hotels to conduct business as usual.

Not everyone was satisfied with the city's position that a vice district was necessary. In August 1910, local property owner James Murphy filed a suit against the City of Seattle in King County Superior Court challenging decisions that were being made by newly-elected Mayor Gill, Police Chief Wappenstein, members of the City Council, and John Crichton as the City's health and sanitation commissioner. The suit alleged that the city was in part responsible for devaluing "legitimate" property that was adjacent to those with vice uses. It was argued that such actions from the municipality essentially "endorsed" prostitution through land use management, designation of a Red Light District, and passage of local ordinances that would encourage illicit behavior.[59]

A 1910 inspection of the Restricted District by three independent real estate and land brokers produced a report that had two primary findings. The first indicated that every sex worker should post a certificate of health in her room. Per city regulation, the certificate was to be issued by the branch bacteriological office of the city's Health and Sanitation Department, an office that was conveniently located on King Street in the Green Light/Russell Hotel that was owned by William Chappell.[60] A second finding confirmed that every floor of all of the buildings was being "used for and devoted to the purposes of public prostitution and immorality [and] congregation of idlers, dissolute, lascivious persons and vagrants, [with] no lawful or legitimate business carried on in said buildings...."[61]

In presentation of witnesses and written affidavits, Judge Mitchell Gilliam ordered a temporary injunction to enjoin and restrain "encouraging, promoting, maintaining or aiding, by and through officials and agents [of the city, and] defining and bounding [the] Red Light or Restricted District."[62] Property owners would likewise be "enjoined and restrained from running, conducting or maintaining the several houses of ill fame, crib houses, parlor houses and bawdy houses...and to cease from operating...renting, leasing, hiring or permitting to be operated the properties owned by them...as houses of ill fame and bawdy houses."[63]

Two years following the announcement of relocation of the second Restricted District, Wappenstein concluded that "theoretically the old district was closed [but that] practically, the conditions were little changed.[64]

Twenty-two saloons remained in the second Restricted District by 1910 as well
as seventeen bordellos and two parlor houses. At the time of the announced third
relocation of the Restricted District, over half of the SRO residential hotels that
were used for prostitution and about three-fourths of the properties and businesses used for vice in the second Tenderloin were owned by William Chappell.

Chappell had initially hired the architecture firm of Spalding and
Umbrecht to prepare preliminary plans for an upscale six-story residential
workingman's hotel that would be constructed on the 105' x 120' lot on the southwest corner of Jackson and Maynard.[65]
But final architectural plans for the new
hotel were ultimately drawn and filed by
the office of John Lawrence McCauley.
McCauley had consulted with East Coast
hotel designs, including New York's Mills
Hotel, in order to comply with Chappell's
request to design a low-cost accommodation but make certain that it was the best
hotel in Seattle and with all materials,
furnishings, and decorative elements
manufactured in Washington State.[66]
Construction began in spring 1915 with
the framing of the building completed
by mid-May.[67] Within five months, the
building was completed and a public
grand opening on 9 October 1915 celebrated the new fireproof building that
was to be the most modern and luxurious
hotel west of Chicago. Initially named the Busch Hotel in honor of Chappell's
wife, Margaret Busch Chappell, it was also the largest hotel south of Yesler
Way at that time with 255 rooms, 75 bathrooms, six commercial storefront
bays, and two light wells that created three bays that were visible from the
south façade of the building.

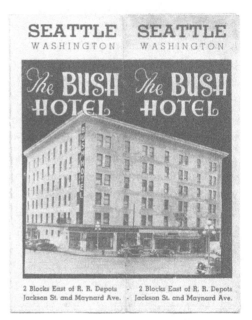

Bush Hotel Advertisement. [Courtesy Takashi Hori]

Each floor had a different color scheme, and all of the furniture was
designed by Chappell, manufactured by F.S. Harmon Company of Tacoma, and
distributed by Kazuo Miyamoto who, as the owner of the Jackson Furniture
Company, had leased one of the larger storefronts and part of the basement in

MAP 3-3: *Prostitution Hotels in the Red Light District, 1910 [Author]*

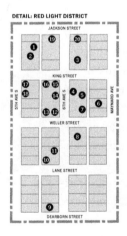

DETAIL: RED LIGHT DISTRICT

▪▪▪▪ Chappell Franchise District

Future Interstate 5 Alignment

FEET: 0   330   660   990   1320

MILES: 0   1/8   1/4

NORTH

VICINITY MAP

Elliot Bay   YESLER   Lake Wash.

❶ St. Paul Hotel (Chappell)

❷ Washington Hotel later named the Diamond Hotel (Chappell)

❸ Dreamland Hotel (Chappell)

❹ Little Casino (Orth Estate)

❺ 512-1/2 6th Avenue S. (Ernest Hester)

❻ Big Casino (Louis Friedman)

❼ Midway Hotel (Sam Pinschower)

❽ 6th Avenue Hotel (Union Trust Company leased to William G. Lowery)

❾ Wayne Hotel (Albert S. Heck)

❿ Eureka Hotel (Thomas Hyde)

⓫ New York Hotel (Sam and Rachel Hyde)

⓬ Paris Hotel (Chappell) (The Paris and LaFrance were later joined and operated as the New Paris)

⓭ La France (Chappell)

⓮ Red Light renamed the Hamilton and finally the Mukilteo Hotel (Chappell) (L-shaped building with entrances on both King Street and 6th Avenue South)

⓯ Tokio House renamed the U.I. Hotel (Chappell)

⓰ Green Light renamed the Russell Hotel (Chappell)

⓱ Dean Hotel renamed the St. Nicholas Hotel (Chappell)

⓲ Emma Norton Parlor Houses/Fashion Hotel (Chappell)

⓳ Welcome Hotel (Chappell)

⓴ Welcome Hotel Annex (Chappell)

the new hotel building. Every room was furnished with a bed, dresser, a rocking and sitting chair, a library table, and a footstool. A phone paging system to
notify guests of visitors and cold water that was plumbed into every room were
part of the luxury stay. Adjoining doorways in every other room provided the
flexibility of creating a two-room suite. The Busch Hotel included two elevators that were the same Otis gearless traction elevators that had been used in
Seattle's Smith Tower and New York's Singer and Woolworth buildings. As a
rarity in residential hotels at the time, the Busch included a reception counter
of mahogany and granite. The spacious lobby used nine steel girders in its
construction to keep the interior plan light, open, and free from pillars or posts.
By the time the Busch Hotel was completed, Chappell had spent $500,000 on
the building and furnishings of the luxury single-room occupancy residential
hotel that was ironically located immediately east and adjacent to his Welcome
Hotel bordello.[68]

For McCauley, the Busch Hotel was the start of a long-term professional association with Chappell, and while he was not the architect on
permanent staff with the power company, he continued to do designs for the
largest residential hotels that would be constructed in the restricted zone. His
work on the Busch Hotel was the first of five other commissions that would
be undertaken for the Rainier Heat and Power Company; the others were the
power company offices (1917), the American Hotel (1925), Governor Apartments
(1926), and Publix Hotel (1927).[69]

In the early years of the Busch Hotel, the general manager and president of the Busch Hotel Company, Jesse F. Russell, made it a point to only hire
white staff, but this was not the sentiment held by Chappell in his preference
of Japanese tenants to lease rental spaces in all of his buildings. In 1919, the
Rainier Heat and Power Company listed 146 leasing and utility accounts of
which 138 were Japanese tenants and service customers with only a single
business, the Mee Chin Low Restaurant, located in the Welcome Hotel and
leased by Chinese. Monthly income from all sources totaled $21,835, with
$13,722 or almost 63% coming from hotel properties.[70]

In 1921, Chappell died in a Baltimore hospital. At the time of his death,
the total value of his estate was in excess of $712,000; the majority of which was
associated with his shares in the Rainier Heat and Power Company and that
represented the hotel properties in Maynard's Plat within the second restricted
district.[71] Chappell's last will and testament attests to his belief that properties

south of Yesler Way would continue to escalate in value, as well as to his obsession for control. Chappell instructed that all of his land and properties be held in a trust with the generated income used to meet support payments to family members and to maintain the properties. Most importantly and supported by laws in the State of Washington, a trust could be held valid for a sixty-year period following the death of an individual, and Chappell's trust was intended to span the full allowable time limit of the law. At the expiration of the trust tenure, all assets would be divided and given to his survivors, including one-third to his widow and the remaining two-thirds to be divided among siblings and their heirs.

It was the sixty-year provision that made the Chappell Trust the longest-running trust of its kind that would ever occur in the history of Washington State or the nation.[72] In the coming years, the greatest challenge and ultimate test of the SRO hotel empire of William Chappell would be retaining financial solvency from the modest rental income of the SRO rooms.

ENDNOTES

1   Ford's book contains a masterful look at the evolution of land uses that comprise and define central business districts and downtowns.

2   Paul Groth, "Marketplace Vernacular Design: The Case of Downtown Rooming Houses," *Perspectives in Vernacular Architecture*, Vol. 2 (1986), p. 179–191 and Paul Groth, *Living Downtown: A History of Residential Hotels in the United States* (Berkeley: University of California Press, 1994).

3   Groth, *Living Downtown*. Single-room occupancy that was rented out in single-family dwelling units were considered to be rooming houses.

4   Harvey Zorbaugh, "Roomers," *The Survey*, 15 July 1926, vol. LVI, no, 8, p. 462. In part, boardinghouses were diminishing because of the cost of providing meals that increased the rental room rate.

5   "Decline and Fall of Hotel Life," *Harper's Weekly*, May 1857, vol. 1, 2, p. 274.

6   Gwendolyn Wright, *Building the Dream: A Social History of Housing in America* (Cambridge, MA: MIT Press, 1983).

7   These painted signs are called "ghost signs." See Marie Wong, "Teaching the Ghost Signs of Seattle," in Stefan Schutt, Sam Roberts, and Leann White, *Advertising and Public Memory* (London: Routledge, 2016).

8   Jefferson Williamson, *The American Hotel: An Anecdotal History* (New York: Knopf, 1930), p. 3. Williamson's work on hotel classification and description is one of the oldest to analyze and review the precedents of the American hotels and the contribution of this building type to central cities and urban history.

9   Data for room dimensions of Seattle's SRO hotel buildings is taken from the author's field surveys of those hotels that are still standing in the C-ID and from original building plans in the private collections of former and current hotel owners.

10 Groth, "Marketplace Vernacular Design."

11 Ibid., p. 181.

12 City of Seattle, Ordinance 17240, June 1909, Section 1.

13 The boarding house provided meals on premises as part of the rental fee.

14 The City's Department of Planning and Development also characterized "duplexes" as a building type that was "understood" but not specifically defined in code.

15 "Dwellers in Furnished Rooms," *Monthly Labor Review*, 91, 1926.

16 "The Word Hotel, Its Use and Abuse," *Hotel Monthly*, March 1922, Vol. 30, No. 348.

17 See Norman S. Hayner, "Hotel Life and Personality," *The American Journal of Sociology*, Vol. 33, No. 5, March 1928, p. 785. Hayner was a professor at the University of Washington who spearheaded a number of studies that examined social interaction, housing, and homelessness. This particular study included a broader spectrum of economies and addressed living in upper class and residential hotels.

18 Robert G. Barrows, "Beyond the Tenement: Patterns of American Urban Housing, 1870–1930," *Journal of Urban History*, Vol. 9, No. 4, August 1983, p. 195–420. From 1890 to 1916 and with minimal fluctuation, new housing starts made a strong appearance in the national economy. Even with a two-year slump and energies concentrated on World War I, the construction of housing was fairly constant, with an average of over 400,000 units added every year between 1890 and 1930.

19 Hayner, "Hotel Life and Personality," pp.784–795. Hayner's ground-breaking work on hotels indicated that data collected from various sources on the number of hotels in a specific city depended on which organization was collecting the data and how "hotel" was being defined. According to Hayner's study, San Francisco ranked first, Seattle second, and Los Angeles third in an assessment of the twenty largest cities in the US in the number of hotel rooms. The figure surpassed New York and Chicago.

20 Ibid., p. 786.

21 Ibid., p. 795.

22 Groth, *Living Downtown*, pp 152–153. Groth points out that skid row districts in cities were recognized by and through the use of street names that reflected both image and identity.

23 The first Japanese person in the state was one female who was recorded in the 1880 US Census.

24 While the gender ratio appears to be improving for Chinese, this does not account for the largest age cohorts that could include very young females and an aging population of males.

25 Cost is based on advertisements in the Polk Directory for years ranging from 1900 to 1930 and advertisements in the *North American Times* for these same years.

26 Ibid.

27 Polk Directory, 1920–23.

28 Groth., p. 158. A room would typically house a number of men, each of whom would take turns sleeping and working in shifts.

29 A.K. Sandoval-Strausz, *Hotel: an American History* (New Haven: Yale University Press, 2008), p. 209–210.

30 C.H. Hanford, ed. *Seattle and Environs, 1852–1924*. Vol. 3 (Chicago and Seattle: Pioneer Historical Publishing Company, 1924), 164–67.

31 As a tributary of the Bonanza Creek, the Eldorado Creek tributary provided Chappell with a nugget and gold dust extraction amounting to a reported $3,000 per day. Over one-half of the 50,000 ounces of gold from Alaska's Chisana area were recovered before 1915 and came from the Bonanza Creek (including its tributaries) and Gold Run areas.

32 Chappell purchased his first piece of Seattle property in 1898 from Judge Arthur Griffith for $55,000. The parcel was developed and leased out to the Seattle Theatre on the northeast corner of 3rd Avenue and Cherry Street and was sold in 1903 to the company for $76,000.

33 "Real Estate and Building News," *The Seattle Times*, 6 April 1902, Magazine Section, p. 6, col. 1, 2.

34 Seattle, City Ordinance 4953 (20 June 1898).

35 The report would list the owner, any changes to a franchise agreement, along with dates of approval and operation of the franchise.

36 Seattle, City Ordinance 7765 (20 February 1902).

37 Seattle, City Ordinance 8696 (6 October 1902).

38 In addition to his larger-scale construction ventures, Chappell purchased nine single-family houses that were in the wide path of the Jackson Street Regrade. Within eleven months and prior to the beginning of regrade construction, he moved the houses to land that he had purchased outside of the downtown and farther to the north and east in the Hill Tract Addition; owning a total of 20 lots by 1904.

39 The hotel was completed by mid-1903.

40 The city's earliest recorded building permit records indicate that repairs were done to this building as early as 1897 and prior to Chappell's purchase of the property.

41 The house cost $110,000 when it was built in 1906. California architect Edgar A. Mathews had to bring legal suit against Chappell in order to collect the 7% fee for the design of the house and the $50 per diem to cover expenses that were associated with supervisory visits to Seattle while the house was under construction. More than two years after the house was constructed, Chappell had only paid $4,000 of the total fee that was in excess of $12,300.00.

42 "Kelley Tells How Nichols Lost," *The Seattle Daily Times*, 8 May 1908, p. 9, col. 4.

43 "The Removal of the Tenderloin," *The Seattle Sunday Times*. In 1898, the property at Sixth Avenue South and Weller had been sold to the Miller Investment Company for $15,000 and in 1901 that same property was sold to Chappell for $75,000. By 1902, the value of the two lots had doubled again.

44 Letter of Marcus Braun, "White Slave Investigations, Subject Correspondence," Records of the Immigration and Naturalization Service, Case File 52484/1-A, 29 September 1908.

45 Ibid. Five saloons were included in this category.

46 The INS report also indicated that there was a difference between "resorts" and "houses of prostitution" since the latter was a specific location of a sex worker where a customer would knowingly go for such service. These could be hotels or single family detached houses that were not categorized as rooming houses.

47 Parlor houses were distinguished from cribs in that the former had residents that lived in the facility all of the time where women employed in cribs lived away from the place of business. The Cosmos was later known as the "Green Light Hotel" and changed again to the "St. Nicholas" by 1930. The Tokio Hotel was later renamed the UI Hotel.

48 "Woman Suspected of Robbery Goes Free," *The Seattle Daily Times*, 5 June 1903, p. 4, col. 2.

49 "Red Light Dance Halls are Closed," *The Seattle Post-Intelligencer*, 13 July 1906, p. 10, col. 3.

50 "Dive Dance Halls Closed," *The Seattle Daily Times*, 11 July 1906, p. 4, col. 4.

51 "Lowest Dive in City Closed," *The Seattle Daily Times*, 14 July 1906, p. 12, col. 4.

52 Ordinance No. 1090, 18 May 1889, To Prevent and Punish Gambling.

53 This time, the bail was set at $1,200 for Chappell, a marked increase from the $500 bail for his first arrest in 1903 for the same offenses.

54 "Chappell's Tenderloin and His Land," *The Seattle Sunday Times*, 8 July 1906, p. 19, col. 7.

55 While acting as Chappell's property manager, Nichols' campaign for office was supported by John L. Wilson and the Seattle Brewing & Malting Company. The company held an exclusive contract to supply all of Chappell's businesses with beer. In 1908, Senator Ralph Nichols was defeated in his re-election to his senate seat, due in great part to his association as Chappell's manager of the properties in the restricted district.

56 After 1910, the New Paris Hotel joined the La France Hotel business that shared the same building and both were operated under the name "New Paris."

57 None of the businesses were insured.

58 Moore was running for an additional term after having been defeated for re-election in 1908 by John Miller.

59 James S. Murphy v. City of Seattle, et al. King County Superior Court, Report of the Grand Jury, Case #75162, 2 August 1910.

60 The city passed Ordinance #23897 in April 1910 that allowed hiring additional physicians and a bacteriologist that would work in the Red Light District. For $2.50, a woman could get an examination and the required certificate of health that would be good for one week. The woman's name, hotel, and room number were listed on the certificate and were not transferable if the woman relocated to another room, even if in the same hotel. The collected monies for the health inspection would go into the city general fund.

61 Ibid.

62 Ibid.

63 Ibid.

64 "Police Chief Begins Fight to Clean Up," *Seattle Times*, 23 March 1910, p. 1, col. 3, 4.

65 The firm's owner, Max Umbrecht, had prior experience working for Chappell.

66 The only material that did not originate in Washington was the antique marble from Vermont that was used in the lobby.

67 Construction of the hotel was originally planned to begin in September 1914.

68 The Welcome Hotel was also the site of a 1922 raid by the police "dry squad." Over 200 gallons of sake and about $2,000 of equipment that included a large press, vats, and barrels to make the liquor were seized from a two-room apartment. Over sixty filled kegs were found in the tiny rooms, but no arrest was ever made of the parties responsible for the liquor that was said to have supplied all of the bars in that side of the city. In 1934, Masajiro Mizuta, manager for the Welcome Hotel, died as a result of a single gunshot from a robbery of the day's receipts.

69 The latter three commissions were done following Chappell's death and under the direction of the board of trustees. The date near the cornice of the front façade of the Publix Hotel indicates that the building was completed in 1928, but it was completed ahead of schedule with the first guests registering in December 1927.

70 These figures are derived from business ledger and accounts payable for January 1919. Rainier Heat and Power Company Businesses, 1919–1922, 1a.2.3. Museum of History and Industry, Collection #2012.3.1.5.2.

71 Preliminary estimates of Chappell's estate were initially given at $681,000.

72 Interview with William K. Goodwin, Attorney at Law, Montgomery Purdue Blankinship & Austin, PLLC, 23 August 2006. Goodwin handled the Chappell Trust up to its time of dispersal.

The Neighborhood of Asian American Hotels

THE BUILDING BOOM OF SROS

In a 1906 real estate report, *The Seattle Mail and Herald* profiled the challenge to the city in accommodating a growing population and the shortage of available housing.

> ...three hundred people had to spend the night in the railroad station because there were no vacant places in the numerous lodging houses [and] hotels...people walk the streets... all night seeking some place to stay even for a night. When one...notes the large number of huge apartment, lodging houses and hotels that are being constantly added to the large number already in use, this seems almost incredible; but the actual facts seem to be that this city is in a chronic condition of overcrowding....[1]

At the time that the Jackson Street Regrade project was nearing completion, the John Davis and Company real estate office predicted that the newly-leveled construction zone would fill with stores, hotels, and rooming houses. In January 1909, only New York and Chicago exceeded Seattle in the amount of money that was being invested in construction projects. Over $17.5 million in new construction had occurred, with permits for future building issued for an additional $5 million.

By 1910, Seattle ranked as the fifth city in the nation to average over $1.5 million per month in building permits.[2] The city had reported its highest construction dollar valuation to date in 1909 and 1910 with over $19,000,000 and $17,000,000 in property development, respectively.[3] The 237,194 population figure for 1910 indicated a near tripling of the 80,671 that was recorded in 1900. In 1909, the majority of the construction dollars was for single-family detached housing, followed by over $4,000,000 spent on the construction of hotels, lodging, and apartment buildings. In 1910, this latter category accounted for over $2,300,000, following single-family housing and office/retail store building categories that each had about $3,900,000 in annual construction.[4] It would take another twelve years before construction values would match the growth of 1910.

As the city, architects, and builders suspected, completion of the regrade and train stations brought a record construction year for Seattle. Real estate brokers were monitoring the number of commissions in architectural offices and escalating property values. With an increase in the population, the construction industry was finding it difficult to keep up with the demands for permanent housing and temporary lodging facilities. The dramatic increase in residents occurred from the growth in trade and commerce that had already begun between Seattle and Alaska and the market connection that was developing with Asia.

The Seattle Post-Intelligencer reported that "in the Jackson Street regrade district, scores of costly new hotels [were completed in 1910] and that this section has become an important addition to rent-producing property of the city."[5] SRO construction that was underway in the Jackson Street regrade area included the Hotel Kanagawa ($50,000), Hotel Norway ($30,000), Eclipse Hotel ($50,0000), Hudson Hotel ($50,000), and Ashima Hotel ($30,000). John Davis and Company acknowledged that a large part of Seattle's success was due to "the disposition of Orientals...establish[ing] a new business district in the South End. Several important purchases had been made in the vicinity of Eighth and King, and a number of the buildings were being constructed—and planned."[6] Such a move was thought to be a benefit to the 2nd and Washington Chinatown area where the Asian American community was vacating and "a better class of retail and wholesale stores" was predicted to move into that location.[7] The commitment to building a pan-Asian community that would be the center of the new Chinatown and Japantown was materializing with the

A wall of residential hotels: (left to right) Eclipse Hotel, Oak Tin building and the Hudson Hotel building.
[Courtesy King County Assessor's Office, Property Record Cards, 1937–1973, Puget Sound Branch,
Washington State Archives]

construction of a number of single-room-occupancy residential hotel buildings on the Jackson Street regrade land. The Wa Chong Company, under the
leadership of Chun Ching Hock and his manager Woo Gen, continued to be at
the forefront in settling a new Chinatown that was migrating to the east and
south of the downtown. From 1900 to 1910, the Wa Chong Company was listed
as owner or long-term lessee for properties that bridged the old with the new
Chinatown location.

Seattle had over 200 SRO buildings listed between Yesler Way and
Charles Street and from the Waterfront to 14th Avenue South in 1910, with ten
such hotels that had been newly constructed from available building parcels
made possible by the Jackson Street Regrade area and immediately to the east
of the Union Pacific Station. The hotels were not isolated structures, but were
frequently built on adjacent parcels; creating an entire neighborhood of SRO
buildings. Half of the block face on the west side of 7th Avenue South between
South King and Weller streets had been totally built with SRO buildings with
the completion of the Hudson, the Gee How Oak Tin building, and the Eclipse
Hotel building.[8] On the southeast corner of the South Weller Street and 7th
Avenue South intersection, another half block had been filled with the three-
story New Central Hotel designed by the firm of Gaffney and Hyde and located
immediately adjacent to the New Kanagawa Hotel. The New Hotel Norway,

New Central Hotel. [Courtesy The Wing Luke Asian Museum, 2006.038.001.024]

located on the block south of the New Central, added another three-story SRO
with fifty-two rooms and four storefronts to the neighborhood. On Maynard
Avenue South, the four-story Freedman Hotel was just beginning construction
under the design of W.P. White. Henry Broderick, one of the city's leading real
estate brokers, had predicted that 1910 would bring more growth and development than Seattle had ever experienced. It was the beginning of a continual
construction zone that would last for the next two decades.

     In addition to architect John L. McCauley's work with William
Chappell, the greatest number of residential hotel commissions in the new
regrade area was awarded to the firm of Thompson and Thompson whose prin-
cipals were father Charles L. Thompson and son Charles Bennett Thompson.
From 1910 to the mid-1920s, their commissions included eight major hotel buildings in Chinatown and Nihonmachi, some of which were done for Chinese and
Japanese clients. Unlike other architectural firms, Thompson and Thompson
built a reputation for the design of prestigious Seattle buildings and houses,
such as the Sartori, Metropolitan, and Hyde blocks, in addition to promoting
their work on residential hotel design.[9]

     In the six-month period that closed 1910, an assessment of real estate
development revealed that in addition to single-family home construction

throughout the city, the area east of the train stations had experienced a phenomenal addition of 200 stores and 2,000 single rooms, the majority of which
were occupied as quickly as the buildings were completed. Fifty-eight out of
eighteen thousand property sales were in excess of $40,000, which included a
Second Avenue and Washington Street Chinatown lot that was sold on behalf
of Chin Gee Hee for $50,000.

THE VISION FOR A NEW CHINATOWN

Chinese entrepreneur Goon Dip rivaled William Chappell when it came to business savvy and acumen in the development of property in the new Chinatown.
Born Goon Yuen-Dip in 1862, he arrived in Portland, Oregon, as a young Chinese
immigrant from Hoyun in the Sun Ning District of Guangdong Province. Young
Goon worked as a servant and ultimately in the employ of Moy Back Hin, one
of Portland's leading merchants and labor contractors. The friendship that
developed between these two men lasted throughout their lives.

Speaking Chinese and with a fluent and skillful command of English,
Goon was an indispensable asset in Moy's business world and a quick learner
when it came to managing people and property. By 1900, Goon had begun his
own dry goods store in Portland along with a highly successful labor contracting company that kept expanding from his reputation as a generous, fair, and
caring employer. He furnished workers for the Oregon-Washington Railroad
and Navigation Company and seven canneries in Oregon and Washington, with
about nine hundred of his employees working in the Alaska fishing industry.[10]
With an excess of two thousand laborers on his payroll during the height of
fishing season, Goon estimated that two-thirds of his employees were white
laborers with the remaining one-third being Chinese.[11] While his personal net
worth was estimated at $500,000, newspapers delighted in speculating his
wealth. "[Goon Dip] is the largest Chinaman, financially, west of the Mississippi
River...[and] one of the shrewdest businessmen on the coast...he has the reputation of never losing out and his immense holdings bear up this statement.
Nobody knows how much Goon Dip is really worth but it is positively known
that he owns Portland business blocks that enable him to write his check in
the seven figures."[12]

With Moy Back Hin as a partner, Goon purchased the Oregon Hotel
in downtown Portland in 1904 under their corporate name of the Western

Goon Dip Certificate of Residence, 1894. [Courtesy Karen Goon]

American Company. The hotel served as a home for his family but was also a financial venture to accommodate throngs of Portland visitors attending the 1905 Lewis and Clark Exposition.[13] As his reputation as a businessman grew, Goon was now spending as much time traveling to and attending his business concerns in Washington State as he was working in his home city of Portland.

Before the turn of the 20th century, Seattle's Chinese residents numbered a modest 438 and only about 15% of the total Chinese population in Portland. Seattle's 1886 expulsion of Chinese and Portland's reputation as a more tolerant city toward this ethnic group had helped retain its population. In 1900, Portland's total city population still exceeded Seattle's with 90,426 and 80,671, respectively. Both Seattle and Portland had experienced remarkable growth attributed to industrial development and manufacturing including the lumber industry, cannery and agricultural growth, and rail and roadway construction.[14] But by 1910, Seattle's population of 237,194 people eclipsed Portland's

207,214 in the US Census count. Seattle Judge Thomas Burke observed that China and commercial competition with European countries and the East Coast were opportunities to compete with Portland and San Francisco. If Seattle did not "get a full share" of trade, it would be "the fault of blundering legislation."[15]

The commercial growth and high population of Chinese residents in Portland had already earned that city a Chinese consular position in 1905 that was filled by Moy Back Hin with Goon serving as his secretary. Into the first decade of the 1900s, business matters between China and Seattle required that all transactions be reviewed through the office of the Chinese minister in Washington, DC, an action that resulted in costly delays of time and money. The Chinese population of Seattle was at a modest 924 compared to the nearly 5,700 who were living in Portland, but trade and industrial development were shifting the importance of these Northwest cities and dictating that political changes be made.

In January 1909, Chinese Minister of Foreign Affairs Wu Ting Fang appointed Goon as the honorary Chinese consul for Washington, Idaho, and Alaska with headquarters in Seattle.[16] Chin Keay of the Quong Tuck Company was assigned to serve as secretary to Consul Goon.[17] With business ventures in Portland and responsibilities throughout the Pacific Northwest, Goon needed to turn over much of the AYP fair responsibilities such as parade chairman and activities associated with the construction of the Chinese Village. His choice for replacement of the Chinatown fair activities was Lew Geate Kay, a young Chinese American and recent graduate of the University of Washington.[18]

On his consul appointment, Goon was instructed to proceed immediately to Seattle to assume his new position, and according to *The Oregonian*, he was heartily greeted by "thirty members of the local Chinese colony, representing nearly every mercantile house in the city, and T. Kikutaka, representing the local Japanese [in] one of the most elaborate Chinese banquets ever served in Seattle."[19]

The core of what *The Seattle Daily Times* referred to as the "first super-structure building of the new Chinatown" was an action of genius and commitment on the part of Chinese entrepreneurs under the leadership of Chinese Vice Consul Goon.[20] In the summer of 1909 and as the AYPE was underway, plans to construct two mixed-use commercial and residential hotel buildings around King Street were announced before the details of location and land purchases were even finalized. Representatives for Chun Ching Hock, Chin

Gee Hee, and Goon Dip planned and executed a brilliant strategy to secure the future of Seattle's Chinese community.

So many properties in the regrade district had already sold, with building permits issued and construction underway for seven residential hotels that were in the immediate area that was under consideration by Seattle's Chinese "syndicate."[21] As a strong leader in property investment, the Wa Chong Company had the unencumbered financial resources that were necessary to buy the land before it was lost to another potential buyer. On 5 December 1909, the Wa Chong Company purchased two parcels at the southwest corner of the intersection of King Street and 8th Avenue South for $33,000, specifically identified as lots 7 and 8 of Block 54 of Maynard's Plat. The neighboring parcels 1 and 2, located immediately to the west of the Wa Chong parcels, were owned by Earl and Alice Young.[22]

In January 1910, Goon, on behalf of a not-yet-registered corporation, assumed options to purchase the four Wa Chong and Young lots. The options gave Goon the time that was needed to file official articles of incorporation with the state and to solicit investors for a major construction project. An office in Chin Gee Hee's residential hotel building at 208 Washington Street served as the first location of Goon's newly-formed corporation as property purchases and building plans were underway.[23] Translated as "for mutual benefit," the "Kong Yick" intended to create a center for the new Chinatown that would include a broad number of participants. On 6 June 1910, the Kong Yick Investment Company (KYIC) became a reg-

Chun Ching Hock, 1902. Chun was 58 at the time this photo was taken. [Courtesy the Woo Family]

istered Chinese-owned Washington State corporation. On 20 June 1910 the Youngs sold their two lots to the KYIC and agreed to carry the $40,000 purchase price in a mortgage. Three days later and after a short six-month ownership of the parcels, the Wa Chong Company sold its interest in lots 7 and 8 to the KYIC for $1.00.

Goon Dip spearheaded the organization of over 600 Chinese shareholders and short-term investors to purchase and construct two residential hotels on the four lots on King Street between 7th and 8th Avenue with total capital of $150,000 from the sold shares.[24] The short-term mortgage from the Youngs was paid in full through a corporate loan before construction began. Goon understood the importance of rallying the support of Seattle Chinese and Chinese investors that were both in and out of Washington State to establish Chinatown. While Goon had the financial means to front the construction of the buildings, he knew that with a great number of shareholders it would be possible to garner the finances to purchase the land, construct, and furnish the buildings. More importantly, a syndicate of owners would lend permanence to the core of the new Chinatown, and the Chinese would be vested in the property. The investment of a single share gave ownership in the corporation, the building, and a part of Chinatown. Goon's greater plan envisioned the Kong Yick buildings as the first to be owned through share investments and upon their completion other such buildings would be constructed in the new Chinatown and under collective Chinese ownership.

The Kong Yick Investment Company followed the technique that the Wa Chong Company had pioneered in 1869. The creation of a corporation would circumvent national law that prevented property purchase and ownership by aliens ineligible for citizenship; specifically those Asian immigrants from China, Japan, and the Philippines. Clear title of property ownership would minimize the possibility of losing homes and businesses that was always a threat for Asian immigrants leasing land and buildings. With the public-works projects of filling the tideflats, building roads and railways, and the south downtown regrade completed, there was little worry that other such major capital projects would threaten the location of the new Chinatown. Each shareholder would be creating a Chinatown home that would not be moved again.

Through the Kong Yick Investment Company's officers J.A. Kerr, Lew G. Kay, and C.H. Kee, the corporation filed a charter with capital stock listed as $55,000 that was divided into 1,100 shares of $50 each.[25] The articles of incorporation gave the Company the right to:

> ...acquire, purchase, lease, own, hold, sell, mortgage or encumber both improved and unimproved real estate wherever situated; to survey, subdivide, plat and improve the same...to construct, erect and operate thereon houses, buildings, light and power plants, machinery and appliances...own and conduct buildings for merchandising, for hotels, lodging houses and to rent, [and]...furnish hotels and lodging houses and places of business.[26]

The corporation assigned five trustees to oversee the management of the real estate and building construction until 1 December 1911 when a seven-member board of directors would administer the operation of the buildings on behalf of the investors. Rent profits during the first year of operation would be used to pay off any amount owing on the building construction and to begin to build capital for future building projects of the corporation. Every person purchasing shares in the company was entitled to a debenture bond certificate that included ten detachable interest coupons. From January 1912 through 1921, one coupon could be surrendered annually for a guaranteed interest payment of $3.00 in gold coin. As a major investor in the Kong Yick Company, Woo Bing was chosen as the treasurer trustee in charge of the disbursements that would take place in the Quong Tuck store in the East Kong Yick Building. After 1921, interest payments would be replaced with dividends at the discretion of the board of directors.

In a 1910 interview about the building project and new Chinatown location, **Ma Hing** commented on the significance of the location and the importance of the building design in creating Seattle's Chinatown.[27] It was specifically stated that the two Kong Yick buildings would serve as a prototype in the construction of buildings in other Chinese American communities.

> The concerted movement of our people to procure a site on which to erect new and modern buildings was begun some months ago. Our first building should be completed by April and a second will be finished by fall. These will be modern in every respect.... The site is an ideal one, close to terminals of both the Great Northern and the Harriman [rail] lines. Seattle Chinese have outgrown the idea of close, cramped, dark quarters. In a few months Seattle's Chinatown will be a model for other cities to imitate.[28]

As was the case with the formation of the 2nd and Washington Chinatown, Chun Ching Hock through the Wa Chong Company and Chin Gee Hee and partner Woo Bing through the Quong Tuck Company played seminal roles in helping establish the new Chinatown. The guarantee that both businesses would take up tenancy in the future buildings endorsed and sealed their participation in Goon's plan for corporate shareholders and Chinese ownership of Seattle property. At the same time, it provided the anchor stores of longstanding familiar identity to the Chinese American community. In October 1910, the Quong Tuck and the Wa Chong companies relocated into

East Kong Yick building. [Courtesy Richard Lew Kay]

the East Kong Yick building. It would be the latter company's final commercial management office from the multiple locations that they had occupied in the city since their establishment in 1868.[29]

The fact that the design of these influential Chinatown buildings would not follow an expression of "Chinoiserie" was a significant statement. At the same time that Seattle's Chinatown was being planned, relocated, and reconstructed, San Francisco's Chinatown was also being rebuilt in the aftermath of the 1906 earthquake and fire. Architectural firms that were hired by San Francisco's Chinese Americans chose building design elements that were very different from those selected by the Seattle Chinese community. Through architecture and engineering firms such as T. Paterson Ross and A.W. Burgren, San Francisco's Chinatown adopted an Asian motif of upturned eaves, gold and red colors, lanterns and pagoda-shaped, non-structurally authentic roofs that created a "new Oriental city [that would] be more picturesque and interesting to travelers than ever before."[30] The image was much like the pagoda pavilions that were built for the tourists of the Seattle Alaska-Yukon-Pacific Exposition.

In 1908, *The Architect and Engineer of California and Pacific Coast States* journal credited Ross and Burgren as the firm that was responsible for "radical changes in style and construction of buildings in the Oriental district."[31] Post-earthquake commentary noted that the residential hotels that previously stood in San Francisco's Chinese quarters had been replaced with an Asian motif. "Where previously the rigid lines of cheap occidental building construction had provided perpendicular walls, now the fantasy of the Far East has been borrowed and in the Chinatown of today the pagoda-style quite generally predominates."[32] But Seattle's Chinese American community chose a typology of mixed-use single room occupancy residential hotel buildings for Chinatown.

SING FAT CO., INC.
LEADING ORIENTAL BAZAAR
S. W CORNER CALIFORNIA ST AND GRANT AVE
CHINATOWN, SAN FRANCISCO, CAL.
So. Broadway, at 6th St }   { Broadway, at 25th S
LOS ANGELES, CAL. }   BRANCHES   { NEW YORK CI1
美國金山正埠生發公司

Sing Fat Building [postcard]

The Kong Yick buildings were designed by the local firm of Thompson and Thompson with Hans Pedersen as general contractor, and constructed at a cost of $70,000 per building. Known as the "twin buildings," they were not totally identical in purpose or appearance. Both of these SROs were four-story brick and concrete structures with the West Kong Yick having arched windows and door entrances to the association room at the northeast corner of the building. The connections between Seattle's Chinese community and passage to China were directly reflected in the usage of the West Kong Yick building. While both accommodated a transient population of workers, the East Kong Yick building was rented out for a general working population that could stay short or long-term while the West Kong Yick building, known as "Building 1," had the additional function of providing quarters for those Chinese who were in wait for ships bound for China.[33] This latter aspect was important for transnational connections of Seattle's Chinese community with families and business concerns in China and it expanded opportunities for businesses in Chinatown that could cater to the needs of Pacific Rim travelers.[34]

The China Mutual steamers connected the commercial maritime trade between the Puget Sound, Asia, Australia, and England. In 1902, British owner Alfred Holt entered into a transportation agreement with the Blue Funnel Line to operate passage that connected Seattle to China and Japan and on to Australia via the Asian ports.[35] In January 1909 and the year before the completion of the Kong Yick buildings, the Blue Funnel line finished construction of their dock in Kowloon, China. An agreement with Seattle's Yick Fung Company established an agent office of the Blue Funnel ship transport line that would be conveniently located in the grocery store and part of the service that was offered for patrons staying in the West Kong Yick building. As the son of the Yick Fung Company founder, James Malcolm Mar recalled the significance of the role of his family's business.

> The Yick Fung was the first business in the West Kong Yick building and my father was one of the first investors in the corporation. The buildings were called "Kong Yick" as it was intended that the Chinese community would come together to build Chinatown and that is just what happened. At the height of our business, we had about 230 customers from across the country. We weren't the only such business in Chinatown. In those days, every business had "a piece of the apple." No one undercut prices—they were consistent and that kept everyone in business. When my dad got the Blue Funnel Line contract, the main branch office was operated out of Hong Kong and he received a commission for the service of selling passages. Dad supplied transportation service to and from the dock and that is how my brother got into operating the China Cab Company. The Blue Funnel Line served freight and about ninety passengers a month...the Chinese couldn't afford to go on the passenger liners so they would travel with the freighters. It would cost $76.00 to go to China and it would take longer than a passenger-only ship... 28 days to get to Hong Kong. It stopped in the Philippines and at eight places in Japan before arriving in China. We could provide accommodations for about thirty people that would stay in the mezzanine level of the store and on cots in a space that was also used for store supplies. Passengers were all men and would typically stay about three days. We'd send the overflow of passengers that we couldn't serve to the other hotels... once a month we'd give business to the Panama or the Publix or some other hotel in Chinatown.[36]

For an additional fee, prospective Chinese passengers could take their meals as part of the service of the Yick Fung or from other commercial

East Kong Yick (left) and West (right) buildings, divided by Canton Alley, 29 September 1911. The photo shows the Shanghai Hotel that opened in the West building upon its completion in 1910. The SRO part of the building was operated under four different business names, including the Niagara Hotel from 1913–1919 under Japanese management, the LVM Hotel from 1925–1930 under Filipino management and the White Star in 1941 (Filipino management) and from 1953–1957 when it returned to Japanese management. The hotel space was vacant from 1938–1940. The vacant lot in the foreground is where the Norway/New American Hotel would be constructed in 1916. [Courtesy Washington State Historical Society at WashingtonHistory.org, Asahel Curtis Collection, 1943.42.22232]

businesses in the two buildings. As grandson of a managing partner of the Wa Chong store, **Jack Peng** remembered his visits to the store and the awaiting travelers.

> The Wa Chong provided two meals daily; one at noon and one at midnight. Two large round tables for feeding the Chinese boarders were placed in the center aisle along with the store provisions and amid people who were trying to shop. Sawdust was under and around the tables and cats were always roaming in and out of the store. When it was mealtime, they knew that there would be plenty of bones and gristle as the Chinese guys spit them out and onto the floor. The cook lived in the basement of the store. He made the egg noodles that would be wholesaled and delivered with the company truck throughout the Seattle area. He'd mix the dough and keep putting it through a roller conveyor until it was flat enough to cut and then hang the long noodles in the basement and on wooden rods to dry. He did this job every day.[37]

East Kong Yick – Hoy Sun Ning Yuen Association on the top floor of the building. Decorative banners and wrought iron railing noted the importance of the use and its function. Upper floors were the Freeman Hotel and was a member of the Seattle Japanese Hotel and Apartment Association in 1915. [Courtesy Richard Lew Kay]

Both of the Kong Yick buildings included family association rooms that gave further cultural identity to the structures as being Chinese American and with functions that served a primarily male population.[38] The East Kong Yick building had the Hoy Sun Ning Yuen Benevolent Association meeting room on the fourth floor in the far northeast corner of the building. The Gee How Oak Tin Association had taken temporary occupancy in the basement of that building and adjacent to the space that was used for the Chinese School. The Oak Tin represented the Chin, Woo, and Yuen families along with members whose names represented a smaller segment of the Seattle Chinese population.

On 13 March 1911, the Seattle branch of the Hop Sing Tong was inaugurated in the association room on the fourth floor in the West Kong Yick building with an elaborate banquet, music and singing performers; over one hundred guests and officers of the organization were in attendance. While the exteriors of the hotel buildings appeared to be very "American" in expression, the interiors of Association rooms allowed for flamboyant expressions of Chinese heritage. On the night of their installation of officers, *The Seattle Daily Times* covered the story of the event of the Hop Sings as they attempted to de-mystify the association.

> The gorgeous draperied trappings of the Orient covered the walls of the tong's headquarters. Red and yellow predominated. About the rooms ran rows of seats—teak and mahogany, inlaid with mother of pearl and ivory. Tables, some plain in the somber tints of the native wood and others bedecked with covers of interwoven silk and gold, occupied the center. On them rested the fragile crockery...of the Flowery Kingdom.[39]

The tong emphasized its purpose as a peaceful and benevolent organization that, in part, gave financial assistance to its members when it was needed. Any actions of violence would only occur in self-defense of the organization and not as the instigator of aggression.[40]

By 1936, fourteen associations and tongs were recorded by the Chong Wa Benevolent Association that represented multiple Chinese districts.[41] The Chong Wa was housed in its own building in 1929, but all of the other associations and tongs were located in residential hotels, with the Kong Yick buildings housing the majority of them. As president of the Lung Kong Tin Yee Association since 1989, **Sen Poy Chew** shared its origins and relocation to the second Chinatown.

> My father was a member of the Association, so I was a member. The association name originates from "Dragon Hill" in Guangdong province. Their land struggles in China go back to the end of the Han Dynasty almost 2,000 years ago. Historically, the Lew, Quan, and Chang families banded together when warriors were needed. Later, these three families were joined by people with the surname "Chew." These warriors became folk heroes and a temple was built about 300 years ago on the top of the hill called "Lung Kong" to honor these ancestors. The Lung Kong Tin Yee Association was established in Seattle in 1890 and was one of the oldest in Chinatown. In 1929, the four families of about one hundred members raised enough money to purchase a building on South Washington Street between 2nd and 3rd Street and owned it until 1954 when it was sold

MAP 4-1: *Chinese Associations and Tongs – 1936 [Author]*

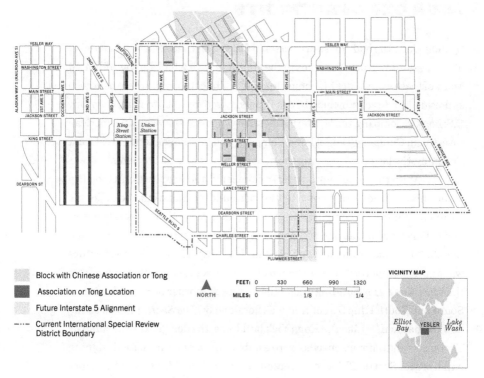

Block with Chinese Association or Tong

Association or Tong Location

Future Interstate 5 Alignment

---- Current International Special Review
District Boundary

FEET: 0   330   660   990   1320
MILES: 0   1/8   1/4

NORTH

VICINITY MAP

Elliot   YESLER   Lake
Bay   Wash.

to move to the new Chinatown. We didn't have enough money to buy another building, but Rosaline Goon Kay, Goon Dip's daughter, told our association that we could stay in the West Kong Yick building for as long as we wanted. We're still here.[42]

Unlike neighboring Chinese-occupied hotel buildings with recessed balconies, the Kong Yick buildings included projecting iron balconies across the King Street primary façade that were accessible from double doors that connected to the association rooms.[43] The importance of associations and their role in the community was evident in the design and placement as these functions were always visible as part of the top floors of the buildings, and in their role as physical reflections of spiritual and cultural significance. Economically, associations would not be located at-grade so as not to compete with prime retail business spaces that were in clear view of the street trade.

HOTEL MILWAUKEE AND THE
GOON DIP APARTMENTS

By 1909, Goon Dip had amassed a personal fortune and had registered a number of business and corporate names in the state and with which he was affiliated. Many of these were under his complete control. The companies where he served as president or director included Goon Dip and Company, G.D. Young & Company, G.S. Long & Company, the Western American Company, the Western American Investment Company, Daniel Land Company, and the Daniel Land Investment Company, the latter two bearing the name of his American-born son.

With the Kong Yick buildings completed and in operation, Goon Dip turned his attention to the construction of a building that would be under his sole ownership and accomplished by the formation of another corporate investment. This time, it was one of Goon's Portland corporations that purchased the $50,000 parcel from the A.A. Schuchard family.[44] The new Seattle venture was a corner property that was located diagonally across the intersection from the West Kong Yick building and at the northwest corner of Seventh Avenue South and South King Street that was heralded by *The Seattle Times* as the "new Chinatown."[45] Like the Kong Yick buildings, the design was executed by Thompson and Thompson, who were establishing a reputation for designing buildings for Seattle Chinese entrepreneurs. Goon's building was a five-story brick hotel containing 150 rooms and nine storefront bays. Work on the $65,000 project began the first week of January 1911 with Hans Pederson as general contractor.

From the primary entrance on King Street, it was the Hotel Milwaukee, and from a secondary entrance on 7th Avenue South for people who were considered to be permanent residents of the building it was the "Goon Dip Apartments." Both consisted of SRO rooms, with doors that made adjoining multiple-room rental possible for extended or expanding families. Both the long-term and short-term rooms shared common corridors in the building with the only discernible difference being a sliding metal-clad door that was intended to be closed and that acted as a hallway divider between the apartments on the north side and the single hotel rooms on the south side of the building. As a long-term resident, **William Chinn** grew up in the hotel.

Our apartment was on the 2nd floor...and looked down on 7th Avenue South. We had the only set of rooms in the entire building that had a private bathroom and kitchen. There was a swinging door that separated the kitchen from a single room. I lived in the Goon Dip Apartments until I was 18 years old. The Oriental Café was operated by Yap Lee on the ground level and at the corner of the building along with the New Butterfly Restaurant. There was a pool hall where we played as kids and there were so many gamblers in Chinatown. In the mid-1930s, Big Hank Wong sat out in front of the New American Hotel across the street. He was a well-known gambler and whenever he won, he'd give all of us kids a quarter. I remember the men staying in the East Kong Yick building... Ray Chinn and I would go over there to play in Canton Alley. The men living in hotels liked having us kids there and they took time to play games with us...they really missed having their own families.[46]

The entrance for hotel patrons was covered with a decorative wrought-iron canopy with entry tiles on the single stair stoop that declared the "Milwaukee" name. The terracotta entrance carving over the King Street door displayed "Goon Dip Young," which translated meant "the seal of Goon Dip." "The lobby with a check-in desk was not visible from the street and was tucked behind the two westernmost King Street storefronts and filled with benches and high-backed rocking chairs for the guests."[47] Like the newly completed Alps Hotel that was one block to the west on King Street, the Milwaukee, as a more luxurious SRO, contained an elevator that was operated by a hotel clerk. An early advertisement for the hotel noted "very low transient rates, rooms with or without bath; desirable rooms for $3.00 and up weekly for permanent guests. Newly furnished. Hot and cold water in every room. Long distance telephones in all rooms.... First-class café. Free bus to trains and boats."[48] Unlike pot-belly stoves that heated each storefront of the Kong Yick buildings, heat for the Milwaukee and the other newer hotels was furnished through steam radiators that were located in all of the rooms and serviced from a coal-burning furnace in the basement. Under the ownership of Goon Dip, the Hotel Milwaukee Café that was located on the mezzanine level of the building offered "the best in Chinese and American cuisine with live music and dancing."[49]

While Goon Dip certainly had the financial means to instruct his architects to integrate a luxurious space for his personal living quarters as part of the design of the building, he did not do so. He and his family occupied a simple suite of rooms on the 6th and top floor of the hotel, facing the Puget

Milwaukee Hotel. [Courtesy King County Assessor's Office, Property Record Cards, 1937–1973, Puget Sound Branch, Washington State Archives]

Sound. The four small but comfortable rooms were along one side of the corridor and connected with doorways. Their quarters served the family well as they traveled between their Portland and Seattle homes until they made their full relocation to the Milwaukee Hotel in March 1912.[50] It offered the family security and privacy with an additional accommodation of one modest room across the hall that served as the quarters for "Charlie," Goon's Irish-American bodyguard.[51] As the only granddaughter of Goon Dip, **Gladys Goon Choi** regularly visited her grandparents in the Milwaukee Hotel.

> My father was Daniel Goon, the only son of Goon Dip. Chinatown was small and [centered around] grocery stores, family associations and tongs and lots of restaurants that were all located in hotel buildings. My brothers and I were all supposed to be studying in Chinese School but I would slip out the back door and run down the alley to the Milwaukee Hotel to see my grandparents. There was a large bearskin rug on the floor and not much furniture in their "apartment." It was the same kind that you'd see in a family association; mahogany and inlaid pearl. My grandfather had steel doors installed for the bedrooms

because at one time someone tried to kill him. My grandmother's feet were bound and she couldn't get around very well, but she was tough and managed to walk to the stores in Chinatown that were across the street.

I had to learn Chinese so that I could talk with my grandmother as she spoke so little English. She never talked about her life in China but she did talk about Angel Island [off the coast of San Francisco] and about the beds that were stacked for the incoming Chinese immigrants and the INS interrogations. She told me that if some of the women didn't answer the questions right, they were sent back to China. They would take a shower and groom themselves carefully before they would leave. The other women knew that they would likely hang themselves before they would land in China because over there, it was assumed that the only reason a woman would be sent back was if she were prostituting herself.[52]

As the Milwaukee Hotel was being constructed, China's changing political life was drawing the attention of the world and focusing more attention on Chinese Americans throughout the United States. It was impossible to ignore the revolution that was sweeping through China and the supportive sentiments of young Chinese Americans growing within American Chinatowns. A storefront of the West Kong Yick building was now used for meetings of the local Kuo Min Tang and those supporters of the Chinese Nationalist Party. As a show of support for the revolution and in recognition of the certainty that the overthrow of the ruling Manchu Dynasty could adversely affect the work of US diplomatic posts, Goon Dip and Chin Keay tendered their resignations to the Chinese foreign minister in November 1911. As war-torn China wreaked havoc on the poor and starving peoples, relief efforts on the part of the local Kuo-Min Tang expanded and monies were collected through fund-raising efforts in and outside of Chinatown. Speaking in an unofficial capacity in a letter to the people of Washington State, Goon expressed his gratitude to have been of service to the Chinese.[53]

Goon's retirement from political service and as the voice that bridged Chinese and US economic development was short-lived when he was asked by the Chinese legation in Washington DC to serve the new government of the Chinese Republic as vice-consul in March 1912. The new position had an expanded territory that included Washington, Idaho, Oregon, Montana, Wyoming, North and South Dakota, and Nebraska. In recognition of his new post, Goon no longer wore the Chinese robes or queue that signified allegiance to the now defunct Manchu rule. There was a larger effort on the part of Goon to actively unite an older generation of Chinese immigrant conservatives with a younger generation of Chinese Americans who were in support of the new Nationalist party of China. Goon invited meetings to take place in his restaurant at the Milwaukee Hotel and donated $200 to the growing political group to help with organization efforts.

With ample financial resources to live anywhere in the city, Goon Dip continued to live in the Milwaukee Hotel that bore his seal. He also chose the Japanese management team of George Nishimura and George Koike to take care of the financial and day-to-day operations of the business. The Nishimura and Koike team provided the longest management tenure of the Milwaukee Hotel from 1915 until September 1933 when Consul Goon died. Up to that point, the Milwaukee Hotel remained as a member in good standing of the Seattle Japanese Hotel and Apartment Association. The event of Goon's passing was one of the most noted to ever occur in the heart of Chinatown. While white pieces of paper were being burned on the streets of Chinatown as a funeral rite for his prosperity in the next life, a caisson led by white horses circulated throughout all of Chinatown and people mourned the passing of Consul Goon. Both *The Post-Intelligencer* and *Seattle Times* noted that all of Seattle had lost one of Seattle's most respected citizens.

> He brought the innate courtesy, the kindly philosophy, the "do unto others" doctrine common to all faiths into his daily life and his contacts with white and yellow, black and brown-skinned friends.... Wherever a friend had occasion for rejoicing or sorrowing—a police chief's birthday, a man wrongfully arrested, a family starving and too proud to ask alms—there would be Goon Dip. ...it was an honor, accorded bankers, newspaper reporters, civic leaders...or lost souls in the backwash of society, to be invited to the Goon home, hung with marvelous brocades, in the Milwaukee Hotel building, for a cup of tea and a friendly heart-strengthening chat.[54]

Unlike William Chappell, Goon did not leave his estate in trust, but rather left his properties and corporate shares in the care of his descendants, including his wife, Yoke Chin Shee, daughters Lillian, Martha, and Rosaline, and son, Daniel. Son-in-law Lew G. Kay assumed the management of the Milwaukee Hotel under the name of the Chung Hing Investment Company where he served

as president. From 1937 until 1941, Daniel Goon assumed absentee management
of the hotel. Unlike Goon Dip, neither of these men ever lived in the Milwaukee
Hotel and instead chose to live in the First Hill neighborhood east of Chinatown.
In many ways, Daniel Goon's death in May 1959 marked the beginning of a loss
in leadership of Goon Dip's prized hotel property and the first in a series of down-
turn events that would ultimately result in the closure of the Milwaukee Hotel.

CORPORATE POWER

The progress of Seattle's growth was measured by *The Seattle Times* in a series
of articles in early 1911 that profiled the fifty best buildings and outstanding
examples of engineering of 1910.[55] Of these fifty, five were single-room occupancy residential hotels located south of Yesler Way, including the West and
East Kong Yick buildings, the Hotel Rex Building, Alps, and Tacoma hotels. Of
these five, only the Kong Yick buildings were under Chinese ownership.

     The one-hundred-room Rex building was a four-story brick structure
with a 120 foot façade of ground-level commercial storefronts facing King Street
that was constructed for Charles D. Wason at a cost of $30,000. The upper three
floors were operated as the Astoria House Hotel with a sundry shop, the Rex
Café, and Hiranaka Tailor shop. Constructed for $85,000, the Alps was one of
the more luxurious SRO accommodations and contained six stories of rooms,
the maximum height of most of the residential hotels.[56] Like the Milwaukee,
the Alps had an at-grade hotel lobby and a paging system to serve its guests.
The four-story brick-and-concrete Tacoma Hotel at the northwest corner of
Ninth Avenue and Jackson Street was built at a cost of $60,000 at the fringe
of Japantown and near the concentrated Chinatown core of residential hotels.

     In the 1920s, there was a noticeable increase in the number of hotels
and businesses that were Chinese-owned. Many of these were operated in
conjunction with and under state-registered corporations that were legally
able to circumvent federal law that prohibited Chinese from owning property.
The corporations accomplished something that no immigrant Chinese could
do as an individual in that the former acted as the recognized legal owner but
still gave the ability to control and manage the property to the Chinese investors or owners. These corporate-owned hotels included the Oak Tin under
the Oak Tin Association (1907), the Freeman Hotel that was in the East Kong
Yick building and under the Kong Yick Investment Corporation (1910), the

Rex Hotel. [Courtesy King County Assessor's Office, Property Record Cards, 1937–1973, Puget Sound Branch, Washington State Archives]

Alps Hotel. [Courtesy King County Assessor's Office, Property Record Cards, 1937–1973, Puget Sound Branch, Washington State Archives]

At the southern fringe of Japantown at the northwest corner of 9th Avenue South and South Jackson Street were the Hotel Tacoma (also referred to as the Tacoma Hotel, left) and the Banzai Hotel (right). The former was under Japanese management from its construction in 1910 to 1960. The Banzai as seen in this photograph indicates Japanese management that lasted until 1932. [Courtesy Seattle Municipal Archives, Photo 606]

This 1915 photograph shows the developing Chinatown core. Taken from a vantage point up the hill from the South Jackson Street and 8th Avenue South intersection are the Western Hotel, Chinn Apartment Hotel, and the East Kong Yick building (left to right). [Courtesy Seattle Municipal Archives, Photo 607]

MAP 4-2: *Chinese Businesses – 1930 [Author]*

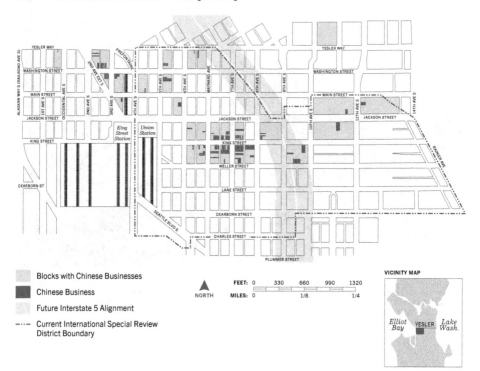

Chinn Apartment Hotel operated by the Leon Yick Investment Company (1910), the New American owned by the Kong Leong Investment Company (1916), the Eastern Hotel under the incorporation of the Wa Chong Company (1916), the Atlas Hotel owned by the Atlas Investment Company (1918), and the Republic Hotel owned by Fang Yick Investment Company (1920).

CONSTRUCTING AND DECONSTRUCTING NIHONMACHI

Before the movement for and construction of the new Chinatown core was underway, the Nihonmachi community was growing with new buildings that included architect-designed residential hotels.

A plan had been launched for construction of a grand SRO at the central node of Seattle's Nihonmachi at South Main Street and 6th Avenue South.

Lot 1 of Block 42 was purchased for $2,025 by Japanese immigrant, Ushitaro Ota, on 24 March 1900 from Arthur Hamilton. Using the corporate model of ownership, the World Real Estate Commercial Company was incorporated in March 1905 with officers of the corporation that each held an investment valued at $100 per share. Ushitaro Ota served as president and treasurer (83 shares), James Hickox as vice-president (251 shares), and Tyojiro Otany (83 shares) as secretary. Ota also served as an initial trustee of the corporation until a permanent board of trustees was elected. In February 1905, Ota was elected to serve as the president of a permanent body of trustees, and in May 1905 he sold Lot 1 of Block 42 to the corporation for $13,000. He held the mortgage on the land and secured it for the new corporation for an additional five years. [57]

Ushitaro Ota. [Courtesy Steve Tsukuno and Linda Tsukuno Hjorten]

With the Jackson Street regrade completed and new buildings being planned and constructed in that part of the city, the time was finally right to build on the parcel. In May 1910, the corporation had received its final permitting for the construction of the Panama Hotel under Japanese immigrant architect and civil engineer Sabro Ozasa with the Manhattan Building Contractors in charge of construction. Ota worked directly with Ozasa on every detail of the building's design and costs, carefully monitoring everything from the wood, plumbing and light fixtures, boiler and radiators to the wall tiling and brass handrail that graced the central entry stairway that led to the building's second floor. The resulting $50,000 five-story wood, brick, and concrete SRO building provided ninety-four rooms with steam heat and hot and cold water in every room. [58] With mezzanine-level business offices, the second floor of the building contained a separate apartment that was specifically designed for use by a resident manager and adjacent to a small hotel business office where guests could register. The Panama Hotel was and would be the only hotel in the Asian American district to include a small apartment with a kitchen for an on-site manager. [59] Only the Panama and the East Kong Yick buildings would include an office space and check-in desk located on the second floor at the top of a long flight of stairs.

Astor Hotel. [Courtesy Washington State Historical Society at WashingtonHistory.org, Asahel Curtis Collection, 1943.42.22226]

In addition to the Chinese-commissioned hotels, the firm of Thompson and Thompson designed the Astor Hotel for the Cascade Investment Company; the SRO was built before those in the new Chinatown and with Japanese corporate partners. The corporation was licensed by the state on 2 March 1906 and was formed under the partnership of William H. Maude, John F. Tenrey, Frank Jobst, George W. Williams, Kuranosi Hirade, and Matajiro Tsukuno.[60] Between 1906 and 1920, the company purchased about thirty properties, only two of which were used for the construction of residential hotels. Built the year before the Kong Yick Buildings, the $40,000 Astor Hotel was permitted for construction in August 1909, a four-story mixed-use hotel that was referred to by the architects as the "Japanese Club House" for its inclusion of a performing arts theater and cultural events center for the Japanese American community that was part of the building design.

The Hotel Puget Sound was the largest residential hotel in Seattle. Located south of Yesler Way, it was under Japanese immigrant development and management.[61] Located at Dearborn and 6th Avenue South, blocks away from the Japantown central core, the hotel was constructed in 1914 by the

A group of Issei men posing for a photo outside the Maynard Avenue main entrance of the Astor Hotel. [Courtesy The Wing Luke Asian Museum, 2000.015.142]

Keystone Development Company. The five-story brick building contained fifteen at-grade retail storefronts, 27 bathrooms and 444 rooms, each of which had its own sink. The hotel had a mixed-clientele population of Japanese, Filipino, and whites and was a popular destination that helped meet the increased demand of housing for shipyard workers in 1917 during World War I. The design included a main lobby with terrazzo flooring and a passenger elevator and was noted by *The Seattle Times* as an "an example of the permanency of Japanese investment in Seattle."[62] In 1926, the hotel was sold to the Puget Sound Hotel Investment Company whose corporate officers were Japanese Americans including manager, Manpei Miyagawa, along with Tsurue and Toki Nasasura.[63]

Corporate titles that masked Japanese ownership became the subject of state and ultimately Supreme Court challenges. Following California's 1913 Alien Land Law, Washington State adopted similar laws in 1921 and 1923 that prohibited property ownership to any person who did not declare an intention to become a United States citizen.

There were two prevalent means for Japanese involvement in SRO proprietorship. One was their having a *leasehold interest* that enabled them to

Hotel Puget Sound. [Courtesy King County Assessor's Office, Property Record Cards, 1937–1973, Puget Sound Branch, Washington State Archives]

physically occupy a building for an intended purpose, such as operating the upper floors of hotel rooms, but not holding title to the real property. A second means was holding a *master lease* of the entire building, which allowed them to operate the residential hotel portion and then sublease commercial storefronts to other building tenants. In the latter, the hotel proprietor had the advantage of controlling the types of businesses that were in the building. The ability to pick and choose appropriate businesses for the SRO storefronts helped build a Japantown that responded to community and resident needs. Through either means, rent was paid directly to the building owner or to a real estate management company that acted as an intermediary. The West and Wheeler Company was one of the most prominent property managers in Seattle and their rentals of hotel properties, such as the Alps Hotel, were rented and managed under a master lease system. Like the Chappell properties, the company had a preference for contracting with Japanese lessees, reportedly because of the skill and care that they employed in the management and upkeep of a building.[64]

Of equal importance to the California Alien Land Law, passage of a similar Washington law came at the heels of over a year of national committee hearings that were focusing specifically on Japanese immigration. Decisions on immigration law were going to be made through the lens of citizenship and property ownership and from the perspective of the West Coast, where the majority of the Japanese Americans were residing. In a House Resolution, Washington Congressman Albert Johnson was called to act as chairman of an immigration committee that would "investigate fairly and impartially, yet thoroughly, the Japanese situation in the Northwest, and particularly in the State of Washington...[including] their possession of hotels, groceries, markets and other places of business."[65] Washington State Governor Louis F. Hart had written a letter to Johnson, emphasizing the need for investigation of Japanese since conditions were so similar to those of California.[66] Hart had publicly declared that the legislature needed to enact laws that would "prevent the ownership, holding, leasing or controlling of real estate by Japanese or Chinese in the State of Washington."[67]

The hearings convened in California from June to September 1919 and continued in Washington State from July to September 1920. The House Committee on Immigration and Naturalization was charged with the task of collecting testimony that would address the "Japanese situation" and for a recommendation of how Japanese immigration should be handled.[68] In a series of public hearings that took place in San Francisco, Sacramento, Stockton, and at Angel Island, California, and in Tacoma and Seattle, Washington, the Committee opened the floor to public testimony regarding the involvement of Japanese in the community, including banking, Japanese fraternal organizations and membership support, and schools, along with pivotal employment sectors that included farming, operating businesses, and hotel management. The latter classification drew specific scrutiny. The Washington State Department of Licensing records that were aggregated from a report for Governor Hart's office indicated that of the "667 hotels inspected in Tacoma and Seattle [in 1919], 264 were owned by Japanese."[69] By the time the federal hearings commenced, another 18 hotels were added to the Seattle list.

At the California hearings, **Miller Freeman**, a Seattle trade journal publisher and president of Seattle's newly-formed Anti-Japanese League, offered his testimony on the city's Japanese. In a lengthy and impassioned plea, Freeman presented his case, recounting an outsider's view of Japanese customs and tradition without ever actually having spoken with any of the Japanese Seattleites. In rural economies, the issue was the perceived spread and domination of crops and consumer goods by the Japanese who were "con-trolling" public markets. In the urban environs, the concern was not addressed in terms of the geography that they occupied in the city, but of the Japanese control of the city's hotel businesses.

> ...I had heard rumors...about Japanese activities in various lines of business, and partic-ularly the absorption of the hotel business.... On April 1,1919, 47 per cent of the hotels in Seattle...were operated by Japanese. ...Grocery concerns...in the hands of Japanese [are] about one-fourth, including their own wholesale grocery. ...They were absorbing laundries rapidly...[and] practically all of the best farming land in the vicinity of Seattle... is in the hands of Japanese. [The hotels] are operated...as chains or mutual associa-tions.... The secretary of the Hotelman's Association of the City of Seattle...cannot tell you all the hotels that have Japanese capital interests, directly or indirectly.... A friend of mine in the real estate business told me that he was approached by a Japanese to buy a piece of property, and the question was asked who the Japanese expected to hold this piece of property, and his answer was that they had just had a child, and the property was to be transferred to that child.[70]

When asked for a "practical solution" to the issues that Seattle was experiencing with the Japanese presence and alleged "business takeover," the issue of property ownership was brought to the forefront and linked with the need for restrictive legislation similar to Chinese Exclusion. The latter had proven to be effective at diminishing Chinese laborers and the need for decisive actions addressing Japanese immigration had not been effective under the provisions of the Gentleman's Agreement. **Freeman**'s testimony continued:

> First, you can deny the right to citizenship to those who come here and possibly those who are born here. Second, it might be possible to approach Japan with a view to their amicable withdrawal. Third, you can surround them...with restrictions, and compel the enforcement of our Federal and State laws, including the laws against corporations and trusts...and...land laws. ...If you shut off immigration, you will greatly relieve the situation.... If you naturalize them, the balance of political power of the City of Seattle... would be in the hands of Japan.... The people of the State of Washington were lulled into false security by the position taken by some of our leading citizens, who stated that cordial relations would help to bring trade to us and make Seattle a great seaport...I think they were hoodwinked.[71]

At the time that the 1919 hearings were coming to a close and as the Japanese American populations reached an all-time high, **Edward Clifford**, the new president of Seattle's Anti-Japanese League requested that the state legislature and Seattle City Council take action by enacting local ordinances that could accomplish what the US Congress would not be able to do. The league asked for enactment of laws that would prohibit the Japanese from engaging in businesses that included any issues involving land tenure, specifically in farming and hotel operation. State law could intervene for areas outside the city limits and in due time other municipalities on the West Coast would follow Seattle's lead. If the avenues of their employment were removed, the city's population of Japanese would be dramatically reduced as they would be forced to seek employment elsewhere. In a letter to the Seattle City Council, Clifford stated that

> … unless radical steps are taken, people now living will see the day when the Pacific Coast will be a Mongolian instead of a White Man's Country…. Seattle will probably be a Japanese instead of an American City. It is the Japanese that have created the rental situation in Seattle, as they pay almost unheard of prices for leases in order to get a foot-hold and then raise rents to heights that if the results were not so tragic, might appear sublime. More than forty percent of the Apartment Houses not in direct control of the owners are held by Japanese lessees. Half of the hotels and rooming houses are under Japanese control…. It is up to us to protect ourselves and our children against these Asiatic hordes.[72]

Clifford enclosed a draft city ordinance that, among other provisions, would require denial of licensing to hotels, rooming houses, or any corporation where owners or shareholders were non-citizens.

The league's accounts were further emphasized the following year when the case was presented a second time to the same immigration committee members and as hearings on Japanese immigration reconvened. This time, hearings were held in Washington State to examine the Japanese presence in the Pacific Northwest and the population centers of Spokane, Portland, Tacoma, and Seattle. In concluding commentary to the committee, Freeman noted that every one of the 700 Anti-Japanese League members believed "that the Japanese [were] nonassimilable [sic], and that this [was] a white man's country...[and] not possible for the two races to mix."[73]

Accusations were made that monies were filtered from Japan to support local associations in an effort to undermine US economies. Representatives from the Seattle Japanese community and Juno Sasamori, the general secretary of the Central Japanese Association of Southern California, described the function and importance of Japanese American associations as social service agencies and protection against vice such as gambling or prostitution that could infiltrate local businesses. The associations offered support that was not available elsewhere, such as aid to families and individuals in times of illness or providing information for immigrants about earning a living in America. Sasamori's comments reinforced an earlier statement by **Tokichi Tanaka** who had served as the Japanese consul in Seattle in 1909. In Tanaka's comment, the benefit of continued association with a person's home prefecture or *ken* and a professional trade organization provided fraternal spirit, unity, and support with the most "conspicuous [example] among them [being the] Japanese hotel-keepers' association."[74]

> ...the Japanese associations are often misunderstood by the Americans. It is a gross mistake to think of them as...founded on the authority of the Japanese government to penetrate the welfare of the American people. Association[s] may organize, disband... elect...or discharge their officers at the will of the members. It is a self-governing body...to protect unnecessary competitions among themselves.... It is an organization to improve the morals...and to assist the distressed Japanese, and promote friendship among their members and with the Americans.[75]

Reverend Mark Matthews contributed his testimony to the proceedings by addressing social justice on behalf of the Japanese. He refuted the sentiments that had been presented by the league, calling them statements that went "beyond the bounds of fairness, justice, local and international peace."[76] Matthews was in favor of restrictive immigration legislation, but addressed this and citizenship as a matter of federal responsibility and not one that should be done out of state or local prejudice and hysteria. Moreover, he drew the parallel of prejudice and what was happening with the Japanese community to its similarity with the passage of Chinese Exclusion that he viewed as "the most un-Christian and un-American act ever committed."[77]

City and county statistics for 1920 that were taken from building licenses and entered into public testimony indicated that Japanese Seattleites were involved in sixty-five different employment sectors with the largest represented by 282 hotel operators and the second largest being 242 farmers with permits to sell produce at public markets throughout the city.[78] The projected number of hotel operators was deemed to be conservative since small lodging house hotels with fewer than fifteen rooms were omitted from the count. Of the 282 that were listed, 60% were located south of Yesler Way, 35% were located in the north downtown, and 5% indicated a name but showed no specific address.[79]

As decisions on addressing Japanese immigration were being discussed, the US Supreme Court handed down a decision in November 1922 on challenges to two local court decisions regarding the right of naturalization for Japanese residents. The first was filed from the Territory of Hawaii in Takao Ozawa v. United States. The second was from Washington State where Takuji Yamashita and Charles Kono filed suit against the secretary of state for reversal of a lower court decision that had granted both men naturalization in 1906. The latter case drew attention when Yamashita and Kono attempted to form the Japanese Real Estate Holding Company in order to purchase agricultural property in the White River Valley and urban manufacturing real estate along the Seattle waterfront. In both cases the high court determined that naturalization was not warranted under Section 2169 of the Revised Statutes of the United States, with further note that the lower courts allowed naturalization before the statute had "been in full force and effect."[80] According to King County Deputy Prosecuting Attorney Ewing D. Colvin, the federal decision opened the possibility for even more court challenges of Japanese owning land under corporation names or serving as trustees or shareholders than the six civil suits that had already been filed locally. He carefully noted that the law was not specifically directed at Japanese, but that as aliens ineligible for citizenship, they could not "directly or indirectly hold land for agricultural or manufacturing purposes."[81] If it was proven that the Japanese had purchased properties in violation of federal law, it would be forfeited to and sold by the state. The key element of enforcement of this law lay in the hands of white Americans who could bring charges of illegal ownership to the attention of the court system. Short of this, the legal system did not check all of the property deeds in the state for possible violations.

For the House Committee on Immigration and Naturalization hearings, the rhetoric regarding Japanese business activities continued to focus on the dire conditions of the inevitable loss of a white economy and a land and hotel takeover of the West Coast by Japan. A more secure mechanism to control Japanese immigration was sought, partly with the belief that controlling immigration would prevent Japanese from further expansion into employment sectors and preserve American financial interests. While it was not as immediate as anti-Japanese interest groups had hoped, President Coolidge signed the Senate bill that put the Immigration Act of 1924 into law on 24 May. It ended Japanese immigration into the United States along with any possibility that the Issei would be permitted to become naturalized or allowed to freely own property.[82]

By 1927 and with the new federal immigration law and the Washington Alien Land Law firmly in place, an independent hotel operation study was conducted for Seattle. Rather than an assumed decline in proprietorship, the Seattle Japanese were recorded as managing over 8,600 rooms in 37% of the city's total number of hotel buildings, a 7% increase from the 1920 pre-legislation figure.[83] Legislation successfully stopped an influx of new Japanese immigrants but it did not discourage the community that was already here from operating residential hotels.

RAISING FAMILIES, APPRAISING "COMMUNITY"

Seattle residents, churches, and city hall had addressed the problems of vice and prostitution in the city for decades. How to handle the issue ebbed and flowed with political platforms and special interest groups over the years. The third and final relocation of the boundaries of the Restricted District had only succeeded in redefining the "official location" on paper, but with no actual effect on moving vice out of the Asian American hotel neighborhood. Vice remained an issue as the second generation of Asian Americans was growing up in the residential hotels. Civic and religious leaders condemned vice, but the politics of finding a space for these "necessary evils" had been accepted since the early land development.[84] Seattleites never gave up their determination to fight the political war for social and urban morality.

In 1916, a special investigation by undercover officers from the Burns Detective Agency was conducted on vice activities and police corruption in the downtown.[85] Over a three-month period of surveillance, one of the agency's investigators had established residence in the Busch Hotel to observe not only vice activities, but the actions of police officers assigned to the area south of Yesler Way. In a series of reports, thirty-seven hotels were confirmed to be involved in prostitution, liquor, and gambling with an even greater num-ber—fifty-seven hotels—equally engaged in the north downtown. Retaining his anonymity and signing his report as "**Investigator #11**," the account noted that

> ...the Nippon Club is a gambling house [in the basement of the Alps Hotel] where the play is frequently for large stakes. It is presumed to be for members only, but everyone goes there after they...secure admission. The city appears to be run on a wide open plan, whiskey and beer is being sold on every hand, prostitutes are working the streets under the very noses of the police and apparently with their sanction.... Gambling houses are allowed to do business...and moderate gambling is allowed publicly in pool halls, cigar stores, etc., with the actual knowledge of the police...all of the sporting element are pay-ing the police large amounts for the privilege of doing business, that certain policemen are actually engaged in the various phases of the sporting business themselves, there appears to be an organization among the uniformed police and also one among the plain clothes men for the collection and distribution of this graft money of which it appears there is perhaps $10,000 collected monthly.[86]

The report went on to note that gambling could be found every day and night in the Chinatown Hotels, including the Louisa Hotel, Hotel Rex, Milwaukee Hotel, and the East Kong Yick building. The war on gambling was exacerbated by the knowledge that if raids were conducted, the design of some hotel interi-ors would lead police "through long, winding halls, and several rooms before reaching a main gambling room."[87] In one instance, it took so long to reach the gamblers that all the police found were "a group of men listening to a lecture on Japanese literature."[88] Admittedly, part of the problem in the war against gambling was due to an ordinance that was passed in July 1922 that allowed licensing of public card rooms by the city council. In less than two months, over one hundred licenses were granted for organizations that were engaging in friendly games and small stakes that fell within the category of "public card games" and short of being defined as "gambling."

In the summer of 1935, a similar series of vice investigations and collection of eighty testimonies was undertaken by a joint effort of the Clean City League and the Seattle Council of Churches and Christian Education.[89]

Paintings on the stairway wall of the Sky-Hi Club in the basement of the Louisa Hotel [Author]

The collected testimonies focused on specific residential hotels throughout the downtown and on gambling operations south of Yesler Way. The few remaining businesses in the old Chinatown at 2nd and Washington and the residential hotels and frame houses in the core of the new Chinatown and Japantown were of particular interest. The Sky-Hi Club located in the basement of the Louisa Hotel, "with its Oriental mural decorations on the wall" and the second floor of the Atlas Hotel, where girls would tap on the window glass to advertise their trade, were specifically noted. The latter included a gambling room where 300 people could play blackjack or the Chinese lotteries.[90] In total, fifteen Chinese lotteries were identified south of Yesler Way with two of them distributing tickets to other locations in the downtown. In a final comment, the committee noted that the "spectacle of officers failing to take police action as to places which they know, or by the exercise of due vigilance should know, are operating illegally, is explainable on no other theory than that these officers, or others above them, are receiving a consideration to protect such places."[91]

The primary difference between civic reformer attitudes toward vice and the Asian American community's viewpoint was the latter's acceptance that the people south of Yesler Way represented a diverse population and that tolerance and diversity included ethnicity, culture, income, and the means by which that income was obtained. On a practical level, engaging in the battle for public morality by removing all vice had no chance of succeeding. For the Chinese, Japanese, and Filipino Americans, judgment regarding the morality of people outside the community was best determined by the private life and spiritual commitments of an individual.

In an early report by the Seattle Ministerial Federation, the authors noted the difficulty of raising Japanese children who lived in neighborhoods where vice was permitted, a problem that was easily extended to all children living in the pan-Asian quarter. "Japanese families...have no desire to attempt to raise a family without children...[yet] the moral conditions...where most of the Japanese live are such that it is almost impossible to raise children properly. In the cities on the coast, conditions are permitted to prevail in the sections where the Orientals live that would not be permitted in the residential sections [of the city]."[92]

For Asian American families, living in the same hotels and neighborhood as the pimps, sex workers, and gamblers was simply a daily part of their surroundings, and the proceeds of such activities were obvious to everyone. It was clear to Asian American parents that their young children who were growing up among vice activities of the residential hotels could not be totally spared from this knowledge. For parents, the greater issue was not the eradication of vice, but how to retain some innocence for their children within an environment that was known to be morally corrupt. **Tyrus Okada** grew up playing in and around the old wooden-framed SRO hotels south of the Chappell bawdy houses.

> My grandfather, Isokichi Mayeda, and grandmother, Masa, operated the Fremont Laundry in the Fremont Hotel on 6th Avenue South before the war years. My grandfather had this old delivery truck that I don't think was ever used for delivery of anything but it sat on the curb as part of the business. It had a crank in the front of it and it was noisy and shook when it started. There were only two storefronts in that building and the other one was the Seattle Noodle Manufacturing Company that was owned by Mr. Tosaya. I spent a lot of time at the laundry with my grandparents. Behind the laundry was a small kitchen area where my grandmother would make lunch for us...they didn't take the time to close the

business and have lunch anywhere else. I was six years old and played with Carl Tosaya, Henry Ozaki, Frank Okada, and his brother John...the guy who ended up writing the book "No-No Boy." Frank's family managed the Yakima Hotel across 6th Avenue South. As kids, we would run in and out of the noodles that were hanging to dry on the dowels overhead until Mr. Tosaya chased us out of the shop and told us to go and play outside. The lot to the north and next to the hotel building was vacant and it was a huge grassy slope. We'd get boxes from the KCW Furniture Shop across the street from the Fremont and flatten them out to make box sleds. That slope used to lead to the tideflat land at the bottom of the hill and after it was filled in, it was all grass that still had some muddy areas. Those were great areas for digging earthworms for fishing. We'd collect a can of worms, get some fishing line and walk down to the pier at the waterfront to fish. We didn't have poles but we always caught something to take home.[93]

Though living side-by-side, the Chinese, Japanese, and Filipino immigrants retained a strong focus on their respective families and community life. The same might have held true for that second generation, as the children engaged in playtime and social activities that were within their own cultural group, had it not been for Bailey Gatzert Elementary School. The school, located at 12th Avenue South and South Weller Street, brought the second generation of Asian American children together and solidified a secondary level of friendships outside of their respective ethnic affiliations. The importance of the school cannot be overstated as it was the most diverse in the city's public school system. By the 1940s, forty-two percent of the student body was comprised of Asian American children, the majority of whom represented the Beacon Hill neighborhood or the residential hotels of Chinatown and Nihonmachi. Across the street from the Bailey Gatzert Elementary School and located in the Moose Hotel was the *Miya Shonien* or Japanese Children's Home that was a preschool for working parents.[94] The major walking routes to Bailey Gatzert for many of the children took them past the hotels and bordellos in nearby houses up the hill from the Chinatown and Japantown cores. Many were clustered between 10th and 12th Avenue South, and along Washington, Main, King, and Weller streets. Women tapping on the glass to advertise their business at night would wave at the children as they walked by the building in the morning on their way to school.

An in-depth discussion of vice was rarely necessary between Asian immigrant parents and their second generation offspring as it seemed to be inherently understood as the children grew up.[95] Overwhelmingly, that first

Fremont Hotel. [Courtesy King County Assessor's Office, Property Record Cards, 1937–1973, Puget Sound Branch, Washington State Archives]

Moose Hotel. [Courtesy King County Assessor's Office, Property Record Cards, 1937–1973, Puget Sound Branch, Washington State Archives]

The Japanese Children's Home pre-school was located on the main floor of the Moose Hotel. [Courtesy Hiro Nishimura]

Prostitution businesses that were located in the above grade apartments at Main and Maynard. The area was prone to landslides from the adjacent hillsides as can be seen in the right foreground. [Courtesy Seattle Municipal Archives, Photo 46250]

generation of Asian immigrants fought vice from within their realm of control as parents and did it with a two-step formula of empathy for others and involvement in teaching their children. It had nothing to do with belittling or ridiculing those who were typically considered by social reformers to be the "dregs" of human society. It had everything to do with the guidance of "respecting and being kind to all people" and reliance on organizations that could provide structure for living when they were away from parental guidance.[96] This was done through affiliations that included sports activities, churches, community-supported schools, clubs, and work responsibilities to home and community.

Hotel owners and operators understood that there were a number of other factors that were characteristic of hotel occupancy, particularly in the decades leading up to WWII. Key among these was the proposition that hotel living was synonymous with a socially-detached life in spite of the close physical proximity to others and low vacancy rates of the hotel residents. Isolation was associated with high incidences of suicide in Seattle with over half of the suicides from 1914 to 1925 taking place in the hotels and rooming houses downtown and among people who were non-residents of the city.[97] It wasn't simply the anonymity that was possible in the SRO living, but also the means for suicide since there were many hotels that used some form of gas as opposed to electric lighting, making death by asphyxiation a possibility.

Criminal activity was also higher in the downtown hotels between 1914 and 1925 with 53 of the city's 212 homicidal crimes occurring south of Yesler Way, 43 of which were reported to have taken place among the Asian population. In 1926 and according to local sociologist, Calvin Schmid:

> ...almost 25 percent of the crimes are concentrated in a very small area, about four blocks wide and ten blocks long. This territory...can be divided roughly into two districts...the upper (east) and the lower (west). The upper part is characterized by a motley number of cheap hotels and rooming houses, old frame residences, many of which are now used as houses of prostitution, and a large variety of retail stores. This section includes Seattle's "Chinatown," typified by its "joss" houses and commercial establishments. The permanent denizens of this district consist chiefly of foreigners, of which the majorities are Japanese and Chinese. Many of the migratory workers and dispossessed transients of various types room in this section, but spend most of their time in the lower section... gambling "joints" are quasi-clandestine in character, and are arranged characteristically in the following fashion: A store-room facing the street, ostensibly a grocery or export

establishment with a few shop-worn goods on the shelves, serves as an entrance; there is usually a man in front of the entrance who plays the double role of look-out and solicitor. From the store-room there is a dark alley or hallway leading into an artificially-lighted, dingy, poorly-ventilated, and...very unsanitary room which is the gambling den proper. The equipment is very meager, consisting generally of a counter or desk, sometimes enclosed in a wire cage, and a few chairs. The living quarters of the proprietor and family are often next to the gambling room.[98]

The common connection of deaths by suicide or criminal activity was identified by local sociologists as being part of the "Oriental environment" where people were living in the "worst part of the city" and where Chinese and Japanese found employment as "keepers of cheap hotels and lodging houses."[99]

In some ways, Nihonmachi developed into three semi-independent Japanese American communities that were divided by Jackson Street; one area north of and a second south of Jackson Street and east of 5th Avenue South occasionally referred to as "Lo-Jack" by the Nisei, and a third area west of 5th Avenue South and the train stations as part of Pioneer Square. Seizo Itoi began operating the Carrollton Hotel at the southwest corner of Occidental Avenue and Main Street. His son, **Henry Seichi Itoi**, was born in that hotel.

When father began running the hotel in 1919, he did all of the work himself since mother was busy caring for us four children. As we got older, she helped my father with chambermaid work. Each day she replenished the water pitcher, cleaned the wash bowl in each of the forty rooms, and emptied and cleaned out the urinal pots. The rooms were swept and the hallways were mopped. The laundry was rolled into a big bundle that was picked up from the Grand Union Laundry Plant that was operated by Japanese partners.

The Great Depression fostered a need for more cheap places to sleep. My father expanded his business by leasing two adjacent large unrented spaces and converted them into dormitory rooms. Each had about eighty beds that were like cots. A bed rented for fifteen cents a night and father accepted King County welfare tickets that were good for a night or two of lodging. It was much different than the early years when a room in the hotel with an outside window rented for fifty cents and an interior room next to the light well was thirty-five cents a night. There were other Asian-run restaurants in the building and many surrounding hotels that were run by Japanese families. There was the Grand

Togo Hotel. [Courtesy King County Assessor's Office, Property Record Cards, 1937–1973, Puget Sound Branch, Washington State Archives]

Panama and N-P Hotels. [Courtesy Steve Tsukuno and Linda Tsukuno Hjorten]

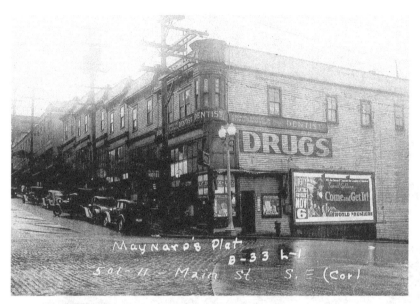

de Europe Hotel. [Courtesy King County Assessor's Office, Property Record Cards, 1937–1973, Puget Sound Branch, Washington State Archives]

Sun Hotel. [Courtesy King County Assessor's Office, Property Record Cards, 1937–1973, Puget Sound Branch, Washington State Archives]

Central Hotel (Okiyama), the New Richelieu Hotel (Sato), the Tourist Hotel (Kuniyuki), Rainier Hotel (Ota), the Regina Hotel (Hayano), Our Home Hotel (Murahashi), the Lucky Hotel (Tokita), Cadillac Hotel (Chikamura), and the Fulton (Kataoka).[100]

Jackson Street was a heavily travelled route, in part because of its post-Regrade direct connection to the waterfront and downtown with the Beacon Hill neighborhood. The train stations and tracks created another geographic boundary that separated the Nihonmachi community living in the Pioneer Square neighborhood from east of the tracks. While Japanese businesses were located throughout the lower downtown and south of Yesler Way, the core identity of the community at 6th Avenue South and South Main Street was defined by Japanese-operated businesses, apartments that were in converted wood-framed houses, and rooms in the residential hotels. While this pattern of land uses was duplicated throughout the Asian American district, 6th and Main developed as an important center of the Japantown community life and commerce. The northeast corner of that intersection had been purchased by the Oriental-American Bank for $60,000 in July 1906. The bank's officers made the decision to move their operations one block east as they believed this would be the center of the Japanese American community.[101]

"TWO FLAGS OVER 6TH AND MAIN"[102]

The 6th and Main location of Nihonmachi served as an important focal point for community gatherings. At the turn of the 20th century, this was the location of the Seattle Buddhist Temple and the Main Street School that was attended by both Chinese and Japanese children in the district. Beginning in 1935, the adjacent Japanese businesses chose and financially supported this central location for the community's annual Bon Odori festival, partly because such an event would encourage business transactions for the numerous Japanese-operated stores in the immediate vicinity.[103] This general location was also the site of a concentrated core group of hotels and storefront businesses that were operated by the Japanese, including the Togo, Panama, N-P, deEurope, and the Sun Hotels that provided a combined total of 391 rooms. **Roy Minoru Hashimoto** recalled daily life for young Nisei growing up in the hotels of the Japantown core.

We called ourselves the Main Street Gang because our families lived or had businesses at 6th and Main in Japantown. We were a "gang" in the good sense of the word…a close group just like the kids in the "Our Gang" movies of the 1930s. There were seventeen of us. Hideji Yamamoto was our leader because his dad had a soda fountain and sundry store that was in the Sun Hotel building. It was our hangout. Every night we'd take our school books and tell our folks we were going to do homework with our friends…it was a good excuse so that we could meet at the store. I don't think there ever was a group of kids that had more fun or were more compatible. There were four stools at the soda fountain. Mr. Yamamoto put a bench in front of the store in the summer so that we could sit outside if we didn't get one of the inside stools…it was okay because it was cooler outside. If you were late getting there, you would have to stand around the light pole or lean on the building because there wouldn't be anywhere to sit. We did this every day.[104]

In 1936, that Main Street central intersection included the Toyo Bank, four restaurants (Gyokko ken, Rose Cafe, Maruman Café, Tenyoshi), two sign-painting companies (Noto Sign, Pacific Printing), two barbers (Uji Barber, Sato Barber), a drugstore (Main Drug Store), two sundry stores (Sato Curio, Hamada Variety), markets and food manufacturers (Sarashina Noodles, Seattle Tofu, Oriental Fish), two tobacco shops (Imaizumi Company, Hosokawa Tobacco), and service businesses that included two labor contractors (Kushi Cannery Contractor, Nagamatsu Cannery Contractor) and a labor newspaper publication (Rodo Koron), a tailor (Tanaka Tailoring), a plumber (Teramae Plumbing), carpenter (Shiota Carpentry), paperhanger (Nakano), a regional association, and one pawn shop. **Ushio "Joseph" Hamanaka** grew up in the Main Street core.

I lived in Japantown and my whole life centered around 6th and Main until WWII. I was born in 1922 in the Empire Hotel at the northwest corner of 5th and Main Street that was operated by the Kamura Family. We moved to the Toyo Apartment Hotel before I started school so that we could have a kitchenette and steam heat. Both the Empire and the Toyo had long-term Japanese residents. The Toyo residential hotel got its name from the Toyo Bank. The windows of our two rooms faced 6th Avenue South across from Sagamiya Confection and the two-story Nikko Low Chinese restaurant. Like many immigrants from Japan, my mother and father only spoke a little English. For a while and until my parents started their own wholesale rice business, my mother worked as a hotel chambermaid at the Alps Hotel and my father washed dishes at the Alaska Café on 1st Avenue in Pioneer Square…in the summer, I picked strawberries on Vashon Island at the Mukai farm. I recall

Main Street Gang on the bench in front of the Sun Hotel, 1939. Photo is of seven of the seventeen friends: "Chick," Hedeji, Tad, Eddy, Franklin, "Slop," and Roy (left to right). [Courtesy Roy Minoru Hashimoto]

Nippon Kan Theater in the Astor Hotel, 7 February 1937. The hanging flags were gifts given to the Taiyo Baseball Club from Japanese universities. This was one of many fundraising performances at the Theater that provided support for various organizations and activities in the community. Club Manager, Bansan Okada is in the second row, far right with his young son, Tyrus, seated in the first row, sixth seat from the left. [Courtesy The Wing Luke Museum, 2007.036.339]

that all of the hotels were legitimate family-operated businesses. Rooms were rented out for Japanese families or single Japanese and Scandinavian men like loggers, pensioners, widowers, and Pinoy cannery workers en route to Alaska. At Japanese-operated hotels in the 1st, 2nd, 3rd, 4th Avenues South and Occidental areas, there were more Caucasian than Japanese renters. Japanese patronized the businesses in the 6th and Main core of Nihonmachi. Many of the Filipinos were "seasonal" tenants of the Japanese-operated hotels, restaurants, groceries, barbers, laundries, dye works and custom tailors—after a season in Alaska, Filipino single men were "rich" and good customers. Some hotels, like the U.S. Hotel at 307 Maynard and operated by the Miyagawas and the Atlas Hotel at 416 Maynard that was operated by the Nakamuras, invited Black American renters... these were favorite locations for railroad train porters and entertainers. Just imagine the Will Masten Trio with father, uncle, and Sammy Davis, Jr. They weren't allowed in the Seattle downtown hotels for whites but they were allowed to perform at stage shows at upper downtown theaters like the Palomar at 3rd and University.

Hotel people needed to cooperate and help each other; it was no different than what was happening in Chinatown. We patronized Japanese shops in our community…if the dollars stayed and circulated within the community, it was for the best interest of everyone. Hotel operators and night clerks operated hotels by *rashiko* or "like Japanese should." Our culture and parents infused us with responsibilities of our conduct; concepts like *shinyo* meaning to be trustworthy, *anzen* for "safety," *kichomen* for "precision,"*kimochi* for "empathetic feeling of others," *reigi* for "etiquette or propriety," and *tadashii* meaning that you would conduct your life in a way that was "just, honest, proper, correct, legitimate"… and this is why the hotels and businesses were successful.[105]

One block north of the Nihonmachi core and up a steep hill was the Astor Hotel building. It included rooms and at-grade commercial stores as could be found in all of the other hotels, but it also housed the Nippon Kan, a large theatre that featured films and live performances with ticket or donation proceeds benefiting the Japanese American community. One block to the south of the core was the Higo 10 Cents Store where any resident or laborer could find anything that they might need. **Paul Murakami**'s family owned and operated the Higo Building.

The Higo Store was one of the at-grade commercial businesses in a professional office building of dentists, doctors, and lawyers. It was built by Sanzo and Matsuyo Murakami who believed that the neighborhood needed a building that would have commercial and office uses that would support hotel residents. The parents and then their children operated the store, and 99% of the office businesses in the building were Japanese-operated. There weren't any leases for the tenants in the offices or the retail spaces…they were all like family so a handshake was good enough. Rents were kept low as it was believed that the success of long-term tenants would make the entire building successful. The original plans for Higo included three storefronts but they removed the walls and separate doors to combine it into one large retail space—almost 4,000 square feet. The store operated 365 days a year. Higo had a little bit of everything…clothing, kitchen wares, hardware, food items like rice and sugar, candy, and *sen bei* (rice crackers) that were treats for the children. Laborers came to the store to buy "taps," those small leather or metal pieces that they'd put on their heels so that the boots wouldn't wear out too quickly.[106] The workers tried to save money wherever they could, and Higo merchandise helped them do that.

Kazuichi Kay Murakami inside the Higo Store that was established by his parents. [Courtesy Paul Murakami]

Whatever disruption occurred to the Japanese-operated businesses at the 6th and Main location during the Jackson Street Regrade had no lasting effect at keeping them from returning and expanding their businesses when the regrade was completed. While the regrade solved a number of the access problems by leveling hillsides, it did not completely remove the steep slopes east of Maynard on South Main, Washington, or Yesler streets. Those areas remained untouched. Amid the new and old buildings there were pockets of empty lots that were used as playgrounds for the young Nisei, and wood-framed housing along the western-sloped hillsides that housed a community of Japanese families, transient laborers, sex workers, and madams.

The core of Japantown also held one of the community's most enduring treasures: the Hashidate-Yu, a Japanese bath that was located in part of the basement on the western side of the Panama Hotel. The idea of providing public bathing facilities or comfort stations was a common practice in many American cities under the firm guidance of urban reformers. From 1890 into the 1920s, public bathing was extolled as a way of providing for the urban poor and pursuing the connection between cleanliness, hygiene, and community health. The most ardent period of this progressive reform coincided with the dates of residential hotel construction.

As architect of the Panama Hotel, Ozasa included the bath as part of the amenities of the hotel design.[107] It was the transplant of a Japanese custom of the *furo*, or public bathhouse, which served as a cultural center where individuals and families could go and as a place for neighbors to congregate to share news. The Japanese tradition deviated in that the original design and construction of the Hashidate-Yu facility provided separate marble bathing tubs in adjacent rooms for men and women. "For fifteen cents or the purchase of eight tickets for one dollar, you could gain admission to the bath with two towels, washcloth, soap, razor, and pumice stones provided."[108]

The bathhouse was viewed as a necessity for Japanese residents who lived in the SRO hotels. With spare facilities in the hotels, and no existing city code to dictate the required number of wash basins, showers, or baths per the number of hotel occupants, plumbing was a rare and valued commodity.[109]

Seattle passed its first ordinance requiring the licensing of bath houses in 1914, four years after the grand opening of the Hashidate-Yu.[110] It wasn't until 1923 when Seattle appropriated $10,550 from the city's general fund in order to construct seven comfort stations, none of which were located "below the line."[111] The following year, Seattle passed its first comprehensive ordinance that addressed the definition and function of public bathhouses. "The term 'public bath house'...shall be held and construed to mean and include any place open to the public where Russian, Turkish, Swedish, hot air, vapor, electric, cabinet or other baths of any kind whatever are given or furnished; provided, that such term shall not include ordinary tub baths where an attendant is not required...."[112]

The definition of a bathhouse fit the Japanese bathhouses that were multiplying in the Japanese American community. At the time that Seattle passed its regulation, the Hashidate-Yu was one of ten bathhouses south of Yesler Way, nine of which were located in SRO hotels that included the Chicago, Panama, Miyajima, Eastern, Markeen, Nippo Ryokan, Yorazuma House, Diamond, and Paris Hotels. Many of the bathhouses, like Hashidate-Yu, capitalized on the bath facility by coupling the use with a laundry. Patrons could leave clothing to be cleaned upon entering the main door and pick them up on a subsequent visit. The baths were in basements that took advantage of the warmth and extra steam that was emitted from heating pipes of the furnace boilers.

MAP 4-3: Japanese Bathhouses in Residential Hotels [Author]

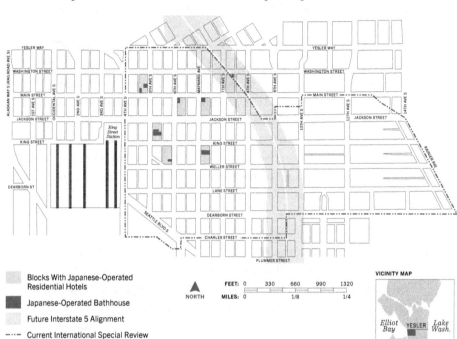

Blocks With Japanese-Operated
Residential Hotels

Japanese-Operated Bathhouse

Future Interstate 5 Alignment

--·-- Current International Special Review
District Boundary

NORTH

FEET: 0   330   660   990   1320

MILES: 0   1/8   1/4

VICINITY MAP

Elliot Bay   YESLER   Lake Wash.

According to City Ordinance, if a public bathing facility was located in a build-ing where prostitution was known and verified as taking place, a license would be rejected or revoked. There was little evidence that this was enforced given that bathhouses in the Paris and Diamond Hotels were owned by Chappell and in the red-light district. By 1928 four of the bathhouses had closed and at the height of hotel operation in 1936, there were even fewer with only Miyako-Yu, Hashidate-Yu, and Hinode-Yu still in operation.

By 1943 and during the Japanese incarceration, Seattle passed an amendment to the ordinance that would now require all bathhouses to be inspected by the city's commissioner of health prior to license renewal and that they "must at all times be open to inspection as to sanitary and moral condi-tions by the Police and Health Departments."[113] Only Hashidate-Yu reopened following the war years. As the Japanese community found homes outside of Japantown, the need for a public bathing facility continued to diminish.

Men's Bath in Hashidate-Yu, Panama Hotel. The cast iron pole with o-ring handle against the wall was used to pull out the tub's plug for drainage. Throughout the bathhouse, the floor is slightly canted toward floor drains. [Author]

Personal lockers for the bathhouse patrons and advertisement signs of Japanese businesses located in the men's section of Hashidate-Yu. [Author]

This and rising costs of water matched with higher sewer fees forced the closure of Nihonmachi's last Japanese bathhouse in 1950.

Japanese American family life revolved around the activities and needs in these immediate neighborhood vicinities, typically defined by the blocks and businesses that were adjacent or across the street. Goods were purchased from the nearest corner stores and it was possible for an Asian American woman to live a lifetime without venturing far from the building where she lived with her family. It was a common instruction for the young Chinese Americans and Nisei to play within the immediate neighborhood, which in turn helped create the neighborhood sports teams. Core community institutions and festivals or celebrations, such as the Bon Odori, Chinese New Year celebration, or dances at Washington Hall, the family associations, ken-jinkai picnics and meetings; churches, temples, and schools; or specialty retail businesses such as the Higo 5 & 10 Cent Store; Maneki, Gyokko ken, or Hong Kong restaurants; all served to draw families and individuals outside of their otherwise closely-knit geographies.

The Japanese School and Chinese School provided a cultural education for their respective groups of young people outside of the Seattle public school system. For most Seattle Nisei, life was a busy balance of attending American schools followed by 90 minutes at the Nihongo Gakko, the Japanese Language School located east of the community's core businesses. The remaining time would be spent on work and play, some of which was also structured. The increased number of Nisei to the Seattle community between 1916 and 1920 was reflected in the attendance records of the Seattle public schools and the Japanese Language School. The records indicated that for Grades 1–8, 126 students attended the Nihon Go Gakko in 1916 with an increase to 251 students by 1920 and the hiring of two additional teachers. In this latter year, the total number of students attending Japanese School was about 31% of the 806 Japanese students who were attending the Seattle Public School system. With such modest financial means, parents paid for the Chinese and Japanese teachers so that their children would learn and hopefully retain knowledge of the customs, history, language, and traditions of their parents' home countries, along with an inheritance of pride and ethical values. For the Japanese community, the test of tradition and challenge of national identity came with their World War II incarceration. **Kamekichi Tokita**, who operated the Cadillac Hotel in the years before the war, reflected on the cultural divide and the bridge between the Issei and Nisei.

There were always complaints within the Japanese/Japanese-American community that the Nisei were too Americanized. Nisei, on the other hand, thought it was natural to deliberately act like Americans…"It can't be helped because they were born in America.".…The Issei have tried all kinds of methods and worked extremely hard to try and seize every single opportunity to achieve that goal [of being an American]. Instead of fulfilling our desires, our efforts only helped increase the distance between Issei and Nisei. In the midst of that crisis, the current war broke out. More precisely, it…reinforced the ties between the Issei and Nisei. [With the war], [t]hey have become aware that they were in fact Japs [sic] themselves. This realization is not something that money can buy.[114]

Life events were taken in stride outside of and within the residential hotels. The community of those living in the hotels included Asian American proprietors who were taking great care of their guests, often to a level that far exceeded those of upper downtown hotel managers. The hotel proprietors became social service workers.

For many of the hotel patrons who frequented the same hotels or chose to make them their "permanent" residences, the children of the hotels became part of an extended family for the single men. Children understood the clientele within the building that they shared. Parents understood the meaning of relationships and fostering a hotel community that was a part of raising children. Both before and after the incarceration, Shokichi "Shox" Tokita's parents and family operated and lived in four different residential hotels that included the Cadillac, Wilson, New Lucky, and Freeman hotels.

After the war, we lived in the New Lucky Hotel. We leased the hotel part but not the commercial storefronts of the building. We had a big lot behind our hotel that was shaped like a bowl with a grassy rim that was like stadium seating…it was a natural draw for kids to come and play and it was one of the reasons that our mother liked the New Lucky. We played baseball and other games and the residents of the nearby hotels would come down and watch us play…they would cheer for us, and drink liquor. There was a Danish carpenter, Mr. Jackson, who was an immigrant and who barely spoke English himself. He built the playground that we had in the lot: a wooden slide, the parallel bars, the swing and teeter-totter. He hung the basket so we could play basketball. Hotels in the neighborhood provided a home to so many people…they served a huge purpose to stave off homelessness. The men in our hotel would give their pension or social security to our

New Lucky Hotel. [Courtesy King County Assessor's Office, Property Record Cards, 1937–1973, Puget Sound Branch, Washington State Archives]

Playing basketball in the empty lot that served as a playground behind the New Lucky Hotel. "Shox" Tokita shooting the basketball. [Courtesy Shokichi Tokita]

mom at the beginning of the month and she would take out $20 for their room, and enough to cover a monthly meal ticket at the local café downstairs. She'd give the balance of it to them and they would buy liquor. There were so many alcoholics and our mother took care of all of them. We knew what was going on with the drinking and women in other hotels who tapped on the windows…our mother never had to explain anything to us. It wasn't what she said…there was just as much in what she didn't say.[115]

ENDNOTES

1   "Seattle Real Estate," *The Seattle Mail and Herald*, 22 December 1906, p. 3, col. 1–4.

2   The Oregon and Washington Railway depot had been issued the largest permit in January 1910 in the amount of $350,000.

3   Statistics on building construction and valuation were kept beginning in 1889,with the reconstruction of the city following the downtown fire.

4   Seattle, Washington Department of Buildings, "Seattle Statistics of Growth and Development," 1910.

5   *The Seattle Post-Intelligencer*, 1 January 1911, p. 3, col. 1.

6   "Dealers Unite in Predicting Spurt," *The Seattle Times*, 6 February 1910, p. 6, col. 5.

7   Ibid.

8   The Hudson Hotel on the southwest corner of King Street and 7th Avenue South was eventually renamed the Louisa Hotel, though there is no information as to why or when this happened. The Gee How Oak Tin also housed the Oshima Hotel.

9   F.T. Harris, ed. "Architecture of Thompson & Thompson." Seattle: Lowman & Hanford Co., n.d. This booklet containing photos of their commissions was published to showcase some of the work of the firm. While no date is given, it can be assumed by the content that it was produced around 1910. The photo of the Kong Yick Investment Company that is identified on Eighth and King was printed backwards, likely to emphasize the King Street façade.

10   Goon provided all of the labor for the Pacific American Fisheries plant in Bellingham, Washington. During the off-season, Goon transported Bellingham's Chinese population by train to live in Portland awaiting the next fishing season. Portland, and not Seattle, was known as the headquarters for labor contractors.

11   An interview that was given by Goon Dip. "Rich Chinese in Bellingham," *Bellingham Herald*, 25 January 1905, p. 5, col. 4.

12   The $500,000 figure was from an earlier 1905 estimate. "Celestials of High Degree in City," *Bellingham Herald*, 25 August 1909, p. 1, 3, col. 2.

13   By 1916, Goon Dip was approached by Amos Benson to discuss purchase of the Oregon Hotel site in order to build an addition to the adjacent Benson Hotel in Portland. Benson offered $375,000 for the property, an offer that included cash and a piece of property across the street from both hotels. Negotiation on the property failed since Moy and Goon wanted $500,000 cash for the property. In September 1929, the Oregon Hotel closed and the businesses on the commercial storefronts relocated. Goon cited prohibition law and the loss of a money-making tavern that was located in the hotel as one of the reasons for loss of revenue to the hotel.

14   Part of that difference was attributed to Seattle's easy access to the Puget Sound and the great opportunity that existed for industrial development and trade with its proximity to the Pacific Rim countries.

15   "China and Its Trade Possibilities," *The Coast*, December 1909, p. 286.

16 Chin Gee Hee had applied for the Consul position in 1897 under Fong Wing Hong of the Consulate Office in San Francisco. At the time, Chin had the endorsement of the Seattle Chamber of Commerce and many of the same supporters who had advocated for Chun Ching Hock's nomination to the diplomatic post. Seattle's Chinese population was estimated to be between four and five hundred and the appointment was never made.

17 Chin Keay was a nephew of Chin Gee Hee and manager of his stores for thirty years. The position of Consul was one that was decided among members of the Chinese community. While there was some speculation that Chin Gee Hee could have been given this assignment, Chin had left America for Sunning, China, in early 1906, with no plan of returning to his former business undertakings in Seattle.

18 The year of the AYP Exposition was also the same year that Lew graduated as the first Chinese American to earn a degree at the University of Washington.

19 Banquet for New Consul," *The Oregonian*, 11 January 1909, p. 2, col. 1.

20 "Chinese Move When Rents Get too High: Orientals Buy Ground and Plan to Erect Modern Buildings on Four Lots at Eighth Avenue and King Street," *The Seattle Daily Times*, 6 February 1910, p. 6, col. 6.

21 These seven SRO buildings included the Freedman, New Central, Kanagawa, Eclipse, Ashima, Hudson, and New Hotel Norway.

22 Early and mistaken reports by *The Seattle Daily Times* (6 February 1910) indicated that lots 1 and 2 were owned by Chin Gee Hee's Quong Tuck Company. No such record exists by the King County Assessor Office to indicate that this was ever the case.

23 Chin Lem, Chin Gee Hee's son, had sold the building to F.C. Johnson in August, 1909 for $50,000.

24 This amount included the cost of the buildings, furnishings, and operating capital.

25 Most accounts refer to Mr. Lew as "Lew G. Kay" where in later years and with the word order, "Kay" became the surname, beginning with his children.

26 Articles of Incorporation of Kong Yick Investment Company, 14135, 6 June 1910, p. 2.

27 Ma Hing was a representative of the Ah King Company that was going to be locating its business to one of the Kong Yick buildings.

28 "Chinese Move when Rents Get Too High," *The Seattle Times*, 6 February 1910, p. 6, col. 6.

29 In part, the relocation of these important companies from the 2nd and Washington Chinatown area was encouraged in that rental fees had become so high that business profits had been steadily declining. The Ah King Company moved to the West Kong Yick building in 1914 after having been in the previous Chinatown location for two years. What did remain in the Old Chinatown area was the central location for picking the winning lottery numbers. Young Chinese runners would transport the daily numbers to the businesses of the King Street Chinatown.

30 *The Seattle Star*, 14 May 1907, p. 11. The Sing Fat and Sing Chong buildings are two examples of the designs of Ross and Burgren.

31 "The Work of T. Paterson Ross and A.W. Burgren," *The Architect and Engineer of California Pacific Coast States*, May, 1908, vol. XIII, no. 1, p 35.

32 Ibid.

33 The West Kong Yick building was known as Building 1 because its building permit was issued before that of the East Kong Yick.

34 The Quong Tuck Company in the East Kong Yick building also had agent offices for the Dollar Steamship Line and the American Mail Line. Both of these shipping companies were under the ownership of Captain Robert Dollar and his family. The Dollar Line was established in August 1900 and the American Line was acquired in 1922 when it was under the name of the Admiral Oriental Line. Dollar's initial years of operation focused on importing and exporting goods to Asia with early ventures including the export of lumber from the Pacific Northwest. Dollar hired both white and Chinese crews on his vessels. In the mid-1920s, the Dollar Steamship Line included passenger service. Both lines ultimately ceased operation in the Pacific Northwest with the Dollar Line serving California beginning in 1937 and the American Mail line stopping regular service in

1938 due to decreased revenues from cancelled mail contracts. See Peter B. Kyne, "Our Maritime Bugaboo" in *The Saturday Evening Post*, Vol. 188, No. 13, 25 September 1915, and "Dollar Steamship Line Travel Brochures, Historical Documents Archives," https://www.gjenvick.com/SteamshipLines/DollarSteamshipLine/index.html. Accessed 2 February 2016.

35 Prior to this time, the only available West Coast shipping connections to Australia were from San Francisco, California, and Vancouver, British Columbia.

36 Interview with James Mar, son of Mar Hing, who managed the Yick Fung Store until its closure in 2008, 3 October 2006.

37 Interview with Jack Pang, grandson of Chin Quong, who was a managing partner of the Wa Chong Company, 21 June 2011.

38 Chinese American associations were organizations that helped provide social services and networking opportunities within the community. These were of particular importance since associations often provided for the needs of individuals that could not be accomplished through other means in the city. District association membership was based on province of origin while family associations were based on common surnames. Tong associations had discretionary or optional memberships and the interest of the organization was more business- and protection-focused, with some involvement in vice activity such as gambling or prostitution. Among other purposes, the primarily male population of Chinatown could rely on the association for loans, dispute resolution among members or businesses, assistance in finding employment and/or housing, assistance with language issues, providing entertainment and recreation, social interaction where news of China could be shared with its members, and funeral arrangements. Associations were also active in hiring attorneys to represent community members in immigration hearings, habeas corpus cases, and wider legal matters of interest such as changes in Chinese Exclusion laws or lawsuits from loss of lives and property from acts of violence against the Chinese.

39 "Hop Sing Tong Now has Seattle Home," *The Seattle Daily Times*, p. 7, col. 3. The Hop Sing, Bing Kung Bow Leong, Suey Sing, and the Hip Sing Tongs signed an agreement in April 1917 that they would not engage in warring activities

that were instigated in other cities. The peace treaty of these four tongs was signed with Mayor Gill and Goon Dip as witnesses. The penalty for breaking the treaty was punishable by deportation of any member who actively violated the agreement.

40 "Hop Sing Tong Now Has Seattle Home," *The Seattle Daily Times*, 14 March 1911, p. 7, col. 3. The membership was estimated to be between 3,000 and 4,000 on the Pacific Coast.

41 Seattle's Chong Wa Benevolent Association was and is a branch of the national Chinese Consolidated Benevolent Association.

42 Sen Poy Chew, personal interview, 27 August 2007.

43 Both projecting and recessed balconies, whether covered or uncovered, were traditional architectural features found in buildings from Guangdong province. As well as being decorative, they served an important function of providing additional living or worshipping spaces in more urbanized areas and as an area to use for hanging laundry or watching community celebrations. See David Chuenyan Lai, "The Visual Character of Chinatowns," in *Understanding Ordinary Landscapes*, ed. Paul Groth and Todd W. Bressi (New Haven, Conn: Yale University Press, 1997), 82.

44 At the time of the $50,000 purchase, Daniel was fifteen years old but already learning the hotel business from his father's ownership of Portland's Oregon Hotel.

45 "Chinese Purchase Two Valuable Lots," *The Seattle Times*, 8 February 1910, p. 4, col. 2.

46 William Chin, personal interview, 11 September 2012.

47 Jack Peng, personal interview, 16 June 2011.

48 Milwaukee Hotel advertisement, *The Seattle Sunday Times*, 3 March 1912, p. 10, col. 7.

49 Milwaukee Café advertisement flier.

50 There have been numerous previous accounts that have stated that the entire top floor of the Milwaukee Hotel was a penthouse that was reserved for the Goon Dip family. This story became more legend than fact as no indication

of a penthouse ever existed. Descriptions of the rooms reserved for and used by the family have been verified by an inspection of the floor plans and room layout of the building by the author and through the interviews of Gladys Goon Choi, the granddaughter of Goon Dip, and grandson, Richard Lew Kay.

51 In the early morning hours of 2 June 1912, visiting Chicago Chinese Charles Kee was killed in the doorway of a store owned by Goon Dip. Kee, who was staying at the Milwaukee Hotel, was visiting Seattle as a representative of the Northern Pacific Railway. It was speculated that the killing was linked with the Hop Sing Tong and their support of a tong war that had begun in San Francisco's Chinatown. A rumor had circulated in the press that also indicated that a contract had been taken out to murder Vice-Consul Goon. Local police believed that the physical similarities of both Kee and Goon indicated that Goon was the real target, particularly so since it was Kee's first visit to Seattle. In spite of the investigation, there was never any proof of Tong involvement. In fact, the Seattle Chinese community publicly denied the possibility. Immediately following the incident, Goon received police protection and retained a personal bodyguard. Bodyguards and protection were common among the more affluent Chinese. The case of the Kee murder was never solved. A second murder on December 1912 occurred in the entry doorway of the Milwaukee Hotel which again aroused suspicion that tong revenge was the motive. While an arrest was made of someone staying in the hotel, no proof was ever presented that linked the murder to a rival tong killing of Hop Sing Tong member, Wah Sing Suey.

52 Interview with Gladys Goon Choi, 7 January 2007.

53 "Goon Dip Sends Thanks," Oregonian, 9 March 1911, p. 7, col. 3. The Oregonian published part of Goon's letter: "The people of this great state have generously responded to the appeals made to them to aid the starving and suffering Chinese of Northern China and my people residing in this state desire to thank the citizens of the state for the great good they have done in this, our time of great need. So to you, as representative of this great state, we desire to extend our heartfelt thanks and hope that this occasion will be the means of drawing our respective peoples closer together."

54 "Goon Dip, Chinese Consul Dies and All Seattle Mourns Passing," The Seattle Daily Times, 13 September 1933, p. 12, col. 2–4.

55 From February through April 1911, The Seattle Times carried updated profiles on the best buildings that had been constructed.

56 The Alps Hotel, located across Maynard Avenue from the Rex Hotel, was owned by Charles Krug of Glendive, Montana.

57 With 83 shares of the corporation, Hongiro Kono was elected to the board of trustees as treasurer in February 1905 but unexpectedly resigned from the position in April of that year. Ota assumed the additional role as treasurer until the expiration of the trustees' terms in January 1906 or upon his resignation of the position.

58 Ozasa permanently left the US for Tokyo in April 1911 to pursue other hotel commissions.

59 The Milwaukee Hotel also had a separate apartment on its second floor that held a kitchen and a private bathroom but there is no evidence that this was ever used for a manager. Its location in the northeast apartment side of the building was rented by long-term tenants. Owner Goon Dip did not use this space for his own family.

60 C.T. Takahashi became a partner in the Cascade Investment Company before the Astor Hotel was constructed. Tsukuno was killed in 1908 when he was hit by a train while trying to cross over the tracks as he headed to Smith Cove. Tsukuno was the President of the Cascade Investment Company, the Oriental American Trading Company and the Oriental American Bank. Takahashi assumed the position of president of the trading company.

61 This hotel was also referred to as the Puget Sound though the building marquee was "Hotel Puget Sound." It was a member of the Seattle Japanese Hotel and Apartment Association.

62 "Example of Permanency of Japanese Seattle Investments," The Seattle Times, 8 July 1917, p. 4, col. 3, 4.

63 Miyagawa tragically died in November 1936 in one of the Hotel Puget Sound rooms as a result of a fumigation procedure that involved a toxic mix-

ture that included cyanide. In 1935, the hotel was sold to Yuki Nishamura who had also operated the Welcome and Indiana Hotels.

64 Shigeko Uno, personal interview, 2 July 2006. Ms. Uno was employed by the Rainier Heat and Power Company for over twenty years in a position that oversaw hotel management, maintenance, and accounting of the Chappell Trust properties.

65 "Civic Mass Meeting Protests Jap Menace," *The Seattle Star*, 12 August 1919, p. 1, col. 6.

66 "Johnson Committee to Investigate Menace of Japanese in this State," *Olympia Record*, 1 July 1920, p. 5, col. 5.

67 "Hart Opposes Japs," *Bellingham Herald*, 7 September 1920, p. 2, col. 3.

68 The Committee consisted of Representatives Albert Johnson (Washington, DC) as chair, Isaac Siegel (New York), Harold Knutson (Minnesota), Roscoe C. McCulloch (Ohio), J. Will Taylor (Tennessee), John C. Kleczka (Wisconsin), William N. Vaile (Colorado), Hayes B. White (Kansas), King Swope (Kentucky), Adolph J. Sabath (Illinois), John E. Raker (California), Riley Wilson (Louisiana), Benjamin F. Welty (Ohio), John C. Box (Texas), and Joseph B. Thompson (Oklahoma). Thompson died shortly after the initial meeting of the committee on 18 September 1919.

69 "Governor Asks Probe," *Bellingham Herald*, 1 July 1920, p. 6, col. 1–2.

70 Miller Freeman Testimony. Percentage Plans for Restriction of Immigration. Hearings before the Committee on Immigration and Naturalization. House of Representatives, 66th Congress, 1st Session, 25 September 1919, p. 220–234.

71 Ibid., p. 234.

72 Letter to the Seattle City Council, Comptroller File 75079, 24 October 1919.

73 Miller Freeman Testimony, Hearings before the Committee on Immigration and Naturalization, House of Representatives, 66th Congress, 2nd Session, Part 3, 20 July 1920, p. 1065. Actual membership was between seven hundred and eight hundred members.

74 Tokichi Tanaka, "The Japanese in Seattle," *The Coast*, November 1909, vol. 19, no. 5, p. 256.

75 Juno Sasamori Testimony, Hearings before the Committee on Immigration and Naturalization, House of Representatives, 66th Congress, 2nd Session, Part 3, 20 July 1920, p. 924.

76 Mark Matthews, Letter to Miller Freeman, 29 July 1919.

77 Mark Matthews Testimony, Hearings before the Committee on Immigration and Naturalization, 20 July 1920, p. 1088–1091.

78 The number of residential hotels had increased by an additional 18 since the 1919 report that indicated 264 total Japanese-operated hotels in Seattle and Tacoma.

79 The remaining 5% of the total hotels included hotel names but did not have specific addresses. These hotels were not included in Polk Directories for 1919 or 1920. Of the hotels listed "below the line," 7% were listed south of Dearborn Street.

80 Takuji Yaashita, et al. v. Hinkle, Secretary of State of Washington. No. 177, 260 US 199 (1922). Justice George Sutherland delivered the decision of the court.

81 "King County Suits Against Japanese to be Pressed," *Seattle Times*, 13 November 1922, p. 5, col. 2

82 This same year marked a further restriction in Chinese Exclusion law, where the wives of Chinese merchants were prohibited from immigrating.

83 This included SRO and upper class hotels.

84 The rare exception was the leadership under Mayor Hiram Gill's first term in office beginning in 1910. Gill's open policy on vice in the restricted district of the city ultimately cost him his position as mayor. A recall election the following year removed him from office, partly from the position of reformers who wanted to see the city clean and clear of vice regardless of location.

85 "Special Report," Mark Allison Matthews, Accession Number 97-3, Box 2, Folder 13, University of Washington Special Collections. The two agents had been hired by the city's leading moral crusader, Reverend Mark Matthews of the First

Presbyterian Church. As a looming public figure, orator, and staunch supporter of the law, it was Matthews's belief that corruption in the form of graft and payoff in the Mayor's office and the city's police department was undermining the eradication of vice in Seattle. With enough evidence, charges could prompt a grand jury investigation on corruption in city hall. Matthews's long involvement with urban politics and reform in Seattle is well documented by author Dale E. Soden in *The Reverend Mark Matthews: An Activist in the Progressive Era.* (Seattle: University of Washington Press, 2001). This account that examined alleged corruption in the city was not the first such involvement for Matthews nor was it the first encounter in opposing the administration under Mayor Hiram Gill. Soden points to a number of examples that indicate Matthews being sympathetic to the Asian American community when it came to issues of education, religion, and immigration legislation. There is also evidence that Matthews was accepting of the indigenous culture of the Igorrote Village during the AYP expo when he summarily dismissed allegations of the inappropriate manner of their dress.

86 Ibid.

87 "Gambling Dives Doomed in City," *Seattle Star*, 11 August 1922, p. 2, col. 3.

88 Ibid.

89 Transcript of Testimony and Majority Report of the Department of Efficiency Committee Investigation of Gambling, Vice and Liquor Conditions in the City of Seattle, 10 July to 30 August, CF 1802-C8, p. 1. The report was done by the Department Efficiency Committee of the City Council as an investigation of gambling, vice, and liquor with the intention that the report would be broadly distributed to inform Seattleites on the moral corruption that was permeating the city. The Committee had been formed in 1911 by city ordinance and had the authority to conduct investigations and collect accounts that were "authentic and personal in nature."

90 Ibid. Testimony of Councilman Robert Beach, p. 184.

91 Ibid., p. 3.

92 Seattle Ministerial Federation, "Report of the Committee on Orientals," 4 June 1917.

93 Hiroshi "Tyrus" Okada, personal interview, 22 April 2016.

94 The building that became the Moose Hotel began as a design for an apartment house with retail storefronts. Constructed in 1910, the building was designed by Seattle architect Charles Haynes, and before completion, the structure was modified to become the Reliance Hospital, "the first and only hospital in Seattle…serving a Japanese immigrant clientele." [Brendan Jonathan Harrison, HistoryLink.org Essay 9078.] The Moose Hotel began operation in 1926 and in 1964 it was listed as the Tokyo Hotel. By 1977, there were no further records as to its operation as a hotel.

95 Hundreds of hours of interviews with second generation Asian American children in the C-ID confirmed a knowledge of prostitution and vice that occurred in the neighborhood, but this was understood without discussion with immigrant parents.

96 Ibid.

97 Calvin F. Schmid, "Suicides in Seattle, 1914 to 1925: An Ecological and Behaviorist Study," *University of Washington Publications in the Social Sciences*, October 1928, vol. 5, no. 1.

98 Calvin F. Schmid, "A Study of Homicides in Seattle, 1914–1924," *Social Forces*, June 1926, vol. 4, no. 4, p. 748.

99 Ibid., p. 750. Throughout the years, the Milwaukee Hotel, as a number of other hotels, were noted for numerous unsolved crimes that included murder, extortion, drug smuggling, and robbery.

100 Henry Seichi Itoi interview and correspondence, 11 April 2007.

101 The bank had been in a building at 5th and Main that housed the Empire Hotel. The sale was made to the Union Pacific Railroad, prior to the completion of their new train terminal. Though not beginning construction of the new building until 1911, the new bank location reflected the highly-respected status and reputation of its bank president and president of the Washington Japanese Association, C.T. Takahashi, who was instrumental in the relocation decision.

102 "Two Flags Over 6th and Main" refers to the title of a newsletter that was distributed by retired journalist Ushio "Joseph" Hamanaka from 2000 until Mr. Hamanaka's death in September 2011. "Two Flags" refers to the Japanese American community that represented both American and Japanese ancestry.

103 The Bon Odori is an annual celebration that honors the ancestors. The festival still occurs, but was relocated nearer the Japanese Language School and in front of the Buddhist Temple at 14th and Main Street. It has been at this location since 1949.

104 Roy Minoru Hashimoto, personal interview, 15 March 2012.

105 Joseph Ushio Hamanaka, personal interview, 28 November 2010.

106 Paul Murakami, personal interview, 27 September 2006.

107 Ozasa has also been referred to as an engineer, though his corporate stationary and journals of the period, including the *Pacific Builder and Engineer*, noted him as an architect of record. The Panama remains as his only known extant Seattle building to date. He is credited with the designs and construction of at least two other building plans, neither of which are still standing in the Chinatown-International District. These include the Japanese Specie Bank (Maynard between Jackson and King Streets that was immediately south of the Bush Hotel) and a single-story commercial building that was located at Maynard and Weller.

108 Eddy Sano, personal interview, 17 April 2011.

109 The Washington Board of Health Rules and Regulations for Labor Camps Code was the standard that was used during a 1950 assessment of the sanitary conditions of hotels and dormitories since the city code only addressed a ratio for water closets and urinals at two for every twenty-four beds.

110 The 1914 ordinance that required an annual license fee was repealed in 1918.

111 It is reasonable to assume that Seattle was influenced by a 1922 report entitled the "Statistical Report on Public Baths, Laundries or Wash-Houses and Comfort Stations for Municipalities" in *The Journal of the American Association for Promoting Hygiene and Public Baths*. The journal included a survey of those cities with a population of 25,000 or greater that had addressed incorporation of public bathing facilities as part of urban redevelopment and as an example of the need for more commitment. Seattle was conspicuously missing from the survey of West Coast cities where only Los Angeles, San Francisco, Oakland, and Spokane were mentioned. For a comprehensive history of progressive reform and public baths in America, see Marilyn Thornton Williams, *Washing "The Great Unwashed": Public Baths in Urban America, 1840–1920* (Columbus: Ohio State University Press, 1991).

112 Seattle, City Ordinance #47237 (25 June 1924). The new ordinance dictated that an application for a $5 per year license would need to be filed with the City Comptroller. The application included sixteen fields of information, including a questionnaire about the premises where the public bath would be located and if the structure met all building, zoning, fire and health, and sanitation codes. Revocation of a license could occur if the owner was convicted of any other city violation or criminal activity. Sections 8 of the code forbid an owner from "permitting a female employee to attend a male patron while such patron is undergoing a massage or treatment, or taking a bath." Admitting anyone who was of "poor moral character," could cost the owner their operating license along with a fine and up to ninety days in the city jail. "Poor moral character" was broadly defined from any activity that compromised public morals, including prostitution and substance abuse.

113 Seattle, City Ordinance #72529 (26 March 1943).

114 Diary of Kamekichi Tokita, Friday, March 20, 1942, p. 117–118.

115 Interview with Shokichi (Shox) Tokita, 3 August 2007.

Behind Those "Ordinary" Walls

Hotel operation required a willingness to work 24-hours a day every day of the week. The daily pressures of operating a business were partially offset with help from family members and specifically with support from organizations that were part of the Asian American community.

Along with management and accounting for a hotel business, operation meant assuming the responsibility for building maintenance and conflict resolution with and between transient guests. The entry doors to the hotels were never locked since access to the hotel proper was most often on the second floor of the building and check-in was any time of day or night. Management often required noninterference and, to a degree, resignation that some activities would occur in the hotel regardless of monitoring. Clean, orderly, and licensed hotel operation also meant the risks that came from drinking, drug abuse, gambling, prostitution, robbery, and occasions when a resident in despair would opt for suicide rather than continue in a cycle of hard labor and poverty. Growing up in the Western Hotel, **Nobue Shimizu** remembered:

> My father had an outside job so my mother ran the hotel: checking people in, taking care of the accounting, and making sure that the linens were cleaned every week. The lamps in the room were gas and sometimes I'd go to Kresse's five-and-dime to buy a

gas mantle replacement to put over the open flames. If my mother went upstairs and smelled gas, she knew that someone had committed suicide...and I was the one to call the coroner. My mother didn't want this to happen anymore so we paid the cost to rewire the building for electricity.[1]

The Issei accepted the hard work and sacrifice of time as a matter of necessity and part of the job. For a Japanese family, the hotel provided shelter, a home, and a stationary means of making a living that allowed a family to be together. Hotel management meant that the family could live in the hotel without paying rent since the other rooms would cover the total cost of the hotel rental space that was charged by the leasing agent or building owner. Any number of rooms on a floor or occupying small office spaces behind check-in counters could serve as the family's residence, and as the family size grew, the spatial needs could conservatively increase as long as there would be enough rooms and paying patrons to cover the hotel costs.

Skilled command of the English language was not a requirement for a Japanese immigrant to be an owner or proprietor of a hotel, just as it wasn't a requirement for Chinese immigrants in the laundry business. As **Takashi Hori**, who grew up in and eventually managed the Panama Hotel, recalled:

It wasn't difficult to be a manager of a hotel. If someone came to the check-in window, you just knew that they wanted a room...why else would they be there? "How many... days?...weeks?...months?" was all you had to know. Anything else that required more English was the responsibility of the children. The Nisei became the "jacks-of-all-trades."[2]

The challenges of language and conducting day-to-day hotel business for Japanese couples was eased with the birth of the next generation, who worked alongside their parents to keep the family business viable. While it relieved some of the stress of the workload for the Issei and bridged the language gap between the Issei and English-speaking patrons, it also contributed to an even busier day-to-day life for the generation of Nisei as they struggled to shape an identity between the cultural worlds of Japanese tradition, values, and duty, and native-born Americans of Japanese ancestry.

Life for the Issei and Nisei was lived in a series of "relationships" or affiliations where each person had both a sense of belonging and duty, and a personal investment in activities that were for the good of the community.

Organizational affiliation contributed to bolstering the strength of the individual during hard times. Inherent to this sense of belonging was the common tie to a person's *ken*, or prefecture, which created a close bond of familiarity, camaraderie, and support. Affiliations were economically, politically, and socially focused.[3] A *ken* would typically be dominant in one sector of the local economy, partly from language dialects that would be spoken from each *ken* and for the help that would be extended to a newcomer joining the same sector of a business. For the Issei, the umbrella organization was the Japanese Association of America (JAA) that was re-organized in 1908 from the Japanese Deliberative Council of America in 1900. For the Nisei, it was the Japanese American Citizens League (JACL) that was established in 1930. These organizations existed wherever there was a growing population of Japanese in an area. The agendas addressed affairs that were socially and politically unique to the immediate community and those issues that affected all Japanese populations in America. The Japanese Association of America served a similar function as the Chinese Benevolent Association in training and helping new immigrants, providing social service and protection, hiring attorneys to fight discriminatory legislation, and retaining connection to old world traditions. In many ways, the JAA established the tone for the development of other organizations in the structuring of bylaws that could respond to the common interests of a focused membership and the Japanese community-at-large. The strength of the individual was reinforced by the presence of the association to which they could affiliate.

SOPHISTICATED SYSTEMS

In the early 1900s as the Japanese population expanded its affiliation to specific business sectors, professional associations formed to represent the major classifications including: barbers, grocers, restaurants, general mercantile stores, laundry and dye-works, shoe shops, produce, photographers, jewelers, auto repair associations, and hotel and apartment operators. Having a successful business that was going to provide for the individual and the family depended on the broad-based support of the community. Every business was provided the opportunity to be affiliated as a member of a respective business professional organization or association. Members could share issues and problems that were specific and unique to their line of work; the result was a highly refined system

The Nakamura Grocery that was in the Jackson Hotel. [Courtesy May Nakamura Sasaki]

of interaction, education, and support. Through annual dues and fundraisers, these associations stayed financially solvent and able to support community services. *Tanomoji* was an internal banking system for the Japanese community where money would be used for loans to start businesses or as a monetary gift to a business or family that was in financial need. The organization provided advice on management skills, clarification of local ordinances and laws that affected the business, employment, or repair and maintenance training. Any of these could be discussed at respective organizational meetings. Each of these organizations elected officers that included a president, vice-president, secretary, and treasurer and they developed bylaws, goals, and fund-raising events for their respective associations. Organizations also monitored the number of businesses by category with the goal that there would never be more than could be supported by the community. It was a way of ensuring financial solvency and a balance of businesses within Nihonmachi. As **May Nakamura Sasaki** recalled:

People that were part of the *tanomoji* would contribute some money every month and the amount was based on what you could afford and intended to save. You could get a loan if you had a good business plan. In the *tanomoji* system, the responsible association kept track of the number of specific types of businesses in the community so that there wouldn't be too many of any one category, such as grocers, drug stores, dry cleaners, launderers, and hotels. My father had a business in the University District and wanted to move to Japantown to start a grocery. At first, the Japanese Grocers Association told him that there were enough groceries and that the suppliers wouldn't be able to provide goods for another. Twenty-seven was the limit for that classification. He ultimately did get permission and opened his store on Jackson Street across the street and one block east of the Bush Hotel. His store was at the corner of the [Jackson] Hotel building and we lived above the store.[4]

In 1908, the Japanese in Seattle were recorded as operating fifty hotels and single-room boarding houses.[5] It was this business sector that formed one of the earliest business organizations in the ethnic community as the Seattle Japanese Hotel and Apartment Association (SJHAA). The first meeting took place at the Uraume Restaurant on 30 January 1910 with a core group of "20 civic-minded individuals." The new association elected officers and established that it would be "the single largest association with the purpose of protecting the authority (*kenri*) and profits (*rieki*) of those involved in the same business (*dogyosha*)."[6] The inaugural meeting of SJHAA members took place on 6 February 1910. The SJHAA consisted of nine

Chojiro Fujii, President of the Seattle Japanese Hotel and Apartment Association, ca. 1902. [Courtesy Minoru Fujii]

officer positions of the organization with Chojiro Fujii, one of the first pioneers of the hotel business, as president of the newly formed association.[7] Risaburo Sunada was elected to serve as vice-president with Shiro Chiba as secretary, Tokio Ota as treasurer, and five other board members.[8]

The Japanese Association of North America and the City of Seattle business licensing office kept data on the number of Japanese-operated hotels, and SJHAA membership directories began being printed in 1915. For about $10.00 a year, the hotel that you operated could be an official member and listed

A 1914 advertisement postcard of three Japanese-operated hotels. Each hotel advertised their prices and the amenities that you could expect. The Hotels Yakima and Tacoma advertised unlimited hot water in each room, upstairs telephone, steam heat and a bathtub, with the latter hotel mentioning the ease of getting tickets to Japan. The Fujii Hotel indicates that Chojiro Fujii was the proprietor and that a car was available for transport to the hotel. [Courtesy Washington State Historical Society at WashingtonHistory.org, 2009.42.2]

in a directory of businesses that was printed annually.[9] In the early years, the business directories listed the name of the business and the proprietors, and like the community newspapers they were primarily published in Japanese with little, if any, English. As the population of Nisei began to exceed the number of Issei by the 1930s, all of these publications transitioned to English with little to no Japanese.

    The SJHAA was a fraternal organization that represented people from various *ken* and where any topic of discussion dealing with hotel management and operation could be addressed to help their members. Sometimes the concerns of the association included legal help, as Henry Itoi remembered in an incident at the Carrollton Hotel.

> The worst problem that my father encountered came from an unexpected source…the two policemen on the Occidental Avenue beat. One day, they came upstairs into the hotel, called father aside into a hallway, and tried to bully him into housing a prostitute in the hotel. He refused. Some months later, the same two policemen barged into our kitchen at dinnertime and began rummaging through the pantry without a search

warrant. They grabbed a bottle, ordered father out into the hallway, and accused him of selling liquor. They didn't know the bottle contained soy sauce. They said that they could forget about jailing him if he gave them some money. Father refused and said that he was willing to go to court. He was in jail for three nights before his court case came up. In the meantime the Japanese Hotel and Apartment Operators Association people called an attorney. When father appeared in court, many fellow hotel operators showed up to be witnesses at the trial. When the prosecutor asked the "star" witness of the two policemen to point out the man who had sold him liquor, the witness pointed to the wrong man. The judge threw out the case. After that, I did not see those two policemen back on the Occidental Avenue beat.

In its years of operation, the SJHAA expanded its interests from being one of business-support to also being a social catalyst for picnics and community events for families that operated hotels. As the city passed new ordinances, the agenda of the association became more proactive in understanding the effect of local laws on the business of operating SRO hotels and leasing the commercial storefronts. Other neighborhood businesses paid for advertisement space in the directory that essentially paid the expenses of publication. Members elected officers at the New Year's dinner and discussed common issues, problems, and challenges and attended the local meetings that were called on an intermittent schedule. The inability to pay the annual fee to be a member never precluded a person from receiving help and training in how to operate and care for a hotel. As manager of the New Central and Eclipse Hotels, Elmer Tazuma recalled the importance of sharing information:

Seiichi Hara, [who operated the Union and later] the Tacoma Hotel, was the secretary of the hotel association for a long time, and after that, it was Hitoshi Taniguchi. Mr. Hara was always willing to teach anyone who needed help. In the old days, you had to know how to start the fire in the hotel boiler and regulate the heat. You also had to be able to pass the exam that was given by the city inspector so that you could get your certificate as proof to show that you knew how to do the required work. You couldn't pay a plumber or contractor every time something would go wrong or need fixing. If you did that, there would be no money left for the family. Sometimes the plumbers and electricians you hired would teach you how to care for things...it was best to know how to do everything yourself.[10]

The greatest number of hotels and rooms that had Japanese proprietors was located throughout downtown Seattle with the vast majority south of Yesler Way.

Like the Chinese, Japanese-member corporations purchased land and developed hotels. As with the Astor and Panama, the N-P Hotel was under Japanese corporate ownership, but it took decades for the immigrant Shitamae brothers to become partial owners of the corporation and the hotel. From 1914 to 1939, the hotel was owned by Seattle attorney James B. Murphy and managed by the Shitamaes.[11] After twenty-five years of saving their money they were able to purchase the building through registration as the N.S. Investment Corporation. Registered in 1939 with $5,000 (one hundred shares of fifty dollars each), the N.S. Investment Corporation's corporate officers and shareholders included Frank N. Shitamae as president (49 shares), Thomas Masuda as secretary and treasurer (50 shares), and Mamie Gregory as a board director (1 share) with the corporation office located in the N-P Hotel.[12] **Miyoko Shitamae Ike** grew up in the N-P Hotel.

My father, Niroku Shitamae, and mother, Moto Okubi, married in Japan in 1902. He was working at a ward office and processing paperwork for people who were leaving Japan for the United States. That is how he got interested in emigrating. My father came to America in 1907…right before my older sister was born. He joined his youngest brother, Shihei, who was already in Seattle. The two of them managed the N-P Hotel.

It was 1915 before my mother and sister were able to come to America and the first home that my parents had was the N-P. We lived in the hotel until 1928 when we moved to a house on 20th and Dearborn that was large enough for my parents, my four sisters and me. My uncle continued to live at the N-P as a live-in manager but as the Great Depression got worse, our family had to move back to the hotel as it was too expensive to live in the house and pay for the needs of the hotel. My father opened up the walls between 218 and 219 so that we'd have a larger living area but the kitchen room wasn't connected and we had to share the bathroom down the hall. There were only six rooms that had baths attached to them. The rest of the rooms used one of the two bathrooms that were on each floor. My mother missed having a yard but had a small rooftop garden at the hotel. As children, my older sisters would go out the window on the second floor and play on the rooftop overhang. It was a lot different to walk through the lobby of the hotel than through a front door to our house on Dearborn. There were big leather chairs in the lobby, a marble floor, and spittoons close by. There was a long, huge counter and my father

The Shitamae Brothers, Niroku (Frank) and Shihei with children Yukiko (standing), Haruko (sitting in front row) and Fumiko (held by Shihei) in front of the N-P Hotel. [Courtesy Miyo Shitamae Ike]

would sit in the back office at a big roll top desk. My uncle, who went by "George," was a very social, affable man and my father, who now used "Frank" as his first name, was very quiet and took care of the accounting. The hotel was such a busy place and one of the best in Nihonmachi. Workers stayed there as well as visitors from Japan who were businessmen, actors, and baseball players. My father would drive our car to the dock to pick up our guests and bring them to the hotel. For people from Hiroshima Prefecture, the hotel was a central meeting place to socialize and to get help if they needed a job.

Even without corporate or property ownership, Japanese controlled a great share of the Seattle residential hotel industry management and operation that lasted for decades. By 1920, hotel and apartment operation accounted for almost 26% of the jobs that were held within and by the Japanese community with over 1,300 Japanese men and women employed in this industry.[13] **Hotoru (Theresa) Umeda Matsudaira**'s diary recounts her experiences as a new bride and her employment in the hotel industry that began with being a chambermaid in the Alps Hotel.

...Our wedding date was May 23 [and]...it was late July in 1921...when I came to the [United] States. We spent a whole day at the Immigration Center. Next day, my sister and her husband came to meet us and took us to the Alps Hotel on King Street.... I started working (that day) as a maid. I worked very hard, even on Sundays and earned forty dollars a month. I was so happy when I got my first monthly salary that I wrote to my mother in Japan. I wanted to send her some money...but I couldn't afford it.... The US economy was falling into a severe economic recession and streets were beginning to fill with jobless people...[14]

Of the city's recorded 762 hotel and rooming houses, 232 or over 30% were being operated by Japanese Seattleites in June 1920 and with over 62% of these located south of Yesler Way.[15] Of these 232 hotels, 82 were listed as members of the SJHAA. By 1927, one-half of the hotels were being operated and occupied by Japanese husband and wife couples and their children.[16] **Martha Kawaguchi Onishi** grew up in the Royal and Standard Hotels.

Kametaro "KK" Kawaguchi. [Courtesy Martha Kawaguchi Onishi]

My father's name was Kametaro Kawaguchi but everyone knew him as "KK." He was raised fishing when he was at home in Japan and in America he fished for pleasure and sport competitions. He was so proficient that other fishermen kept their eyes on him and would follow wherever his boat went. Still, he would catch fish when no one could. His pole would be still and he'd tell us where there would be a fish below the water. One day, he said, "It's time for lunch." At noon he'd get out the rice balls that mother had prepared, lower his line in the water and would reel in a cod, fillet it right there and put it on the rice...and we'd have sashimi for lunch. It was so fresh, that the fillet would still be moving!

My father made his own poles and nets. At one time he had a fishing tackle store on First Avenue but it had to be registered in someone else's name. There used to be fishing derbies and *The Seattle Times* sponsored a Salmon Derby...he won two cars and a television set in these competitions. There were a lot of Japanese who were fishermen before the war... and after the war they formed the Tengu Club, a membership of Japanese fishermen. He'd come home with shrimp, red snapper, and octopus and share what he caught with friends and people he knew. He'd pickle salmon heads and cheeks, and tie up salted salmon in guinea sacks and hang it in the hotel basement on a line to dry. He would go out at 3:00 a.m. to fish as that was his quiet time and he'd get back by 9:00 to help my mother make up beds...there were forty-two rooms in the Standard Hotel.[17]

There is little information about the reasons for how names were selected for these hotels. Notable exceptions are the Bush Hotel which was named for William Chappell's wife or the N-P Hotel that was named in honor of the Northern Pacific Railroad by the hotel manager, Noroku Shitamae.[18] What is observable is that the names of some of the hotels, particularly in the late 1900s, reflected the operating family's name, such as the Nakanishi Hotel, Yamamoto Hotel, or the Fujii Hotel. Very few hotels had Japanese names after 1915 and all but one of the hotel names were anglicized by the end of World War II, presumably to attract American patrons and avoid any possible repercussions from latent negative post-war sentiments.[19] Like the marketplace design that attracted clientele, hotel names could follow the proprietor if the family opted to relocate to another SRO building or be sold along with the tenancy to a new owner. It was a personal decision at the discretion of the proprietor.

TABLE 5-1: *Hotels in the Seattle Japanese Hotel and Apartment Association [Author]*

	1915	1928	1932	1936	1949	1964	1977	1983
Hotels within Study Area	84	113	106	86	79	48	6	4
% Within Study Area	94.3	79.5	79.1	62.3	60.7	46.1	31.6	40.0
Hotels Outside of Study Area	5	29	28	52	51	56	13	6
Total Hotels in The Association	89	142	134	138	130	104	19	10
Total Hotel % Change	—	59.6	-5.6	3.0	-5.8	-20.0	-81.7	-47.3

The records of those members that were affiliated with the SJHAA provide a glimpse into both the importance and longevity of this sector of employment that sustained the economic livelihood of this community, along with geographic distribution of where the community was living. The number of residential hotels that were being operated by members of the association saw a substantial increase of over 59% from 1915 to 1928 with only minor fluctuation in the total number of hotels in the next three decades.[20] From 1915 through the 1950s, the majority of these hotels were located south of Yesler Way and shared the area of town that had earned the reputation for the worst vice that the city

The New York (415 Washington Street) and Montana Hotels (417 ½ Washington Street) seen in the farthest right wooden-frame building shared the same structure but with separate entrances to the rooms on the second floor. Both of these hotels were under Japanese management and two of the earliest members of the Seattle Japanese Hotel and Apartment Association in 1910. The tailor shop in the Montana Hotel building was operated by K. Tai, a Chinese immigrant. The center frame building is the Hotel Welton that had an at-grade restaurant owned by Japanese proprietor K. Tsuda and adjacent to another restaurant under the Japanese ownership of K. Kawamoto in the frame building on the far left. Immediately across Washington Street (out of this photo) were the Quong Chong Chin Mercantile, a Japanese barber (U. Kuntsugu), The Gom Hong and Company merchandise, a Japanese Employment Agency, and the Hop Gee Chinese laundry. The immediate neighborhood was changing with the completion of the five-story, masonry Alki SRO Hotel (far left) in 1910 by architects Thompson and Thompson. With 86 rooms, the building also housed the Hong Chong Company Chinese merchandise. [Courtesy Washington State Historical Society at WashingtonHistory.org, Asahel Curtis Collection 1943.42.20064]

had to offer. From the pre- to post-depression years, there was less than a 6% decline in the number of Japanese hotel operators, indicating both the need for low-income housing and reasonable stability of the SROs in providing a home and financial support for the Japanese proprietor either with or without a family. As **Takashi Hori** recalled:

> Running a hotel during the Depression was so difficult but what else could we do? It was our business and if you lost the hotel, you also lost the home for your family. People were struggling so much and it was hard to turn someone away if they couldn't pay...

and sometimes people just left without paying. If customers wouldn't pay for their room and they wouldn't leave, a hotel operator might give them a week's rent just so they would go somewhere else. There were issues of theft in the rooms, like food or shoes. In the hotels that had large dormitory style rooms, you could see a number of beds all lined in a row and you could rent one for five or ten cents a night. You'd put your shoes next to the foot of the bed with the leg of the bed frame inside the shoe…if anyone tried to steal them, they'd have to "jostle" the bed and you'd wake up to protect what may have been the only property you had left. [21]

In 1932, hotel operators represented eight of Japan's nine regions and thirty-five of the forty-seven total prefectures of the country. Twenty-four hotel men were from the Hiroshima Prefecture in the Chugoku Region, followed by eighteen from Shiga in the Kinki Region, and sixteen from Kumamoto Prefecture in the Kyushu Region. Fourteen hotel members were represented in both Wakayama Prefecture in the Kinki Region and the Yamaguchi Prefecture in Chugoku Region. There was only one instance where a prefecture was represented by a single member and that was for Okinawa.

The forced removal of Japanese from Seattle during their WWII incarceration placed a hold on all Seattle Japanese associations and organizational structures of the community with the SJHAA ceasing operation from 1942 until 1949. When the Japanese community received the official word that they had to evacuate, there were literally only a few days in which to sort, store, and divest of all personal properties. Hotel operations were sold for sums that were far below market value, or arrangements were made for temporary management by real estate firms or individuals who were hired to care for them during the period when the family was gone. In no instance were any of the hotels closed during the war. In fact, the hotel business was busier than ever as defense workers in Seattle's port industries sought inexpensive and convenient housing.

In the case of the Panama Hotel, the Hori family sublet the hotel with John Davis and Company real estate to manage the collection of rents, with part of the basement being used for storage of personal goods by members of the Japanese community who had relocated to incarceration camps. **Takashi Hori** recalled the single request that was made to his father by a family friend who wanted to store his personal belongings, along with the difficulty in reclaiming their hotel from the lessees when the war was over.

MAP 5-1: *Seattle Japanese Hotel and Apartment Association (SJHAA) – 1915 [Author]*

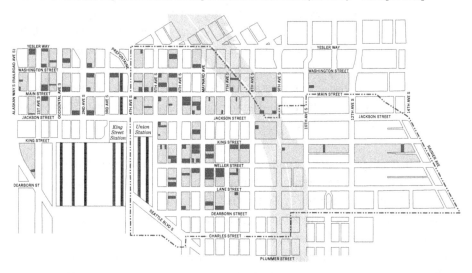

MAP 5-2: *Japanese-Operated Hotels, SJHAA members and Non-SJHAA Members – 1920 [Author]*

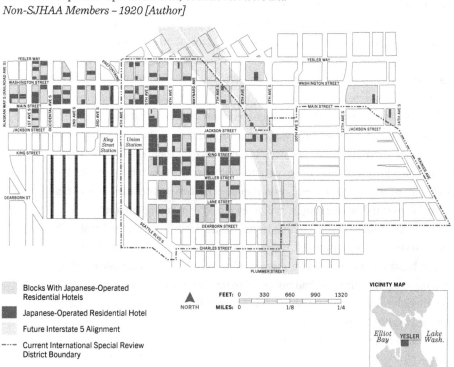

MAP 5-3: *Seattle Japanese Hotel and Apartment Association (SJHAA) – 1928 [Author]*

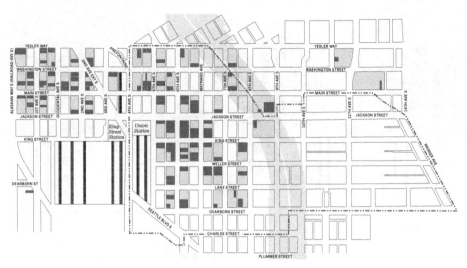

MAP 5-4: *Seattle Japanese Hotel and Apartment Association (SJHAA) – 1932 [Author]*

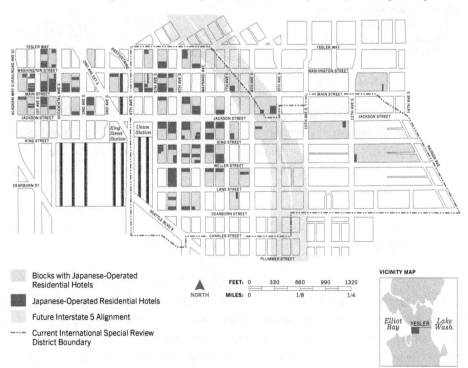

Blocks with Japanese-Operated
Residential Hotels

Japanese-Operated Residential Hotels

Future Interstate 5 Alignment

Current International Special Review
District Boundary

FEET: 0   330   660   990   1320

MILES: 0   1/8   1/4

NORTH

VICINITY MAP

*Elliot
Bay*   YESLER   *Lake
Wash.*

MAP 5-5: *Seattle Japanese Hotel and Apartment Association (SJHAA) – 1936 [Author]*

Lots of churches stored things for people during the war. One day Mr. Fujii, who operated the Gyo-Gokken Chinese restaurant on Main Street, came to see my father and asked him if he could store some of his things in the basement. By word of mouth, our friends found out and before you knew it, the hotel basement was full. Some people had things they stored sent to the camps. Fred Darnell of the Davis Company took care of this and found a family to lease the hotel during the war. When we returned, they refused to give the building back so we had to hire an attorney to get the keys returned to us so we could come back to our home. My father spent a lot of money for that.[22]

In the days between the bombing of Pearl Harbor and the evacuation of Japanese communities from the West Coast, Cadillac Hotel operator Kamekichi Tokita kept a written account of his observations as anti-Japanese sentiments and the tensions within Nihonmachi escalated in Seattle.[23] With the 7 December 1941 radio announcement about the events that occurred at

Cadillac Hotel. [Courtesy King County Assessor's Office, Property Record Cards, 1937–1973, Puget Sound Branch, Washington State Archives]

Pearl Harbor, Tokita wrote about international events, reflections and the struggles of Japantown, along with the fragile nature and uncertainty of the hotel community in Seattle. As he noted in the first entry, "In a moment, we lost all the value of our existence in this society. Not only have we lost value, we're unwanted. It would be better if we didn't exist."[24] Local authorities had arrested 120 Issei who were assumed to have potentially dangerous connections with Japan, including operators of the Tacoma and Regina hotels.[25] Tokita carefully observed the changes in Seattle's Nihonmachi while he continued to care for his hotel and help his wife Haruko's parents with their work as proprietors of the Wilson Hotel nine blocks away.

Blackout conditions from the war dictated that hotel operators assume the additional expenses to bring their buildings into compliance. From a functional perspective and since all SRO hotels contained light wells that provided lighting for interior rooms, interior hallways would now be permanently dark.

Tokita tried to retain the dignity of his business and felt a responsibility to his patrons amid the uncertainty and prejudice. He never sacrificed the personal attention that was a part of the management style of operating his hotel.

With the majority of his guests being elderly people on Social Security, Tokita empathized with the hardship to them if the Japanese were forced out of the hotel businesses and ownership replaced by people who wouldn't understand the needs and financial limitations of the seniors.[26] At the same time, the Cadillac was facing increasing operating costs when the City's Department of Health made the decision that all hotels without central heating would be required to have room radiator heaters on all day; the additional expense would leave the operators no recourse but to pass it on to the tenants.

> As reasonable as [leaving the heaters on]…may sound, it is an indication that they are beginning to put indirect pressure on the Japanese hotels. Most Japanese hotel owners run economy hotels. If we are required to keep the heat on all day everyday during winter, economy hotels like ours wouldn't be able to make any profit at all. "The hotels on Yesler Way are using their central heating systems, and charging their guests $5.00 a week. If you start using yours, you can charge $4.00 to $5.00 a week, too," the official said. It seemed like the official wasn't able to differentiate economy hotels from the hotels downtown. Hotels like ours, whose guests are elderly people…can't charge [this] for the heaters. Our guests wouldn't have any money left for food. At a hotel like ours, it is also kind of dishonest to charge that much merely for steam heat. By the time the current war is over, all Japanese will be left penniless….[27]

Tokita's diary reveals the angst that plagued the community in the early days of the war. The rumors of the Japanese community being moved were being printed in the local newspapers, partly because of Seattle's coastal position and national defense concerns. On a visit by newspaperman and community leader James Sakamoto, Tokita learned that authorities were considering assigning a custodian manager for Japanese-owned businesses, beginning with hotel owners since they were "the largest segment among Issei Japanese."[28] While it was initially a consideration, ultimately hotel custodians never were assigned.

By mid-February, relocation was still an unclear issue, which made it extremely difficult for any hotel operator to know whether improvements to the hotel would be warranted compared to saving money that might be desperately needed later. Articles in the local Japanese newspapers indicated that once a relocation plan was announced, there would be very little time for the community to comply.

The evacuation debate was answered on 3 March 1942 when it was decided that both Issei and Nisei would be removed from the western half of Washington State, which was designated a military area. With the anticipation that relocation to a yet-unknown location would occur within the month, every Japanese-operated business in the West Coast's military area faced the grim reality of how to dispose of personal property, shops, and residential hotel businesses with the impending certainty of an economic loss. **Shikego Sese Uno** recalled the response of the Rainier Heat and Power Company as it faced a loss of Japanese American hotel operators and tenants.

> There were a great number of Japanese tenants who leased from the Rainier Heat and Power Company. A number of the commercial businesses asked if they could leave their personal things with the company office and the trustees decided to designate a couple of rooms for storage. During the incarceration, people would write the company and ask them if they would please check a specifically marked box that they had left behind and if they would send the item…and the company did it.[29]

Tokita faced pivotal and urgent decisions beginning on Thursday, 5 March 1942 as he prepared to pack personal belongings, move his wife and five children, and sell the hotel business that was a home to them and the many patrons they had cared for over the years. Like the Hori family and other Japanese hotel operators, there was little time to negotiate for true market value of the business. **Tokita** noted that in a non-war market, the business could have been sold for about $3,000 but with the current conditions, the offer that was accepted was $1,500.

> In order to protect the property people leave behind after relocation, the government… set up consultation offices in different regions. …As it turned out, the…offices were virtually useless. It's a shame to sell, but it's too ridiculous to throw it all away. Other people in the hotel business must also be driven into similar situations that require them to give their businesses away at bargain prices. Right now I feel as if my clothes have been stripped off by force.[30]

What is striking about comparing the numbers of hotel operators before and after their WWII incarceration is that the Japanese American community managed a strong return to the operation of the residential hotels.

With so little money, few possessions, and beginning their lives and livelihood again, many were aided by the local churches and the Japanese Language School after their release from Minidoka. The interior spaces on the first and second floors of the school were partitioned with temporary divider walls that created makeshift "apartments" for twenty-seven families in spaces that were smaller than the internment barracks.[31] Perhaps it was the size and sparseness of the accommodations of the Minidoka internment camp near Hunt, Idaho, that had housed the majority of Seattle's Japanese community or their intention to return to this line of business that caused the Japanese Seattleites to label the school building as the "Hunt Hotel." Some families stayed at the "Hunt Hotel" for weeks, and others, like the Tokita family, stayed there for years until they were able to re-establish themselves financially so that they could return to residential hotel living and management.[32] So often, the return was a step backwards in what the Japanese American families had accomplished before the war years. **Henry Itoi** remembered their return to the Carrollton Hotel.

> In 1937, my father started looking for a house to rent in Beacon Hill...somewhere where each of us could have our own bedroom and close enough to keep operating the hotel. After the bombing of Pearl Harbor, there was only one guest who yelled that he "would not pay money to a Goddam' Jap!" The other patrons...calmed him down and convinced him to leave. This was really the only trouble that we had with residents of the hotel during the beginning of the war years. We lost the rental house during the incarceration and it was difficult for my father to find someone to run the hotel in our absence. We stored our household possessions at the hotel and were so disheartened to find that some of our things had been stolen while we were away. After the incarceration, it took a while for Japanese restaurants and small shops to begin to reappear along Main and Jackson Street. My father had returned to Seattle in early 1945 to resume operating the Carrollton Hotel; ill from the Minidoka Internment Camp. Within a year, he became too sick to continue so he sold the business to another Japanese family. My father died in 1948 at the age of 69....[33]

After over forty years of life in the US, Chojiro Fujii left Seattle in 1935 to live the remainder of his life in his home city of Hiroshima, Japan. He entrusted the Fujii Hotel to his adopted son, Hisato, and mother, Shige. Grandson, **Minoro Fujii** recalled his grandfather, and the changes from the war years.

It was 1894 and my grandfather was 17 when he came to America with his father, Kojuro. My great-grandfather, Kojuro, returned to Japan but Chojiro stayed. He was young but a very independent person who was attracted to the opportunity that was available to him in America. It was still the "Wild West" back then and not too long after the Civil War. My grandfather used to carry a walking cane with him that had a sword in it for protection. The cane was made by his father who was a sword maker for the samurai in Japan.

Chojiro got his first job on a dairy farm in the Kent area and for a while, he was a labor contractor for Japanese coming to America. He got into the hotel business in 1899, thinking that it would be a good idea since the immigration station was so close by and laborers from Japan would need a place to stay. For a while, he operated two other hotels including the Yakima on Maynard and Dearborn, and the Tacoma on Jackson and 8th. The Fujii Hotel became a subcontracting office for the Nippon Yusen Kaisha steamship line. My grandfather worked hard at everything he did...he was 23 when he helped establish the Buddhist church.

When my grandfather went back to live in Japan, my parents managed the hotel, corner grocery store, and the bar. At one time there was a barber shop in the store. They were all places where people would come together to visit. My younger brother, Hisashi, and I were both born in the Fujii Hotel...Mrs. Beppu was a midwife and she delivered both of us. I would play on my tricycle and my brother peddled his go-cart. We would ride back and forth in front of the store and when I was older, I would roller skate around the block.

In 1935, when I was ten years old, my brother and I went to Japan for part of our education and to be with our grandfather. We were there for twelve years and didn't see our parents during that time. When the war broke out, we weren't allowed to come back to America. My parents never saw my brother again...he died from the bombing in Hiroshima in 1945. When my parents were released from the [incarceration] camps, they returned to the Fujii Hotel and bought an apartment building in Capitol Hill. I returned to the United States in 1947 and after being in Japan for so long, I had to learn English all over again.[34]

The 1950 Census indicates that in the years after their release, the Japanese had returned to Seattle, and while the numbers were the lowest recorded since 1900, almost 5,800 or 82% of the Japanese community had been

Chojiro Fujii's grandchildren; Minoru (left) and Hisashi (right). [Courtesy or Minoru Fujii]

restored from the 1930 figure. With the SJHAA back in business in 1949, the
members were only eight hotels short of the pre-war figures. **Janet Sakamoto
Baba**'s family entered the hotel business after the war.

> My father, Noburo Sakamoto, bought the Star Tofu Shop on Main Street across from the
> Panama Hotel. There were four of us children by then and my parents and grandparents.
> Our business relocated to Weller Street between Maynard and 6th Avenue and it was
> on the same block as the Mar Hotel. That's how he knew that the hotel business was for
> sale and dad bought it in 1950. Our family had the entire second floor of rooms where
> we lived right next to the lobby. We children didn't go upstairs to floors where the guests
> were staying. At the top of the stairs from the first to the second floor was the lobby with a
> check-in desk, mailboxes, and a switchboard system that connected to the rooms. There
> was also a huge kitchen and a ballroom floor that was once part of a restaurant. It wasn't
> used when we bought the hotel and hadn't been for years. We rode our bicycles on that
> marble dance floor. Most of our residents were either white or African Americans who
> worked in the neighboring train stations or in the jazz clubs. Sarah Vaughn and Count
> Basie stayed at our hotel along with other Black entertainers who weren't allowed to stay
> in the other downtown Seattle hotels. . . .[35]

MAP 5-6: *Seattle Japanese Hotel and Apartment Association (SJHAA) – 1949 [Author]*

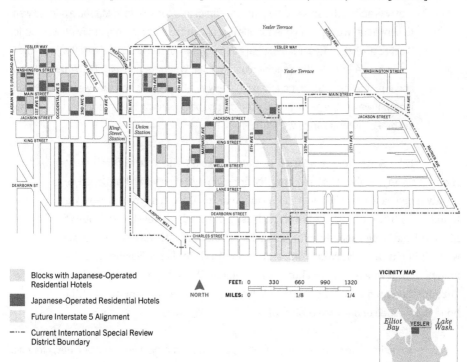

Even with the encouraging post-war numbers that showed a return of Japanese operation of hotels, there were some who could not return to the hotel businesses that they had once managed. **Shea Aoki**'s family had operated the Alps Hotel for decades.

> Before the war, my husband's family managed the Alps Hotel with the Matsudaira and Ichigoshima families. My father-in-law, Seita Aoki, had been a businessman in Japan before he came to Seattle. He and his wife, Sei, worked in the hotel with their sons, Taro and Jiro, who were both born in the hotel. After Jiro and I married, we lived in the Alps on the second floor facing King Street and occupied five rooms—a living room, dining room, two bedrooms and a kitchen that was across the hall. In the early days, a lot of Japanese families lived there but by the 1930s, there were a lot of Filipinos living in the hotel… maybe because we were so close to the Rizal dance hall on the corner. My mother-in-law and Mrs. Matsudaira took care of the laundry in our hotel and my father-in-law did the

accounting and management. He also owned and operated the Atlas Theater business that was across the street. When the war came, they took Seita to Missoula and we went to Minidoka. We'd been gone for a few years and the new managers [who worked for West and Wheeler Real Estate] didn't care for the hotel in the same way that we did...it made a difference to the condition of the hotel. When we met with Mr. Wheeler to ask about managing it again, he told us that it was all run-down and that we wouldn't want it now. It wasn't the same and we couldn't go back...losing the hotel in the way that we did broke my father-in-law's heart.[36]

Like Seita Aoki, who died in 1947 at age 53, the Tokita family lost their father in October 1948 to complications of what was later diagnosed as an advanced case of diabetes. After so much hardship and nearly three years living in the "Hunt Hotel," the family had just purchased the New Lucky Hotel at Maynard and Weller shortly before Kamekichi Tokita's death. As a young widow with eight children, Haruko Tokita, stayed with the only profession that she knew and that was residential hotel management. With the loss of their father, **Yuzo Tokita** remembered the hard work, long hours, and a moment in his childhood that helped encourage their mother.

Sometimes we'd find a few coins in the playfield near the hotel...but one day, I found a small Buddha statue...a face of a monk, a *dharmasa*. The story of the image was that he was a monk who prayed in the mountains and who sat in one position for so long that he couldn't move. If he was pushed over, he would always sit back up, stationary, and strong. I showed the little statue to our mother and she was so happy and asked where I found it. She told me that she knew that from that time on, things would be okay for us. She placed it at papa's altar in our hotel and alongside our picture of Jesus, Mary, and Joseph...she prayed at both every day and so did we.[37]

Through discriminatory legislation, the Great Depression, war, incarceration, and the pain of personal family loss, the Japanese American community returned and retained a steadfast foothold in the hotel economy that built Nihonmachi and Seattle's low-income housing alternative. The 1959 receipt records of the SJHAA indicate that the Japanese in Seattle were controlling over 8,000 residential hotel rooms in the downtown and throughout the city with 53% of these, or over 4,300 rooms, located south of Yesler Way.

PAYING THE PRICE: DANCE HALLS AND CABARETS

In addition to the rise in SRO hotel construction and associated commercial services near the turn of the twentieth century, there were land and business uses that drew people from other parts of the city and that were interspersed throughout the neighborhood and in some of the hotel buildings. Neighborhood businesses offered an opportunity to leave the small and spare rooms of a hotel to engage in the active life of the community. In part, the vice district included the operation of speakeasies, restaurants, bars and musical clubs, most of which had dancing.

In the early years of development, the Restricted District, dominated by William Chappell's hotels, the neighborhood dance halls, and the Arcade Dance Hall, was partially responsible for perpetuating a broad assumption that dancing was equated with liquor and that all dance hall women were nothing more than sex workers.[38] Proof to the contrary was the responsibility of club owners and it was believed by the City Council that any legitimate business would have no problem passing through a "gauntlet" of investigation and regulation.

The city updated its ordinance on dance halls in 1914, changing the previous classification of dancing and liquor establishments as a punishable "nuisance" into an activity that could be regulated via police control. The new classification determined conduct, a minimum age requirement for female admission, proper lighting of the facility, and a license requirement. Dance halls were divided into categories of those that taught dance, those that had a dance that was controlled by a club or fraternal organization, or those considered to be cabarets. The latter was the more problematic when it came to regulation because any eating establishment could include dancing as an incidental and not a primary activity, and as such it would not fall under the license requirement as a dance hall.

In 1917, Seattle was one of forty-seven cities that were surveyed as part of a national study of prostitution. Published by the Bureau of Social Hygiene, the findings indicated that it was easy to find sex workers in dance halls; one only had to ask a bartender, waiter, or porter. The report also cautioned that "the cabaret and open dance floor was...a particularly dangerous attraction for young people...and that the majority of halls were controlled by liquor interests.[39] In fact, of the forty cities surveyed for specific businesses that attracted vice, Seattle was one of eight where dance halls were found to be vice resorts.[40]

A 1919 report by the Women's Social Hygiene Department of the Washington State Board of Health found that the city's policemen could not have the best interest of the citizenry if they were hired by dance hall managers in their off-duty time. Without further description, the findings only referred to payment of dance instruction as "not desirable."[41] Three cabarets, all of which were owned by non-Asians, were surveyed south of Yesler Way: the City Grill and the Columbus that were in old Chinatown, and the Little Dreamland Cabaret that was in Chappell's St. Paul Hotel at Sixth Avenue South and South King Street. In part, the report found that the

> "Little Dreamland" Cabaret is a low rambling, shabby white building in the old trap door part of Seattle. . . . The place resembled pictures of gambling dens one sees in "movies" [with] twenty or thirty round bare tables, a little raised platform for the orchestra, a bar, and a space of floor for dancing. . . . The only women. . .were those who were evidently in the employ of the cabaret. There were five or six of these women, who at the arrival of each new man, would go over and sit down and order at his expense. . .most of the men seemed too doped, too unintelligent to know what had taken place. . . . No doubt most of the profits of the place are, as in the old Alaska rush days, made by exploitation. The costumes. . .were so shabby and unattractive that they seemed rather disgusting. Perhaps it was due to the hard lined and almost fiercely painted faces of the girls. The songs were old and the voices hard and unpleasing. The worst thing about the cabaret was the degraded, degenerate class of patrons. . .the utter lifelessness and sordidness about the whole place. In fact, everyone, dancers, singers, and patrons, seemed to appear absolutely disinterested and indifferent.[42]

While surveys of the condition and activities of dance halls were evaluating morality, the 18th Amendment to the Constitution was ratified in 1920, declaring that the sale of alcohol would be prohibited and that the country would be "dry." In thirst and defiance, the means of making and selling liquor became a large illegal business in towns and cities across America, one that was both dangerous and profitable for otherwise unemployed workers. The 1920s were christened with bootleg whiskey, speakeasies, and gambling and dance halls where drinks could be served by young women of the establishments. While Seattle grappled with the enforcement of national temperance, the city was also being challenged with national hygiene reports and local morals committees that were looking at the great potential for decay and human degradation if uses that were common to the Restricted District were allowed to continue. The dance hall became a place for sociological study and numerous investigations by mayors, city council people, clergy, and private interest groups. It launched over thirty years of public meetings and experimentation with various ordinances and regulatory measures for any "likely" business where dancing might occur.

Councilwoman Bertha Landes was a particularly outspoken and relentless opponent of Seattle's dance halls and was a staunch proponent of a "dry" Seattle. [43] After decades of open policies and half-hearted efforts to address vice in the city, Seattle was tainted with a reputation as a prime location for graft and corruption across the country. Landes and the council were going to change this by closely examining changes to the dancing ordinance.

The first effort began when Landes invited three of the thirty-one girls from the Liberty Dance Hall to her home in 1922, in what *The Seattle Times* referred to as a "heart-to-heart discussion of alleged vice conditions" and one that she had found both "pleasant" and "enlightening."[44] Just days after the meeting, Landes was elected as chair of a committee of moral reform that had been organized as the Seattle Federation of Churches and consisting of members of thirty of Seattle's churches. In her double role as committee chair and councilwoman, Landes did not excuse herself from discussion or votes on policies involving dancing. She advocated for a change in the dance ordinance that would give discretion to the City Council in revoking or approving a business license. Robert Hesketh, chair of the council's License Committee, was fully supportive of the action, declaring that "the days of the dance hall are over."[45]

While Mayor Edwin Brown was relying on the council to make decisions that would satisfy the business representatives of the Seattle Council of Churches, there were also varying opinions on what really constituted a "dance hall" versus a "cabaret" and if the two should be addressed separately. The current ordinance was open to subjective interpretation. Brown's stance toward dance halls as part of the city was much more moderate, a position that caused regular friction with Landes and her constituents. It was Brown's opinion that the dance halls served an important function for working men and that it was not really the dance hall that was at fault and that more mindful management would take care of any concerns regarding the reputation of a business. The number of people who attended them and the licensing fees helped build the local economy.

By mid-December the King County grand jury was hearing testimonies of members of the Council of Churches, the mayor, and Police Captain E. C. Collier to determine whether proper evaluation and permitting had been followed in the issuance of licenses. The debate continued, and Landes, as a member of the city's license committee, drafted a comprehensive dance hall ordinance that had a number of provisions. If passed by city council, the ordinance would allow the comptroller office to have control over the issuing of licenses after approval by council and the mayor, an ability to inspect the business, and to require proof that the hiring of a matron as approved by the chief of police had been done in order to monitor the dance hall establishment. Final approval would result in an ordinance for the applicant business. Sunday dancing would be prohibited in all venues and on other days dance halls would close at 12:30 a.m. Dance halls that focused on male patrons only would be prohibited, which affected at least three dance halls south of Yesler Way. Women would now be required to be charged an entrance fee equal to those that were already being paid by men. The greatest measure of control came with cafés that were previously exempt from dance hall regulations. Under the new ordinance, the guidelines and requirements for licensing cafés would be the same.

The new legislation was "highly necessary and desirable" according to advocates such as the Women's Civic Club and the PTA, and viewed as "vicious class legislation" by opponents representing the dance halls and the local Musician's Union.[46] Even more than public dancing, Seattle's moral standing as a city was up for challenge, as was whether it would continue to retain an "open policy" when it came to conducting businesses that were considered to be harbingers of vice. The ordinance, referred to as the "Mrs. Henry B. Landes Dance Ordinance," supported the more restrictive stance based on recommendations that were made by previous reports on national hygiene and public health. Attorneys for the Hippodrome and the Dreamland dance-teaching studios protested what could have been the end of their lucrative businesses. Public hearings were contentious and in one incident a local businessman referred to all of the women dance hall employees as "scarlet women," while the *Seattle Post-Intelligencer* described the "flushed faces and flashing eyes of girls from the dance halls...in a murmur of protest... as a chorus of hisses and cat-calls."[47]

With broad support from Landes' constituents and in a five to three vote, the ordinance was passed by council on 20 February 1923.[48] Any violation of the ordinance would be subject to a $100 fine and/or thirty days in jail and forfeiture of one's license to operate.

The law went into effect in April 1923, which also marked the beginning of more trouble as the city was met with resistance from the dance hall employees and supporters. Various suits were filed against the city, including a joint complaint when the north downtown Hippodrome and Butler Hotel Café filed suit against the city in King County Superior Court for prohibiting Sunday dancing. There was also a debate as to whether private dances held in public halls should be considered "public" or "private" since the latter would be considered a nonprofit event. Considerable discussion took place on how dancing on boats and barges should be classified. The question of monitoring and enforcing conduct came to the forefront as businesses with dancing applied for licenses.

The basement-located Dreamland Dance Hall had the reputation of being an establishment of the "lowest order" and one where a patron could expect to find female companionship and be led to either the St. Paul Hotel in the top two floors of the building or the Diamond Hotel next door. *The Seattle Daily Times* noted that the most serious charge against the Dreamland was that it catered to a large and predominantly Filipino crowd.

> [The] Dreamland [is] the slum of slums...old rugs at the entrance, a few artificial palms, paper garlands and trellis work of wood give the hall a rather gay though tawdry appearance. The walls are dirty...and around them are a lot of old oil paintings, formerly hung in tenderloin saloons of old days. A policeman takes tickets at the entrance. There were twenty-five girls in the place.... Many of them were mere children. But the principal patrons of the place, we were told, are Filipinos. We saw fifty or more Filipinos in the hall. They far outnumbered the whites. No girl solicited us to dance or buy a drink. The dancing was proper. The music was good. The central floor was good. The bar was in evidence, but it was doing no business. We saw no girls drinking with men and none soliciting men to buy drinks or to dance.[49]

While the mayor and council had conflicting opinions on which businesses should be denied licenses, too many denials would open the door for further challenges and lawsuits. The council gave approval for the Dreamland Dance Hall to receive its license.[50]

While the Liberty Dance Hall, which was owned by the Liberty Amusement Company, was considered by the mayor to be a "legitimate" dance hall operation "below the line," it was not without its problems. As its license came up for renewal, stockholders, citizens, and employees attended the council meetings in order to lobby for the Liberty to remain open. Without any tangible evidence on violations of the Dance Ordinance, council members Campbell and Landes attempted to challenge whether the building itself met city codes for construction. The decision was weeks in coming and barely passed with five votes for and four votes against renewal.[51]

In 1924, Seattle amended the dance hall ordinance so that dance halls would now be included as one of a number of places of "amusement."[52] While passing the council vote, Mayor Brown did not sign or veto the law, letting it pass, instead, by default. The new ordinance addressed licensing and conduct of public dance halls, cabarets, massage parlors, public bath houses, and card, billiard, and pool rooms in a collective title. With respect to dance halls, the ordinance forbade "prostitutes, drinking, liquor, and narcotics to be on or about the premises," all of which were broadly defined. Any rumor of bootleg whiskey on a dance hall premises would provide an opportunity to investigate other requirements and potentially revoke a license. Women were forbidden to leave the dance floor at any time during employment, and in order to keep an eye on activities in the hall, no one was allowed a "pass" that would allow them to leave the hall and then return the same evening. The previous provision that skirted the issue of cafes needing dance hall licenses was also addressed and now required a "Café Dance License" that had the same approval process and requirements.

Before the 1924 ordinance, cabarets had been handled under separate ordinances. Now they would be included as a business of amusement. The definition of a "cabaret" continued to be "a place of public resort or assemblage, operated for gain or profit, where refreshments of any kind are served, and where theatrical performances, exhibitions, shows, vocal music or exhibition dances are maintained or permitted."[53] Any indication that a cabaret had "box house" spaces that were being used was strictly forbidden.[54] No licenses would be issued to individual applicants who were not citizens of the United States or to corporations where the majority of stockholders were not citizens. By definition, virtually any business with even a potential for dancing could arguably be considered a "cabaret."

The 1924 amended ordinance included creation of a "Supervisor of Dance," a position that would be filled from among the officers and selected by the chief of police. The supervisor would investigate the validity of the business and report to the city council, investigate any complaints filed against a dance hall, keep a log of visitations, and ensure that each dance hall had an approved chaperone on the premises. The chaperone monitored all dances, but having a matron or chaperone that was approved by the police department was not a requirement to receive a cabaret license. If all of the conditions were satisfactorily met, the applicant would be granted a license through city council approval and an ordinance specific to the applicant and business would be passed in recognition of the approved license. A properly lit dance hall was a requirement to facilitate the work of the chaperone and "shadow and moonlight dances [were] prohibited and declared to be unlawful."[55]

The taxi dance hall was both a popular and suspiciously-viewed enterprise in the 1920s and 1930s. In Seattle, it was specifically scrutinized when Landes became the city's short-term social reform mayor between 1926 and 1928.

Unlike other dance halls or cabarets, taxi dance halls were blatant when it came to soliciting money for a dance partner. It was a "closed dance hall" and operated as a business where a man could purchase an infinite number of tickets for ten cents each in order to dance with women employees whom he chose to be his dance partner.[56] The taxi dancer was paid through the ticket sales.[57] On collecting the ticket, a woman would get half the cost of the ticket with the remainder going to the house. As the dancing commenced, a manager on duty would walk through the dance floor and collect the tickets to keep track of the tally. A woman could also get as much as 25% of the liquor bill total for the evening.[58] On a good night, a dancer could earn over $5.00, which was estimated to be over twice the earnings of a store clerk. Thursdays through Saturdays were the best nights for salary and tips at the taxi dance halls and particularly during the cannery off-season from November through March. It was lucrative for the establishment owner, and it made a living for the women who danced and for the musicians who relied on the regular gigs that they would play as the dance hall orchestra. In one short night, a laborer's weekly earnings could be spent on tickets.

Music and any dancing in public places was considered a potential venue for, and indication of, the presence of other vice. Along with prostitution, dance halls and music raised the same moral concerns as drinking and gambling, particularly since these activities were typically combined in the storefront businesses of the hotel buildings. Whether they were community dances such as those that were sponsored by organizations and in places such as the Finnish or Washington Halls, or in the night clubs of Seattle, the dance hall was a place of courtship for Filipino men. As such, the dance hall became a catalyst for the revival of segregation politics as people viewed the setting that incubated mixed-race relationships.

In an early sociological study of taxi dance halls, reflection was also given to the characteristics of Filipino immigration, and the anti-miscege-nation laws in California, Arizona, Idaho, Nevada, and Oregon that left little alternatives for companionship outside of such establishments.

> These young [Filipino] men, more than half of them under twenty-five years of age when entering America and very few married, are quickly attracted to these halls. Alone in a foreign land, far from the rather simple family and community life in the Philippines... to which they have been accustomed, and with very few young women of their own race in the United States, it is not surprising that many have been drawn to these resorts...the all important factor of race prejudice must not be overlooked. The Filipino finds himself in a racially hostile society where not only his occupational and professional opportunities are restricted but where he is denied the usual social contacts with young women.... The Filipino gravitates to the taxi-dance hall because he is already familiar with [them]. Under the name of "cabarets" taxi-dance halls are...found in the larger cities of the Philippines. They are run on much the same plan as the American taxi-dance halls.[59]

Landes's crusade against taxi dance halls culminated in a 1926 amend-ment to the 1924 ordinance that made it illegal for a dance hall owner or any woman in its employ to be paid as a dancing partner by salary or commission. An owner or manager who knowingly allowed it stood to lose his business license and could not reapply for a license for one year. In the next three years, attempts were made to keep the taxi dance halls open, but as legal actions against the city were exhausted, all but one of the dime-a-dance businesses remained closed. Subsequent amendments to the ordinance reaffirmed prohibition in that no giving or selling of alcoholic beverages would be tolerated in any dance hall.

Though damaged by Landes's crusade and the ordinance, the dance hall business interest was not completely eradicated. Organized in 1929, the Woman's Dancing Entertainer's Union (WDEU), Local 17943 was officially affiliated with the American Federation of Labor.[60] The union would enable the regulation of the profession with a licensing fee that would help prevent women from entering the profession who were using dancing as a front for prostitution. The preamble of the WDEU was to "create better understanding of social integrity, working conditions and wages, inspire mutual protection and confidence of members, and develop protective resources for ourselves and dependents."[61] By the early 1930s, there were 300 members of the union. Union officers were elected and rules of the organization provided that a member pledge to stay sober, prompt, and arrive at work on time.

In October 1929, the WDEU and AFL came together before the Central Labor Council to address the high number of unemployed musicians, dancers, and janitors from the dance hall ordinances. Charles Doyle, as secretary of the council, noted that after visiting some of the dance halls, "the whole trouble [was coming] from the fact that a majority of the patrons were Filipinos" and that one solution to reopening the dance halls might happen with "the under-standing that Filipinos and other dark-skinned peoples be denied admittance."[62]

At the end of Landes' term in office, Frank Edwards, who shared the same viewpoint that dance halls were a "moral menace," was elected as the city's mayor in 1928.[63] Under his administration, the taxi dance halls were ulti-mately closed through police enforcement of the ordinance that forbade hiring women to solicit dances for money. The effort to accomplish these closures was a difficult one since there were attempts to circumvent the ordinance. The Columbia dance hall had attempted to put the selection of dance partners as "men's choice" dances and placed signs in the dance hall that said "Solicitation not allowed—men select their own partners." The Breakers, Columbia, and Bungalow dance halls ultimately had their permits revoked.

In 1932, Earnest Dowd, who had been the manager of the Liberty (1922) and The Bungalow (1928) dance halls, was hired to manage The Breakers as it attempted to reopen at 102 Cherry Street with the support of the Musicians' Association of Seattle. Many of the dance hall operators attempted to reopen with a provision that women would be salaried and not paid on a commission basis or through a share of collected tickets. In the end, the council and police chief held firm that no dance hall would be allowed to hire women who solicited dance partners.

The victory of the taxi dance hall closures only lasted for a short time. New city administration in the coming years had a more tolerant viewpoint on dance establishments.[64] This, combined with the 1933 repeal of prohibition, helped to revive the dance hall business in Seattle. In October 1936, the Dance

Rizal Club on the second floor with entrance on King Street with the New Manila and Estigoy Cafés and a barber shop along 6th Avenue South. [Courtesy King County Assessor's Office, Property Record Cards, 1937–1973, Puget Sound Branch, Washington State Archives]

Hall License provision that prevented women from working on commission in dance halls was repealed.

In the 1930s, some of the more popular night clubs and dancing halls south of Yesler were the Black and Tan, which catered to Blacks, Whites, Asian Americans, and other minorities, and the Hong Kong Chinese Society Club that was commonly known as the "Bucket of Blood" and located in the Mar Hotel.[65]

THE RIZAL CLUB...MABUHAY![66]

The Casino and Columbia dance halls that were close to the core of old Chinatown were favorite locations of the Filipino community, but between 1935 and 1942, the Rizal Club on the second floor of 605 King was *the* place to go for Filipino men.[67] Its location was ideal as it had a barber shop and a couple of cafés at the ground level that included The New Manila Café and the Estigoy Café.[68] **Delores Sibonga**, whose parents owned the Estigoy Café on 6th Avenue South between King and Weller streets, recalled the liveliness of the café.

MAP 5-7 : *Filipino Business Map – 1941 [Author]*

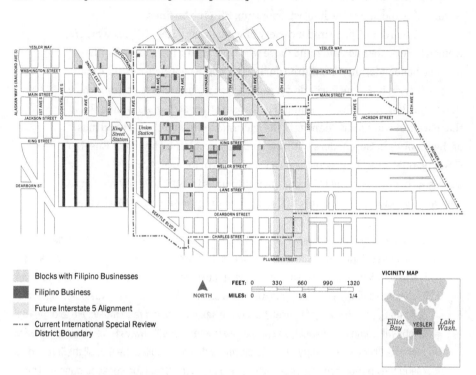

Blocks with Filipino Businesses

Filipino Business

Future Interstate 5 Alignment

---- Current International Special Review
District Boundary

VICINITY MAP

FEET: 0   330   660   990   1320
NORTH   MILES: 0   1/8   1/4

Elliot YESLER *Lake*
Bay   *Wash.*

We had meal tickets for the laborers that would be punched for each meal...a lot of times
my parents would give them credit for a meal and for the most part, they paid their bill
when they came back to Seattle at the end of the cannery season. We kept mail for a lot
of the Filipino workers since they would stay in different hotels and didn't have a regular
permanent address. In the summer, the hotel rooms would be so hot and stifling...a lot
of the Filipinos played musical instruments and so they'd come to the café. At the front
and near the juke box there was room for them to play—bass, violin, mandolin, guitar,
and harmonica...such incredible music. When we would make deliveries to the hotels,
you could often hear the Manongs playing their guitars in their rooms as you walked up
the long staircases.[69]

The Rizal Club was a recreational escape. While there may not have
been an officially recognized Manilatown, there was definitely a concentrated
core of Filipino-operated and specialized businesses on South King Street

between 5th and 6th Avenue South in 1941. The Rizal Club was the heart of the community and one of the longest-operating Filipino businesses.

The Rizal Club hired a variety of women that included sex workers, women looking for husbands, and those who were trying to support families of parents, husbands, and/or children during the Depression years. Unlike many of the other clubs in the lower downtown, it was a place where patrons knew they would listen to a Filipino band. The Zapata Orchestra was a popular band that played at community dances in the fraternal halls, and the big band music of the Moonlight Serenaders with the smooth saxophone playing of Eusebio Francisco "Frank" Lopez Osias as a regular favorite. **Don Francisco Lopez Osias**'s father came to the US from the Philippines in 1929 to study medicine but had to abandon that dream during the Great Depression to earn a living.

> My dad was nineteen years old when he came to the United States. He worked in the canneries during the fishing season and in the offseason he was in California working in a bakery. While he was there, he was living with other young Filipino men in an SRO. They convinced him to go on the road with them as a musician. He was always learning how to do things and he taught himself to play the saxophone and read music. He told me that "jobs will come and go but if you play an instrument, you'll always have music to fall back on. You'll never be hungry." He was playing with a band called the Moonlight Serenaders and they performed in grange halls up and down the Coast for weekend dances. That's how he met my mother who was taking tickets at one of the dances in Cave Junction, Oregon. Eventually, she came to Seattle with a girlfriend and my dad came up here with the band. She was white, they were in love, and could legally marry in Seattle, which they did in 1933. Dad got a job managing the Yesler Apartments hotel and owned a grocery business. But at night, he played music. During Prohibition, speakeasies needed bands and Filipinos were their preferred choice. In Seattle, he played at the Rizal Club...and this was *the* place to go for entertainment. When you got to the main stairway, you'd have to check in your weapons—guns or knives—before you bought your tickets to dance. In those days, everyone was carrying weapons...they did this in the Philippines...and if you knew everyone had a weapon, you wouldn't mess with anyone and ironically, everyone felt safe. They played six nights a week and non-stop from sundown to sunrise...that's how you'd keep money coming in for the taxi dancers and the house. Two musicians could break at any one time and go and lay down in the back to rest. A lot of the girls who danced there were from broken homes, some were prostitutes...but a lot of longstanding relationships and marriages came from those dances.[70]

The Moonlight Serenaders at the Rizal Club. Eusebio Francisco Osias with his saxophone (far left). [Courtesy Don Osias]

The Osias family outside the Yesler Apartment Hotel. Front row, left to right: children, Don and older sister, Anita. Back row, left to right: family friend with father Francisco Osias, and mother Letha Jane Tresham Osias. The hotel management was registered under Letha Tresham. [Courtesy Don Osias]

In April 1935, the *Philippine Advocate* reported on a celebration that had occurred in the Rizal Club. The newspaper gave great detail of the taxi-dancing that was taking place and the social standing of the women dancers who awaited patrons.

> ...The Rizal Dance Hall is a melting pot, where one's money, health and honor melt in a progress of social decay. Taxi-dancing is not a healthy amusement.... Many taxi-dancers are not physically and morally healthy. Some of the self-reconciled inmates of the Rizal Dance Hall [are] stray girls, washed up ladies of joy, destitute widows.... Undoubtedly, most of the taxi dancers have their own social pride and family background of which they come to think sometimes. Perhaps circumstances had initiated them to play as amateurs in the 10-cent-store of amusement. However, the lure of the profession won their hearts, until life meant nothing to them but the glitter of the ballroom, the drowsy music and the warmth of an embrace. There are sweet professional taxi dancers who are dancing their way through life, supporting an invalid non-employed husband and a couple of more offspring. These command my admiration for they are, of a nobler sort, possessing a morally sound body and a morally sound mind....[71]

The Rizal did not go through the normal channels to acquire a license to operate any kind of dance facility. While the repeal of the taxi-dancing ordinance did not occur until at least eighteen months after it was written, it is likely that the Rizal, like the majority of the businesses in the heart of Asian American Seattle were "paying out a great deal of money...with the cop on the beat [coming] in for his free round of drinks three or four times a night."[72] The Rizal was able to remain open and avoid being cited by the supervisor of the Dance.[73]

The rhythm of day-to-day life for the Filipino men on a typical day in Chinatown had little variation, according to the editor of the *Philippine Advocate*. The paper highlighted the contribution of Filipino businesses to the daily scene of Chinatown with the notable mention of Filipino dance halls and specifically the Rizal Club.[74]

> Eight o'clock in the morning. Chinatown is just dead—dead as a deserted ballroom in the morning after the night before. Ten o'clock and the crowd begins to form around street corners and in the lobby of the Alps Hotel. By noon King Street is like a barrio street in the Philippines.... Filipino pool halls open about this time and the crowd begins their diversion of pool and cards. Gossips go the rounds. Labor's latest news is read

and discussed. Last night's date is reviewed and critically considered. Seven o'clock in the evening and the barber shops begin to get busy.... The crowd on King Street is augmented and Jackson Street is like Second Avenue during a parade...lotteries, the card games...pleasure and business become [sic] the order of the night. Ten o'clock in the evening. The tantalizing music at Rizal Hall tickles the eardrum and makes the feet itchy. The crowd moves around the corner and in the neighborhood. "There is pleasure in them thar [sic] houses" becomes a silent melody in the young men's hearts. One o'clock in the morning. Rizal Hall orchestra plays the "good-night" and Filipino sheiks with blondes and brunettes and half-ways come out still pleasure-bound. Atlas Theatre is just next block and is open all night. The chop suey houses are open until three o'clock in the morning. These places have seen dates made and remade, romances flourish and decline. Half-past three in the morning and the day is officially ended...."[75]

Other editorials and commentaries provided a picture of the allure of what was happening within the closed rooms and behind the building walls in what many passersby could not see. The Rizal Club took center focus again with the mystique of Chinatown attracting a diverse socio-economic population both in and out of the pan-Asian neighborhood.

Chinatown is essentially a part of the American city...the shadows of Chinatown beckon American society, for it has a superficial grandeur of its own which the superficial American wants to experience and possess....For Chinatown nourishes a cauldron of vice, where the Chinese, Negroes [sic], Japanese, Italians, Swedes, Americans and Filipinos are united in... mercenary feast. From 11:00 p.m. to 2:00 a.m. a parade of drunken couples...give color to the enchanting shadows of the Chinatown. Chop Suey—dancing and drinks! Under the subtle management of the Chinks [sic]....Amateurs of adventure from America's social register, come night after night to Chinatown where they can be nasty dames and nasty men...Nasty dames of the "houses" around the neighborhood, walk furtively at sundown with a pet lap dog stringed to one hand. A waft of perfumed air blows...Mae Westian [sic] hips wiggle on two feet at 8:00 p.m. towards the...center of Filipino pleasure—the Rizal Club Dance Hall. Stray girls, destitute widows, and washed up ladies of joy, furnish their streamlined waistlines to the lascivious embraces of the pleasure seekers. A piano, a drum and a saxophone create a frenzied harmony that inspires a dozen or more paired bodies, undulating in a passionate embrace while they trip haphazardly at the even tenor of the music. One has to live through experiences behind paneled doors to understand and see the tragic and comic exultation of life as staged in the grim shadows of Chinatown...."[76]

SHIFTING SETTLEMENTS OF
PAN-ASIAN SEATTLE

A very small number of Filipinos were in Washington State in the early years of their immigration: three in 1900 and seventeen in 1910. In 1920, the numbers had increased to 958 in the state with 458, or almost 48% of that total number, living in Seattle.[77] Given that the practice of engaging in Census counts commenced after 1 April of these decennial years, it is reasonable to assume that the figures did not include the high number of transient Filipino laborers who would have been in the city had the Census count not coincided with the seasonal work that took them out of Seattle. A 1927 labor report confirmed that "Seattle [had] a large floating population during the winter months [and that] each fall...Alaska turn[ed] thousands of men from the fisheries, canneries and mines" into the Seattle port along with "fruit pickers and packers of eastern Washington and the grain harvesters as far east as Montana [with an] estimated...twenty-thousand itinerant laborers here each year."[78]

What the Census numbers do begin to indicate is the beginning of a social and economically viable core of community settlement and services for these laborers and that there were opportunities and accommodations within the city that compelled some Filipinos to stay. There was never any doubt that the Filipino population and their businesses were a vibrant part of a growing pan-Asian district. [79]

As the number of Filipino businesses in Chinatown and Nihonmachi fluctuated from 1930 onward, *The Philippine American Chronicle* noted that "Usually the life of our business[es] is limited to a month. Any venture that survives [beyond] that time is in a safety zone. In the making of a reputation not only for themselves alone but for the people with which they are identified, [they] should be credited for the fine showing they have done."[80]

The Filipino businesses that developed south of Yesler Way were typically small in number and created a pattern of shifting settlement throughout Chinatown and Nihonmachi with commercial development primarily consisting of gambling clubs, barber shops, and restaurants, many of which occupied the storefronts of the hotel buildings. 1938 was one of the peak years for Filipino-owned businesses; twenty-eight were recorded south of Yesler Way, including nine barbers, eight cafés, four entertainment establishments that included gambling and dancing, three newspapers, two labor contractors,

and one each of a mercantile and grocery business. Of this total, seventeen were
located in residential hotel storefronts including the *Filipino Forum* as one of
Seattle's longest running Asian American newspapers (1928–1969).

The node of social interaction of the Filipino male community was
a part of Chinatown in front of the Alps Hotel. According to the *Philippine
Monthly Review*:

> ...the intersection of King Street and Eight[h] Avenue...is the only street in the city that
> is China.... Chinatown really never sleeps...it keeps awake at all hours of the day be-
> cause the dollar rolls in at all hours.... Expensive cars and luxurious limousines testify to
> Chinatown's prosperity, even in these days of economic reversions and Hooverian [sic]
> optimism. For Chinatown gets its money and does not care how it gets it, and expects
> you and me not to care.... The mystery that is Chinatown's fascinates and intrigues us.
> King Street is really a two-way street, the Orient and the Occident. Inscrutable Chinatown
> is slowly absorbing Western culture but at the same time keeping its own...and in the
> Yankee town of Seattle, only a few blocks away....[81]

There were two cores of the Seattle Filipino American community. If
you were married with a family, you'd settle in the Central District to the east
of Chinatown and Nihonmachi areas and around Immaculate Conception
and Maryknoll Catholic churches. But the vast majority of the predominantly
single and male Filipino community lived in the neighborhood residential
hotels "below the line" that included the N-P, Eastern, Publix, New Central,
Crescent Hotels, and the Hotel Puget Sound. Kinship caused many, if not all,
of the Filipino families to open up their homes at various times to relatives and
people who shared regional ties from the Philippines that included Illocanos,
who represented the majority of Filipino Seattle, Pangasinans, Tagalogs, and
Visayans. Kinship and a sense of hospitality also extended itself to the possibility of a stay in a residential hotel free of charge if you were willing to share the
floor space of a small room with multiple occupants. It was this same regional
connection that was experienced in the Chinese and Japanese communities
as they gave assistance to community members who were in need.[82]

In terms of 1930 population expansion, the number of Chinese continued to hover around 1,300 people while the Japanese population reached
over 8,400, an increase of almost 600 people since the 1920 Census. As the
Japanese population increased, most of their new businesses were located

MAP 5-8: *Chinese and Japanese Businesses – 1910 [Author]*

Blocks with Chinese/
Japanese Businesses

Chinese Business

Japanese Business

Future Interstate 5 Alignment

Current International Special
Review District Boundary

NORTH

FEET: 0   330   660   990   1320
MILES: 0   1/8   1/4

in the commercial storefronts of the residential hotels with at least six of the Chinese restaurants being Japanese owned and operated.[83] Between 1920 and 1930, the numbers of Filipinos had more than tripled to 3,480 in the state with 46% of this number, or 1,614, in Seattle, but the figure also shows how few Filipina women were part of this ethnic community profile in this latter year and that they represented only 3.2% of the population. While this period marks an increase in numbers for this community, their arrival in America was also the beginning of a very stressful time as both businesses and individuals responded to the stark hardships of the Great Depression in 1929. "Unskilled cannery positions occupied by Filipino workers dropped by 40 percent" and competition with the masses of other ethnic and Caucasian unemployed workers made landing seasonal agricultural work even more difficult.[84] In addition to the loss of positions, pre-Depression wages for work in the salmon canneries were $60 to $100 a month, which plummeted to less than half that amount after the Great Depression began.

Geographically, the new Chinatown at 7th Avenue South and South King Street was about the same modest size as it had been at the prior 2nd Avenue South and South Washington Street node, with about ten Chinese businesses still located at the first Chinatown core. Between 1910 and 1938, there was a notable shift of these two communities with respect to the number of Chinese and Japanese businesses and the incorporation of Filipino businesses amid Japanese enterprises. All three of these communities lived in and among one another, creating a scattered geographic pattern in pan-Asian Seattle.

The foothold of the flagship buildings of old Chinatown took a dramatic turn in 1926 when the City of Seattle began plans to provide a direct connection between the downtown business district and the train stations. Beginning with a discussion by members of the business community and ending with the city's exercise of eminent domain, the estimated million-dollar property procurement project included a new fire station, modern street lighting, and a diagonal street that would connect Yesler Way to Jackson Street between the two train stations. By May 1927, condemnation hearings were underway for the new 2nd Avenue Extension, and in less than a year, the city's Board of Public Works served notices of vacation to building owners whose structures would be affected by the alignment, including lots 3 and 4 that housed the 1889 Chinese-constructed SROs in the Lexington, Phoenix, and Chin Gee Hee

MAP 5-9: *Chinese, Japanese, and Filipino American Business – 1938 [Author]*

Blocks with Japanese, Filipino, or Chinese Businesses

Chinese Business

Japanese Business

Filipino Business

Future Interstate 5 Alignment

Current International Special Review District Boundary

NORTH

FEET: 0   330   660   990   1320

MILES: 0   1/8   1/4

VICINITY MAP

Elliot Bay   YESLER   Lake Wash.

The construction of the 2nd Avenue Extension and the Razing of Old Chinatown. On both images #1 is the Lexington Hotel, #2 is the Phoenix Hotel, and #3 is the Chin Gee Hee Building. The dashed line in the right photo overlays the previous location of all three buildings before the alignment diagonally connected to Jackson Street, near the King Street Station. [Courtesy Seattle Municipal Archives, Photos 2886 and 3455]

buildings. Ordinance 50867 stated that no part of the project would be paid from the city's general fund and that the entire project cost would be paid in assessment fees levied on those properties that would benefit from such a roadway.[85] The Wa Chong buildings that were now under the ownership of partners of Chun Lung Key received a total of $84,000 for the land and "adjustments" to the buildings that included severely altered facades and the entire removal of the residential hotel floors of the Phoenix Hotel. The Lexington Hotel retained two of its floors, but lost the entryway and decorative cornice that had displayed the building's name and function as an SRO. The Chin Gee Hee building, which was now under ownership of the Kong Yick Corporation, sacrificed a smaller amount of land with a "clipped" corner of the building that included $4,840 in land and building alteration damages. With other neighboring Chinese-owned properties that were affected to a smaller degree, the total property damages to old Chinatown totaled an excess of $91,000 and one-tenth of the moneys paid in condemnation. The price of lost property was compounded by an even more severe loss of old Chinatown's identity.

As the number of Japanese businesses continued to grow throughout the area, the near-poetic 1935 editorials entitled "I Cover Chinatown" in the *Philippine Advocate* reflected on international politics and overseas military action between Japan and China, and how a similar spatial phenomenon was happening with the expansion of Seattle's Nihonmachi.

> A carbon copy of Japanese encroachment in Manchuria is noticeable by any impersonal observer of Chinatown. The best locations of Chinatown's business district bear the Nippon trademark. Hotels, groceries, hardware stores, drug stores, restaurants, medical and dental, as well as cannery and labor contractor's offices out-number and out-influence the Chinese signs in their chop suey houses and well-disguised lottery "stores."

> The Filipinos have their own modest contributions to the superficial grandeur of Chinatown. Pool halls, dance halls, coffee shops and barber shops.[86]

HOTEL AND HOOVERVILLE

With few Filipino businesses as part of the neighborhood, there were even fewer Filipinos involved in SRO hotel ownership and management. No papers of incorporation were filed in the state that would have allowed for Filipino corporate ownership of a hotel building as had been done by Chinese and Japanese in Seattle. There was some involvement with hotel management by Filipinos that occurred because of or after WWII and directly related to the loss of hotel businesses by Japanese who were forced to leave. For the most part, Filipino-operated hotels were typically of short duration. In 1935, the Hotel Patron, located at 3rd Avenue South and South Maynard Street amid the Japanese-owned businesses and hotels, announced its grand opening as the "only hotel managed by Filipinos."[87] While it was Filipino-operated, it was not the "only" Filipino Hotel as the advertisement indicated, nor did its single year of operation prove to have business longevity. The Havana Hotel building at 618-1/2 South Jackson Street that had been built in 1900 and was saved and elevated from the Jackson Street Regrade project had been under Japanese management from 1929 until 1948, when the hotel was purchased and briefly operated under Filipino management as the Leyte Hotel.[88]

The most noted Filipino hotel management occurred with two SROs in the heart of new Chinatown, one of which became the longest-running hotel business by a Filipino entrepreneur. The LVM Hotel business was under the management of Valeriano N. Sarusal from 1925 through 1930. Named in honor of the three regions of the Philippines (Luzon, Visayas, and Mindanao), Sarusal leased the hotel space from the Kong Yick Investment Corporation. The West Kong Yick building had always functioned as a workingman's hotel, but by the 1920s, exclusion law had effectively depleted the community and stopped Chinese laborers from leaving and returning to the United States. There simply was no need for a 158-room hotel that specifically catered to Chinese immigrants.

Sarusal duplicated the successful formula of operating a labor contracting business and renting hotel rooms to workers. Along with the hotel, he started the LVM Trading Company and the Fish Cannery and Labor Contractors, Local 102 that was initially located in the Rainier Heat and Power Company building. The Contracting Agency operated under various other names, including the Filipino Employment Agency (1927–28), the LVM Employment Agency (1929), and the Filipino Reliable Employment Bureau (1930), all of which were at the same address and operated by Sarusal.[89] By 1930 these businesses were relocated to a storefront space in the Chinese tong-owned American Hotel across the street from the West Kong Yick building and a more convenient location for the Filipino workers living in the LVM Hotel. A second hotel under Filipino management in the core of Chinatown was the Mint Hotel from 1951 through 1954.[90]

Occasionally, one of the more spare apartment buildings would function like an SRO, offering single-night stays, as was the case with the Yesler Apartment Hotel in the 1940s. The most noted intersection of the lives of Filipinos in Seattle with the residential hotels came with their patronage of off-season accommodations as a majority population of transient agricultural, lumber, and fishing industry labor and in their support of the commercial storefronts where specific goods and services catered to the young laborers. The Murakami family's Higo Store, as one of the largest variety stores of Japantown, regularly carried shoelaces, work shirts, and shoe repair kits that were the most popular purchases of Filipino workers.

Like the Chinese and Japanese immigrants before them, Filipinos became part of the annual northerly migration from the US to Alaska during the late spring to early fall months of every year. Known as the Alaskeros, the Filipino Alaskan cannery workers quickly came to outnumber all other ethnic groups in that line of employment within a decade. Filipinos represented four times the number of Chinese cannery workers and over twice the number of Japanese by the end of the 1920s, but had a much smaller share of the market when it came to the labor contracting businesses that were responsible for salary negotiations and caring for the welfare of their workers.[91] When the work season ended and with their earnings in their pockets, the Filipinos would return to the cities and remain in the residential hotels of Chinatown, Nihonmachi, and Pioneer Square, sometimes working temporary jobs or waiting for the next season of work to begin.[92] For those few who were lucky enough to have families in Seattle and some financial backing, there was the possibility of being a tenant of a commercial business in one of the hotel building storefronts or finding employment in service industries, such as cooks, waiters, or domestics.

In many ways, the decline of jobs and wages, the high number of unemployed hourly workers, and a history of poor working conditions and treatment in the canneries and agricultural belts of the West helped launch the grassroots dreams of early community labor organizers into powerful social change. Discussions of organizing took place in hotel lobbies, cafés, restaurants, and on the street corners of the SRO hotel core at 7th Avenue South and South King Street. The early attempts for recognition and acceptance by the American Federation of Labor (AFL) in the mid-1920s proved to be unsuccessful, partly because, like the Chinese and the Japanese before them, Filipinos were targeted as the cause for few jobs and low wages. The Filipinos planned and organized efforts to have a voice in the politics of economic development.

Seattle's Filipino population may have been small, but the commitment to be heard and to organize was very strong. A core group of Filipino agricultural workers started the Filipino Laborers' Union (FLA) in Seattle in 1930, the same year that the Cannery and Agricultural Workers Industrial Union (CAWIU) was organized in California.[93] While the success and recognition of Seattle Filipinos came with their hard-won acceptance into the AFL as the Cannery Workers and Farm Laborers Union (CWFLU), Local 18257 in June 1933, the struggle to define the roles of contractors, laborers, and the division of Filipino, Chinese, and Japanese along ethnic lines would last for another five years as the focus of union membership and goals became based less on ethnicity and more on the labor itself.

While Filipino labor unions were clearly identified with organizing better employment conditions, salaries and fair treatment for their workers, they fought alongside other Asian American groups and lobbied for issues that affected all of them. In April 1938, the Hotel, Restaurant Local Union 844, which included 200 Filipino, Japanese, and Chinese members, was in negotiation with Seattle businesses. Salvador Lazo served as the local leader. Seattle Filipino newspapers such as the *Cosmopolitan Courier, Philippine Advocate,* and *Philippine American Chronicle* served as the voices for labor and social justice. The newspapers addressed the issues of gambling as an activity that did not contribute to the welfare of the workers, and attempted to unite the efforts of pan-Asian Seattle workers against the unscrupulous practices of labor contractors and openly protest state-initiated legislation that would infringe on civil liberties.

As labor struggles continued in the city, other civil liberties were also being challenged in the state. In the absence of an anti-miscegenation law that would bar Asian Americans from marrying white women, King County Congressman Dorian Todd introduced a bill to the Legislature in 1935 that would prevent and declare as illegal any marriage between whites and "...Negroes, Mongolians or 'Oceanics' in the State of Washington."[94] A committee of four from the local labor union went to Olympia to voice opposition to the proposed anti-miscegenation H.B. 301. Rallying attention and support to defeat the bill, representatives announced that it was "unfair for any government to manage the affairs of one's heart" and that the "bill was unconstitutional in the sense that it deprive[d] either party of their rights in the pursuit of happiness."[95]

The Cannery Workers and Farm Laborers' Union also initiated a fight to "save Filipino workers from losing all of their wages at Chinese gambling establishments."[96] Opportunities for gambling were too easily available in and near the residential hotels. **Union President Virgil Duyungan** testified at the Department Efficiency Committee Investigation of Gambling, Vice and Liquor Conditions hearing in the summer of 1935, telling the investigators of the severity of the situation for the Filipino workers when wages were lost gambling and the threat of homelessness, hunger, and the potential increase in crime that could result.

> ...when [Filipino workers] are broke, they become vagrants in the streets... last year we had three hundred in the bread line, and [in only the first half of] this year we [already have] 175.... they become petty thieves...pick-pockets and purse snatchers and burglars, and a brush of them now are in jail. [If these places were closed], my people

would be encouraged to save up their money, and would be able to go back home to
the old country…[then] the majority of them, would have a chance to go back to school
and make a decent life.[97]

In a follow-up letter and petition to Mayor Charles L. Smith, Police
Chief Walter B. Kirtley and members of the City Council Vice and Gambling
Investigation Committee, Union President Duyungan noted that the worst gambling establishments were located at 221 Washington Street in Old Chinatown
and in basements of the Milwaukee, Louisa, and Rex Hotels on King Street in
Chinatown. The Boston Gambling House in the Louisa Hotel could accommodate 300 patrons with its $50,000 in operating capital. The Tin Yee Society was
the cover name for the Hong Fook Gambling House in old Chinatown and could
serve as many as 200 patrons with $30,000 in operating monies and millions of
lottery tickets per week. The union also identified these businesses as the "central
headquarters of all lottery joints where lottery tickets [were] manufactured" and
distributed to other locations in Chinatown.[98] In addition to the headquarters,
other lotteries were in the Alps Hotel, the Eagle Hotel at 4th Avenue South and
South Main Street, and Chappell's Dreamland Hotel around the corner.

In total, the lotteries had capital assets of $87,000. While games in
the Atlas Hotel had ceased, other establishments were still in violation of city
and state law. The petition indicated that Filipinos were losing an estimated
$500,000, or half of all of the money that was taken in at the end of every work
season, to games of chance. "Hundreds of our workers lose their earnings every
year…. Hundreds of thousands of dollars which would be spent for necessities
and for legitimate business are grabbed by the Chinese racketeers and their
lieutenants and protectors….We hope that the authorities will change their
policy and close the Chinese lotteries….If they are not closed, we will be forced
to place 'Pickets' on the premises of these gambling resorts. By so doing we
firmly believe that we are not only aiding the law in their location, but we are
also destroying the foundation of the corner-stone of crime."[99]

The picketing was modest, calling for notice on the part of cannery
workers to stay away from businesses where gambling was present. But resistance and defeat of the effort came with stern warnings to the picketers by the
police department that any demonstrations would be considered disturbing
the peace. An anonymous letter forwarded to the union stated that while the
motives of the union were solid, the effort would not win the fight.

The *Philippine Advocate* ran similar editorials criticizing the opportunity for gambling, but also noting that these were pastimes that robbed not only their income but their future and would likely result in an aging population of Filipino males living in residential hotels. "Seattle's Chinatown operates some of the most efficiently organized gambling rackets on the Pacific coast...[but] if [Filipinos] want a good time or recreation, they must seek it in wholesome and socially-approved channels...they cannot always be young and strong...now is the time...to lay the foundations of life before they get old and weak. The optimism of youth must face squarely the stark reality of life."[100]

In the final blow to the movement to rid Chinatown of gambling, Duyungan was discredited under charges of grand larceny in allegedly accepting $50 of vouchers from the Washington Emergency Relief Administration (WERA), which was considered to be an ethics breach while he was accepting $35 a week as the union president. Gambling "below the line" would and did continue with some of the well-known gambling establishments being Filipino-operated, such as those that were located in the Freedman and Alki Hotel buildings. **Robert "Uncle Bob" Santos** recalls a kind of philanthropy that was also part of the gambling and the life for the Manongs that included his father.

> Lobbies of the hotels were everyone's living room. All of my dad's friends lounged in the N-P lobby in their favorite chair with a spittoon sitting next to it. I was "Sammy's boy" to all of these men. Every Saturday, I took my dad from the N-P Hotel on a walk through the district...our "family outing." Dad would always want lunch at the "Filipino Social and Improvement Club," a gambling hall in the basement of the Freedman Building where the Adams Hotel was located. It was the biggest Filipino gambling club in Seattle with blackjack, poker, and Pai Gow. The stairwell had artwork that had been painted on the walls in the 1920s with men in top hats and women who were dressed elegantly or as flappers. The club was owned by Rudy Santos, known to all of us as "Uncle Rudy." There was gambling but it was also a popular place to get a free lunch every day of the week: rice and a couple of entrees like adobo...something that you could keep heated all day. You could listen to the Seattle Rainier's baseball game on the radio, sit on couches and drink coffee that was often laced with whiskey and the guys would tell stories. The guys might lose all of their paycheck gambling somewhere but they knew that they could always get a free meal and share stories at Uncle Rudy's. Patrons to these clubs represented different parts of the Philippines. Uncle Rudy grew up in the metropolitan area of Manila, so more town mates would come to his club. Kids couldn't gamble but they

could hang out with their "uncles." The guys would give me a nickel or a quarter if they were winning and I'd buy candy or a soda pop. The other club was Dan Sarosol's "Bataan Improvement Club" at the southwest corner of 5th Avenue and Washington Street in the Alki Hotel. That club was in one of the storefronts...the drapes were always drawn with a lot of plants in the window. If you saw this in any of the Filipino storefronts, you knew what was going on...."[101]

The corporate establishment of Chinese hotels and the broad-based management of Japanese-operated hotels had created a monopoly within the SRO hotel market and a safety net that, at a minimum, provided accommodations for these two groups during the Depression. The hotels offered some element of security and control that was not experienced by Filipinos who were tenants to the hotel economy. In a reflection of the cycle of life as a Filipino newcomer to Seattle, **Emeterio C. Cruz** offered his observation in a 1932 edition of the *Philippine Monthly.*

The Filipino immigrant's problems really begin the moment he steps off the boat that has carried him across 7,000 miles of watery wastes to the shores of America.... When he leaves the customhouse he is met by over courteous taxicab drivers who offer to take him to a Filipino hotel....He finds himself in Chinatown—and he feels at home again. His room is bare except for a chair, a table and a bed... he goes to the pool hall where he sees most of his countrymen, and sometimes meets a long-lost friend. If he is industrious and willing to do domestic work he may find "houseboy," hotel or restaurant jobs during the winter. If he is not fortunate enough to be able to do these things he rents a room in some cheap hotel, pays his rent for five or six months in advance, buys his provisions, and waits for Springtime to go to Alaska again, or to the farms around Seattle...every Fall he starts again, and by the following year completes the cycle.[102]

As the effects of the Great Depression deepened, conservative estimates of transients and homeless in the US put the number at well over a million.[103] As **Dorothy Laigo Cordova** remembered:

The Filipinos didn't have formal associations like the Chinese or Japanese, but families and people helped one another as much as they could. I remember that our house was filled with "aunties" and "uncles"...just like the other Filipino families in Beacon Hill but there just wasn't enough room for all of the Filipino men who didn't have a place to stay.

Some of them would bunk with friends who were in the hotels...ten to fifteen Filipino men would stay in one hotel room because someone was able to pay the rent for a single night. The one who could pay for the room got to sleep in the bed and everyone else took a place on the floor until there wasn't any more floor space left. Sometimes you could go to an all night movie at the Atlas Theatre on Maynard Avenue in Chinatown if you couldn't find anywhere else to stay.[104]

In the midst of the Depression, a number of homeless camps began to spring up in cities across the United States. Referred to as "Hoovervilles," the shanty homes were built by those people who were either unemployed or underemployed and otherwise homeless.[105] Seattle's Hooverville was in an area that had once been part of the tideflat fill project, north of Royal Brougham Way (then Connecticut Street) and west of Alaskan Way (then Railroad Avenue) to the waterfront on what was part of the abandoned Skinner and Eddy shipyard site. Seattle's Hooverville was the largest of several homeless camps that had settled in the city.

A small group of forty men began to settle in this location in December 1930, growing to a 100-man community by the fall of 1931. Initially, the public health authorities had closed Hooverville in 1931 for sanitation reasons, burning the make-shift homes and scattering the population. But the closure was short-lived when the evicted members of the community returned to the waterfront location and began to rebuild. The shelters numbered over 300 units at the height of the community and were constructed of any available materials that could be found; some shelters were partially or totally underground in a development that was considered even more transient than the SRO residential hotels.[106]

The shacks themselves are examples of ingenuity. The men who built them being laborers...their dwellings show their experience...boards were obtained from wrecked buildings or discarded packing boxes. Tin for roofs was made by splitting open oil cans. The roofs were made waterproof in many cases by melting pieces of asphalt and smearing the tar over the cracks in the roof. Inside, many of the shacks are papered with scraps of wallpaper, newspaper, or wrapping paper to keep the wind out.... The [homeless camps] are away from main travelled routes for the most part—with the notable exception of the one so ironically named Hooverville, which is the highest class and most populous of all...[107]

In February 1932, the Hooverville community was housing 235 men. The three largest represented groups of the community included seventy-eight white men, followed by thirty-seven Filipinos and eighteen Norwegians. By October of that same year, the total number of residents had increased to 416 men with white residents increasing by 65% to 129, Filipinos increasing by 116% to 80 men, and Norwegians by 50% to 27 men.

> The age of the men...varies greatly, but the great majority...are from thirty to fifty-five, the most productive years of their life....Race and nationality are important considerations....There is a block of Filipino shacks on the south side of Hooverville. Amusement is fairly limited. I have seen many men playing cards and reading old magazines. A few in the poorer jungles indulge in "dehorn"—denatured alcohol, which kills them off if they keep it up.[108]

In May 1933, Filipino men represented the majority of the 840 total Hooverville residents with a seven-month increase of 160% or 208 men. This exceeded all other nationalities with no Chinese or Japanese ever recorded as living in Hooverville.[109] Like the residential hotels of pan-Asian Seattle and homes of the Filipino families, the shanties of unemployed Filipino men housed as many of their countrymen as was possible. As Dorothy Laigo Cordova recalls, "It was not possible for the few Filipino families in Seattle to house all of the Filipino single men during the Great Depression but the community did its best."[110]

Not even living in Hooverville could contain their spirit for organizational structure as the Filipinos helped mobilize the homeless community to organize and operate the shanty population and to have a voice with the Health Department in the city. At one time, the mayor of Hooverville was Filipino.[111]

In the midst of the Great Depression, as many people were focused on the sheer act of daily survival, the United States revived a discussion in 1933 of repatriating Filipinos and ultimately curtailing their free immigration to America by offering neither the continuance of protectorate status nor true independence for the Philippines. As California prejudice mounted against Filipino workers on labor issues, national anti-miscegenation laws were also proving ineffective. Relationships were being forged between Filipino men and white women. Clearly, the central city dance halls had provided a setting and the opportunity for interracial relationships.

Seattle's Hooverville, 1931. [Courtesy Washington State Historical Society at WashingtonHistory.org, June Hayward Fifield Collection, 2009.48.10]

Congress was faced with addressing public outcry and drafting a law that would exclude Filipinos and circumvent the issue of their right to enter America as US Nationals. Introduced as House Resolution 7233, Public Law 73-127 was drafted by Senator Millard Tydings of Maryland and Representative John McDuffie of Alabama. Known as the Tydings-McDuffie Act or Philippine Independence Law, the law passed on 24 March 1934. It allowed for a number of major provisions and conditions to the Philippines that would be met within a ten-year period of transition to final independence. The law granted the continued arrival of US goods to the Philippines with restrictions on Philippine exports to America; with only the former being duty-free for the first five years. The Philippine Legislature would draft a constitution within the first two years of the transition period that would be approved by the Filipino people and President Franklin Roosevelt. It allowed for US military and naval bases to remain on the islands and the retention of a school system that taught classes in English. Both programs had been put in place thirty-five years earlier. *The Philippine Monthly* called the drafted Independence Law "a delusion, a mockery, and a snare. It does not grant independence at all; it merely promises it, after certain explicit provisions have been met by the Filipino people. It possesses the

single virtue of granting ultimate independence, but that is not even certain....
It is evident that the United States does not intend to give up the Philippines
entirely."[112]

The debate on whether free immigration of Filipino laborers should
be continued was decided with a limit of fifty Filipinos per year that would be
admitted during the transition, with the Asiatic exclusion law being enacted
afterwards. Though independence would not be granted until 1944, the status
of Filipinos in America instantly changed from being Nationals to resident
aliens. It was hoped and assumed by exclusionists that the passage of the law
would eliminate Filipino immigration and decrease the population in the same
way that the Exclusion Law had addressed Chinese and the Immigration Act
of 1924 had taken care of Japanese.

As aliens and deemed "non-white," Filipinos joined other Asians in
America in being ineligible for naturalized citizenship and unable to apply for
federal work programs or receive any public assistance during the remainder
of the Depression years. Rising unemployment and discrimination against
Filipinos continued beyond passage of the Tydings-McDuffie Act when
Congressman Dickstein of New York presented his resolution to Congress to
repatriate Filipinos. It was the third attempt at the legislation and this time it
was approved. The resolution provided an option for the removal of Filipinos
from American cities and the labor force under the assumption that their unemployment was a drain on city social services. As it was, any unemployed Filipino
was encouraged to seek help from an immigration officer and voluntarily apply
to the secretary of labor for removal from the United States.[113] Transportation
and maintenance would be provided by US military vessels or private transport
companies with the cost borne by the US Treasury with "authority...granted
to the legislature of the Philippine Islands to initiate necessary procedure to
appropriate from the treasury of the Philippine Islands, sufficient funds to reim-
burse the government of the United States such amounts as may be expended"
along with any applicable taxes.[114] Had cities, such as Seattle, been effective at
eliminating gambling as Duyungan had lobbied for over a decade earlier, the
addiction to games of financial chance may have been reduced to a point that
the Congressional "drain on social welfare" argument would have been moot.

By the early 1940s, the effects of legislation were evident with
US Census figures that indicated a 9% national decrease to a population of
98,535 Filipino Americans, with a majority of over 68% living in California.

Washington State's Filipino population had declined from 3,480 in 1930 to 2,222 in 1940, amounting to about 2.3% of their total US population. Seattle's Filipino population had declined by 14% in these same years. But the national figures also indicated a potential for long-term changes in that 25% of Filipino marriages were mixed racial unions. While Filipinos in Seattle were only a small percentage of the national Filipino population figures, the city census count indicated that there was a marked shift in the gender disparity where the male to female ratio had improved from 30:1 to 7:1.[115]

In 1948, and at the insistence of Filipinos in the Pacific Northwest, the Philippine Consulate office was opened in Seattle. It joined the ranks of other such offices for the Chinese and Japanese as a place to help monitor and assist the 100 person quota of incoming immigrants and to obtain certificates of identification for residency that still indicated a population of pan-Asian Seattleites who were living in the city's residential hotels.

By 1970, one third of the additional Filipino population consisted of new births as United States citizens. As the gender ratio continued to improve and as more families represented the profile of Filipino America, the need for single male transient living in the residential hotels correspondingly declined to only a small population of the aging Manongs. *The Seattle Times* speculated on the disappearance of the dance halls and the taxi dancers.

> [What became of] the girls from the Liberty Dance Hall? It could be that they are represented among the wives and mothers who have proudly watched their children progress through college. They were, after all, victims of the same social-economic conditions that put their male contemporaries [south of Yesler Way].[116]

ENDNOTES

1   Interview with Nobue Shimizu about the Western Hotel, 20 March 2009. It is important to note that at the time Ms. Shimizu was calling the coroner, she was a young teenager.

2   Interview with Takashi Hori, 27 July 2006.

3   Religious organizations included the Young Christian Association (1892) that changed its name to the Japanese Baptist Church (1899), Young Buddhist Association (1901), Methodist Church (1904), Japanese Christian Church (1906), Japanese Congregational Church (1907), and St. Peter's Church (1908).

4   Interview with May Nakamura Sasaki, 21 June 2007.

5   Charles D. Raymer & Company, 1908. *Raymer's Dictionary of Greater Seattle*.

6   University of Washington Special Collections, Seattle Hotel Operators Domekai Records, 1910–1961. Manuscript Collection No 1896, Accession No: 1896-001. Written in old Japanese, the translation was provided by Mr. Robert Hori, Gardens Cultural Curator and Program Director, Huntington Library, Art Collections and Botanical Gardens, Los Angeles, CA, 25 January 2013. At that first meeting, the initial name of the organization was proposed as "Seattle Inn Keepers Alliance." There is no evidence to support that the SJHAA was ever a civil rights organization.

7   Fujii was only thirty-two at the time but had spent fifteen years in the United States and had learned how to run a business from his experiences in the dairy industry, labor contracting, and with the Fujii Hotel. His organizational skills made him a highly respected leader of the growing Seattle Japanese community and specifically from his role as co-organizer of a committee that founded the Seattle Buddhist Church in 1901.

8   Kazuo Ito, *Issei: A History of Japanese Immigrants in North America*. Translated by Shinichiro Nakamura and Jean S. Gerard. Japan Publications, Inc., 1973, p. 519. The five board members included Uichiro Ikeda, Mampei Miyagawa, Shiro Chiba, Daitaro Fujita, and Tokio Ota. The

information about the members of the board was provided by Yoshito Fujii, the younger brother of Chojiro Fujii.

9   The cost of membership was between $5 and $10. There is no indication on how this was assessed since there is no direct correlation between the number of rooms, quality of the hotel, or its location in assessing the fee. Receipt records of the SJHAA indicate that in 1959, there were 259 members operating 8,305 single rooms and 4,168 apartments. The annual membership dues totaled $1,950 of which $868.75 was collected from apartment operators.

10 Elmer Tazuma, personal interview, 20 March 2009. Mr. Tazuma managed and operated the New Central and Eclipse Hotels in the 1940s and 1950s.

11 Seattle architect John Graham, Sr. designed the hotel. Graham was responsible for a number of Seattle building commissions in partnership with David Meyers and as an independent firm. He is credited with the Physics Building on the University of Washington Campus, as well as the Frederick and Nelson, Dexter Horton, and Joshua Green buildings in downtown Seattle. Heather MacIntosh, HistoryLink Essay 124, http://www.historylink.org/index.cfm?DisplayPage=output.cfm&File_Id=124. Accessed 14 July 2014.

12 Masuda's parents operated a hotel on West Third Street in Seattle. At the time of the N.S. Investment incorporation, Masuda and Gregory were in business together.

13 The total employment figure that is being used in this report was prepared by the Japanese Association of North America in their Census Report that was provided to the House Committee on Immigration and Naturalization in September 1920. On 4 June 1917, the *Report of the Committee on Orientals* prepared by the Seattle Ministerial Federation indicated that the hotel industry provided employment for 250 persons. "Laborers" was listed as a second category that included 2,700 men and women. It is reasonable to assume that "laborers" may account for part of the discrepancy in the numbers between these two sources and within this three year time differ-

ence. The second largest employment sector was in the dye works and dry cleaning business that accounted for another 26% of the population.

14 "Memoirs of Theresa Hotoru Matsudaira, 1902–1996," Martin Matsudaira, ed. Translated by Yuka Matsudaira (2006), Chapter 6, p. 1–2.

15 Rooming houses were identified by the City Fire Marshal's Office as establishments with up to 20 rooms while hotels were defined as any building with over 20 rooms. The figure includes all classifications of rental housing including hotels, rooming houses, lodging houses, apartment hotels, and other temporary dwelling units.

16 Norman S. Hayner, "Hotel Life and Personality," *The American Journal of Sociology*, March 1928, vol. 33, no. 5, p. 786. Hayner's research on transient living examined Seattle's hotel population based on Washington State's definition of a hotel as a "building or dwelling which contains five bedrooms to be rented out to transient guests, i.e., by the day or the week" and the transient nature of the guests. At the time of Hayner's survey, he was refuting the modest official count of 74 that was quoted for Seattle by the New York Hotel Association (NYHA) to include both lodging and rooming houses in Seattle. In his adherence to his two parameters that provided a definition of hotels, he also included those facilities that might be frequented by prostitution and that would otherwise be omitted from the NYHA's count of only "legitimate" hotels. Hayner calculated that 203 children under the age of 12 were living in hotels, which was one-ninth the total number of children in all of Seattle and in this age bracket.

17 Martha Kawaguchi Onishi, personal interview, 30 March 2007.

18 Chappell's wife's name was Margaret Busch Chappell. Presumably, the spelling of "Busch" was changed to "Bush" during WWII as an effort to disassociate the name with Germanic ancestry.

19 The Fujii Hotel's name changed to the Beck Hotel under the new operators of the business during WWII and remained under that name until the building was demolished in 1971. The Tokiwa Hotel at 655 South Jackson retained its name until the mid-1960s when its name was changed to the Evergreen Hotel.

20 When Goon Dip was overseeing the operation of the Milwaukee Hotel, he had chosen Japanese resident managers beginning in 1914. The Milwaukee Hotel was also a member of the Seattle Japanese Hotel and Apartment Owners Association until 1928.

21 Interview with Takashi Hori, Panama Hotel, 27 July 2006.

22 Takashi Hori, 10 August 2006.

23 A family man and respected proprietor of one of the Seattle Japanese Hotel & Apartment Association SRO hotels, Tokita was also a gifted poet and artist who managed to steal some personal time in late night or early morning hours in which to write or paint the landscapes of the Seattle Japantown community.

24 Kakuko Imoto, translator, editor. Kamekichi Tokita, *Conflict of Loyalties: A Personal Memoir of Life and Internment During World War II*. Seattle: Tokita Family, 2005, p. 6.

25 Ibid., p. 12.

26 Social Security amounted to $40.00 per month according to Tokita's account, p. 56–57.

27 Ibid., p. 64–65.

28 Ibid., p. 16. James Sakamoto is referred to in an honorific as "Sakamoto-kun" in Tokita's diary. Sakamoto was a Nisei and the founder of the *Japanese American Courier* newspaper and co-founder of the Japanese Progressive League that ultimately became the Japanese American Citizens League.

29 Shikego Sesu Uno was employed by the Rainier Heat and Power Company while it was operating under the trust of William Chappell. In this capacity, she acted as a business manager and accountant. Personal interview, 2 July 2006.

30 Ibid., p. 115–116, 132–133.

31 The average size of barrack units was about 450 square feet for a family of six.

32 The classroom spaces served as units for families, and sometimes multiple families, with a shared kitchen.

33 Henry Seichi Itoi correspondence, 11 April 2007.

34 Minoru Fujii, personal interview, 22 and 23 May 2007 and correspondence 14 and 16 July 2007. The Nippon Yusen Kaisha line began service between Kobe, Japan and Seattle in 1896 with the sailing of the Miike Maru.

35 Janet Sakamoto Baba, personal interview, 19 September 2008.

36 Shea Aoki, personal interview, 19 September 2008.

37 Shokichi (Shox) Tokita, Yuzo Tokita, Yoshiko Tokita Schroder, personal interview, 28 November 2010.

38 The City already had an ordinance in place that had declared dancing in any establishment that served alcohol as a nuisance and punishable by a fine. Ordinance No. 3152 prevented and punished the conducting, managing, carrying on and taking any part in any dance in any saloon or drinking place. 26 December 1893. "Every dance, which shall take place in any saloon or other place where intoxicating or malt liquors are sold, given away or otherwise disposed of, or in any room or place connected, directly or indirectly, with any such saloon or other place where intoxicating or malt liquors are sold, given away or otherwise disposed of, is hereby declared a nuisance."

39 Howard B. Woolston, *Prostitution in the United States*, (New York: The Century Company, 1921), p. 149–151.

40 Ibid.

41 Women's Social Hygiene Department of the Washington State Board of Health, "Survey of Seattle and Bremerton District," 1 April 1919.

42 Ibid., p. 52–53.

43 Real estate mogul Henry Broderick recalled that during prohibition, speakeasies were located throughout the city and that "[prohibition] was an ignoble experiment breeding lawlessness and crime, but worst of all a great erosion of American morals...otherwise law-abiding people picked out the dry law as one to disregard...when the ogre of Prohibition arrived...morals deteriorated with

a bang." Henry H. Broderick, *The H.B. Story and Seattle's Yesterdays* (Seattle: Frank McCaffrey Publishers, 1969), p. 155, 157.

44 "Mrs. Landes Meets 3 Girls of Dance Hall," *The Seattle Times*, 16 October 1922, Part 2, p. 1, col. 7.

45 "Inquiry to Continue," *The Seattle Times*, 18 October 1922, p. 8, col. 1.

46 "Dance Hall Bill Delayed after Battle," *Seattle Post-Intelligencer*, 9 January 1923, p. 3, col. 5.

47 "Dance Halls Hearing Ends in Near Riot," *Seattle Post-Intelligencer*, 16 January 1923, p. 3, col. 1.

48 On the night before the ordinance vote was to have taken place, Roy Thornton, the manager of the Liberty Dance Hall "below the line," was shot at his home in what appeared to have been a staged burglary. The police department did not immediately file a report of the incident. In normal course, Mayor Brown had ten days to sign the ordinance into law, but on his refusal to approve or veto the dance hall ordinance, it returned to Council and became law thirty days later.

49 "The Saturday Nighter," *The Seattle Daily Times*, 3 March 1923, p. 1, col. 5, p. 5, col. 6.

50 The license was granted in 1924.

51 Like the hotels, dance hall names would change, which would entitle the business to a new application filing. When faced with more legal trouble in 1928, the Liberty closed and reopened as the Columbia, only to close again later in the year.

52 Seattle, City Ordinance 48022 (28 November 1924).

53 In 1921, Ordinance No. 42395 had already supplied a definition of a cabaret that also included the possibility of dancing on the premises. Applications for license would be investigated by an officer for validity before approval would be granted.

54 "Box House" uses refer to musical performance spaces that could sometimes include small, enclosed, and private areas that would use curtains or folding screens. These were areas where sexual services could be obtained.

55 Seattle, City Ordinance 48022, Section 76.

56 "Closed dance" was an early term that was evidently coined by social workers of the early twentieth century and referred to dance halls where only men would be allowed admittance since all dancing employees were women. "Taxi dancing" was a term that was popularized in the early 1930s. Prior terms to describe this type of dancing included "dime-a-dance halls," "stag dance" and "nickel hopper," all of which describe the activity. Paul G. Cressey's work entitled *The Taxi-Dance Hall: A Sociological Study in Commercialized Recreation and City Life*, (Chicago: The University of Chicago Press, 1932) is an incredible research study that examines activities, definitions, and interactions of taxi dance establishments in Chicago.

57 Taxi halls differed from the businesses of the early 1900s that combined saloons with a small dance floor, where a dancer was compensated through a percentage cut of the profits for all of the alcohol sold, or the larger dance palaces of the teens and 1920s, where dancers were compensated as teachers for paid lessons. Some taxi dance halls also provided a commission percentage on the amount of alcohol that a dancer could convince a patron to purchase, particularly after prohibition had ended.

58 One notable exception was the Columbia dance hall where women received 40% of the money that was collected for drinks.

59 Cressey, p. 145, 153.

60 In 1922, Seattle Mayor Edwin Brown had suggested the formation of a professional union for the estimated 200 girl dancers who worked in the dance halls and cabarets as dance teachers and hostesses.

61 "Dance Clubs of Seattle," unpublished student paper, Norman S. Hayner papers, Accession 2706-001, n.d. To remain in good standing, monthly dues of $1.00 a month would be paid, which entitled the member to sick leave benefits after two months.

62 "Dance Hall Ban is Taken before Organized Labor," *The Seattle Daily Times*, 31 October 1929, p. 16, col. 5.

63 Ibid.

64 In 1924, attorney John F. Dore had represented the Casino dance hall as it sought a restraining order to keep the police from closing the business. Dore became mayor in 1932 as the dance halls were beginning to resurface in Seattle.

65 The Mar, Eclipse, and Tokiwa Hotels catered to Black patrons who were musicians in the clubs or who worked in the King Street and N-P rail stations. The "Bucket of Blood" was a name that was coined from a murder that took place near the entry. The club was located at 511 ½ -7th Avenue South. The Turf was at 6th Avenue South between Jackson and King Streets and the Black and Tan was at 12th Avenue South and South Jackson Street.

66 *Mabuhay* is a Tagalog word meaning "to live or thrive." It is also used as an expression of welcome.

67 The building that housed the Rizal Club replaced a similar commercial building that was frame construction. That earlier building held a number of commercial uses that included a residential hotel from 1911 to 1925 and the M. Furuya Company in 1903.

68 According to the Polk Directory for 1941, the Estigoy Café was called the Rainier Café but Victor Estigoy was the owner of record.

69 Interview with Delores Sibonga, 26 July 2006.

70 Interview with Don Osias, 3 November 2007.

71 Simeon Doria Arroyo, "I Cover Chinatown," *Philippine Advocate*, April 1935, p. 4, vol. 1, #2, col. 1–3.

72 M. Hollowfield, "Dance Clubs of Seattle," Norman S. Hayner Collection, Accession Number 2706-001, University of Washington, unpublished paper.

73 The knowledge that the Rizal was a dance hall was also referred to in the *Seattle Daily Times* and *Post-Intelligencer* when both papers carried articles in May and August 1935 about violence between Filipino men or for disorderly content.

74 The Rizal Club and Rizal Hall refer to the same business.

75 Willy Torrin, "I Cover Chinatown," *Philippine Advocate*, May 1935, p. 4, col. 1.

76 Simeon Doria Arroyo, "Chinatown...As it Looks to An Interested Bystander," *Philippine Advocate*, Rizal Commemorative Edition, April 1935, p. 8, col. 1, p. 14, col. 1,.

77 US Bureau of the Census, Table 2: Color, Nativity, and Sex for the State, Urban and Rural, 1910–1930.

78 Capitola Pinches Allen, "Seattle's Jobless," 1927–28, *Survey*, 15 September 1928, p. 593.

79 Interview with Dr. Fred Cordova, 18 June 2009.

80 "Parodical [sic] Signets," *The Philippine American Chronicle*, 1 March 1935, col. 2, p. 4.

81 Jay Cee Dee, "Seattle's Chinatown—Mysterious and Fascinating," *The Philippine Monthly Review*. October 1932, vol. 1, no. 1, p. 6.

82 From 1932 to 1933, the account ledger of the Kong Yick Investment Corporation noted that a number of businesses and residents were unable to pay their rents. One exception was a madam and sex worker known only as "Gracie" who lived on the second floor of the building. Even in the depression years, Gracie's rent was never delinquent.

83 These included the Atlas Chop Suey, Gyokko Ken, Kinka Low, Nikko Low, Manshin Low, and Hin Pu Ken. Of these, five were located north of Jackson Street and one was located south of Jackson Street and in the Chinese-owned and -operated Atlas Hotel.

84 Hyung-Chan Kim and Cynthia Meija, comps. and eds., *The Filipinos in America, 1898–1974: A Chronology and Fact Book* (New York, 1976), 12; *United Cannery, Agricultural, Packing and Allied Workers of America (UCAPAWA) Newsletter*, July 1939, p. 4.

85 Seattle, City Ordinance 50867 (26 November 1926).

86 Simeon Doria Arroyo, "I Cover Chinatown," *Philippine Advocate*, April 1935, p. 4, vol. 1, #2, col. 1–3.

87 Advertisement in the *Philippine Advocate Commemorative Edition*, April 1935. The hotel was named by its owner Henry C. Patron. Prior to this, it was known as the Olympus Hotel and was a member of the SJHAA. Patron had at least one other short-lived business venture in the area as the manager of the ABC Employment Agency at 412 Main in 1929.

88 During the interim period between Asian American management, the hotel was vacant for a year and then operated by the Jacobs family.

89 There were other Filipino employment agencies at this time, and some owners, like Sarusal, were involved in other businesses as well. Aquelina Nator operated the Philippine Recreation Parlor, which was also in the Rainier Heat and Power Company building, and the Filipino Employment Agency from 1927–1930. The Philippine Investment Company was a cannery contractor business that was operated by V. Martinez and Pedro Santos at 803King Street from 1929 to 1935. The Filipino Enterprise that was run by Vincent Agot was in business in 1934 at 523 Main.

90 During its operation under Filipino management, the official name of the business was the Mint Hotel, but the building was known as the "Louisa Hotel." The hotel building is at 665 ½ King Street.

91 Chris Friday, *Organizing Asian American Labor: The Pacific Coast Canned Salmon Industry, 1870–1942*. (Philadelphia: Temple University Press, 1984), p. 127 as originally found in US Bureau of Fisheries, *Alaska Fishery and Fur-Seal Industries*, 1928 (Washington, DC, 1928), 273. Figures used in these sources indicate that Filipinos represented 3,916 while Japanese totaled 1,445 and 1,065 Chinese.

92 Some agreements between the labor contractors and workers would include holding back salaries until the fishing season had ended.

93 Vicki L. Ruiz and Virginia Sanchez Korral, eds, *Latinas in the United States: A Historical Encyclopedia*, (Bloomington: Indiana University Press, 2006), p. 117–118. The Cannery and Agricultural Workers Industrial Union (CAWIU) was primarily

active from 1931 to 1934 in organizing agricultural workers strikes in Southern and Central
California. As an agricultural branch of the
communist party, the CAWIU joined forces with
Mexican laborers in organizing strikes to improve
wages and worker conditions.

94 "Filipino Labor Union Local Sends Delegates to
Olympia; report Findings on Bill 301," *Philippine
American Chronicle*, 1 March 1935, p. 1, cols. 5, 6.

95 Ibid.

96 Clean City League and the Seattle Council of
Churches and Christian Education, *Department
Efficiency Committee Investigation of Gambling,
Vice and Liquor Conditions in the City of Seattle
Summary,* Seattle Municipal Archives, 1935.

97 Ibid.

98 Seattle Municipal Archives, Comptroller File
Number 147559, letter dated 15 July 1935.

99 "Vigorous Picket Against Gambling Resorts
Launched by Union Local," *Philippine American
Chronicle*, 2 August 1935, p. 1, col. 7, p. 2, col. 5.

100 Larry Miranda,"Gambling in Chinatown," *Philippine Advocate,* June 1935, p. 4, col. 5.

101 Interview with Robert Santos, N-P Hotel, 22
February 2007. Robert Santos was not related to
"Uncle Rudy."

102 Emeterio C. Cruz, "In the Land of Promise: Filipino Life in Seattle as a Newcomer Would Live It,"
Philippine Monthly, November 1932, vol. 1,
no 2, p. 5–6.

103 Samuel Wallace, *Skid Row as a Way of Life.*
(Totowa, New Jersey: The Bedminster Press,
Incorporated, 1965), p. 21 as cited in Ellery F.
Reed, *Federal Transient Program: An Evaluative
Survey, May to July, 1934.* (New York: Committee
on Care of the Transient and Homeless, 1934),
p 6, 18–22.

104 Interview with Dr. Dorothy Laigo Cordova,
18 June 2009.

105 These homeless camps were called such in
reference to President Herbert Hoover.

106 Interview with Todd Kuniyuki. 18 December
2009. Kuniyuki delivered groceries to Hooverville
residents as a young man.

107 Selden Menefee, "Seattle's Jobless Jungles,"
unpublished paper, 14 November 1932, p. 3.
Norman S. Hayner Papers, 1913–1970, Accession Number 2706-001, University of Washington
Special Collections. Hayner was a Sociology
professor at the University of Washington and
engaged in a great deal of community-based
research with his student classes. This particular
collection included original student field research
and notes that were taken of Hooverville. Files
also contain limited interviews with Hooverville
residents. The research indicated a very high
level of interaction within the Hooverville community and the establishment of self-government
and representation when it came to interaction
with city officials, including the health board and
police department.

108 R. Ferrandini, "Hooverville," unpublished paper,
13 May 1933, p. 5. Norman S. Hayner Papers
– 1913–1970. Accession Number 2706-001,
University of Washington Special Collections.

109 Ibid. "Homeless Man," May 1933.

110 Interview with Dr. Dorothy Laigo Cordova,
18 June 2009.

111 Ibid.

112 "And they call it Independence," *Philippine
Monthly*, vol. 1, nos. IV–V, p. 1, col. 1, 2.

113 "Resolution of Repatriation is Again Revived in
Congress," *The Philippine American Advocate*,
p. 1, col. 1.

114 Ibid.

115 Some of this shift is due to a decline in the number of Filipino males from 1,563 in 1930 to 1,213
in 1940. While the ratio improved overall, it does
not reflect data of age cohort in both of these
groups.

116 Ross Cunningham, "The Passing of the Skid
Road," *The Seattle Times*, 7 November 1963, p. 5,
col. 4.

The Death Knell of the SRO Residential Hotels

PUBLIC PROJECTS, PUBLIC GOOD, AND THE EROSION OF "JAPANTOWN"

Even before the incarceration that uprooted all of the Japanese Americans from Seattle, the plans of pre-World War II urban renewal and city redevelopment projects were already beginning to erode Japantown. In an effort to stimulate local economies in the post-Depression years, the Franklin D. Roosevelt administration instituted a number of federal programs that were geared toward revitalizing both rural and urban areas. One of the agencies under Roosevelt's "New Deal" legislation was the United States Housing Administration that was established under the United States Housing Act of 1937.[1] The new agency was charged to work with Local Public Authorities (LPA) in efforts to provide quality low-income public housing in city areas that were deemed to be "slums." The LPA was responsible for identifying and clearing the designated area of the city in order to make way for new construction. Project financing would come from the federal government as low-interest loans and ownership would be under the control of a city's public housing authority. The act stated that a public housing agency would designate a project and determine its need "to meet the housing needs of the low-income population of the jurisdiction."[2]

In terms of geography and location, Yesler Hill was a steep area with a western-facing slope that was characterized as a slum because of the old Victorian homes that had defined the neighborhood since Seattle's early days of settlement. It was an area that had not been included during the Regrade project but urban renewal included that part of Yesler Hill that was the eastern portion of Japantown.

In 1939, Seattle established the Seattle Housing Authority (SHA) as the first local public housing authority in the state. As its first project, the SHA was given a $3,000,000 low-interest loan from the United States Housing Authority for a project to construct eighty-four two-story housing units on a 43.5-acre site of Yesler Hill. The Yesler Terrace Housing Project would be the first public housing development in the state and the first in the nation to be racially integrated.

The SHA identified that 95% of the buildings in the area were "substandard," which resulted in razing 158 buildings and displacing over 1,000 residents in a little over one year. In a 1941 report, the SHA supported the need for the redevelopment project. "A blighted district such as this, in the very heart of our city, is socially and economically injurious to the community's welfare. Its advantageous position, however, makes it desirable from a residential viewpoint....Seattle shall soon see one of its most ugly and disreputable areas transformed into a carefully designed and constructed residential district."[3]

There were restrictions on who would be eligible to live in the new housing project once it was completed; income and marital status requirements would disqualify single people from renting. Many of the Japanese families were deemed ineligible for having multiple incomes per household, a byproduct of extended families and adult Nisei who worked and lived with parents. Only families whose members were citizens were allowed to live in the new housing project; that immediately disqualified Asian immigrants and forced the displaced into the SRO hotels that were down the hill from the new project.[4]

The profile of the project area mimicked that of the rest of property "below the line" in its multiethnic population living in houses, tenements, and residential hotels that were interspersed with bars and bordellos. Relocation proved a challenge for city staff that were charged with the responsibility of addressing the needs of this diverse population.

The houses of prostitution presented...a problem...[where some] found their own places, [and] some persisted in staying on after others had moved away....Relocation of houses of prostitution had some advantages, for they moved to a more segregated district on the edge of Chinatown, except for two houses where the inmates had grown weary of window-tapping, and had taken over hotels on the skid-row....Sandwiched in between the houses of prostitution...children played under open windows where pretty girls brazenly shouted to their prospective customers. Many of the Japanese families purchased their own homes after renting property on the hill for twenty or thirty years, [finding] it particularly difficult to leave their gardens.[5]

Among those displaced, the SHA recorded that 127 of the 359 displaced families were Japanese, with five Chinese families, and twenty married and single Filipinos.[6] A representative from the city noted that "moving the Filipinos with white wives was a headache all its own, as few landlords were willing to accept them as tenants."[7]

In addition to homes, the well-established Japanese community lost the Seattle Buddhist Temple, Japanese Episcopal Mission, and the Japanese Methodist and Seventh-day Adventist churches; seven residential hotels, including the Miyajima, New Seattle, Newton, Broadway, Sprague, Sankai, and Sunrise Hotels; along with four grocery stores—the Hajame Michihira Grocer, Furuta Grocers, Shoshi Grocers, and Yoshioka Grocers; and the Ishii Chu Sho School, Yesler Laundry, and the Ito Shoe Repair shop. The project site had an irregular shape but included an area roughly defined as between 7th and 12th Avenues South, Fir Street to the north and the Main Street alignment to the south. Yesler Terrace had, for all practical purposes, razed the entire eastern side of Nihonmachi.

As the Great Depression was helping to shape policy and housing design, issues of private versus public transportation, travel means, and routes were also changing American cities. As the job market declined, so did the need for public transportation that relied on ridership for operation funding. It was the beginning of decades of decline in public transportation dollars and support that was only made worse with post-WWII suburban development and the rise of automobile ownership. The population shift out of central cities by people of means left an urban core profile that was characterized by a high number of minorities and the urban poor, which left a dramatic shortage in central city municipal dollars through taxation.

Seattle had completed a comprehensive plan that identified routes for urban arterials in 1947, the most striking addition of which was controlling the movement of traffic by means of a limited access expressway system. In 1951, the city was looking at a proposed alignment that would create a ten-mile, north-south freeway corridor to facilitate the projected increase of automobile use and alleviate the congestion of through- and local-traffic. City Engineer Ralph Fiske, D.D. Forgy with the Washington State Department of Highways, and real estate appraiser Earl F. Dickinson were looking at the projected cost of acquiring properties on which such an expressway system could be built. As an independent appraiser, Dickinson was charged with cost estimates and identifying a route "of various real properties to determine the most economical location for the highway from a standpoint of right-of-way cost."[8] Identified as Primary State Highway No. 1 or Highway 99 East, the exact alignment was approximated with a portion of the south downtown properties to be acquired that included some in the newly constructed Yesler Terrace Housing Project and other land parcels east of 8th Avenue South.[9]

Route planners looked at traffic patterns that would serve the greatest number of motorists while preserving the business and major retail districts of the city. The city's geography between the Puget Sound and Lake Washington made it impossible to design a freeway system that would encircle the downtown as was being done in other US cities. An alignment would need to skirt the far eastern side of the downtown that included properties in Japantown and Chinatown. It was estimated that $977,000 would be needed to procure properties between Yesler Way and Dearborn Street for construction, with over half of this amount needed for lots that lay between Yesler Way and Jackson Street in Japantown. Residents and businesses had voiced concern over what such a system would mean to the local economy of small business owners, but statistics and visits to similar developments in Sacramento and Los Angeles had indicated that adverse effects were minimal and that business trade had actually improved. Seattle was going to join the list of American cities that had or were in the process of limited-access freeway construction.[10]

The idea for the $100,000,000 Seattle project received wide support from the Washington State Highway Commission and had been the topic of discussion for a decade without any clear idea of how such an ambitious endeavor could be financed. Two major pieces of federal legislation put transportation issues at the forefront of metropolitan redevelopment and set the construction of the Seattle freeway system in financial motion. The Highway Act of 1954 required local transportation planning in order to qualify for matching funds and the Federal Aid Highway Act of 1956 established design standards and helped provide the funding for construction.[11] Seattle included recommendations for a freeway system in a 1957 Comprehensive Plan. In compliance with the 1956 act, the final proposed route through the city was the subject of a public hearing in April 1957. Almost 90% of the needed construction funding was provided through federal funds, and Primary State Highway 1 was now going to be part of a national freeway system that would connect major metropolitan areas throughout the nation. Seattle's link through the city was to be part of the state's plan to have a freeway system that would traverse the state from Vancouver, British Columbia to Oregon on the west side of the Cascade Mountains.

The process of property purchase began north of the city and was slow getting to the Chinatown-International District with the first procurements beginning in 1963, more than seventeen years after the freeway construction discussion began. Until properties were specifically identified, owners were only willing to put minimal investment for property upkeep, which translated to a lower purchase price as a consequence. For someone leasing property, prospects for a building owner to contribute to the upkeep of a structure were likewise grim and unlikely since any financial return on improvements would go unrealized. The ability to sell private property that was in the general corridor was unlikely as no potential buyer was interested in purchasing a building that was surely slated for demolition. If property was purchased by the state, but not immediately needed for freeway construction, an owner could keep leasing it from the state until evacuation was ordered.

Neither the City Planning Commission nor the majority of council members encouraged a detailed study on adverse effects to the downtown. Local architect and Commissioner Paul Thiry and Commissioner Gilbert Mandeville held the only dissenting opinions, arguing that the ramifications of the freeway project on the downtown were unknown without further investigations. The discussion that did occur involved access to the city's medical facilities in the First Hill neighborhood. With the state's interest being only the land, houses could be auctioned and relocated, but the larger structures, such as the hotels and large commercial buildings, would need to be torn down. In addition to single-family houses, rooming houses such as the Okazaki Housekeeping Rooms at 8th Avenue South and South Weller Street, the Coast Hotel (1909),

Hotel Western. [Courtesy King County Assessor's Office, Property Record Cards, 1937–1973, Puget Sound Branch, Washington State Archives]

Hotel Western (left) and Chinn Apartment Hotel (right). The latter was the home to the Hip Sing Tong with their meeting room and adjoining kitchen on the 4th floor in the northwest corner of the building, highlighted by a decorative awning and projecting iron balcony. [Courtesy Washington State Historical Society at WashingtonHistory.org, Asahel Curtis Collection, 1943.42.22228]

Tacoma Hotel (1910), and commercial buildings in the Asian American District were razed. The Tacoma Hotel, owned by Yukiko Kawakame, was the larger of the two hotels with four commercial storefronts and 211 rooms that would be lost as low-income housing stock. The Western (1910); the Chinn Apartment Hotel that housed the Hip Sing Tong (1910); and Astor (1909) Hotel lost at least one-half of their land to the freeway right-of-way, but the buildings remained standing in the shadow of the noisy and elevated road. The welcoming main entry façade of the Astor Hotel that had fronted the neighborhood street of Maynard Avenue South now sat immediately facing the six-lane freeway.

The interstate freeway project officially opened in September 1966 and for the most part it followed the alignment that had been proposed twenty years earlier.[12] Four of the east–west street connections between Beacon Hill and the International District that had been made possible from the Jackson and 12th Avenue Regrade projects were lost with the Yesler Terrace housing and I-5 construction, including access connections via Washington, Main, Weller, and Lane streets. The two mega-improvement projects dramatically divided the Asian American community and succeeded in creating a more isolated neighborhood.

FORTUNES WON AND LOST: THE HOTELS OF WILLIAM CHAPPELL

Under the William Chappell Trust, the Rainier Heat and Power Company owned the Governor Apartment Hotel, the St. Paul House, American, Welcome, Publix, Paris, St. Nicholas, Russell, Hamilton, UI, Dreamland, Bush, and Welcome Annex Hotels.[13] Chappell's will had given the trustees permission to sell any other holdings of the estate for management and upkeep, but with strict instructions that the hotel properties could not be sold or conveyed during the sixty-year trust period.[14]

Over the years, the low rental fees for the rooms were not keeping pace with inflation and the increasing costs of operation and maintenance of the buildings. The hotel accounts were also depleted when the trustees made personal loans for repairs and taxes to the buildings of the Chappell Trust, a lending practice that carried substantial interest penalties as part of the repayment. A $40,000 loan that was made in 1923 by Chappell's widow, Margaret, depleted the estate of over $18,000 in interest over a ten year period as part of the repayment.

The Chappell Hotels — Paris Hotel with the Hinode-Yu Japanese Bathhouse and Laundry, the L-shaped Mukilteo Hotel (formerly known as the Hamilton Hotel) that had entrances on 6th Avenue South and at South King Street, UI Hotel with the Bison Café at the corner, Russell House Hotel, and the St. Nicholas Hotel. (left to right) Eventually, Chappell's holdings would include the construction of the Publix Hotel on the empty lot west of the St. Nicholas. [Courtesy Shigeko Uno and Tomio Moriguchi]

Governor Hotel Apartments. Commercial businesses included the Strand Dance Hall, Home Bottlers Supply, the Alaska Grill, Oriental Optical, and the Hirada Dry Goods store (operated by Kiyo and Yoneo Hirada) (left to right). The Man Shin Low Chinese Restaurant was on the second floor of the building with entrance around the corner on 6th Avenue South. The 'E' in 'Suey' in the electric blade sign that advertised "Chop Suey Noodles" was mistakenly fabricated backwards. [Courtesy Shigeko Uno and Tomio Moriguchi]

Similar charges of personal loans, interest charges, and excessive distribu-
tions to the beneficiaries drained the financial reserve of the trust year after
year. The Bush, American, Welcome, Publix, and Governor Apartment hotels
had all been mortgaged and the Paris Hotel was razed in 1936 due to its failing
condition. Some of Chappell's smaller properties in Beacon and the First Hill
neighborhoods had been forfeited to King County in January 1939 for taxes
that hadn't been paid in almost a decade, as was the case with the Dreamland
Hotel. In a strategic move to reclaim the Dreamland property, the Rainier Heat
and Power Company bought it back from the county at the end of that year
through a public bid at auction.[15] Its return to the trust's ownership did little
to improve the financial viability or condition of the hotel as a leasable space
and in 1944 it was demolished.

At the beginning of 1942, the tenant rental of $156,319 for all of the
Chappell properties was the greatest source of income followed by $16,448
that was collected for the sale of steam heat and water to properties outside of
those owned by the Chappell Trust. By the early 1940s, the total mortgage liens
of all of the properties were in excess of $260,000. When all of the immediate
expenses were paid, only $550 was left in the company account.

In the 1950s, four of the oldest Chappell Trust hotel buildings were
demolished, including the buildings that housed the Welcome, St. Nicholas,
Russell, and UI Hotels. The latter three hotel buildings were razed in 1952,
leaving the 6th Avenue block face between King and Weller streets vacant for
the first time since 1903.[16] Total rental income revenue for the properties had
declined from approximately $17,000 in the 1940s to less than $11,000 per
year in the 1950s due to a combination of escalating maintenance costs and
the razing or vacancy of many of the Chappell hotel properties. One attempt
at financial solvency occurred in 1956 when the trust constructed a small
concrete structure where the Dreamland Hotel had once stood at a cost in
excess of $98,000 with all but $5,000 paid for through a loan. Security for the
loan was based on a twenty-year renewable lease to the federal government for
use as a US Postal Station.

The Welcome Hotel had essentially lost the original first floor of its
building when the 1907 Jackson Street Regrade raised that section of the
intersection by 15 feet. After the regrade, no appreciable use of what used to
be the first floor had given any financial return. With only two useable floors
remaining, the "new" first floor was used for commercial retail and only the

second floor was used for hotel rooms. The compounded settling and shifting of the Welcome Hotel's wooden frame over the years made it too costly to repair in order to bring it up to building code. Repeated violations of city ordinances that regulated construction and safety standards threatened condemnation of the building.[17] The only reasonable course of action that was allowed by William Chappell's will was to follow what had been done to raze the Dreamland and that was to seek court approval for demolition of the hotel and construction of a new building that would help keep the ailing trust solvent. It was believed that a long-term lease would provide an income that would help take care of the remaining Chappell properties.

In 1958, thirty-seven years into the sixty-year time requirement of the trust, the Welcome Hotel was approved for demolition with the land to be retained by the Rainier Heat and Power Company as an instrument of the Chappell Trust and to be the site of a new building constructed for a branch of the First National Bank.[18] With a fifty-year lease agreement, the bank held the option to purchase the building with the expiration of the trust instrument in 1981. Construction of the new building fit well with the city's plan for a sixty-block urban renewal area that included the South Jackson Street and 6th Avenue South intersection where the Welcome Hotel had once stood.

Like the aging hotels, the three-story frame powerhouse building needed extensive repairs that could not be permitted or feasibly paid for by the trust. The old building had been damaged and patched following a 1955 fire and was replaced with a smaller building that was connected to the Publix Hotel as the last SRO hotel that was constructed by the Rainier Heat and Power Company in the pan-Asian community.[19]

The Rainier Heat and Power Company was still providing steam heat and hot water to the buildings of the trust and other buildings that were connected from the maze of underground pipes that were part of the Chappell franchise agreement from 1902, including Union Station. But from 1953 to the 1963 report, total revenue from the sale of steam heat was declining, in part from the discontinued passenger service from the Milwaukee Railroad that no longer required a heated area of the train station. Within this ten-year period, utility revenues plummeted from an excess of $51,000 to under $15,000 per year.

The Publix Hotel and powerhouse occupied the western half of a city block. While the land where the St. Nicholas once stood remained vacant, the trust borrowed money to construct a small tilt-up concrete building that was placed under a ten-year lease by Piston Services, Incorporated, as collateral for the loan.[20] Income from all of the properties owned by the Chappell Trust could barely meet the cost of upkeep to the buildings and increases in local property taxes. As each of them fell into disrepair, the ability to absorb escalating maintenance costs became more challenging with the annual declining revenues. In 1960, all of the trust properties had a total net profit of $3,400 and by the close of 1964, and for the first time in the history of Chappell's holdings, the costs exceeded revenues for a net loss of $2,396.

Some of this deficit was attributable to the loss of the two-story, wooden-framed Welcome Hotel Annex building. In 1962 and as the oldest remaining hotel in the district, the building was cited with 23 violations to the city's building codes. The City of Seattle found that the

> Inspection of the premises reveal[ed] an old building, poorly maintained, which has settled badly and is leaning dangerously. The wooden walks surrounding the building on all sides are in poor repair and some are exceedingly dangerous. Evidence of rot and disintegration is visible throughout the structure. The structural members supporting the building and the walkways are rotted and unsafe. This structure is unsafe structurally, a fire hazard, a health menace, and should be vacated and torn down. We are posting the building "Unsafe and Unlawful to occupy."[21]

The old hotel was condemned in 1964 and demolished in 1966. Of the eight hotels that were once part of Chappell's property empire, only the Bush, American, and Publix were left.

In a 1970 end-of-the-year "Report to the Heirs of William Chappell," the trustees outlined operation management problems and necessary cost cuts that had been implemented in an effort to effectively operate the hotels and minimize the certain financial losses for the buildings. With so few tenants in any of the Chappell hotels, there was no dividend for payment to the trustees or money to address the necessary hotel upgrades that would bring the American, Publix, and the Bush hotels in compliance with fire, safety, and building codes. With citations in hand, the city's fire department gave the trust two years to address the list of violations.

Like Chappell had done in the early years of hotel construction, the trust turned to Japanese management in an attempt to bring the former luxury of the Bush Hotel back to prosperity and promoted longtime bookkeeper Shigeko

Uno, to oversee the operation of the hotels and to manage the office. The trust's legal firm of Montgomery, Purdue, Blankinship, and Austin reported the dire circumstances.

> ...the present cash position of the estate is critical. The [lessee] in the Bush Hotel was unable to pay its rent for two months, walked out on its lease and closed the hotel... it would be a serious mistake to attempt to operate the hotel ourselves [and] we were fortunate to find two Japanese brothers (experienced hotel men) who took it over on a cooperative basis to see if they could build up the business to a profitable level. While it is not returning any income, it is not costing us as much as if it were closed entirely. Seventeen comparable hotels have closed during the last six months and we understand that several others will close shortly. The long-range problems of our hotels are very critical.... Most of the individual rooms have no plumbing other than a wash bowl or a small sink. Restrictions on sale and long-term leases contained in the Will make future planning difficult. [The Tokiwa Hotel,] a federally financed rehabilitation of an old hotel across the street...is nearly completed. It took the owner over two years to get this far and it appears it will take several more months to complete the job. As these newly renovated hotels with federally subsidized rent become more numerous, the old operators will find it more and more difficult to compete.[22]

In a 1971 legal memorandum to the King County Superior Court, the trustees outlined the bleak financial future of the properties along with seeking relief from the provision of the Chappell will that prevented the sale of the hotel building. The argument reflected on the prosperity that was once the history of the hotels and neighborhood along with the inability for Chappell to have foreseen such a dramatic decline in conditions "below the line." In part, the memorandum stated that "During the past fifty years...the character of the neighborhood has deteriorated and the area no longer is conducive to successful business operations [with] continuing difficulty in obtaining tenants...several of the buildings are old and dilapidated, and the trust does not have sufficient cash to make appropriate alterations...each of these hotels contains structural defects which render them unsafe for occupation in present form. Unless substantial alterations are made, the City will prohibit further operation of those buildings as hotels [and] taxes on the properties will dramatically increase in 1972."[23]

The petition relied on the explanation that the two intentions of the will were acting in a manner that was mutually exclusive. The first intention was to provide an expressed financial benefit to the beneficiaries and the second prescribed an administrative method that would produce that income. Chappell's will dictated that the properties not be sold and yet this same provision was making any financial solvency impossible. The solution that was presented and approved for this problem lay with a petition to the court to allow for "an orderly liquidation of properties" that would commence immediately and continue for the remainder of the trust's sixteen-year term. The sale of some of the properties might produce enough money to save the better SRO hotel buildings that were left.[24]

THE OZARK HOTEL AND 7TH AVENUE APARTMENT ORDINANCES

The fire and building code compliance that was referred to in the final days of the Chappell Trust turned to an immediate issue on 20 March 1970 when an arson fire destroyed the Ozark Hotel, one of the SROs on the north side of the downtown. At the time, it was given the distinction as the "second-worst fire in city history and the worst arson fire ever" with twenty people dead and another fourteen injured and hospitalized.[25] Until then, Chappell's Tokio rooming house fire of 1919 had claimed this second position when ten people had died. The investigation of the Ozark Hotel incident indicated that fires were set at both entry points of the building that included the main entry stairwell and second floor staircase landing on the opposite side of the building; classic design elements of an SRO hotel.

Compared to the hotels south of Yesler Way, the five-story building was a small facility with sixty rooms. The day of the fire, forty-two of the rooms were occupied. It was not only a tragic fire responsible for deaths, injuries, and a ravaged building with over $130,000 in damages, but it was also the beginning of the city's reassessment of fire code enforcement, housing conditions of SRO hotels, and potential municipal liability.

Seattle Mayor Wes Uhlman and Fire Chief Gordon Vickery had been notified by federal authorities that there had been a series of hotel arson fires in metropolitan areas across the US with a similarly suspicious fire in Olympia two months earlier. The traditionally unlocked front doors and transient tenants made SRO hotels a prime target, but with so many such buildings in Seattle's downtown, official monitoring of each one was impossible.

The SROs that had been built according to city building code at the turn of the 20th century were no longer meeting the regulations for safety. They did not have fire doors to separate long hallways or fire walls to stop the spread of fires in stairwells. Transom windows above doorways that had initially been installed to give rooms with no or minimal direct access to fresh air were standard features. But these windows would also allow a fast moving fire direct access into any room where the transom was left open. There were no sprinklers, alarm systems, or peepholes in the doors in which to see whether there were flames or smoke in a hallway. Some of the hotels, like the Ozark, did not have emergency egress, which made fire on staircases and landings almost a certain death trap. The matter of public safety for hotels and apartment hotels became a priority discussion with the state insurance commissioner's office and in administrative offices throughout the state.

Within three days of the fire, Vickery and Uhlman drafted a building and fire code ordinance for consideration by the council that included fire response upgrades for multiple resident buildings that were four or more stories in height. The proposal for the new ordinance would allow hotel owners one year to fully comply with all the new standards, but fire safety provisions needed to begin immediately. Ordinance 98868 was an amendment to current fire codes and while its official title related to improvements in safety standards, the new code became commonly known as the "Ozark Hotel Ordinance." In addition to defining a hotel as "a building in which is conducted the business of lodging the public and which contains six or more guest rooms," the provisions for fire code safety included having "two fully enclosed stairways that had a one-hour fire resistance rating, interior corridors and egress ways, improvements to doors and transoms and other openings into corridors, approved automatic fire sprinkler systems installed in all janitor rooms, storage closets, utility rooms, and other usable spaces in which combustible materials are or may be stored or kept."[26] Compliance with the ordinance had to be started by 1 January 1973 and completed by 1 January 1974. If buildings were considered to be an "imminent" threat to occupants, the extended time in which to respond would not apply and all improvements would be ordered done immediately.

At the time of the initial review of the 1970 Ozark Hotel ordinance, there was discussion in city hall that approving such legislation could have a devastating economic effect on the owners of the estimated 350 downtown residential hotels. The prominent challenge was to strike a reasonable balance between a demand for improvement, the cost of upgrades, and the preservation of down-town low-income housing as a proactive measure, though interviews with the mayor indicated that economic considerations were not going to override the responsibility for public safety. *The Seattle Times* published an early editorial that became a self-fulfilling prophesy of the events to come. It pleaded for some "flexibility" in the solution before enacting a code that would be another form of community devastation. "The problem...is an economic one of winning compliance from landlords whose rental revenues may not be sufficient to warrant costly rehabilitation of old structures. An 'instant compliance' order would cause some landlords to close their hotels, thus forcing into the street up to 5,000 persons of low income...certainly a revision of the city's housing code is indicated....The city's professional inspectors need a code that can be applied with common sense."[27]

Within weeks of the new "Ozark Hotel Ordinance" being approved, Seattle experienced a second fire, this time to the Seventh Avenue Apartments that was also in the north downtown; the building had combined long- and short-term rentals. Twelve lives were lost. The National Fire Protection Association had completed a report of the growing problem of residential hotel buildings, citing the Ozark Hotel fire as the second of three of the worst in terms of loss of lives.[28] While the building qualified under the definition of apartments and hotels, it was only three stories and so not affected by the newly approved Ozark ordinance. In response, the city enacted quick legislative measures again in July 1971, this time passing an ordinance that addressed the same fire protection standards for residential buildings of four and fewer stories. The new legislation would include all of the SRO hotels in the Asian American district. Legislatively, the new fire ordinances showed other cities that Seattle was capable of quickly responding to what was becoming a nationwide concern.

As the ordinances were being passed, eight survivors and two relatives of the victims of the Ozark Hotel fire filed lawsuits in King County Superior Court against the building owner and manager. The suit cited owner negligence in not responding to the interim measures for repair of the hotel that had been submitted through a city inspection that had occurred one day before the fire. A second lawsuit in March 1971 was filed against the city for $1.7 million under the claim that the city was partially liable for not enforcing safety regulations. If the city were to avoid potential suits in the future, strict and swift enforce-ment would have to be done. Under the assumption that there was a surplus of housing for the urban poor and that other housing could be found for those who were displaced, Fire Chief Vickery saw no reason to recommend phasing a program and the directive became "compliance or closure" for the hotel owners.

Protests to and appeals of the swift adoption of the ordinance were filed by the Apartment Operators Association and through the Seattle Chinatown Chamber of Commerce that was representing fourteen petitioning hotels in Nihonmachi and Chinatown under Japanese and Chinese owners and managers. The petitioners included the Kong Yick Investment Company, Seattle Japanese Hotel & Apartment Association, and the Rainier Heat and Power Company under the Chappell Trust. No one disagreed on the goal of safety for the residents, but the question of how to finance such an immediate, large, and expensive project was at the forefront. The SRO hotels had always furnished accommodations at a price that was affordable for lower-income people. Living in a hotel allowed people on small pensions or welfare to pay about one-third of their monthly check on rent and still have some money left for food. The costly upgrades under the ordinance would make operation of the hotels impossible for hotel business operators to afford and would essentially eliminate hotel operation as a way to earn a living. Passing the cost on to tenants was also impossible due to the spare and utilitarian accommodations and the market profile of people who sought the inexpensive residential hotels as a place to call home.

Some appeals were based on timing, but the majority focused on costs and quandaries on potential sources of money. For the larger hotels, compliance of door replacement alone was estimated to cost over $11,000 per building.[29] Sprinkler systems, in lieu of the fire wall construction, were also proving to be a financial burden to both the hotel owner and the city. The city's Water Department could advance a loan to cover service connections for sprinklers, but such financing would only benefit less than one-third of the hotels, and with a ten-year amortized plan, payments would be too high for most hotel operators. Then too, the city would have to do the initial funding of such a project. Banks were not interested in approving rehabilitation loans to building owners who were barely making enough money to cover the expenses of hotel operation. Owner cash flow just wasn't high enough.

The Federal Department of Housing and Urban Development (HUD) wasn't entertaining the idea of a comprehensive effort of financial assistance to hotel owners because they didn't perceive low-income housing as a critical issue. With anticipated closure of "severely hazardous" rated hotels, there appeared to be enough available low-income units in buildings that were identified as "least hazardous" for anyone needing to move. This assumed that the owners of the latter category of buildings would opt for costly renovation rather than closure. Oddly, the desirability of the hotels and the emotional connection to the neighborhood by the residents was not part of the consideration or discussion as the buildings were classified as "transient facilities" and not really considered a permanent home.

Another challenge to the new fire regulations was whether certificates of occupancy should be denied to those businesses that had always been in the same operation and with the same occupants. Some owner representatives argued for a "grandfather clause" that would only make the ordinance applicable to new occupancy applications and not to those hotels and rooming houses that had remained in business and that met the fire standards at the time of their initial construction. While there was a less-enforced section in the building code that stated that any unsafe building could be abated, scrambling for compliance in order to remain open had never before been an issue.[30]

The growing crisis of individual economic livelihood for the Japanese and Chinese hotel operators, and the role of being a voice for the elderly, low-income residents helped forge new alliances between the Chinese, Japanese, and Filipino community advocates. The new national movement that recognized the commonalities of the Asian immigrant experiences, as opposed to emphasizing group differences, was taking root. Collectively recognized as "Asian Americans," these groups began to further that unified vision in Seattle because of the residential hotel closure issue. The city's Filipino population was instrumental in this new movement to ensure social justice by keeping the Asian American residents informed and contributing a community-centered voice to City Hall and meetings with the Seattle regional office of Housing and Urban Development. The publication of the *Kaibigan* newsletter was a mechanism of update and change for the entire community with the same fervor that had been expressed in the Filipino newspapers forty years earlier.[31] The pan-Asian neighborhood was not only fighting for the retention of SRO housing, but was also engaged in protesting the impending construction of the Kingdome. The multi-purpose stadium would boost the municipal budget, but place an even greater strain on traffic and parking, as well as attracting land redevelopment potential that would jeopardize the character of the neighborhood. A 1972 issue of *Kaibigan* reported:

The Domed Stadium will be built at the King Street Station site. With the erection of this edifice, our city can gain entry into the NFL's sacrosanct world of jock-worshipping elite....Within Chinatown, there are approximately 340 elderly Filipino residents. These men, but pioneers, often subsist only on welfare or social security. Their homes are... in any of the numerous run-down hotels in the area. The dilapidated condition of these dwellings has forced...several owners to conform to safety regulations or face closure. Noncompliance would bring condemnation, and condemnation would necessitate the eviction of the residents. One can easily see the next possible step [as] conveyance of the properties to business interests—the presence of the stadium cannot help but increase the value of the surrounding areas. Filipinos comprise only a percentage of the Chinatown population. Hopefully, other communities will unite in our protest. If they choose to ignore their people, we will stand for them also.[32]

The call to action was already in progress and a number of organizations were being formed in alignment with the national Asian American movement. The International District Improvement Association under the acronym "InterIm" began community development work through grassroots participation in 1968. Led by long-time resident Bob Santos, InterIm became the voice of the neighborhood's low-income residents. Other organizations such as the International District Housing Alliance (IDHA), which was established in the early 1970s as a spinoff of InterIm, helped in the effort for community mobilization. Santos knew that if the hotels were slated for certain closure, a plan to combat resident displacement was critical. The Chinatown Chamber of Commerce, backed by InterIm, made a request to extend the ordinance deadline as part of a neighborhood-wide collective project that might be eligible for part of the funding that Seattle had received under an extended federal grant.[33] The Seattle Model Cities Program was also looking at potential sites to alleviate the low percentage of open space in the neighborhood with a hardscape park for residents of the district. After a year and a half of meetings and negotiation, the site that was chosen was where the Fujii and Great Wall hotels stood. The construction of Hing Hay Park would require the relocation of thirty low-income residents and five businesses so that demolition of the buildings could commence in 1971.[34]

As part of the second phase of the Model City Program, funds were available for planning and implementing programs for neighborhood revitalization. Such a plan could include strategies to help owners with the cost of hotel renovation. But both time and money were closing in on the viability of the hotels as the new fire code was not going to be delayed.

In January 1972, all standards of fire safety from the Ozark and Seventh Avenue fires were included in an amendment to the Housing Code, including some additional requirements that created an even greater economic hardship for hotel owners. The Office of the Superintendent of Buildings was engaging in an immediate survey of all residential buildings in the downtown and any building that was deemed "high hazard" would be closed for residential occupancy by order of the city. Decisions of the superintendent that dictated the condition of the hotel could be appealed and would be heard by the Seattle Housing Advisory Board.[35] In addition to previously outlined renovations, transom windows above doorways would now be required to be permanently closed and door glazing would be removed, all room doors that led to a corridor would now be required to be 1-3/8 inch thick and solid wood with "visitor observation ports" or peepholes that would not affect the fire retardant standard of the door. Elevator shafts would have to have the same fire protective standards as stairwells. Main entrance doors would now be required to be self-locking with keyless release bars on the inside of the door and have windows of non-shattering glass. For the first time in their history, the residential hotels would now be required to be inaccessible to the public from locked main entry doors. The economic hardship of meeting ordinance remodeling standards was compounded in finding a solution that would provide some means to notify second floor resident managers of guests who were waiting at ground level to come in, ascend the stairs, and register for lodging. This would require the additional expense of a paging system.

The original estimate was that about 1,000 units could be adversely affected by the new ordinance. By the end of April, fourteen of the older hotels had closed from the new fire code and previous condition standards of the city's hotel stock were being re-evaluated. Those buildings that had been reclassified as "high hazard" had one year to incorporate the necessary changes.[36] Deemed as an economically infeasible prospect, another eight buildings were closed by March 1971.

The eleven largest hotels and the core of the Asian American community were facing a crisis situation with the potential loss of over 1,600 housing units, 444 of which were located in the Hotel Puget Sound. While none of the hotels were completely filled, the 741 hotel residents would be in competition for less than half or 327 available downtown hotel rooms in buildings that had already met the compliance standards. Economic feasibility assessments were being done by William Montgomery as acting attorney for the Rainier Heat and Power Company hotels of the Chappell Trust, which included the Bush, Publix, and American hotels. Economic studies were also being conducted by the owners of the Milwaukee, N-P, Sun, Panama, and Atlas Hotels, and the Hotel Puget Sound.[37] The Chappell Trust was investigating the possibility of selling one or more of its hotels in order to facilitate upgrades to its other buildings, though the terms of the estate made this a challenging prospect—the trust was to remain in control of the buildings for another ten years and legal proceedings would take longer than the ordinance compliance date. The Eastern, Alps, and Hotel Puget Sound intended to comply by the deadline date and stay open if at all possible. By the end of 1971, the Bing Kung Tong's New American Hotel had joined the list of closures along with the Mar Hotel that was more popularly known as the "Hong Kong building" in honor of the storefront restaurant that had been there for decades. **Ron Chew** recalled being a 13-year-old busboy and working alongside his head waiter father in the 1960s.

> The Chinese men had very Spartan lives…a lot of the kitchen help lived in the Mar upstairs or other hotels in the district. You learned things from paying attention to the men you worked with…you'd just know some things without their saying a word. Picture yourself…12 hours, non-stop with a few breaks for food…standing and running back and forth with trays that weighed 50 pounds. You could do it in your twenties and thirties, but forties, fifties, sixties, seventies…it wasn't a way to live your life. Some of the waiters faded away because they couldn't continue to handle the ten to fourteen hour days on their feet. Both waiters and busboys would be so tired at the end of the day…you'd open up the door and smell the air outside of the kitchen along with your own clothes that smelled of grease and sub gum.[38]

In two internal memoranda of the city's Department of Community Development, it was acknowledged that things were going to rapidly change in the district and that rising land values from the proposed construction of a nearby multi-use stadium facility had the potential to raze large sections of the Asian American community. A two-person team was charged with performing a quick analysis of conditions in the Asian American District with no indication that the multi-ethnic profile of residents or social significance of the hotels and neighborhood was understood.

If the hotels are closed, the resulting spin-offs are: (1) individuals will be displaced and could potentially be scattered throughout the city and (2) if the resident population is reduced, many of the resident-oriented services will suffer, thereby bringing on their decline or demise....The moving of people would...have an immediate effect on the Asian population scattered throughout the metropolitan area.... The majority of housing facilities are situated in the section between S. Main Street and S. Lowe St. and 5th Avenue S. and 7th Ave. S. In recent years the International District has lost much of its traditional life. Younger Orientals with families have chosen to move to other parts of the city where there is more open space and better public facilities. Slow deterioration has eroded housing in the area and as a result the population has declined...[and] has become a complex mix of ethnic groups within a high concentration of unattached elderly persons living in older residence hotels...36% of the residents are Japanese, Chinese and Filipino; Negroes [sic] comprise 19% and the remaining are Caucasian, Chicano, American Indian and other. A high degree of skid roaders utilize the ID for housing accommodations. It probably can be said that progress is a road of many deaths. Right now the ID is dead or very close to it....the future of this area is dependent upon the actions of the property owners. The property in the [Asian American] District is valuable from a speculative viewpoint heightened by the impending construction of the nearby King County Domed Stadium.... This brings us to the current problems faced by the property owners: 1) To comply with the fire and building code regulations and/or 2) Speculate on the land use spin-offs of the King County Domed Stadium. Any economic return is probably unrealistic for the hotel owners due to 1) the demand for housing in the International District is not great with the exception of those older individuals now residing there, 2) the hotels are not worth rehabilitation on the whole, 3) most of the existing residents could not afford the potential increase in rents and 4) rehabilitating for residential use is uneconomic. The hotel owners have until May 21, 1972 to comply with fire code regulations, after which the Fire Department will take action against the owners resulting in closure of hotels...[39]

No financial help on the part of the city was part of the analysis, but rather the responsibility rested with the owners and their desire to rehabilitate rather than their financial ability to do so. The final opinion was that there would be no reprieve in compliance and that for all intents and purposes, the land was valuable and not the hotels. The memo concluded with a recommendation that stopping land speculation and preserving the Asian American community could be done if another ordinance was developed that would make the community a "Special Use District." Such an area would ensure a limitation or prevention of uses that would cause speculative development to occur due to the uncertain effects from the Kingdome Stadium and hotel closures. Such an ordinance could focus on design aspects of the community and property investment and, according to the Seattle Department of Community Development, it would put the "City on record as supporting an International District."[40] In the meantime, both the Building and Fire departments believed that the majority of owners would choose to comply with the fire code rather than face certain closure.

By May 1972, fourteen hotels had complied, but none of them were located south of Yesler Way. Seventeen hotels had closed in the downtown, nine of which were in the Chinatown-International District. These included the Hip Sing Association, Sun, Atlas, Adams, Union, Alki, and Sun Yen hotels along with the Mar and New American Hotels from the previous year. It was clear from the owner-generated economic analysis report that the $6.00 per week rental charge was not going to help keep the doors open to the Hotel Puget Sound. The intention to renovate the hotel was withdrawn and by mid-July 1972, the contents of the Hotel Puget Sound were placed on public auction and the hotel permanently closed. The Eastern, Publix, Bush, American, and N-P hotels had not responded to the city's request for an intention statement or an updated progress report.

There was no public or city administrative perception that the loss of hotels was creating a housing shortage, at least not one that couldn't be easily addressed. As fire ordinance compliance was underway, an independent research inquiry called the "Skid Road Housing Study" was examining the Pioneer Square and Chinatown-International District neighborhoods. It intended to bring attention to the area "below the line" because of the belief that there was insufficient public awareness and that "problems would not be dealt with as long as housing data showed a surplus of housing in the Seattle area."[41] The findings noted the distinction on the discrepancies that existed in defining the concept of "housing units" and questioned the consistency of how lost units were classified. Under the Federal Office of Management and Budget and the US Census, an entire SRO hotel building might be counted as a single housing unit if kitchen facilities were available to the tenants. Under the Seattle Building Department, "a single room available for rent regardless of kitchen facilities" could be counted as a "housing unit." It meant that an SRO hotel would contain as many housing units as there were rooms in the hotel. Yet many of the counts of hotels that were closing were being presented as single housing unit closures, one that created a misleading impression of total units that would no longer be serving a low-income population. Within the most populated core of the Asian American district, the Census indicated 447 housing units while the city's Building Department reported 1,024.[42]

When the ordinance compliance deadline was only five months away, the City Council approved a "Special Review District Ordinance" for the Chinatown-International District in August 1973; a suggestion that had been made the year before and under a different title as a "Special Use District."[43] The new ordinance was intended to address land uses and ameliorate impacts of the stadium. It added an overlay of zoning with new restrictions, design review, and compliance that would now be the standard procedure for changes that would occur to the exterior of any of the structures within its boundaries. A neighborhood review board made up of community members would be responsible for reviewing compliance with the ordinance on an individual project application basis. While this new ordinance was intended to mitigate negative community impacts and "preserve the District's unique Asian American character," it was too late to address the loss of use and certain devastation that was occurring in the SRO hotel buildings that had created the community in the first place. Other subsequent city efforts to preserve and enhance an already ailing Asian American district included chartering a nonprofit organization in 1975. Known as the Seattle Chinatown-International District Preservation and Development Authority (SCIDpda), it was the second such corporation in the city and charged with the authority to own and manage properties in the C-ID.

The Office of Housing Policy in the Department of Community Development issued a report in August 1973 that surveyed low- and moderate-income units in the central city due to what they called a "renewed interest in the residential communities of central cities."[44] Only those units with a rent structure of $150.00 per month were included, using data from previous reports and what was referred to as an "exhaustive visual inventory of the downtown" that took only one month to complete. While some of the managers and owners filled out a survey of basic information, the critical missing piece of the analysis was failure to communicate with the people who relied on these units as "home."

Between 1960 and 1973, a total of 148 residential hotels had closed, with 126, or the majority of these, being in the central business district. It was estimated that 3,000 units of downtown housing were lost from Chinatown and Nihonmachi alone.[45] Of this total number, 50 hotels had been razed for parking lots and the construction of Interstate 5, which had cut a wide swath through the downtown in what was identified as an area of "physical isolation" in the Asian American community. Seven hotels had been razed and the sites left undeveloped. Fifty-nine vacant hotels represented the highest category of hotel changes with over half of these hotels under operation by the Asian American community. City officials acknowledged that code enforcement was the primary reason for the closures. The owners and managers of the hotel buildings that were left standing admitted to being uncertain on whether long-term operation would be possible. In the end, only two of the surveyed hotels, the Bush Hotel and the American Hotel, expected to remain operable and were in the process of code compliance. If projected closures on those that were designated as "uncertain" came to pass, 872 residential hotel rooms would be lost to the district's residents; in fact, that figure would be exceeded in the next five years. While no owner disagreed on the need for public safety, passing the Ozark Ordinance was not equally met with any kind of financial assistance to bring the buildings to code nor was there any plan to help find other low-cost housing for the residents who were or would be displaced. Neither the location within the International Special Review District boundary or the accompanying ordinance could address hotel closures as part of the legislation. It was a foregone conclusion on the part of owners that a room rent structure of between $35 to $50 per month would never allow such costly repairs of compliance by the 1 January 1974 deadline and that the hotels would ultimately close.

In early 1974, city statistics indicated that over half of the downtown housing units had closed since 1960. Ninety-three SRO hotels had closed south of Yesler Way, accounting for 5,072 rooms or units of lost housing, according to the building department's definition. Only fourteen buildings remained open in the Chinatown-International District, accounting for about 1,100 total units of housing.[46] Of William Chappell's hotel empire, only the American and Bush Hotels remained open. The Publix Hotel remained open, but was now under ownership of Uwajimaya, Incorporated.[47] The East Kong Yick building had closed its hotel, but the West building had remained open with a partial second floor compliance renovation and closure of the third and fourth floors.

The Panama Hotel was the only C-ID hotel that was in close compliance with the Ozark requirements and this had been done decades earlier. Many members of the Japanese community never claimed their personal effects from the basement of the hotel after the incarceration. At his own expense and for the

sake of building insurance that would cover these items, hotel owner Takashi
Hori withdrew money from years of savings in order to install a sprinkler
system in his building. There was always a possibility that the owners or their
descendants would one day want to collect their property. The Panama Hotel
had become the repository of hundreds of pre-war Nihonmachi artifacts. As
Mr. Hori put it, "The Panama was always much more than a hotel."[48]

The Astor Hotel had closed its residential hotel floors. The building
was a less attractive prospect for residential restoration after having lost its
gracious Maynard Avenue entry to the freeway construction with the building
being so close to the view and noise of so much traffic. The building that had
provided the Japanese American community with housing and the Nippon
Kan performance hall was changing the single rooms to office spaces, a use
that supported the intention of the Model Cities program. The 1970 proposed
reuse project was touted as meaningful to an area that was now a "stagnant
part of the city" in a "significant economic slump."[49]

On 5 August 1976, the New Central Hotel became the twenty-ninth
hotel to close its doors. The installation of a $12,000 sprinkler system by long-
term manager Elmer Tazuma wasn't enough to keep the hotel open according
to the Golden Land Investment Company, which owned the building.[50] With
escalating fuel oil costs and other needed structural improvements, the building
had lost its profitability. The Asian American community viewed the Milwaukee
Hotel as the most likely candidate to become the thirtieth hotel closure. Residents
of the Bush Hotel anxiously watched the activities of the Milwaukee, particularly in light of the fact that their own hotel was the subject of sale negotiations
that would transfer the building ownership from the Rainier Heat and Power
Company to the SCIDpda. Eviction was a frightening probability.

In 1976, the loss of low-income hotel housing was slightly diverted
with two newsworthy opportunities. Low-interest loans became a possibility
to some hotel owners who chose to renovate and restore their hotel if they were
willing to participate in the Section 312 federal program of the Housing Act of
1964 that would rehabilitate multi-family structures. The loan could be procured
at 3% below market-rate interest. Qualification for the program required the
hotel owner to show a consistent and regular stream of income in order to get
the loan, which made obtaining one extremely difficult.

The second opportunity came through the Section 8 Program of the
1974 Housing Act. The federal government would subsidize rents for low-income

individuals and families as much as 75%. Payment would be made directly to the landlord in exchange for a long-term lease from the Department of Housing and Urban Development (HUD) that would designate a specific number of units for low-income residents. But there were formidable obstacles for Section 8 housing that included waiting for the city to prioritize areas that were potential properties, a decision that wasn't completed until 1979. Moreover, few hotel owners were willing to undertake extensive and expensive renovation that would encumber the property with a long-term, low-income commitment.[51] The owners of the Rex Hotel had considered Section 8 as a means for restoration, but the determination of rent subsidy did not take into consideration higher rental or construction costs for central city properties.[52] In the words of Raymond Chinn, the Rex Hotel owner, "there were tremendous risks and after all the figures were tallied it was far from realistic."[53]

It wasn't until 1980 and four years into the discussion of rehabilitative loans when the owners of the Tokiwa Hotel at the southeast corner of South Jackson Street and Maynard Avenue South became the first hotel in the C-ID to apply for a loan under the Section 312 program.[54] This federal loan program made low-interest loans available for qualifying property owners with the Seattle Housing Authority acting as the processing agent.[55] The $800,000 restoration would convert the sixty-two room SRO hotel to sixteen apartments of market-rate housing. It was a first and significant step of investment toward balanced housing in the district.

It was believed that Section 8 housing opportunities were more feasible in new large-scale, big developer construction projects than for restoration of SROs. The International District Housing Alliance (IDHA) also viewed the Section 8 possibilities as being ineffective given the grave nature of hotel closures. In a newsletter editorial, IDHA noted that it was not addressing thirty-three hotels that were in need of rehabilitation. "CLEARLY, the government hasn't even begun to 'scratch the surface' of the housing crisis we face! Meanwhile, the pace of hotel closures and evictions are ever increasing....Owners are looking at 'other uses' for their buildings...trying to cope with skyrocketing property taxes because of developments such as the Domed stadium,...trying to dodge increasing pressure to make necessary repairs of their occupied hotels...residents, let us beware of what is happening before our eyes! Hotel evictions are a reality...."[56]

Unlike the other hotels, the Milwaukee Hotel assumed a central position in a fight for social justice and low-income housing and became a tangible

Tokiwa Hotel. [Courtesy King County Assessor's Office, Property Record Cards, 1937–1973, Puget Sound Branch, Washington State Archives]

example of mobilizing the diverse community of the C-ID. Milwaukee residents, InterIm, IDHA, and young Asian American activists began to replicate a model of political activism that had been inspired by a similar mobilization that occurred in San Francisco in 1968. The latter city's battle to save the International Hotel as the last vestige of Filipino-occupied hotels in San Francisco was an ongoing and highly publicized battle from which Seattle activists could learn.

Like other hotels, the Milwaukee had been cited with numerous fire code violations. Its owners had borrowed $42,000 to help bring the building up to code in 1972, but there were no other avenues by which to borrow the money that would complete rehabilitation by the deadline. One of a series of appeals by InterIm and the IDHA to extend the deadline in order to find the funding to keep the hotel open and in compliance with the ordinances was eventually approved.

In the midst of negotiating, the Milwaukee fell victim to an arson fire on 9 August 1976. While no lives were lost, damage to the hotel exacerbated its condition with an additional estimated repair cost of $25,000. Fire doors had been recently installed, but over the years lack of maintenance had put the building into serious decline. The list included sixty violations of the fire and building department codes with eleven violations that were deemed to be the most critical on the list. Among the violations, the hotel was cited for not complying with installation of a front door locking system, broken glass, and no locks on the tenant doors. Sanitation and plumbing systems were poor and wiring was faulty. Gas had been disconnected three years earlier so the central heating of the hotel had not been working and all of the rooms were without heat. Seven families and eighteen rooms of single residents were scattered between the second, third, and fourth floors of the hotel, occupying only a small portion of the 150-room building. The Building Department imposed a six-month deadline of 5 February 1977 for the Milwaukee to be brought up to code or face closure. The estimate for upgrading the hotel was approximately $300,000, twice the cost that was paid when the hotel changed ownership from the Goon family.[57]

Milwaukee Hotel residents organized a three-member Milwaukee Tenant Council in October 1976 and came to a joint agreement with Bill Vance of the Building Department that three of the violations would be corrected by the city deadline with the remaining eight violations to be completed by 5 August 1977. The ten-month delay would allow for repairs to continue, but more importantly, the time could be used to bring broader attention to the need to save the city's low-income housing, which would in turn save the C-ID. It would allow time for negotiations to commence between the Milwaukee owners and InterIm or the IDHA to possibly purchase the building. An army of committed volunteers managed to address forty of the sixty-item compliance list by September 1977. As efforts to find funding continued, the volunteers succeeded in meeting Fire Department requirements within a week. Twenty tons of debris was removed, the west side of the hotel was closed with tenants relocated to a more concentrated and manageable rental area, and a 24-hour fire watch was activated by community volunteers that lasted fourteen months. Some of the volunteers kept journal entries of the experience, including community activist **Donnie Chin**.

> *June 2, 1978, 6–8 a.m. shift*
> It's been said, for many of us who are active in the social life of the district or who work here, that this is our roots, even though we may not live here. That's true; we feel a belonging, influenced by our parents, our parents' parents, or our culture. My friend's great grandfather, Goon Dip, used to own the Milwaukee…and…[it] used to be a grand hotel, one of the finest in town. It would be good if all the hotels for our elderly could be that way. No?[58]

InterIm and the IDHA were given a short-term lease of the building, but in order to qualify for federal loans under Housing and Urban Development programs, a long-term lease was required. In 1978, the city's Downtown Council and Department of Community Development received $150,000 of funding in a block grant to be used for SRO hotel rehabilitation, an amount that could not begin to address the needs of one hotel let alone those of the entire community. Both money and time were running out for the Milwaukee Hotel to meet the deadline for the rest of the upgrades. Negotiations to buy the building among InterIm, IDHA, and the Preservation and Development Authority, with the partners of the Louie & Wong Investment Company who owned the building, were deadlocked. In September 1979, and with no other recourse available, the residents were relocated and the Milwaukee Hotel doors closed. An anonymously-written poem was written on a second floor room wall, part of which read:

> When I think of the Milwaukee
>   I think of ghetto
> and all the people down here
>   who have convinced themselves
>   that they can do without.[59]

As the spokesperson at the end of the three-year battle to keep the hotel open, **Bob Santos** vowed stronger support of low-income housing efforts for the future of the C-ID and a statement that kept negotiations open should Louie and Wong ever decide to reopen the residential hotel.

> Money in the thousands was poured into the building the last two years just for the maintenance of basic necessities like water, heat, and light [and] it was discovered that the building would not last through the next winter. Other problems started to occur in the heating plant, the electrical and plumbing systems. For the safety factor alone, the responsibility to the residents has become too great of a risk...the time has come and we must leave. We have taken the responsibility to provide relocation funds and are now securing other shelter for the Milwaukee residents. Some day in the future, the owners may want assistance...to pursue rehabilitation of the hotel for low-income renters.[60]

As the Milwaukee Hotel closed its doors, a report on multi-family housing in the downtown was released by an independent consulting firm. Central city neighborhood statistics indicated that 59 percent of all one-person, low-income households were living in the downtown and that single room occupancy units were

> ...often the easiest to care for and the most affordable for these households and that retention of these units was critical. Low-cost housing in the downtown area is especially important for the elderly because of the close proximity to services and the free public transportation. Unfortunately, much of the rental housing in the downtown area has faced the wrecking ball or has been closed over the past years...about 50% of downtown residential structures have been lost in downtown [and] the housing that does remain is becoming more costly. The City of Seattle is suffering a housing crisis.[61]

In the aftermath of the Ozark Hotel fire, the roof had collapsed on the upper two floors, water had leaked down the walls, and the furnace that heated the building was inoperable, but since the ground floor retail spaces were not used for residential purposes, it was possible to still collect rent for the remaining two commercial storefront spaces. Mimicking the building and rental conditions of the Ozark Hotel, SRO commercial storefronts were allowed to remain open as long as the ground floor retail spaces were not used as sleeping chambers and emergency egress and safety codes were met in commercial spaces. The history and tradition of families and retail managers living behind their commercial storefront space was broken, but the SRO buildings would at least provide owners with a small income. For the buildings that remained in the possession of the same Chinese corporations and family associations that had initially built them, the smaller incomes would allow for payment of property taxes, but little else and certainly not enough money for restorations that would revive the hotel portion of the buildings to reopen for business.

JAPANTOWN SROS WITHOUT THE JAPANESE

Even before passage of the Ozark Hotel Ordinance, hotel operation for the next generation of Japanese Americans was waning. With new opportunities for employment, education, and lives outside of the C-ID following the war, the

Sansei, or third-generation Japanese Americans, had little interest in managing hotels in the C-ID. Membership in the SJHAA had declined 20% from 1949 to 1964 with 104 Japanese-operated hotels. With passage of the Ozark Ordinance, membership declined by over 80% between 1964 and 1977 with only nineteen affiliated members. Six of these nineteen hotels were located "below the line," including the Waldon Hotel, Panama, Bush, American, Publix, and Ohio hotels. By 1977, it was dramatically clear that the Ozark Hotel Ordinance managed to do something that even the war had not been able to accomplish and that was to permanently close the hotels as a residence and as a means to earn a living. In 1983, only ten hotels were part of the SJHAA, three of which were below the line: the Panama, Publix, and Ohio hotels.

The ultimate irony came from a 1980 report of the Downtown Human Services Council as they made an assessment of the challenges of being a hotel operator and observed the declining number of hotels and rooms that were open to low-income and elderly residents of the downtown.

> One cannot minimize...the tremendous day-to-day pressures and demands upon the managers. They never know from minute to minute whether the next problem is information giving, coping with a critical illness, stopping a fight or argument, investigating a theft, cleaning up after someone, fixing a broken fixture, etc. In coping with all of this they do so at a very nominal wage and with very few back-up community resources. In most businesses and professions there is usually some type of association or organization which brings the group together periodically. Our study indicates that no such organization exists among hotel and apartment house managers in the Downtown area. RECOMMENDATION: Organize some type of formal or informal association for the purpose of information sharing and problem solving.[62]

There was no expressed knowledge on the part of any office in the city that just such a well-organized hotel association led by Seattle's Japanese American Issei and Nisei had existed "below the line" for seventy years before the Housing Needs Assessment report was written. With the exception of a brief period from 1942 to 1947 and due to the WWII incarceration of Japanese Americans, the Seattle Japanese Hotel & Apartment Association disbanded in 1989 after what amounted to almost 80 years of operation.[63]

MAP 6-1: *Seattle Japanese Hotel and Apartment Association (SJHAA) – 1964 [Author]*

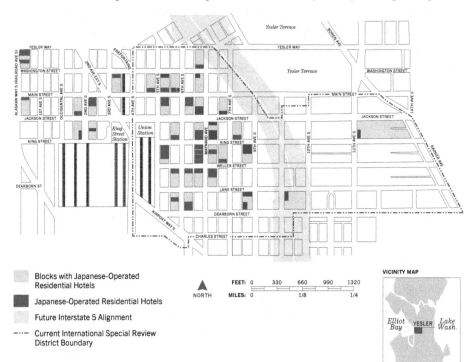

Blocks with Japanese-Operated
Residential Hotels

Japanese-Operated Residential Hotels

Future Interstate 5 Alignment

---- Current International Special Review
District Boundary

FEET: 0   330   660   990   1320
NORTH   MILES: 0   1/8   1/4

VICINITY MAP

Elliot Bay YESLER Lake Wash.

THE COLLATERAL DAMAGE
OF URBAN RENEWAL

According to the City of Seattle, the number of residential hotel buildings
declined from 289 to 77 in the downtown between 1960 and 1980.[64] Of the eight
downtown neighborhoods that were included in a conditions report, the highest number of vacant housing buildings was in the Chinatown-International
District and it was noted that SROs were a "particularly rich source of potential
housing units."[65] By the end of the first quarter of 1980, forty-six hotels were on
the city's list of closures with twenty of these hotels located in the Chinatown-
International District.[66] Yet, single-room rentals were the units with the highest
demand in the downtown and a vacancy rate of less than one percent. As it
was throughout the history of their development, the SRO residential hotels

MAP 6-2: *Seattle Japanese Hotel and Apartment Association (SJHAA) – 1977 [Author]*

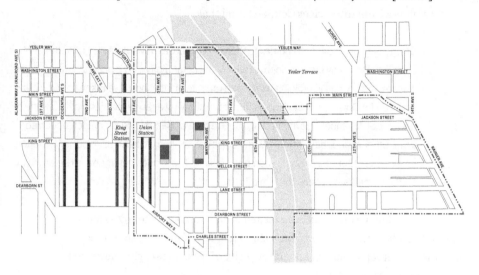

MAP 6-3: *Seattle Japanese Hotel and Apartment Association (SJHAA) – 1983 [Author]*

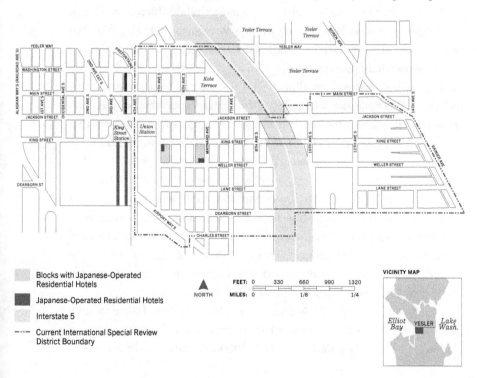

provided housing that satisfied personal need and independence. A report of the Downtown Human Services Council found that:

> Downtown is just as much "home" to those who choose to live there as it is for those who choose to live in any other residential area of the community. ...The bulldozer, the building closure, the change in building usage and the rate of inflation, have taken their toll...the situation for Downtown residents is from one of having a residential "choice"...to one of residential "chance" in even finding a place to live. Had this phenomenon occurred in some other residential community the citizenry would have been up in arms. ...There is no evidence that this phenomenon has peaked. There does not appear to be anything on the immediate horizon to stem this trend.[67]

Sixty demolition permits had been issued in the decade of the 1970s for residential hotels in the C-ID with only three lots developing into low-income housing project replacements and the majority of these vacant parcels turned over to surface parking lots.[68]

Various housing studies were conducted about housing conditions in the 1960s and into the 1970s, each of which had a slightly different number of buildings, closures, and housing units that were reported as having vanished or been retained in the downtown and the C-ID specifically. But all of the major studies agreed that at least half of all of the low- to moderate-income downtown housing had been lost, with the Chinatown-International District representing half of all of these closures. In a 1980 retrospective report that analyzed the cause of so many losses, the Department of Community Development cited that the four major causes of dramatic downtown housing loss were attributable to the freeway construction, urban renewal, public-development projects, and fire and housing ordinances that were adopted because of the Ozark Hotel fire.[69] Land development and private investments were intensifying the demand for more lucrative commercial developments, including tourist hotels as an upscale replacement for the sparseness of an SRO. Hotel chain affiliates such as the Sheraton, Holiday Inn, and Hilton Park Plaza had replaced some of the privately-operated small-scale SROs in the north downtown, and the Kingdome had removed low-income housing in the C-ID.

According to the US Census, the population of the C-ID had steadily declined between 1960 and 1980, with the district losing about 61% of its population to 1,320 people by the latter date. In 1980 over half of the residents were elderly and of low-income and with slightly less than half of the community represented by Asian American residents. Over 2,000 housing units had been lost in this twenty-year period. Even if the remaining hotel buildings would have been brought up to building and fire codes, restoration and renovation would have only provided 620 units of replacement housing. While over half of the residential hotels had closed by 1980, the city's Department of Community Development reported that the residents who stayed in the C-ID did so because of "cultural and linguistic barriers, the attractiveness of relatively inexpensive rents, the availability of ethnic foods and services, and because the District had always been their home."[70]

As quickly as the hotels had been constructed, the few that were left in operation were rapidly losing their foothold in the community. A prediction that had been made in a 1937 article in the Filipino community *Cosmopolitan Weekly* newspaper was seemingly coming to pass as the character of residences and businesses that created the "place" that was the Seattle Chinatown-International District changed.

> The mills of time grind slow but they grind exceedingly fine. For years the people of Seattle have taken their out-of-town guests on tours of our fair city and it has been one of our boasts that we have one of the most elaborate and interesting "Chinatowns" in the United States...how true that was a few years ago. But now things have changed. The venerable gentlemen from the land of Confucius no longer grace the walk before their storefronts...none of the Old China to tell us "The spirit lives on." Is it that the old mandarins have gone to the land of yesteryear, is it that the younger generation is growing away from these traditions that make this old world as livable as it is or is there something deeper, more austere than that which appears on the surface? Today our "Chinatown" has lost the glamour and romance [of] a few short years past....Gradually but with the tenacity and daring of an octopus who has seized its prey, and slowly begins draining the life blood are these merchants who are edging in little by little until one fine day there shall be no Chinatown left.[71]

THE JEWELS OF CHINATOWN: FEDERAL ARREST OF THE MILWAUKEE HOTEL AND THE KONG YICK BUILDINGS

While the Milwaukee Hotel had ceased to be part of the city's low-income housing stock with its 1979 closure, the struggles associated with the building had begun twenty years earlier with the death of heir Daniel Goon in May 1959. In quick succession, the building fell subject to mismanagement of funds with a number of subsequent personal debts that forced the sale of the hotel in February 1965. The hotel was purchased for $150,000 by husband and wife teams Jordan and May Wong, and Donald and Jeannie Louie, with each person having a one-quarter interest in the property. With the closure of the residential floors, only the storefronts were still operating, along with two suspected gambling businesses: the International Club in the basement of the building and the 415 Club located at-grade. Gambling had been integral to the building and the neighborhood's history. Vice raids on the Milwaukee Hotel had happened as early as 1912, just two years after its opening, when customs agents found 156 tael cans of illegal opium that had been found in a trunk in the manager's fourth floor apartment. Still, it was astonishing to members of the community that the FBI had taken such a keen interest in reports of gaming in both the Milwaukee Hotel and the Kong Yick buildings in the 1990s.

At the time of government surveillance, the residential floors had been vacant for twelve years and only 22% of the Milwaukee Hotel was being used in rentable commercial space. The appraised value of the building was estimated at $1.3 million. The Seattle Police Department initiated the investigation of gambling in the Milwaukee in March 1991, which led to a long monitoring process and plan for a "sting" operation between the local police and the FBI. With the help of a Chinese undercover FBI agent, Sa William Liu entered the International Club on 16 December under the guise of wanting to play poker, not knowing that this game had never been played at the club. This mistaken request was just enough to alert the patrons inside. There were two entries to the club: one from a new doorway that had been added to the building on the Maynard Alley side for patrons, and a second from Louie's Broiler that was used only by the gambling bosses. On arrest, one of the Pai Gow dealers identified the club owners as Donald Louie and Andy Wong along with Be Van Truong.

Testimony of the FBI special agents assigned to the case identified that the gambling establishment had:

> ...two video cameras mounted outside the club in the alley positioned so that both the outside door to the club and the alley approaches...could be monitored. The outside door was the first of three doors through which people must pass to enter...the second door, also monitored by a video camera, had a sign on it that said "Members Only." There was also a video camera located above the club...[72] The search resulted in over $5,000 cash, video cameras, monitors, "three gambling tables, two of which were not in use [and one] with a tray full of gambling chips, playing cards, dominoes, dice and Mah Jong tiles and a stack of US currency approximately three inches thick."[73]

It was enough evidence to begin court proceedings against the owners and begin the process of seizing the building. Under violation of federal statute that forbade illegal gambling, the building was now in the control of federal marshals and in essence, it was the building itself that was "under arrest" and the subject of a civil complaint. If the complaint was substantiated, the Milwaukee would come under "forfeiture law" and become the property of the federal government and out of Chinese ownership for the first time since its construction. In the meantime and until a decision could be rendered, no modifications or improvements could be made to the building.

The club at the Milwaukee was found to be in violation of state and federal law that defined illegal gambling as activity "involv[ing] five or more individuals who conduct, finance, manage, supervise, direct or own all or part of such business; and operates continuously for more than 30 days or [having] a gross revenue of $2,000 in any single day."[74] A ledger book of dates, games, payouts and profits indicated that in one five-day period, the club's profit balance ranged between an excess of $6,000 to almost $15,000. Witness testimony confirmed that gaming participants were required to pay a percentage of winnings to the house or owners of the club, an action that was defined in Washington State Law as "professional gambling."[75] The crux of the case that would preserve individual ownerships was based on whether each of the owners could substantiate that they did not know that gambling was taking place on the premises.

In January 1993, and fifteen months after surveillance began, the court determined that the affidavits and testimony of the Wongs and Jeannie

Louie exonerated each of them from being liable for gambling activities and they were able to each keep their share in the building. The testimony of dealers and restaurant workers that identified Donald Louie as one of the house owners and his previous arrests for gambling resulted in the forfeiture of his quarter interest in the building to the federal government.[76] The terms of the judgment dissolved the partnership of the Wongs and Louies. The Wongs subsequently bought Don Louie's forfeited share from the United States Marshal's Office for $294,000. There would be no more gambling in the Milwaukee Hotel.

Like other hotels in Seattle, all but half of one floor of the West Kong Yick building had been vacated following the Ozark Hotel Ordinance. The partial remodeling allowed for tenancy in a mix of twelve single rooms, three studios, three one-bedroom, and one two-bedroom apartment. The company directors had affirmed that rental fees in the building would be kept nominal in order to provide low-cost housing for elderly Chinese immigrants on fixed incomes. Since both buildings had been owned outright for decades, none of the shareholders felt the need for residential profits that exceeded the purpose for which they were constructed.

In June 1994 and in a similar monitoring and sting operation as in the Milwaukee Hotel, the files and records of the Kong Yick Investment Company were seized by the Seattle Police and FBI agents under allegations that professional gambling was occurring on the premises along with organized crime activities that violated Washington State laws. At the time of the raid, gambling was allegedly occurring in the offices of the Wong and Woo Family Associations, and the Lai Kuen Club at 508-1/2 7th Avenue South in the West Kong Yick building. The associations had been under surveillance for two years with Officer L. Shirey, a detective in the Gambling/Special Investigations Unit of the Vice Squad, relying on information from five confidential informants who had participated in other gambling raids for the Seattle Police. Officer Shirey described the activities of the associations in the affidavit for the search warrant.

> ...people participating in the games wager monies on the outcome...and are required to pay a fee to the "house" for the privilege of participating in the games...[of] Mah Jong and 13 card poker...the club also operated the game of Pai Gow for a few days....This club is open 7 days a week and has been operating since at least 1992.... The club opens around noon each day. At that time, the Mah Jong games start...13 card poker is started between 2:00 p.m. and 4:00 p.m...and continues until the club closes, usually around

midnight each night....Individuals obtain cash loans from one of the managers and then use the borrowed money to gamble...the interest charged ranges from 2.5% to 30% per month....The City of Seattle Business Licenses office has advised me that no business license has been issued to the [Wong or Woo] associations.[77]

Evidence was taken from the associations and club, along with all of the historical records and files that were kept in the cabinet and safes of the Kong Yick board room in addition to sundry office supplies. Unlike the Milwaukee Hotel and contrary to articles that were published in the *Seattle Times*, the Kong Yick buildings were not seized by the government, and the company retained control and management of rental spaces while the case was pending. Through their attorney, William Hines, the Kong Yick Investment Company "asserted that they were the lawful owner of the properties but denied allegations of the complaint."[78] Evidence presented in the search warrant notes indicated that "only employees had been observed as having keys to locked club areas," which verified that none of the board members of the Kong Yick Investment Company had access to the association room entry doors.[79] After copious examination of bank, business, financial records, ledgers, by-laws, and correspondence in English and translations of Chinese records dating back to 1910, there was no evidence to link the company with any gambling activity.

At the time of the proceedings, 37% of the East and 52% of the West Kong Yick buildings were producing income. The rental fees for the SRO units ranged between $60 – 75 a month, a small sum given that both buildings totaled nearly 145,000 square feet of leasable space. Neither building was making substantial money for the corporation and both were in need of repair and restoration. In some ways, the case of the Kong Yick buildings was further complicated in that the buildings were still under the corporate shareholder ownership model but now owned by 144 descendants of the original founders holding a total of nearly 900 shares.[80] In the interest of retaining the long heritage that the buildings represented, the company agreed to a Consent Judgment for Forfeiture, paying the Federal Marshal's office $325,000 in settlement rather than risk a protracted legal proceeding, the potential loss of the buildings, and displacement of the elderly renters and long-term commercial tenants. The case against the Kong Yick Investment Company was closed in June 1995, eleven months after the raid.

ENDNOTES

1 The United States Housing Act is also referred to as the Wagner-Steagall Housing Act; named after Senator Robert F. Wagner of New York and Representative Henry B. Steagall of Alabama who drafted the legislation.

2 United States Housing Act of 1937, Sec. 7 [42 U.S.C. 1437e], Authority to Provide Designated Housing. The act was intended to meet the needs of very-low-income individuals with stringent requirements, partially in an effort to ensure that there would not be competition with market-rate housing.

3 City of Seattle, "Yesler Terrace," Seattle Housing Authority Annual Report, 1941.

4 Trevor Griffey, "Yesler Terrace: A Housing Project Like No Other," *South Seattle Star*, 11–24 February 2004, vol. 3, no. 3, p. 5.

5 Irene Burnes Miller. "Relocation of Tenants on the site of Yesler Terrace." Housing Authority of the City of Seattle, 1941. Miller was the Tenant Relocation Supervisor who was stationed in one of the hotels during the relocation process. According to her report, help with relocation was only done by residents who directly requested assistance.

6 Ibid. In Miller's report, she noted that other displaced residents included sixty-six African American families, 161 white families and single people who were "Indians, Greeks and Eskimos."

7 Ibid., p. 6.

8 Letter of Earl F. Dickinson to R.W. Finke. 6 June 1951. Seattle Municipal Archives, Microfiche 2615.02.

9 The alignment of the new freeway was initially called Highway 99 East because the plan was to connect the new route with the existing Highway 99 at a point south of Georgetown and north of Marysville.

10 When the plan was announced, Seattle, Chicago, Cleveland, Denver and Detroit were already in construction. A statewide freeway system had already been approved in Texas with costs that were less than one-third of those of Chicago, at

$2.0 million as opposed to $7.0 million. The difference in cost was attributed to a higher number of private property purchases and building condemnations associated with the construction.

11 John Levy, *Contemporary Urban Planning*, (New Jersey: Prentice Hall, 2009), p. 352,

12 Phelps, p. 116.

13 The trust also owned a few low-rise commercial buildings along with a couple of single-family detached houses in the Central District neighborhood that were moved during the Jackson Street Regrade project. The houses were bringing in about $20.00 per month in income, a sum that could neither maintain the structures nor pay the property taxes.

14 Last Will and Testament of William Chappell, 22 December 1920.

15 The Rainier Heat and Power Company ended up paying about $2,400 less to buy the property back than had they paid the $8,424.93 in taxes that were owed the County.

16 When Chappell purchased these properties in 1903, the three frame building hotels were known as the Cosmos, the Red Light, and the Tokio hotels.

17 This included Ordinances 31578 (1913) that was superseded by Ordinance 72200 (1942) and Ordinance 85500 (1956).

18 The bank had been leasing property in the Governor Apartment Building across Jackson Street.

19 The new powerhouse structure was framed by building a concrete retaining wall from the ground level to the height of Fifth Avenue and extending from the southeast corner of the Publix Hotel in a southerly direction a distance of approximately 90 feet. From that point it continued directly west to Fifth Avenue, a distance of 60 feet. The enclosed area was covered by a lightly constructed roof...the contract included the construction and placing of concrete slabs against the foundations of the Publix Hotel to retain a

dirt fill. "Report to Beneficiaries of the Estate of William Chappell," Courtesy William Montgomery, Attorney at Law, 20 May 1958, p. 7.

20 Under the terms of the loan that paid for the construction of the building, the Trustees needed to take the smallest amount of payment allowed under the provision of the Trust.

21 Letter to the Rainier Heat and Power Company from Fred B. McCoy, Superintendent of Buildings, City of Seattle Department of Buildings, 26 June 1962.

22 William G. Montgomery, Archival Files of Montgomery, Purdue, Blankinship & Austin. Report to the Heirs of William Chappell, 31 December 1970.

23 William K. Goodwin and Robert A Purdue, Montgomery, Purdue, Blankinship & Austin. *Memorandum of Authorities in Support of Petition for Instructions to Commence Liquidation*, Superior Court of the State of Washington, Cause No. 522067. 29 July 1971.

24 Ibid.

25 Lou Corsaletti, "Many Questioned in Fatal Fire," *The Seattle Times*, 21 March 1970, p. A4, col. 3. One more person died at the hospital, making the total fatalities 21.

26 City of Seattle, Ordinance 98868, 6 May 1970.

27 "City's Fire-Code Need," *The Seattle Times*, 25 March 1970, p. 2., col., 1, 2.

28 Office of the State Fire Marshal, "Fires in Multiple-family Residential Occupancies,"18 June 1971.

29 $11,000 in 1971 is the equivalent of an excess of $68,500 in 2018 dollars.

30 Section 3.02030 of the Building Code stated that "All buildings or structures which are structurally unsafe or not provided with adequate exits, or which constitute a fire hazard, or are otherwise dangerous to human life…by reason of inadequate maintenance, dilapidation, obsolescence, damage by fire or other causes or abandonment as specified in this code…are unsafe buildings and may be declared a public nuisance and may be abated."

31 *Kaibigan* is a Tagalog word meaning "friend." Contributing authors of the bi-monthly newsletter included Vic Pineda, editor, and Ally Alfonzo, Peter Bacho, Silme Domingo, Carol Topacio and Dona Young. The journal was a publication of the Filipino Youth Association, an organization that was founded by Fred and Dorothy Cordova and dedicated to civil rights activism in the 1960s and 1970s.

32 "The Struggle is On," *Kaibigan*, 3rd Issue, 9 April 1972, p. 4, 5.

33 Interim was comprised of a pan-Asian and multiethnic membership. The Demonstration Cities and Metropolitan Act of 1966, Public Law 754 (PL 54), was adopted in November 1966; commonly referred to as the Model Cities Program. As an increasing number of people were leaving central cities for what was viewed as a more attractive life in the suburbs, cities were increasingly in danger of losing not only population but the tax base that went with it. Many cities, including Seattle, were becoming centers for those who could not leave, including the poor, elderly, and minority populations. At the time of its passage, 61% of Seattle's central city population was comprised of minorities. The program was meant to revitalize central cities by focusing on joint planning efforts between city officials and neighborhood citizen participation. The intention was to address social and economic problems of respective neighborhoods through adoption of urban programs and comprehensive plan development. Seattle was the first city to be awarded one of these grants to address these issues that were occurring in the Central District, Pioneer Square, and the Chinatown-International District neighborhoods. The boundaries of the neighborhood application were 5th Avenue South, South Yesler Way, 12th Avenue South, and South Dearborn Street. Administered by the Federal Department of Housing and Urban Development, the program was renewed in 1972, but was terminated in June 1975 due to a loss of program funding on the national level, with some of the city's project programs being transferred and eligible for support under the federal Community Development Block Grant (CDBG) program. While developing some successful neighborhood plans, the Model Cities Program lacked the money to implement the majority of the objectives and goals that were identified by the neighborhoods.

34 Located on the Northwest corner of the Maynard Avenue South and South King Street intersection, the Great Wall Hotel was a building addition to the Fujii Hotel and had been constructed following the Jackson Street Regrade. In translation, "Hing Hay" refers to the park as being a place for "pleasurable gatherings."

35 This 11-member board had been called the Citizens Housing Board prior to the adoption of the new housing ordinance.

36 The original draft dictated changes to be done within ten months.

37 Ironically, the Hotel Puget Sound was under investigation in 1969 for three small arson fires that had been set on the third and fourth floors of the building. Damages were isolated to the property and building, with no loss of lives.

38 Interview with Ron Chew, 28 March 2007

39 Internal Memo of Gerry Jones, Department of Community Development, to James Braman, Director of the Department of Community Development. InterIm Community Development Association files, 6 April 1972, and James Braman Collection, Seattle Municipal Archives, 13 April 1972.

40 Ibid.

41 Lawyers for Housing, "Skid Road Housing Study," 1972, Introduction.

42 Ibid, Section II.D. The most populated area was nine blocks, bordered by Yesler Way, I-5, 8th and 7th Avenues South, South Weller Street, and 5th Avenue South.

43 In 1972, Mayor Wesley Uhlman appointed members of the community that included individuals representing the Pioneer Square and Chinatown-International District neighborhoods, as well as Interim members and business and property owners of these two neighborhoods. Called the Citizen's Action Force, they worked in conjunction with the Seattle Department of Community Development (DCD) to make recommendations on how to preserve and enhance both of these south downtown neighborhoods. This included efforts to mitigate adverse impacts of the construction of the Kingdome Stadium. The combined efforts of

both the Citizen's Action Force and DCD led to a recommendation to the City Council to create the International Special Review District.

44 "Low and Moderate Income Housing in Downtown Seattle," City of Seattle, Department of Community Development, August 1973, cover letter of James Braman, Director.

45 Ibid. One of the key pieces of primary research that was used by the city in this report was "The Changing Hotel Pattern in Seattle, 1960–1973" by Kay Peterson and James Katzenberger that was done by the University of Washington Urban Data Center. The boundaries of the studies were slightly different, with the City of Seattle study focusing on the central business district and the Peterson and Katzenberger report including portions of the Capitol Hill and First Hill neighborhoods. This latter study accounted for 21 hotel closures, but the city noted that the number was considerably higher based on their owner/operator survey. Another study that was completed in 1974 by the Skid Road Community Council showed that 3,120 housing units had been lost in the I.D., including apartments and sleeping rooms.

46 In the 1970s, three low-income housing projects were added to the CID neighborhood; that added 205 units, which only replaced about 4% of the over 5,000 units of hotel rooms that had been lost. The Seattle Housing Authority constructed International Terrace (1973), which added 100 one-bedroom apartments and twelve at-grade storefront spaces to the CID. The other two housing projects were added in 1979 included Imperial House (96 units) and International House (99 units), both of which were designated as Section 8 housing.

47 The Publix had been sold by the Rainier Heat and Power Company in 1970 as a part of a "package deal" to acquire the land for development of Uwajimaya, a new retail store on 6th Avenue South.

48 Interview with Takashi Hori, 27 July 2006.

49 "Renovation Aimed at Blight in Model Cities Backwater," *Seattle Post-Intelligencer*, 2 August 1970, p. 7, col. 7. Financial setbacks from another national recession and compliance with local and state bureaucratic offices delayed the work on the project until 1980. The restoration work of architect Edward Burke and his wife Elizabeth included the Nippon Kan Theatre that reopened in 1981 along with a name change of the building from the Astor Hotel to the Kobe Park Building. In 1991 the stewardship of the building under the guidance of the Burkes ended along with the use of the theatre space. The interior of the theatre was renovated again when the main floor was converted to office space that was leased by a messenger service.

50 Tazuma had operated the New Central hotel since 1956.

51 Long-term contract commitment of properties could be as much as forty years.

52 Elaine Ko, "Something Wrong with HUD-subsidized Housing; The Rex Hotel, for Example," *International Examiner*, July 1977, vol. 4, no. 6.

53 Interview with Ray Chinn, 22 August 2006.

54 The Tokiwa Hotel was renamed the Evergreen Hotel.

55 US Department of Housing and Urban Development. "Methods of Urban Impact Analysis: HUD's Section 312 Program," September 1978. These 3% interest loans were repayable in 20 years. Interest and repayment of the loans were then used as a revolving fund for other loan applications. The program ended in 2001.

56 "199 Units—Only a Fraction of Housing Need," *International District Housing Alliance Newsletter*, September 1976, vol. 1, no. 4.

57 The Roberts Hotel at 108 4th Avenue South had similar problems where the structural repairs alone were in excess of $450,000. Razing the building would be less than one-tenth of that cost. It was demolished in May 1983.

58 "Milwaukee Hotel Journal," *International Examiner*, June–July 1980, vol. 7, no. 6, p. 6, col. 1.

59 This poem was discovered by the author on a walk through the Milwaukee Hotel after it had been closed twenty-three years.

60 Bob Santos. "We Must Leave the Milwaukee Hotel," *Inter*Im's Corner*, September 1979.

61 Environmental Works. "Denny Regrade and Multi-Family Housing Potentials," 1979, p. 1.

62 Downtown Human Services Council, "Needs Assessment of Downtown Seattle Residents and Hotel/Apartment House Managers," 17 December 1980, p. 9, R-4.

63 The first recorded Japanese-operated hotel in Seattle was the Cosmos House that opened in 1896. No record has been found of its precise location. In 1897, Seattle mail carriers listed 158 lodging houses and 39 hotels throughout the city with only 2 hotels that were Japanese-operated.

64 "Downtown Population and Housing Data," City of Seattle, Department of Community Development, June 1980, p. 29.

65 Ibid, p. 33.

66 Downtown Human Services Council. The survey and data collection were done from late1979 into the first four months of 1980. The study area included Denny Way as the northernmost boundary, Alaska Way on the West, the C-ID southern boundary, and I-5 on the East. Interviews were done of fifty-eight buildings, about 2/3 of the ones that were estimated as still being occupied within the study area boundaries. Managers and a sampling of tenants were done for each hotel interview. The closed hotel listing included the Cadillac Hotel and Boston Hotel that were south of Yesler Way, but not within the boundaries of the Chinatown-International District. The twenty hotels were listed as the Alki, Atlas, Adams, Evergreen Eclipse, Freeman, Hip Sing Tong, Idaho, Louisa, Milwaukee, Mar N-P, New Central, Oak Tin, Hotel Puget Sound, Pacific, Rex, Roberts, Standard, and Terrace View Hotels.

67 Downtown Human Services Council, p. 8.

68 None of the three projects were residential hotel buildings and only one continued with a pattern that included commercial storefronts. These low-income housing projects were the International House, International Terrace, and Imperial House, the latter two of which were ready for occupants in 1979.

69 The four major studies included Lawyers for Housing, "Skid Road Housing Study," 1972, which examined conditions between 1965 and

1970; City of Seattle Department of Community Development, "Low and Moderate Income Housing in Downtown Seattle," 1973, which covered conditions between 1960 and 1973; Skid Road Community Council, "Changes in Downtown Seattle 1960–1974," 1974; and Kay Peterson and James Katzenberger of the University of Washington Urban Data Center, "The Changing Hotel Pattern in Seattle, 1960–1973," 1973.

70 "Downtown Population and Housing Data," City of Seattle, Department of Community Development, June 1980, p. 59.

71 "Our Chinatown has Lost its Glamour and Romance," *Cosmopolitan Weekly*, 15 May 1937, vol. VI, no. 9, p. 1, col. 2, 3.

72 US v. The Milwaukee Hotel Building, No., C91-1791R, 17 September 1992, Testimony of Special FBI Agent Roberta Burroughs.

73 Ibid. Testimonies of Michael Mahoe Adams, Special Agent, FBI, and Special FBI Agent Roberta Burroughs.

74 Title 18 US Code, Section 1955 (b)(1).

75 Ibid. Accounts by gambling participants of the amount of money that was taken from the house ranged from 5% of the total winnings to $0.50 for every increment of $10.00 that was won, depending on the game that was played.

76 Ibid. According to the testimony of FBI Agent Michael Adams, Donald Louie had been arrested for attempted bribery of two Seattle Police officers in 1973 involving a request for advanced notice of raids on a former gambling den in the Milwaukee Hotel. This case was dismissed, though no information on the reason for dismissal was available. The record revealed a second record in 1976 with the operation of an illegal gambling business that was located in the same commercial space as Louie's Broiler, known as the Modern Pool. In February 1976, the local

office of the FBI raided and arrested members of the Thling Saam Wot for operating an illegal gambling club in the Milwaukee Hotel. Judgment in the latter instance resulted in a $1,000 fine and a one-year suspended sentence. In June of 1987, evidence of illegal gambling was found at the 415 club when a police raid recovered $319 dollars in a shoebox. No arrests were made in the latter raid.

77 Affidavit for Search Warrant, Detective L. Shirey, Seattle Police Department. Issuance of Warrant Approved by Norm Maleng, Deputy Prosecuting Attorney, 1 June 1994. Bill Hines Papers held at the Kong Yick Investment Company. The Wong Family Association had previously been investigated in 1988 for illegal gambling activity.

78 US v. Real Property located in King County: Parcel #1: 701 South King Street, Seattle, Washington, Parcel #2: 725 South King Street, Seattle, Washington; Together with their Buildings, Improvements, Appurtenances, Fixtures, Attachments and Easements., No C94-0826R, 15 May 1995.

79 Search Warrant notes, Bill Hines Papers held at the Kong Yick Investment Company, n.d.

80 While the original Articles of Incorporation called for 1100 shares of stock, over the years the numbers of shares decreased for a number of reasons, including death of a shareholder with no heirs or shares that were unclaimed by descendents. With subsequent generations, whole numbers of shares have been frequently divided into smaller increments if an original owner left them to more than one descendent as part of an inheritance. The corporate bylaws did not include any provision for buying or selling of shares or regulations that would prevent fractional shares. While bylaws required that anyone transferring shares notify the Kong Yick Investment Company, this has not always happened in practice. New company bylaws were adopted in December 2017.

Epilogue: The Legacy of the SRO Hotels

REPEALS AND REVIVALS

The wholeness of community exists in the synergy between the buildings and the people who identify and vest themselves over time in their businesses and what they identify as "home." In the midst of hotel closures and with so much lost in the character of Seattle's Asian American neighborhood, a plan for the Chinatown-International District's future was adopted as part of the 1973 Model Cities Program. The study area stopped short of 12th Avenue South where many of the Japanese American businesses had been, defining the eastern boundary of the district as ending at the freeway. The first comprehensive plan for revitalization of the C-ID was entitled "The International District: An Action Program for Physical Development." The plan was seen as a way to

> ...perpetuate Asian characteristics [as] reminders of a once vigorous commercial and residential neighborhood. To each Asian, the International District represents a concept, a feeling, and perhaps a [place] memory....The preservation of our cultural heritage must be encouraged...sensitive planning is required for this district. We undertook this plan for the following reasons: the community lacks comprehensive planning for a redevelopment program; the community requires a plan which can convey to its members the

images of the long range concepts…the community has a good potential of utilizing the existing Asian character to expand residential, commercial, and social activities catering to a larger Asian clientele….The marginal retail trade, old hotels, apartments, and the low-income residential base are now remnants of a once vigorous community.[1]

Rehabilitating the residential hotels was recognized as central to reviving the district, but strong action plans to do so were weak to non-existent. The document recommended adoption of a "Special Review District" that would begin to identify some criteria and qualities that made the C-ID so uniquely a part of Seattle's Asian American heritage. Under consideration by City Council, such an adopted ordinance would mean that "no persons [would] make alterations, demolish, construct or reconstruct, restore, remodel or make any changes in the exterior appearance of any existing structure in the special review district or change the use of any building, structure or lot without a Certificate of Approval."[2] The majority of what was the remaining building stock consisted of the SRO hotels.

Significantly and for the first time, the pan-Asian Seattle neighborhood was given an officially designated boundary to define its place in the city. The boundaries, as invisible walls, defined the community as an "island" with borders that were determined from the outside as opposed to a focus on key locations of place memory to provide a guide for cultural identity.[3] Doing the latter would have been more inclusive by allowing for a more fluid definition and interpretation of the historic layering that had taken place in this multicultural community. The current eastern ISRD boundary falls short of including the historic Japanese Language School or the Betsuin Buddhist Temple and could not embrace the breadth of the SROs that were so integral in the identity of pan-Asian American settlement in Seattle. Cordoning a community is an easy way to define geographic considerations and address community need, but it is also limiting in that so much concentration is given to identifying an "island" and saving history without understanding how that history was made.

The exodus of the Asian American community from the district was, like the original formation, a combination of coercion and choice. Undeniably, city legislation and urban redevelopments in the name of "progress" influenced the closure of the hotels and businesses, and the demographic profile of the community changed with increasing opportunities to live and work outside of the non-clave that had been created by and for the Chinese, Japanese, and Filipinos of Seattle.[4]

The right of naturalization came as a reward to the Chinese and Filipinos for their status as US allies in WWII, granted to the Chinese in 1943 with the repeal of Chinese Exclusion laws and followed by the Filipino Naturalization Act of 1946. The right of naturalization for the Issei was granted in 1952. With naturalization it was now possible to legally own land. Even so, the alien land statutes remained on the books much longer in Washington than in other states. Washington State followed California's lead in the latter state's 1952 repeal of the Alien Land Law. After two failed attempts in 1960 and 1962, Washington State finally repealed the alien land use laws that had forbidden ownership of property by non-citizen Asian Americans in 1966. It occurred one year after passage of the 1965 Immigration Act that abolished the national origins quota system that had kept the number of incoming Asian immigrants in check. As legislation made the ability to own a portion of the American dream of land and a home a possibility, each group in turn moved to other neighborhoods to raise families and a new generation of Asian Americans soon far outnumbered their immigrant parents. Neighborhoods like Beacon Hill, the Central District, First Hill, and the Rainier Valley offered modest housing opportunities and an ability to remain close to the commercial businesses that were still part of the identity that made the C-ID home. The Chinatown-International District was still recognized as the Asian American core of the city, but the majority of the SRO housing was vacant.

As in the tale of Sleeping Beauty, it was as if a curse had been put on the SRO hotels that had put them in a deep slumber through forced and eerie vacancies. With the passing years turning to decades, the buildings became targets for vandalism and roosts for thousands of pigeons and rats; with neglect breeding more neglect and compounding the initial problems of costly rehabilitation from the Ozark Ordinance. Passersby who would walk the streets of the Chinatown-International District frequently blamed the vacancies and boarded-up windows on building owners who didn't care about their properties, an easy, understandable, but very inaccurate conclusion.

The first comprehensive plan for the district in 1973 was right in its recommendation to seek stakeholders who could help change the identity of the district back to a living and working neighborhood. Change came slowly with the vision and talent of entrepreneurs who were willing to take a chance, and

The Atlas Hotel (front center) and the Milwaukee Hotel (right). [Courtesy King County Assessor's Office, Property Record Cards, 1937–1973, Puget Sound Branch, Washington State Archives]

with private and public partnerships that monitored financial opportunities to help revive some of the twenty-eight residential hotels that were remaining in the C-ID.[5] It was not just a matter of securing funding; it was a race against time to stop vacancy, safety, structural, and cosmetic problems of the hotels from turning into structural decay that was beyond the hope of restoration.

Housing and Urban Development (HUD) funds for rent subsidies were not available for the Rex, Panama, N-P, or Eastern hotels, but the Atlas Hotel, owned by the descendants of founder Shue Mar, became a pilot project for a thirty-year low-interest loan that combined monies from a HUD block grant and a neighborhood housing rehabilitation grant. The Mar family agreed to reciprocate with moderate rents to enhance affordability for a thirty-year period. While the plan for rehabilitation was proposed in 1976, funding wasn't approved until December 1979. What made the rehabilitation of the Atlas Hotel an amazing occurrence is that for the first time in the history of the Asian American community, owners were willing to take a chance and borrow the money that was needed for work on a residential hotel. The $825,000 loan and plan converted the 88 single rooms into 46 studio and one-bedroom units with repayment going into a revolving account that would be available for similar loans.[6]

In the early 1980s, only eleven of the SRO hotels were still operating in the C-ID and far below their capacity with a total of 722 rooms. These included the Bush, Alps, Jackson, Panama, Ohio, American, Eastern, New American, and Publix hotels and the Kong Yick West building. The New Central Hotel had been sold to the SCIDpda and in 1983 the building reopened with a conversion of the original 126 rooms into twenty eight apartment units of low-income housing.

The Rainier Heat and Power Company managed to sell the American, Publix, and Bush hotels, all of which were partially occupied at the time of sale. The American Hotel was purchased in April 1980 and the single rooms renovated to serve as an emergency shelter for women and children operated by the Union Gospel Mission. In 2008 the building was sold again and opened as a youth hostel under private ownership of the American Hotel Building, LLC. As a nonprofit, community-based developer, SCIDpda purchased and rehabilitated the Bush Hotel in 1979, restoring 160 single rooms for low-income residents. Most recently, the US Postal Service rented space in one of the commercial storefronts of the hotel building to provide a local station for C-ID residents when the full-service post office was torn down and redeveloped as an extension of Hing Hay Park.

In 1987, a small portion of the once-bustling Asian American community as defined by the ISRD boundaries was acknowledged by the National Register of Historic Places as the "Seattle Chinatown Historic District," an area that exemplified the history of Seattle's Asian American community. But by its title, the new designation omitted the recognition that so much of that area had really been Nihonmachi and that a node of the Filipino community lay in the 6th Avenue South and South King Street core. Short of public safety considerations and condemnation proceedings by the City of Seattle, the remaining buildings within the boundaries of the multi-layered historical and protective designations would be difficult, if not impossible, to raze without sufficient cause, and verification of the financial infeasibility of restoration. At the same time and on a national level, Seattle had been a participant in the loss of SRO hotel units in major American cities that was contributing to the urban housing crisis. Between 1970 and 1983, New York had lost 113,000 rooms, and between 1970 and 1987 Atlanta had lost 1,757 rooms, with Portland losing 2,426 SRO rooms.[7]

Cities were just beginning to awaken to a new charge that preserving these hotel buildings meant providing a viable alternative of central city housing that could be done through permitting, restoration, and preservation. The lack of understanding on the part of urban renewal proponents had taken a hefty toll on the urban landscape of central cities and adhered to the idea of "home" as a single-family dwelling outside of the downtown and preferably in the suburbs. Planners, sociologists, and cultural anthropologists in the 1970s supported a history of theories that hotel living attracted and emphasized a state of loneliness and cultural isolation in a building type that was neither house nor home by definition.[8] It was ironic that city administrators and planners were finally beginning to understand the very purpose that had created residential hotels—affordable housing close to work and services. In its essence it was a neighborhood whose function and multiple land uses were at the core of the popularized idea of "new urbanism" and sustainability that would take cities by storm by the late 1980s.

HUD launched the Stewart B. McKinney Homeless Assistance Act in 1987 in a series of fifteen new programs signed under the Reagan administration in an effort to help reverse the tide of increasing urban homelessness across America.[9] The act targeted assistance for food banks, emergency social services, mental health programs and substance abuse treatment, and the need for emergency transitional housing. The loss of SRO units in the downtowns of cities across America was recognized as the reason for critically depleting low-income housing with a direct connection to the homeless crisis that was facing the country. In part, the McKinney Act championed serious consideration of SROs in its purpose "to provide funding to rehabilitate existing structures to create SRO housing for homeless individuals of very low income,...provide affordable, secure housing on a relatively permanent basis...[and that] the lack of preservation policies will make the SRO an endangered form of affordable housing in many communities. And yet, it provides an effective housing alternative for many homeless individuals."[10]

Title IV of the Act specifically included a program that addressed rehabilitation of buildings to serve as SRO units along with a Section 8 voucher system that would guarantee rental payments to the owner by the qualifying residents. Grant monies could be applied to rehabilitation costs for any building that was or could be converted to SRO units as long as the cost for conversion or renovation exceeded $3,000 per unit. The program itself was supervised by the Seattle Housing Authority that had spearheaded the Yesler Terrace

Family Housing Project. Between 1987 and 1992, funding that was used in Seattle represented seventy-two cases of assistance to emergency shelters and transitional housing projects, sixty-four food bank programs and four SRO projects. A report from the Section 8 Moderate Rehabilitation Program for Single-Room Occupancy Dwellings for Homeless Individuals indicated that the program had funded thirty total buildings nationwide. **Ray Chin** shared his family's history with the Rex Hotel.

> In 1947, my family bought the Rex Hotel building from Mr. Waisen who was the original owner of the building. Russell's Meat Market had been a commercial store in the Rex Hotel since 1907, and it was there until the 1990s. After the Ozark Hotel fire, everything had to be brought up to code so quickly but the amount of rent we were collecting was so minimal and would never have covered a conventional loan to repair the buildings. We had about 99 rooms in the Rex. Even putting a sprinkler system in the hallways and common areas was so costly. We had no choice but to close the rental section of the building and it stayed closed for almost twenty-five years. My brothers and sisters and I looked at Section 8 opportunities but they just weren't working very well. There were so many different programs with little bits of money and the program requirements would come and end…it was unpredictable.[11]

In the 1990s, InterIm Community Development Association spear-headed the effort to restore four hotels as low-income housing through the formation of private-public partnerships in grant and loan funding, with InterIm acting as owner or developer. With the Gee How Oak Tin Foundation, the Oak Tin opened with 21 units from its original sixty single rooms in 1991. The N-P Hotel was sold by the descendants of the Shitamae brothers to InterIm and reopened with 63 units in 1994 with eighteen rooms that were still a part of the original hotel design. The Rex Hotel reopened in 1995 with thirty affordable apartments. The last to be renovated was the Eastern Hotel. Opening in 1998, the Eastern Hotel replaced the single 100 rooms with forty-seven apartment units. A commemorative mural and photo exhibit located in the former first floor lobby paid tribute to author Carlos Bulosan and the Filipino laborers, cannery workers, community activists who had left an indelible legacy in the hotel and the district.

In the largest residential hotel that had ever stood in the C-ID, a June 1992 fire department inspection of the Hotel Puget Sound found numerous hazards and conditions that deemed the structure "unfit for human habitation

[with] an estimated cost of repairs [that would] exceed fifty (50) percent of the replacement value of the building."[12] Twenty years of closure compounded an even longer fight to repair and maintain the building when it was open. Seeking relief from the problems that were beyond any potential for repair or restoration of the hotel, the owners filed a permit for demolition and the case went to the ISRD for a review that was presented in a public hearing. The report from the Department of Neighborhoods indicated that "all of the plumbing had been removed from the building...the roof is virtually non-existent and the building has severe structural problems...the Fire Department has issued orders that in the event of fire no one can enter the building to fight a blaze because structural deficiencies make it an imminent danger to the firefighters."[13]

The ISRD granted a Certificate of Approval for the demolition of the Hotel Puget Sound on 15 September 1992 with a stipulation "that any future temporary or permanent use or development of the property [was] subject to Board approval."[14] By November, the gateway hotel at the southern entry of the C-ID was gone.

The Publix Hotel was part of a larger land purchase by one of Seattle's pioneering Japanese American families. In 1975, the Moriguchi family's Uwajimaya Corporation had planned for a larger Asian American foods and goods store that would be built on lots adjacent to the Publix and on the site where Chappell's Paris and St. Nicholas hotels once stood. The Publix Hotel building was added to the land sale by default according to then-CEO Tomio Moriguchi.[15] It wasn't so much that the family wanted to purchase or operate a hotel, but their commitment to stewardship of the greater Asian American community was part of their own history in the district. The Publix Hotel was the last of the Rainier Heat and Power Company hotels to open and it was the last one to close in the C-ID from escalating maintenance and repair costs. The concrete that was used throughout the 1927 building, including room wall construction, may have been the latest and most efficient material for its day but it was also the cause of some of the astronomical restoration estimates that included tearing out walls to access plumbing and electrical wires and replacing the original elevator. Many of the total 211 small 8' x 10' rooms did not lend themselves to easy expansion for structural reasons. In August 2003, the Publix Hotel closed its doors.[16] Under three successive generations of hotel management by the same family that began with Seizo "James" Hashiwara, his daughter, **Taeko Hashiwara Taniguchi** recalled:

Razing the Hotel Puget Sound. A Filipino immigrant laborer works at cleaning off the mortar from the bricks of the hotel so that they could be reused. He was paid $1.00 per brick. [Courtesy Dean Wong Photography]

My father bought the hotel business that was the Publix in 1945. The hotel had always been operated by Japanese from the Kagoshima Prefecture, even before my family and when it was owned by the Rainier Heat and Power Company. My father bought it from Mr. Funimori...they were both members of the Kagoshima kenjinkai and this is how my father learned that the business was for sale. My husband and I moved to Seattle from Hawaii in 1949 to help my parents with the hotel and we stayed to manage the building. We had a home in Beacon Hill but we spent so much time in the hotel...our children grew up in the building, talking with the residents and playing on the hotel awning and in the basement where we had a basketball hoop. We retired from the hotel business in 1970 and our son, Don, took over as co-manager after that and became the manager in 2001. The Publix had a huge lobby, a place where everyone could come to play cards and just talk with one another. There would be chairs in the front of the lobby to sit and watch people walk by and spittoons sat by the chairs for our patrons...when Don was little, one of his jobs was to keep them clean. Some people stayed a long time...Mr. Hatana stayed with us at least twenty years. There were Filipino cannery workers in the hotel when they weren't in Alaska. Some of them would make reservations in advance but most would just come. There was always someone at the desk 24-hours a day so they knew there would always be someone waiting for them to check in.[17]

Only seventy-three residents were living in the available 120 hotel rooms of the Publix at the time it closed; a total that was fewer than the ninety-two guests who had checked in for the hotel's grand opening on 29 December 1927. A feasibility study for the restoration of the Publix was undertaken in 2013 with a plan to begin construction in 2014. Like its neighbors to the east, the "new" Publix Hotel would contain a mix of studios and one-bedroom units and restore the at-grade commercial storefronts. It returned to the gateway status that it once held as the key entry point of the King Street Chinatown core with a grand opening and move-in of residents in August 2016.

Nearly one hundred years after the Asian immigrants began to occupy the C-ID, another wave of revival has been taking place with a handful of the SRO buildings, two that were intended for market-rate rental housing and two that would be part of architectural preservation in adapting the buildings for an alternative use. James Koh, himself a self-made pioneering Chinese immigrant, undertook the task of private redevelopment when he purchased the Milwaukee, Alps, and Mar hotels in 2003. The Mar opened in 2008 with office spaces and the Alps Hotel was remodeled to reuse the same small footprint of SRO rooms as efficient studio units. Goon Dip's Milwaukee Hotel reopened with a new configuration of the floors into studio, one-and two-bedroom apartment rentals in 2010. Only the familiar at-grade level commercial retail storefronts remained a part of these three original buildings.

In 2005, the Kong Yick Investment Company garnered the support of its 240 shareholder votes in a decision to sell the East Kong Yick building. With three bids, the company took the one that was going to retain the history of the structure. The building was sold to the Wing Luke Museum of the Asian Pacific American Experience with plans to refurbish the old hotel into a living history museum and one that would commemorate the spirit of the pan-Asian American community that had lived and worked to build the Chinatown-International District. For the museum, it was the first permanent home in a building that they would own outright. With a $24.7 million capital campaign led by then-Executive Director Ron Chew, the museum opened its doors to the public in 2007. Members and supporters of the Asian American community flooded into King Street and raised their hands toward the building to bless its future and to commemorate their common ground of the past. Converting a building intended for housing to a museum needing large exhibit spaces resulted in the removal of the majority of the floors, rooms, spaces, and hallways that had once been occupied by Asian immigrant workers. A small cluster of carefully furnished rooms was retained that marks the passing of the pan-Asian SRO "home." In meeting the standards of the National Register of Historic Places, the exterior of the building remained true to its original design.

Around 4:00 p.m. on Christmas Eve 2013, a fire on the top floor of the Louisa Hotel started from what investigators declared as an unknown cause. The blaze on the western side of the building along Maynard Alley lasted into the early morning hours with the building continuing to smolder into the holiday. On Christmas morning, people from the community filed by the cordoned-off area and watched and wondered if the 105-year-old structure would collapse. With at-grade businesses closed and the two residential floors vacant, there were no lives lost, but the building sustained critical damage that compromised the roof structure, floors and structural frame on the west side before the fire could be extinguished. The larger questions were whether the damage would necessitate razing the entire building and what this would mean to the identity of the historic Chinatown core of which the Louisa Hotel was an integral part.

Local newspapers repeatedly and inaccurately referred to the hotel as the "Wah Mee" building to emphasize the name of a gambling club that was once located in the lower levels of the building. The private card room business was a location of grief in the Louisa's history that included a robbery and multiple homicides, which had occurred one night in 1983. The Wah Mee reference angered much of the Asian American community for the sensationalism of a story that was but a small part of the building's history and a sad moment in the district. Articles assumed and mistakenly portrayed the building as one that was in ruin without any firsthand knowledge of the building's condition. No mention was made of the hotel's qualities, including its being the last SRO of its kind in the C-ID to have window bays on its street facades. The others with that feature had been owned by William Chappell and had long since been torn down. Little, if any, mention was made that the Louisa was home to the Mon Hei, the first Chinese bakery that ever came to the C-ID, and that the bulletin board on the building's east façade continued a tradition of serving and posting news and notice of China that began in the Chinatown-International District

Mural painted on the wall of the community room in the Louisa Hotel, now lost to the 2013 Christmas Eve fire. [Author]

The abandoned Association Room in the West Kong Yick building that was closed at the same time as the residential hotel portion of the building following the passage of the Ozark Hotel Ordinance. [Author]

around 1890. The colorful murals of the hotel's community room that brought the former residents of the 149-room hotel together for conversation, cards, and occasionally for dancing was lost. The Woo family, as owners of the building, vowed to salvage and shore up what was possible and restore the structure to use as they had begun to investigate a few years before the fire. In March 2014, building inspectors determined that the west wall of the building and much of the internal corridors and rooms on that side would need to be removed, including the site of the Wah Mee incident. The historic façade of the building has been saved and repaired and supported with buttresses while restoration of the building continues in a plan that will fully restore it to housing, beginning with construction in January 2018.

The Kong Yick Investment Company completed their first preservation and development plan for the West Kong Yick building in 2016, outlining one possibility for restoring the building. Financial means and escalating costs of restoration of a single building are as critical now for the Kong Yick Investment Company as they were when the Rainier Heat and Power Company was faced with a similar challenge. The disposition on which path will be taken for its restoration lies in the hands of its board of directors and the 160 remaining shareholding descendants of the original investors that supported the Goon Dip, Chun Ching Hock, and Chin Gee Hee 1910 vision for Chinatown. **Curtis Woo** has been a director of the Kong Yick Investment Company for forty years and reflects on the responsibilities of what it means to be associated with the flagship Chinatown building.

When I joined the board, I had barely graduated from college when my father, Woo Din Poy "Daniel" encouraged me to become an active member in the corporation. My father was the president of the board of directors and he was until he died in 1987. My family had been one of the first Chinese immigrants to settle in Seattle's old Chinatown. My great grandfather was Woo Quon Bing, one of the partners of Chin Gee Hee that started the Quong Tuck Company. It was one of the first mercantile stores to move to the East Kong Yick building in 1910 as a sign of their commitment to the new Chinatown...in 1977, my father changed the business to a restaurant but kept the name and restored a lot of the fixtures. That was the same year I joined the board...I wasn't really sure what to expect as a director and everyone else was 40–60 years older than me. There were thirteen directors that included two secretaries; one to take the minutes in Chinese and one in English. We signed our Chinese names as part of the meeting attendance

The Sam Yick Co. Express delivery that was part of the Quong Tuck Company in the East Kong Yick building. The window sign of the Quong Tuck advertises the company as an "Importer and Exporter, Tea and Rice, Wholesale and Retail." [Courtesy The Wing Luke Museum, Donation by Daniel Woo, 1991.100.506]

records. Eventually everything was in English. Then as now, I feel an obligation to the tradition and history that this building represents and I believe we can restore it...it is the legacy of Chinatown.

In the summer of 2014, the City of Seattle passed the Rental Registration and Inspection Ordinance (RRIO). The intention of the ordinance was to ensure that "all rental housing in Seattle is safe and meets basic housing maintenance requirements."[18] All units are registered with the city and properties are inspected by independent contractors for "livability" compliance. For the first time, Seattle's Department of Construction and Inspections has specifically noted that "units with shared kitchens and baths such as those in a single-room occupancy (SRO), rooming house, or micro-housing property are considered individual rental housing units."[19] Not surprisingly, the ordinance comes at the heels of a 2009 American Housing Survey that indicated "10% of Seattle rental housing having 'moderate to severe' physical problems."[20] Less than two years into the ordinance, there are signs that the remaining SRO building owners will consider selling the buildings in order to meet the checklist of standards within the constantly-shifting deadlines. In the absence of financial assistance these Asian American-owned buildings may be sold to outside development interests who can renovate and comply with the code. In 2015, this did happen with the sale of the Republic Hotel that began with the Fang Yick Investment Company almost 100 years ago. The Chew Lun Benevolent Association that represented the Chinese family association that commissioned the building is now gone and searching for a new home in the C-ID.[21] Slated for market-rate housing, the low-income tenants who lived in the building also had to leave. As property values continue to escalate, vacant parcels and structures that are deemed non-contributing to the historic district are seeing an increasing number of interested developers and pre-design proposals.

Most recently, the mayor and city council launched new efforts to address the lack of affordable housing in a rapidly growing city through the Housing Affordability and Livability Agenda or "HALA." One result was the Mandatory Housing Affordability (MHA) program, which is changing a number of working-class neighborhoods in the city, including the fragile C-ID community. As a multi-faceted program, the MHA proposes to increase densities in neighborhoods that have greater access to mass transit by upzoning the land. The latter action to increase density by allowing construction of taller structures began in 2011 with upzones to the Japantown neighborhood. Unfortunately for the C-ID, upzoning actions did not stop there and began again in earnest in September 2014 when considerations of broader-based rezone and affordable housing measures were proposed along with formation of a HALA Advisory Committee. The city announced their intentions for implementing MHA in November 2015 and spent the next five months doing what they termed "significant public outreach and engagement."[22] Between November 2015 and December 2016, the city adopted ordinances that established the procedural steps and requirements that would be needed for passing additional upzoning without actually implementing actions in any specific neighborhood.[23] In April 2017, the HALA Advisory Committee recommended "implementing MHA requirements in conjunction with increases in development capacity" as their "key recommendation."[24]

In July 2017, Council Chambers of City Hall was packed with organizational leaders of the C-ID, who expressed their fears of gentrification and a loss of small independent businesses should MHA be passed without mitigation measures. Simply stated, upzoning would increase the value of land in the neighborhood and make the small-scale buildings outside of the historic core attractive targets for redevelopment. Some comments in the Council Chambers were concerned that no language translators were present or requested at the hearing and that this indicated a lack of outreach to those non-English speaking residents of the C-ID who would be most affected. Council agreed to delay the final vote for one month to allow community stakeholders to make sure that people in the neighborhood were informed of the impending change. Asian American organizations in the C-ID mobilized to unify their voice in an effort to retain the community amid development pressures as they had done during the hotel closures of the 1970s. Interim CDA, the Japanese American Citizens League (JACL), Friends of Little Saigon, and the Filipino American National Historic Society circulated fliers of information in the neighborhood businesses and SRO hotels.

The town hall meeting with City Council was scheduled in August 2017 with the venue held in the C-ID in the Nisei Veterans Committee Memorial Hall auditorium space. This time, there were many more voices that included residents and business owners and with a clear majority of people who did not support the measure. At the closing of the thoughtful public testimony by the community, upzoning and the MHA Ordinance 125371 for the Chinatown-International District was approved by a unanimous vote of the council and signed into law.[25] The concessions that council offered the community came in the form of a companion resolution that included the veiled language of vague solutions to "continue investment...which builds creative anti-displacement, community driven solutions, explore strategies to encourage community control of land,...[and] consider ways to prioritize the City's spending of cash contributions made through the payment option of the Mandatory Housing Affordability program...."

Under MHA, developers are now required to provide a percentage of low-income units in a new commercial or mixed-use construction or pay into a fund that will be used for such a purpose. The monies would then be competitively offered to nonprofit housing associations who would build affordable housing units "somewhere" in the city. While the MHA plan sounds like a reasonable one, it is already showing signs of unraveling the special places that remain in the C-ID.

The pressures of "highest and best use" of the land are beginning to alter the district and most notably in the Little Saigon neighborhood that developed as Southeast Asian refugees became part of the C-ID in the mid-1970s and at the same time that the Ozark Ordinance was being passed. It is not part of the historic core. Properties with two-story buildings are attractive commodities for redevelopment purchases and there is fear that the displacement of small and independent businesses and nonprofit agencies is imminent. Despite the option for residents to return to a new building on its completion, the increased rental fees make the invitation more pro forma than genuine. There is also no assurance that the low-income housing fund will be used for replacement of units that have been and will be lost in the C-ID. The increased densities are not supposed to affect the historic core of residential hotels but RRIO is already showing signs of undermining the social character and cultural history of this area.

In order to adopt the MHA resolution, the Land Use, Zoning, and Development committee of the City Council moved ahead with the same swiftness and myopia that passed the Ozark Ordinance over five decades ago. The council has attempted appeasement to the neighborhood by expanding the influence area of the International Special Review District zone to match the neighborhood boundaries, an action that would have no bearing on what will be built but will allow comment on appearance. The new buildings will have to "look" the part of contributing to the "Asian character district" as it is defined in the ISRD ordinance, evaluating visual characteristics of a building that the original founders did not find necessary. But is the effort of ISRD expansion too little, too late since nothing can stop the more substantive issue of development rights that come with higher density zoning that is already in place? Housing is still a commodity that is driven by the private market and nonprofit housing and community development organizations will be trying to competitively bid on the purchase of expensive land. With no meaningful mitigation measures included in the MHA, displacement can continue.

There are large issues that loom over the neighborhood as to what happens to the identity of a pan-Asian district with ownership that is no longer Asian American. Gentrification of these ethnic districts is being addressed nationwide in cities such as Los Angeles, San Francisco, Boston, Philadelphia,

Washington, DC, Portland, and Seattle. With so much of Japantown gone, will the core SROs of Chinatown remain in Chinese American ownership in light of the same economic pressures that took Seattle's first Chinatown buildings?

HOME IN AN SRO

Living in a single room occupancy residential hotel was neither fully private nor public, and certainly not as absolute as people imagine either domain to be. While so many articles have referred to the life of these residents as "lonely," this is also a characteristic that is too broadly and easily accepted as the standard measure and norm, and one that doesn't really seem to fit those hotels where Asian American management or patronage was a part. There was no lack of social connection in hotel living, but rather an opportunity for an individual to choose the level at which personal interaction could occur and according to the situation that presented itself. In this way, community life in a hotel was one that could be like a spectrum of contact and participation, and on a continuum from no to regular involvement.

There is a certain amount of irony that the Ozark Ordinance, which was intended to save the lives of hotel occupants, did such broad damage to the social and physical community that it was intended to protect. The goal of "public safety" found no balance with other equally pressing needs to provide housing for the low-income, downtown population. In countless reports by city and federal offices, newspaper accounts, private consultants, and nonprofit agencies, it was the ordinance that was blamed for the loss of housing. But believing this and blaming the law that was written on paper makes the loss of affordable housing far too simplistic and inaccurate. While the ordinance was the law, the extensive loss in great part was due to its administrators, who lacked planning and forethought regarding the consequences of complying with the provisions of the regulation.

For Asian Americans "below the line," it was another in a series of near-fatal legal blows that would act to remove their cultural connection with the hotels and businesses that had been their homes, heritage, and livelihood for over a century. The elimination of housing for a fragile population of Asian Americans, elderly, and low-income people and the structural damage of countless buildings that have been left vacant for decades, continues to be an uphill struggle for owners of the SRO hotel buildings amid new and evolving city policies that are redefining "home."

ENDNOTES

1 The District Design Group, The International District: An Action Program for Physical Development, 30 June 1973, Introduction.

2 Ibid., Special Review Districts, no page number.

3 Dan Abramson, Lynne Manzo, Jeffrey Hou, "From Ethnic Enclave to Multi-Ethnic Translocal Community: Contested Identities and Urban Design in Seattle's Chinatown-International District," *Journal of Architectural and Planning Research*, 23:4 (Winter 2006), p. 341–360. http://taz.tamu.eud/Press/japr2.html.

4 The term "non-clave" was developed to describe the presence of an ethnic community where the physical indicators of community are not geographically defined or possessing contiguous land uses such as expected in urban ghettos or enclaves, but where the social community ties remain very strong. The term was coined by the author in *Sweet Cakes, Long Journey: The Chinatowns of Portland Oregon*, p. 267.

5 In *The American City, What Works, What Doesn't*, author Alexander Garvin presents strong arguments for what he has termed "ingredients of success," or factors that contribute to the success of projects and cities. One of the ingredients discussed includes the significant role of entrepreneurship.

6 In 2009 at the end of the thirty-year time commitment, the Mar Family could decide on the future course of rentals.

7 Patricia King, "Help for the Homeless," *Newsweek*, Vol. 111, Iss. 15, p. 58.

8 E. Hertz and O. Hutheesing. "At the Edge of Society: The Nominal Culture of Urban Hotel Isolates," *Urban Anthropology*, Vol. 4, (4), 1975, p. 324. The research came to the conclusion that the social isolation of hotel living began early in the life of the individual. The scope of the work was using a five-month study in a single Manhattan Hotel. The idea of the hotel creating a life of strangers was further supported in the early work of Dr. Norman Hayner, who looked at social isolation in his sociological studies of hotel occupants in Seattle beginning in the 1960s. Hayner

contended that living in hotels was more a result of the breaking of relationship structures than the creation of such.

9 The Act was renamed the McKinney-Vento Act on 30 October 2000 in recognition of the support and work that Minnesota Congressman Bruce F. Vento had given the Act since its initial passage.

10 "Stuart B. McKinney Homeless Programs," Housing and Urban Development, http://www.huduser.org/publications/homeless/mckin/sro.html. Accessed 9 April 2009.

11 Interview with Raymond Chinn, 22 August 2006.

12 City of Seattle, Department of Construction and Land Use, Order of the Director, File No. AB92219, 23 June 1992.

13 City of Seattle, Department of Neighborhoods, Office of Historic Preservation, Nikkei Manor Project File, Meeting minutes of the ISRD board, 8 September 1992.

14 Ibid.

15 Interview with Tomio Moriguchi, 24 August 2006.

16 The Uwajimaya Corporation helped each of the seventy-three remaining residents with over $2,000 in financial relocation assistance.

17 Interview with Taeko Tanaguchi, 25 October 2006.

18 Seattle Municipal Code, Chapter 22.214: Rental Registration and Inspection Ordinance. Section 020 clarifies the housing definition and includes single-room occupancy units as housing.

19 www.seattle.gov/dpd/codesrules/licensingregistration/RRIO/aboutrrio — Accessed 9 September 2014.

20 Ibid.

21 This association includes the surnames of Huie/Hui/Huey/Hoy, Hom/Tom/Tam, and Der/Che/Chea/Tse.

22 "Response to Public Feedback on Mandatory
Housing Affordability (MHA) Implementation in
Downtown and South Lake Union," May 23, 2016.
http://www.seattle.gov/Documents/Depart-
ments/HALA/Response%20to%20Public%20
Feedback%20on%20MHA%20DT%20SLU%20
Implementation%202016-05-23.pdf. Accessed
August 2017.

23 "Implementation of Mandatory Housing Affordability Requirements in the Chinatown/Interna-
tional District – Director's Report." April 2017.
These included Ordinances 124895, 125108,
and 125233. https://www.seattle.gov/Docu-
ments/Departments/HALA/SLU_DOWNTOWN/
Director%27s%20Report%20-%20MHA%20
ChinatownID%20Implementation.pdf. Accessed
August 2017.

24 Ibid.

25 Passed by a unanimous vote of the Seattle City
Council on 31 August 2017, Resolution 31754
that supported the MHA Ordinance 125371,
struck the words "Historic Manilatown" from the
list of C-ID neighborhoods; without considering or investigating the long history of Filipino
settlement in the Chinatown-International District.
Community members subsequently mobilized
to establish the Filipino Town Coalition and with
supporters petitioned the council to correct
this decision and revise the original companion
Resolution to include "historic Filipino Town" by
Resolution 31769. Final approval was given on 8
September 2017.

ACKNOWLEDGEMENTS

This has been a very long and complicated project to research and one that has been a consuming and captivating life activity. It has made my relationships with those involved and aside from the book all the more dear and meaningful. I have been blessed with the company and support of so many people who have given all measures of confidence and support, and lent both their expertise and advice. I am most fortunate to have the faith, friendship, and love of my husband and fellow scholar, Daniel Dombrowski. In all of the years of his listening about this project, I believe that he knows as much about the hotels as I do.

I am grateful to everyone in the Chinatown-International District who shared their lives and community with me for over thirty years. I am particularly indebted to the Tokita family, Shox, Yuzo,Yoshiko, Kurt, and Kara, Takashi and Lily Hori and to Hiroshi Tyrus "Fish" Okada. Two dear friends have been behind me on this research journey for the past eleven years. Rod Shutt began as a dedicated research assistant on this project and taught me Illustrator software so that I could produce the maps for this work. Throughout the years, he took any number of phone calls and text messages day or night so that I could simply talk about the project. If he ever tired of it, he never let me know. When I met Gary Davis, he was a reporter for KPLU who took a special interest in the community and the hotels. He was one of the first people to find the topic newsworthy. No one could ask for kinder or more caring friends than these two men.

My thanks to Robert Hori, Gardens Cultural Curator and Program Director, of The Huntington Library for his talent in Japanese language translation. Deep appreciation goes to the talents of librarians and archivists Greg Lange, Phil Stairs, Midori Okazaki, Susan Karren, Jeannette Voiland, Julie Kerssen, Anne Frantilla, Bob Fisher, and Carolyn Marr. They are all gifted with skill, tenacity, and patience, as is Rebecca Frestedt, International Special Review District Board Coordinator and planner for the Chinatown-International District, Seattle Department of Neighborhoods. I am grateful to research repositories that hold a wealth of documentation, including the Seattle Municipal Archives, Wing Luke Museum of the Asian Pacific American Experience, King County Archives, Museum of History and Industry, Densho, Washington State Historical Society, The National Archives at Seattle, Japanese Cultural and Community Center of Washington (JCCCW), Seattle Public Library, and the University of Washington Special Collections.

This list would be incomplete without special thanks to Cali Copczick, a tireless copy editor, and Bruce Rutledge, Managing Editor of Chin Music Press, who understood this project and envisioned its greater meaning, and to Dan Shafer for his artistic talents. I am grateful to them for making this book a reality.

Finally, I add a special thank you and brief explanation about the dedication of this book. I was three years into the research of the project when I heard about a group of gentlemen who grew up in Seattle's old Japantown. They called themselves the "Main Street Gang." I began to search for them with only a thread of a connection that they would sometimes meet at the Panama Tea House on an irregular basis.

The teahouse manager allowed me to leave an envelope with a note taped to the outside of the cash register and I hoped that one of the Gang would see it, read it, and reply. I addressed the envelope to the "Main Street Gang" with a big "PLEASE read" on the front.

It took about a month for a reply and it was Roy Hashimoto, who phoned me to find out who I was and why I was looking for them. I described this research and asked if the Gang would meet with me and allow me to interview them. Mr. Hashimoto explained that the Gang now consisted of the four remaining members who were left of the original seventeen and that they had a friendship that spanned 70 years.

He was fine with scheduling a meeting and his only concern was that maybe the other guys, Joe Hamanaka, Eddy Sano, and Tad Sato, might be reluctant to talk to someone they didn't know. He took care of this by devising a plan to introduce me; a scheme where he and I would briefly meet before the others would arrive at the teahouse. If he knew what I looked like in advance, he could introduce me as "an old friend."

It was the first of many meetings that we would have together with conversations that occurred over lunch followed by tea. It began as research and became much, much more as we grew into a friendship. We met about once a month for eight years at the Bush Garden restaurant, sitting at the same table and each of us in chairs that became our designated places. Sometimes other people would join us either by an invitation beforehand or someone who just happened to be there and who the guys knew...and they knew everybody. We sat there, ate, and visited until the waitress told us the restaurant was closing to prepare for the dinner crowd and that we had to leave. After a couple of years of lunches, they inducted me into the Gang on Chinese New Year by giving me the "#5" designation along with a $25 gift card to the Uwajimaya store. From that day forward, I was known as "five."

No topic of conversation was off-limits, not even the ones that I feared were too sensitive to discuss, such as the years of Japanese incarceration. We talked about their lives, experiences, and recollections of the Japantown that they all knew so well; every street, alley, sidewalk, lot, buildings and businesses, ball fields, and friends, some of whom did not come back after WWII. I learned to see the community through their eyes. I still see it this way.

Mr. Hamanaka died in September 2011, Mr. Sato in March 2013, followed by Mr. Hashimoto in April and Mr. Sano in September of that same year. I regret that they didn't get to see this work in print, but I don't think that this was ever as important to them as the time that we spent together. They all knew that this book would be completed and dedicated to them as one small thank you for their friendship and all that they shared.

BIBLIOGRAPHY

Books and Articles

Abramson, Dan, Lynne Manzo, Jeffrey Hou, "From Ethnic Enclave to Multi-Ethnic Translocal Community: Contested Identities and Urban Design in Seattle's Chinatown-International District," *Journal of Architectural and Planning Research*, 23:4 (Winter, 2006): 341–359.

"The Alaska-Yukon-Pacific Exposition," *The Coast*, Vol. XVIII, No. 3 (September 1909): 3.

Ambrosio, Christine. "Individualizing Space: Artifacts and Decoration found in Pilipino American Homes and Residences." In *Filipino American Architecture, Design, & Planning Issues*, ed. Anatalio C. Ubalde, 93–108. Flipside Press, 1986.

Anderson, Nels. *The Hobo: The Sociology of the Homeless Man*. Chicago: the University of Chicago Press, 1923.

Andrews, Mildred Tanner, ed. *Judge J.T. Ronald: Reflections Along the Wayside of Life*. Shoreline, WA: Shoreline Historical Museum, 2003.

Azuma, Eiichiro. "The Politics of Transnational History Making: Japanese Immigrants on the Western 'Frontier,' 1927–1941." *The Journal of American History*, Vol. 89, No. 4 (March 2003): 1401–1430. http://www.jstor.org/stable/3092548.

Bacho, Peter. "The Tragic Sense of Filipino History." In *Filipino Americans: Transformation and Identity*, ed. Maria P.P. Root, 1–10. Thousand Oaks, CA: Sage Publications, Inc., 1997.

Bagley, Clarence B. *History of Seattle From the Earliest Settlement to the Present Time*, Vols 1–3. Chicago: The S.J. Clarke Publishing Company, 1916.

Bahr, Howard M. *Skid Row: An Introduction to Disaffiliation*. New York: Oxford University Press, 1973.

Barrows, Robert G. "Beyond the Tenement: Patterns of American Urban Housing, 1870–1930," Journal of Urban History, Vol. 9, No. 4 (August 1983): 195–420.

Baumohl, Jim ed. *Homelessness in America*. Phoenix: The Oryx Press, 1996.

Berner, Richard C. *Seattle 1900–1920: From Boomtown, Urban Turbulence, to Restoration*. Seattle: Charles Press, 1991.

_____. *Seattle 1921–1940: From Boom to Bust*. Seattle: Charles Press, 1992.

Bogardus, E.S., "Social Distance in the City," *Journal of Applied Sociology*. Vol. 22, July 1926, p. 40–46.

Borja-Mamaril, Concordia R. and Tyrone Lim. *Filipino Americans: Pioneers to the Present*. Portland, OR: Filipino American National Historical Society-Oregon Chapter, 2000.

Brewster, David and David M. Buerge. *Washingtonians: A Biographical Portrait of the State*. Seattle: Sasquatch books, 1988.

Broderick, Henry. *The "HB" Story*. Seattle: Frank McCaffrey Publishers, 1969.

Burgess, Ernest W. "The Growth of the City," *Publications of the American Sociological Society*, Vol. XVIII, p. 85–86.

_____. *The Urban Community: Selected Papers from the Proceedings of the American Sociological Society*. Chicago: The University of Chicago Press, 1926.

Burgess, Jacquelin. "Place-Making: The Contribution of Environmental Perception Studies in Planning," *Geography*, Vol. 64, No. 4 (November 1979), 317–326. http://www.jstor.org/page/info/about/policies/terms.jsp.

Burke, Edward and Elizabeth. *Seattle's Nippon Kan: The Discovery of Seattle's Other History*. Seattle: CreateSpace Self Publishing, 2011.

Burns, L. "Splendid Dancing: Filipino 'Exceptionalism' in Taxi Dance Halls," *Dance Research Journal*, 40(2), 23–40. http://search.ebscohost.com/login.aspx?direct=true&db=a9h&AN=34853599&site=ehost-live

Buruma, Ian. *Inventing Japan, 1853–1964*. New York: Modern Library, 2004.

Cacioppo, John T. and William Patrick. *Loneliness and Human Nature and the Need for Social Connection*. New York: WW Norton, 2009.

_____. "Race, Ethnic Culture, and Gender in the Construction of Identities among Second-Generation Chinese Americans, 1880s to 1930s." In *Claiming America: Constructing Chinese American Identities during the Exclusion Era*, eds. K. Scott Wong and Sucheng Chan, 127–164. Philadelphia: Temple University Press, 1998.

Chang, Iris. *The Chinese in America: A Narrative History*. New York: Penguin Group, 2004.

Chang, Kornel. *Pacific Connections: The Making of the US-Canadian Borderlands*. Berkeley: University of California Press, 2012.

Chappel, Edward A. "Vernacular Architecture and Public History," *Buildings & Landscapes: Journal of the Vernacular Architecture Forum*, Vol. 14 (Fall, 2007): 1–12. http://www.jstor.org/stable/20355393.

Chase, John. "The Role of Consumerism in American Architecture," *Journal of Architectural Education*, Vol. 44, No. 4 (August, 1991): 211–224. http://www.jstor.org/stable/1425143.

Chew, Ron & Cassie Chinn. *Reflections of Seattle's Chinese Americans: The First 100 Years*. Seattle: Wing Luke Asian Museum, 1992.

Chin, Doug. *Seattle's International District: The Making of a Pan-Asian American Community*. Seattle: International Examiner Press, 2001.

Choy, Philip P. "The Architecture of San Francisco Chinatown." In *Chinese America: History and Perspectives, 1990.*, 37–66. San Francisco: Chinese Historical Society of America, 1990

Chuman, Frank F. *The Bamboo People: The Law and Japanese-Americans*. Del Mar, CA: Publishers, Inc., 1976.

Cordova, Dorothy Laigo and the Filipino American National Historical Society. *Filipinos in Puget Sound*. San Francisco: Arcadia Publishing, 2009.

Cordova, Fred. *Filipinos: Forgotten Asian Americans*. Seattle: Demonstration Project for Asian Americans, 1983.

Cressey, Paul G. *The Taxi-Dance Hall: A Sociological Study in Commercialized Recreation and City Life*. Chicago: The University of Chicago Press, 1932.

Cresswell, Tim. *Place: A Short Introduction*. Oxford: Blackwell Publishing, 2004.

deBarros, Paul. *Jackson Street After Hours: The Roots of Jazz in Seattle*. Seattle: Sasquatch Books, 1993.

DeParle, Jason. "Build Single Room Occupancy Hotels," *Washington Monthly* (1 March 1994). http://www.thefreelibrary.com/_/print/PrintArticle.aspx-?id=14882984

Dobie, Charles Caldwell. *San Francisco: A Pageant*. New York: D. Appleton Century Company, Inc., 1934.

Dubrow, Gail Lee. ""The Nail that Sticks up Gets Hit:" The Architecture of Japanese American Identity in the Urban Environment, 1885–1942." In *Nikkei in the Pacific Northwest: Japanese Americans and Japanese Canadians in the Twentieth Century*, eds. Louis Fiset and Gail M. Nomura, 120–145. Seattle: University of Washington Press, 2005.

_____ and Donna Graves. *Sento on the Corner of Sixth and Main*. Seattle: Seattle Arts Commission, 2002.

Entrikin, J. Nicholas. "Democratic Place-Making and Multiculturalism," *Geografiska Annaler*. Series B, Human Geography, Vol. 84, No. 1 (2002): 19–25. http://www.jstor.org/stable/3554398.

Erickson, Jon and Charles Wilhelm, eds. *Housing the Homeless*. Rutgers: The State University of New Jersey, 1986.

Erickson, Rosemary and Kevin Eckert. "The Elderly Poor in Downtown San Diego Hotels." *The Gerontologist*, Vol. 17, No. 5 (October 1977): 440–447.

España-Maram, Linda. *Creating Masculinity in Los Angeles's Little Manila: Working-Class Filipinos and Popular Culture, 1920s–1950s*. New York: Columbia University Press, 2006.

Feuchtwang, Stephan. "Theorizing Place," In *Making Place: State Projects, Globalisation and Local Responses in China*. ed. Stephen Feuchtwang, 3–32. London: UCL Press, 2004.

Flewelling, Stan. *Shirakawa: Stories from a Pacific Northwest Japanese American Community*. Auburn, WA: White River Valley Museum, 2002.

Friday, Chris. *Organizing Asian American Labor: The Pacific Coast Canned-Salmon Industry, 1870–1942*. Philadelphia: Temple University Press, 1994.

Friedmann, John. "Place and Place-Making in Cities: A Global Perspective," *Planning Theory & Practice*, Vol. 11, No. 2, (June 2010): 149–165.

Fukei, Budd. *The Japanese American Story*. Minneapolis: Dillon Press, Inc., 1976.

Fugita, Stephen S. and David J. O'Brien. *Japanese American Ethnicity: The Persistence of Community*. Seattle: University of Washington Press, 1991.

Fujita-Rony, Dorothy. *American Workers, Colonial Power: Philippine Seattle and the Transpacific West, 1919–1941*. Berkeley: University of California Press, 2003.

Fulton, William. "A Room of One's Own," *Planning* (September 1985): 18–21.

Gallagher, Mary Lou. "A Small Room at the Inn," *Planning*, Vol. 59, Iss. 6 (June 1993): 20–26. http://proquest.umi.com/pqdweb?did=728392&sid=3&Fmt=3&clientID=19912&RQT=309&VName=PQD

Garvin, Alexander. *The American City: What Works, What Doesn't*. New York: McGraw Hill, 1996.

Gee How Oak Tin Association. *Gee How Oak Tin Association 90th Anniversary & Building Re-Inauguration Journal, 1900–1990*. Seattle: Gee How Oak Tin Association, 1991.

George, W.L., "What is a Home?" *Good Housekeeping*, April 1923.

Grant, Frederic James. *History of Seattle, Washington*. New York: American Publishing and Engraving Company Publishers, 1891.

Groth, Paul. "Generic Buildings and Cultural Landscapes as Sources of Urban History," *Journal of Architectural Education*, Vol. 41, No. 3, Urban History in the 1980s (Spring 1988): 41–44. http://links.jstor.org/sici?sici-1046-4883%28198821%2941%3A3%3C41%3AGBACLA%3E2.0.CO%3B2-V

_____. *Living Downtown: The History of Residential Hotels in the United States*. Berkeley: University of California Press, 1994.

_____. "Making New Connections in Vernacular Architecture," *Journal of the Society of Architectural Historians*, Vol. 58, No. 3, Architectural History 1999/2000 (September 1999) 444–451. http://www.jstor.org/stable/991538.

_____. "Marketplace Vernacular Design: The Case of Downtown Rooming Houses." In *Perspectives in Vernacular Architecture, II*, ed. Camille Wells, 179–191. Columbia, MO: University of Missouri Press, 1986.

Guevarra, Rudy P., Jr. "Skid Row: Filipinos, Race and the Social Construction of Space in San Diego," *The Journal of San Diego History*, Vol. 54, No 1 (Winter 2008): 26–38.

Habal, Estella. *San Francisco's International Hotel: Mobilizing the Filipino American Community in the Anti-Eviction Movement*. Philadelphia: Temple University Press, 2007.

Hamburger, Robert. *All the Lonely People: Life in a Single Room Occupancy Hotel*. New Haven and New York: Ticknor & Fields, 1983.

Hart, Joseph. *Down & Out: The Life and Death of Minneapolis's Skid Row*. Minneapolis: University of Minnesota press, 2002.

Hayden, Dolores. "The Meaning of Place in Art and Architecture," *Design Quarterly*, No. 122, (1983): 18–20. http://www.jstor.org/stable/4091078.

_____. *The Power of Place: Urban Landscapes as Public History*. Cambridge: MIT Press, 1996.

Hayner, Norman S. *Hotel Life*. College Park, MD: McGrath Publishing Company, 1969.

_____. "Hotel Life and Personality," *The American Journal of Sociology*, Vol. 33, No. 5 (March 1928): 783–792.

_____. "Hotel Life: Physical Proximity and Social Distance," In *Contributions to Urban Sociology*, eds. Ernest Burgess and Donald Bogue, 314–323. Chicago: the University of Chicago Press, 1974.

_____. "People Who Live in Hotels," *The Survey* (15 May 1928): 225–228.

_____. "Social Factors in Oriental Crime," *American Journal of Sociology* (May 1938): 908–919.

Hemmens, George C., Charles J. Hoch and Jana Carp, eds. *Under One Roof: Issues and Innovations in Shared Housing*. Albany: State University of New York Press, 1996.

Hertz, E. and O. Hutheesing. "At the Edge of Society: The Nominal Culture of Urban Hotel Isolates," *Urban Anthropology*, Vol. 4(4) (1975): 317–332.

Hildebrand, Grant. "John Graham, Sr." In *Shaping Seattle Architecture*, ed. Jeffrey Karl Ochsner, 90–95. Seattle: University of Washington Press, 1994.

Hildebrand, Lorraine Barker. *Straw Hats, Sandals and Steel: The Chinese in Washington State*. Tacoma: The Washington State American Revolution Bicentennial Commission, 1977.

Hoch, Charles and Robert Slayton. *New Homeless and Old: Community and the Skid Row Hotel*. Philadelphia: Temple University Press, 1989.

Hodgson, Barbara. *Opium*. London: Souvenir Press, 2000.

Hofer, E. "The Problems of Seattle," *Pacific Monthly*, Vol. 11 (Jan–Jun 1904): 114–117.

Hosakawa, William. *Nisei: The Quiet Americans*. New York: William Morrow and Company, 1969.

Huston, Peter. *Tongs, Gangs, and Triads: Chinese Crime Groups in North America*. Lincoln: NE: Authors Choice Press, 2001.

Ito, Kazuo. *Issei: A History of Japanese Immigrants in North America,* translated by Shinichiro Nakamura and Jean S. Gerard. Seattle: Executive Committee for publication of *Issei: A History of Japanese Immigrants in North America*, Japanese Community Service, 1973.

Joya, Mock. *Mock Joya's Things Japanese*. Tokyo: Tokyo News Service, Ltd., 1960.

Jue, Willard G. "Chin Gee Hee, Chinese Pioneer Entrepreneur in Seattle and Toishan." In *The Annals of the Chinese Historical Society of the Pacific Northwest,* 1983, ed. Edward H. Kaplan: 31–38, Bellingham, WA. Center for East Asian studies, Western Washington University, 1983.

_____ and Silas G. Jue. "Goon Dip: Entrepreneur, Diplomat, and Community Leader." In *The Annals of the Chinese Historical Society of the Pacific Northwest,* 1983, ed. Edward H. Kaplan: 40–50, Bellingham, WA. Center for East Asian studies, Western Washington University, 1984.

King, Patricia. "Help for the Homeless,"*Newsweek,* Vol. 111, Iss. 15, p. 58–59.

King, Peter. *Private Dwelling: Contemplating the Use of Housing*. London and New York: Routledge, 2004.

Kitano, Harry H.L. *Japanese Americans: The Evolution of a Subculture*. New Jersey: Prentice Hall, 1969.

Kiuchi, Atsushi and Dee Goto, eds. *Omoide IV: Childhood Memories*. Seattle: Nikkei Heritage Association of Washington Project, 2005.

_____. *Omoide V: Childhood Memories*. Seattle: Nikkei Heritage Association of Washington Project, 2009.

Kinnear, George. *Anti-Chinese Riots at Seattle, Washington, February 8th, 1886. Twenty-Fifth Anniversary of the Riots*. Seattle: Washington, 1911.

Klara, Robert. "Residential Hotels: Return of a Golden Oldie," *Architecture*, 94 (8) (Aug 2005), 27–28.

Klingle, Matthew. *Emerald City: An Environmental History of Seattle*. New Haven: Yale University Press, 2007.

Krafft, Katheryn Hills. "James Stephen." In *Shaping Seattle Architecture*, ed. Jeffrey Karl Ochsner: 58–63. Seattle: University of Washington Press, 1994.

Kurashige, Scott. *The Shifting Grounds of Race: Black and Japanese Americans in the Making of Multiethnic Los Angeles*. New Jersey: Princeton University Press, 2008.

Kyne, Peter B. "Our Maritime Bugaboo." In *The Saturday Evening Post*, Vol. 188, No. 13, 25 September 1915: 3–5, 34.

Lee, C.Y. *Days of the Tong Wars: California 1847–1896*. New York: Ballantine Books, 1974.

Lee, Douglas. "Sojouners, Immigrants, and Ethnics: The Saga of the Chinese in Seattle." In *The Annals of the Chinese Historical Society of the Pacific Northwest*, 1983, ed. Edward H. Kaplan: 40–50, Bellingham, WA. Center for East Asian studies, Western Washington University, 1984

Lee, Douglas W. "Sojourners, Immigrants and Ethnics: The Saga of the Chinese in Seattle," *Portage*, Vol. 2, #3 (Summer 1981): 12.

Lee, Shelley San-Hee, *Claiming the Oriental Gateway: Prewar Seattle and Japanese America*. Philadelphia: Temple University Press, 2010.

Lenhart, Harry A., Jr. ""Attacking Homelessness:" Portland's Strategy," *Journal of Housing*, Vol. 51, Iss. 3 (May/June 1994): 16–23.

Levy, Herbert, "Needed: A New Kind of Single Room Occupancy Housing," *Journal of Housing*, No. 11 (December 1968): 572–580.

Leong, Russell C. and Kyeyoung Park. "How Do Asian Americans Create Places?: From Background to Foreground." In *Amerasia Journal: How Do Asian Americans Create Places: Los Angeles and Beyond*, pp.vii–xiv, UCLA: Asian American Studies Center Press, vol. 34, no. 3, 2008.

Levy, Herbert. "Needed: A New Kind of Single Room Occupancy Housing," *Journal of Housing*, No 1 (Dec 1968): 573–580.

Levy, John. *Contemporary Urban Planning*. New Jersey: Pearson/Prentice Hall, 2009.

Lin, Jan. *The Power of Urban Ethnic Places: Cultural Heritage and Community Life*. New York: Routledge, 2011.

Little Tokyo Historical Society. *Los Angeles's Little Tokyo*. Charleston, SC: Arcadia Publishing, 2010.

Loewen, James W. *Sundown Towns: A Hidden Dimension of American Racism*. New York: Simon and Schuster, 2005.

Lyman, Stanford Morris. *Chinatown and Little Tokyo: Power, Conflict, and Community Among Chinese and Japanese Immigrants in America*. New York: Associated Faculty Press, Inc., 1986.

Ma, L. Eve Armentrout. "Chinatown Organizations and the Anti-Chinese Movement, 1882–1914." *In Entry Denied: Exclusion and the Chinese Community in America, 1882–1943*, ed. Sucheng Chan: 147–169. Philadelphia: Temple University Press, 1991.

Mabalon, Dawn Bohulano. *Little Manila is the Heart: The Making of the Filipina/o American Community in Stockton, California*. North Carolina: Duke University Press, 2013.

Melendy, H. Brett. "Filipinos in the United States." In *Asian Indians, Filipinos, Other Asian Communities and the Law*, ed. Charles McClain, Charles: 20–48. New York: Garland Publishing, Inc., 1994.

McClain, Charles J. and Laurene Wu McClain. "The Chinese Contribution to the Development of American Law." In *Entry Denied: Exclusion and the Chinese Community in America, 1882–1943*, ed. Sucheng Chan: 3–24. Philadelphia: Temple University Press, 1991.

McClain, Charles. *Japanese Immigrants and American Law: The Alien Land Laws and Other Issues*. New York: Garland Publishing, Inc., 1994.

Merrifield, Andy. "Lepers at the City Gate," *Dissent*, 48, #2 (Spring 2001): 78–84.

Milholland, Inez. "The Changing Home," *McClure's Magazine*, (March 1913).

Miyamoto, S. Frank. *Social Solidarity among the Japanese in Seattle*. Seattle: University of Washington Press, 1984.

Morgan, Murray. *Skid Road: An Informal Portrait of Seattle*. Seattle: University of Washington Press, 1982.

Nee, Victor G. and Brett de Bary. *Longtime Californ': A Documentary Study of an American Chinatown*. Stanford, CA: Stanford University Press, 1986.

Neiwert, David A. *Strawberry Days: How Internment Destroyed a Japanese American Community*. New York: Palgrave MacMillan, 2005.

Newell, Gordon and Don Sherwood. *Totem Tales of Old Seattle: The Town that Couldn't be Tamed*. New York: Ballantine Books, 1956.

"No Room for Singles: A Gap in the Housing Law," *The Yale Law Journal*, Vol. 80, No. 2, Dec (1970): 395–432.

Nicola, Patricia Hackett, "Day of the Dragon: The Chinese Community's Participation in the Alaska-Yukon-Pacific-Exposition," *Columbia*, 24, 2, (Summer 2010): p. 14–17.

Nippon Yusen Kaisha. *Golden Jubilee History of Nippon Yusen Kaisha, 1885–1935*. Tokyo: 1935.

Norberg-Schulz, Christian. "The Phenomenon of Place." In *The Urban Design Reader*, eds. Michael Larice and Elizabeth Macdonald: 125–137. New York: Routledge, 2007.

Pascual, Romel, "Pilipino Towns." In *Filipino American Architecture, Design, & Planning Issues*, ed. Anatalio C. Ubalde: 41–58. Flipside Press, 1986.

Pan, Lynn, ed. *The Encyclopedia of the Chinese Overseas*. Cambridge: Harvard University Press, 1999.

Peterson, William. *Japanese Americans*. New York: Random House, 1971.

Pfaelzer, Jean. *Driven Out: the Forgotten War Against Chinese Americans*. New York: Random House, 2007.

Pfiffner, Herbert A. *More than a Thousand Points of Light*. Seattle: Union Gospel Mission, 1992.

Putnam, Robert D. *Bowling Alone: The Collapse and Revival of American Community*. New York: Simon and Schuster, 2000.

Phelps, Myra L. *Public Works in Seattle: A Narrative History The Engineering Department, 1875–1975*. Seattle: Seattle Engineering Department, 1978.

Riesman, David. *The Lonely Crowd*. New Haven: Yale University Press, 2001.

Rollinson, Paul A. "Elderly Single Room Occupancy (SRO) Hotel Tenants: Still Alone," *Social Work*, 36, 4 (July 1991): 303–308.

Salyer, Lucy E. *Laws Harsh as Tigers: Chinese Immigrants and the Shaping of Modern Immigration Law*. Chapel Hill: University of North Carolina Press, 1995.

Sandmeyer, Elmer Clarence. *The Anti-Chinese Movement in California*. Chicago: University of Illinois Press, 1991.

Sandoval-Strausz, Andrew K. *Hotel: An American History*. New Haven: Yale University Press, 2008.

Sandweiss, Eric. "Building for Downtown Living: The Residential Architecture of San Francisco's Tenderloin," In *Perspectives in Vernacular Architecture*, eds. Thomas Carter and Bernard L. Herman, Vol. 3, 160–173. Columbia: University of Missouri Press, 1989.

Santos, Bob. *Humbows, Not Hot Dogs! Memoirs of a Savvy Asian American Activist*. Seattle: International Examiner Press, 2002.

Schmid, Calvin. *Social Trends in Seattle*. Seattle: University of Washington Press, 1944.

_____. "A Study of Homicides in Seattle, 1914–1924," *Social Forces*, Vol. 4, No. 4 (June 1926): 745–756. http://www.jstor.org/stable/3004456.

_____. "Suicides in Seattle, 1914–1925: An Ecological and Behaviorist Study," *University of Washington Publications in the Social Sciences*, Vol. 5, No. 1 (October 1928).

_____ and Maurice D. VanArsdol, Jr. "Completed and Attempted Suicides: A Comparative Analysis," *American Sociological Review*, Vol. 20, No. 3 (June 1955): 273–283. http://www.jstor.org/stable/2087385.

Schwartz, David C., Richard C. Ferlauto and Daniel N. Hoffman. *A New Housing Policy for America: Recapturing the American Dream*. Philadelphia: Temple University Press, 1988.

_____, Charles E. Nobbe, Arlene E. Mitchell. *Nonwhite Races: State of Washington*. Olympia: Washington State Planning and Community Affairs Agency, 1968.

"Seattle and the A-Y-P Exposition," *The Coast*, Vol. 18, No. 1 (July 1909): 50.

Shapiro, Joan. "Reciprocal Dependence Between Single-Room Occupancy Managers and Tenants," *Social Work* (July 1970): 67–73.

Shimabukuro, Robert Sadamu. *Born in Seattle: The Campaign for Japanese American Redress.* Seattle: University of Washington Press, 2001.

Sketches of Washingtonians. Seattle: Wellington C. Wells, 1907.

Soden, Dale E. *The Reverend Mark Matthews: An Activist in the Progressive Era.* Seattle: University of Washington Press, 2001.

Solenberger, Alice Willard. *One Thousand Homeless Men.* New York: Russell Sage Foundation, 1911.

Sone, Monica: *Nisei Daughter.* Seattle: University of Washington Press, 1979.

Squier, Gary. "SRO Housing," *Urban Land,* (January 1988): 10–13.

"The Status of Hotels under the Federal Housing and Rent Act," *The University of Chicago Law Review,* Vol. 16, No. 3 (Spring 1949): 554–567.

Stephens, Joyce. "Society of the Alone: Freedom, Privacy, and Utilitarianism as Dominant Norms in the SRO." *Journal of Gerontology,* Vol. 30, No. 2 (1975): 230–282.

Stutz, Frederick P. "Adjustment and Mobility of Elderly Poor Amid Downtown Renewal," *Geographical Review,* Vol. 66, No. 4 (October 1976): 391–400. http://links.jstor.org/sici?sici=0016-7428%28197610%2966?3A4%3C391%3AAAMOEP%E2.0.CO%3B2-5.

Takami, David. *Divided Destiny: A History of Japanese Americans in Seattle.* Seattle: Wing Luke Asian Museum, 1998.

_____. *Executive Order 9066: 50 Years Before and 50 Years After: A History of Japanese Americans in Seattle.* Seattle: Wing Luke Asian Museum, 1992.

Tchen, John Kuo Wei. *Genthe's Photographs of San Francisco's Old Chinatown: Photographs by Arnold Genthe.* New York: Dover Publications, 1984.

Teaford, Jon C. *The Twentieth-Century American City.* Baltimore: The Johns Hopkins University Press, 1993.

tenBroek, Jacobus, Edward N. Barnhart and Floyd W. Matson. *Prejudice, War and the Constitution: Causes and Consequences of the Evacuation of the Japanese Americans in World War II.* Berkeley: University of California Press, 1954.

Thomson, R.H. *That Man Thomson.* Seattle: University of Washington Press, 1950.

Tsutakawa, Mayumi and Alan Chong Lau. *Turning Shadows Into Light: Art and Culture of the Northwest's Early Asian/Pacific Community.* Seattle: Young Pine Press, 1982.

Tyler, Sydney. *San Francisco's Great Disaster: A Full Account of the Recent Terrible Destruction of Life and Property by Earthquake, Fire and Volcano.* Philadelphia: P.W. Ziegler Co., 1906.

Vellinga, Marcel. "The Inventiveness of Tradition: Vernacular Architecture and the Future," *Perspectives in Vernacular Architecture,* Vol. 13, No. 2, (2006/2007): 115–128. http://www.jstor.org/stable/20355388.

Wallace, Samuel E. *Skid Row as a Way of Life.* New Jersey: The Bedminster Press Incorporated, 1965.

Ward, David. *Cities and Immigrants: A Geography of Change in Nineteenth Century America.* New York: Oxford University Press, 1971.

Williams, Marilyn Thornton. *Washing "The Great Unwashed": Public Baths in Urban America, 1840–1920.* Columbus: Ohio State University Press, 1991.

Williamson, Jefferson. *The American Hotel: An Anecdotal History.* New York: Alfred A. Knopf, 1930.

Willis, John W. "The Federal Housing and Rent Act of 1947," *Columbia Law Review,* Vol. 47, No. 7, November 1947, 1118–1159.

"The Word Hotel, Its Use and Abuse," *Hotel Monthly,* Vol. 30, No 348 (March 1922).

Wong, Marie Rose. *Sweet Cakes, Long Journey: The Chinatowns of Portland, Oregon.* Seattle: University of Washington Press, 2004.

_____. "Teaching the Ghost Signs of Seattle," *Advertising and Public Memory,* Stephen Schutt, Sam Roberts, and Leanne White, eds. London and New York: Routledge Press, 2016.

Woolston, Howard B. *Prostitution in the United States. Vol. I: Prior to the Entrance of the United States into the World War.* New York: The Century Company, 1921.

"The Work of T. Paterson Ross and A.W. Burgren," *The Architect and Engineer of California Pacific Coast States,* Vol.XIII, No. 1 (May 1908): 35–46.

Yans-McLaughlin, Virginia. *Immigration Reconsidered: History, Sociology, and Politics.* New York: Oxford University Press, 1990.

Yip, Christopher L. "Association, Residence, and Shop: An Appropriation of Commercial Blocks in North American Chinatowns," *Perspectives in Vernacular Architecture,* Vol. 5, Gender, Class, and Shelter (1995): 109–117. http://links.jstor.org/sici?sici=0887-9885%281995%295%3C109%3AARASAA%3E2.0.CO%3B2-J

Zorbaugh, Harvey W. "Roomers," *The Survey,* Vol. LVI, #8 (15 July 1926): 461–463.

———. "The Dweller in Furnished Rooms: An Urban Type," *Proceedings of the American Sociological Society,* Vol. XXXII, #1, Part 2.

Interviews

Aburano, Sharon. Interview by author, 4 April 2007.

Akiyama, Tak. Interview by author, 17 July 2007.

Aoki, Shea Shizuko. Interview by author, 14 February 2008, 19 September 2008.

Arai, Jerry. Interview by author, 6 December 2010.

Baba, Janet. Interview by author, 9 June 2008.

Groves, Fumiko, Satoru Ichikawa, Yoshi Mamiya, Nobue Shimizu and Elmer Tazuma. Interview by author, 20 March 2009.

Chew, Ron. Interview by author, 28 March 2007.

Chew, Sen Poy. Interview by author, 27 August 2007.

Chin, Donnie. Interview by author, 14 August 2006, 16 August 2006

Chinn, Ray. Interview by author, 22 August 2006.

Chinn, Ray and Tomio Moriguchi. Interview by author, 24 August 2006.

Chinn, Tony, Art Wong, Doug Chin. Interview by author, 25 April 2007.

Choi, Gladys Goon. Interview by author, 7 January 2007.

Cordova, Dorothy and Fred Cordova. Interview by author, 18 June 2009.

Eng, Tuck. Interview by author, 11 May 2007.

Fujii, Minoru. Interview by author, 23 May 2007, 25 May 2007.

Gee How Oak Tin Association Members. Interview by author, 10 October 2006.

Goodwin, William. Interview by author, 27 July 2006, 23 August 2006. 2 February 2007,

Hashimoto, Roy and Eddy Sano. Interview by author, 15 March 2012.

Hori, Takashi and Lily Hori. Interview by author, 27 July 2006, 10 August 2006, 11 February 2009.

Huie, Richard. Interview by author, 10 February 2011.

Ike, Miyo. Interview by author, 3 August 2005, 11 August 2005.

Itoi, Henry. Interview by author, 4 April 2007.

Kay, Richard Lew. Interview by author, 17 September 2009.

Kazama, Sally. Interview by author, 18 July 2006.

Kuniyuki, Todd. Interview by author, 18 December 2009, 17 January 2010, 28 November 2010.

Lew, Lily and Mari Eng. Interview by author, 28 September 2007.

Louie, Show Wah. Interview by author, 23 March 2007.

Main Street Gang: Joseph U. Hamanaka, Roy Hashimoto, Eddy Sano. Interview by author, 18 July 2007 (with Tad Sato), 23 October 2008, 24 October 2008, 20 November 2008, 13 December 2009, 1 January 2010, 12 February 2010, 19 February 2010, 5 May 2010, 7 July 2010, 31 July 2010, 4 March 2011, 25 March 2011, 13 May 2011, 27 May 2011, 23 September 2011.

Mamiya, Yoshiko. Interview by author, 23 October 2008.

Mar, Barry. Interview by author, 19 April 2007.

Mar, James. Interview by author, 3 October 2006, 10 November 2006.

Mar, Paul. Interview by author, 18 August 2006.

Matsudaira, Martin. Interview by author, 29 July 2008.

Miyamoto, Frank. Interview by author, 19 June 2007.

Murakami, Kazuo (Gus) and Michi. Interview by author, 27 November 2006.

Murakami, Paul. Interview by author, 27 September 2006.

Nobuyama, Shizukoi. Interview by author, 6 November 2006.

Okada, Tyrus H. Interview by author, 28 September 2010.

Onishi, Martha. Interview by author, 30 March 2007.

Osias, Don. Interview by author, 3 November 2007, 17 June 2012.

Peng, Jack. Interview by author, 16 June 2011.

Santos, Bob. Interview by author, 10 February 2005, 21 April 2005, 22 February 2007.

Sasaki, May. Interview by author, 21 June 2007, 11 July 2007.

Sibonga, Delores. Interview by author, 26 July 2006.

Taniguchi, Taeko and Don Taniguchi. Interview by author, 25 October 2006.

Tokita, Shokichi, Yuzo Tokita, Yoshiko Tokita Schroder. Interview by author, 3 August 2007, 28 November 2010, 27 June 2011.

Uno, Shikego. Interview by author, 2 July 2006.

Wah, Raymond, Albert Lee, Tony Chinn, Ed Wong. Interview by author, 22 July 2007, 27 July 2007.

Wong, Art, Ray Soo Young, Doug Chin. Interview by author, 11 April 2007.

Wong, Dean. Interview by author, 17 August 2006.

Wong, Homer. Interview by author, 31 August 2007.

Woo, Jack and Beverly. Interview by author, 12 October 2008.

Yoshida, Don. Interview by author, 30 August 2007.

Manuscripts and Public Documents

Advisory Committee on Social Security to Board of County Commissioners. Single Homeless Men on Relief. King County, Washington, November 1937.

Articles of Incorporation, State of Washington, 1906, 1907, 1910, 1911, 1915, 1916, 1927. Washington State Archives, Puget Sound Regional Branch.

Chinese Exclusion Case Files. Seattle, Washington, District Office. Records of Immigration and Naturalization Service. RG 85. RS 399, RS 1609, RS 1672. National Archives, Pacific Alaska Region, Seattle.

Chong Wa Benevolent Association Directory. Seattle, WA. 1936.

City of Seattle. Department of Community Development. *Downtown Population and Housing Data*, June 1980.

_____. Department of Community Development. *Low and Moderate Income Housing in Downtown Seattle*, August 1973.

_____. Department of Planning and Development (DPD). Microfilm Library, Permit History Cards and Plans.

_____. Department of Planning and Development (DPD). Side Sewer Cards.

_____. Downtown Human Services Council. *Needs Assessment of Downtown Seattle Residents and Hotel/Apartment House Managers*, 17 December 1980.

_____. Seattle Housing Authority. *First SHA Annual Report*, 1941.

_____. Seattle Municipal Archives. Council Bills and City Ordinances, 1887–1975.

_____. Seattle Municipal Archives. Clerk/Comptroller Files, 1890–1990.

_____. Seattle Municipal Archives. *Department Efficiency Testimony*, Office of the City Clerk, Vol. I, II, Exhibits, 1802-B5, July 1935.

_____. "Yesler Terrace," Seattle Housing Authority Annual Report, 1941.

Commemorative Booklet of the Seattle Japanese Language School, Post WWII "Home" Reunion. *Remembering "Tip" School*. 26 October 1997.

Cordova, Fred Dr. and the Filipino American National Historical Society. *Historic Pinoytown Walking Tour Guide*, Seattle 1916/35–75.

District Design Group. *The International District, Seattle: An Action Program for Physical Development*, 1973.

Fujii, Yoshito. *Study of the Early Japanese Immigrants of the Seattle Area: Their Organizations and Businesses, 1890–1930*, ca. 1930.

Howell, I.M. *Session Laws of the State of Washington, Thirteenth Session*, 13 January–13 March 1913.

King County Real Property Assessments and Tax Rolls, 1892, 1900, 1905, 1910, 1915, 1920, 1925, 1930, 1935, 1940, 1945. Washington State Archives, Puget Sound Regional Branch.

King County Superior Court, Report of the Grand Jury, James Murphy vs. City of Seattle, November 1911.

Lawyers for Housing, *Skid Road Housing Study*, 1972.

Matsudaira, Martin, ed. *Memoirs of Theresa Hotoru Matsudaira, 1902–1996*. Seattle: M. Matsudaira, 2006. Translated: Yuka Matsudaira.

National Coalition for the Homeless. *McKinney-Vento Act, NCH Fact Sheet #18*, June 2006.

Neighborhood Planning Office. *Chinatown/International District Strategic Plan*. City of Seattle, 15 June 1998.

Pascua, Reynaldo Jr. *Rural Asian Americans—An Assessment*. A Report of the Yakima Valley Asian American Task Force. Olympia, WA: State of Washington Commission on Asian American Affairs, July 1976.

Peterson, Kay and James Katzenberger, *The Changing Hotel Patterns in Seattle, 1960–73*, 14 March 1973.

Photograph Collection. Buddhist Temple Archives, Seattle.

Rollins, C.H. "Work of the Seattle & Lake Washington Waterway Company," Pacific Northwest Society of Engineers, Proceedings, Vol. III, No 1.

Schmid, Calvin F., Charles E. Nobbe and Arlene E. Mitchell. *Nonwhite Races State of Washington*. Olympia, WA: Washington State Planning and Community Affairs Agency, 1968.

Seattle Chinatown Historic District. National Register of Historic Places Inventory Nomination Form, 1979; 1982–83. Department of Community Development, City of Seattle.

Seattle Japanese Hotel & Apartment Association Member's List, various years.

Skid Road Community Council. *Changes in Downtown Seattle, 1960–1974*.

_____. *Housing in Downtown Seattle, A Compilation of Original Research*.

Strong, Sydney, Chairman. *Report of the Committee on Orientals*. Seattle: Seattle Ministerial Federation, 4 June 1917.

Superior Court of King County, Washington. Case No. 75162, 4 August 1910, King County Court Records, Seattle.

_____. Cause No. 50960, 9 April 1906, King County Court Records, Seattle.

_____. Civil Case 50960, Condemnation for Jackson Regrade, 11 November 1905. King County Court Records, Seattle.

Tokita, Kamekichi. *Conflict of Loyalties: A Personal Memoir of Life and Internment During World War II*. Seattle: The Tokita Family, 2005.

Tokita, Shokichi & Elsie Yukiko Tokita. *A Biographic Resume and Artistic History of Kamekichi Tokita, July 16, 1897 – October 7, 1948*. December 25, 1992.

US Department of Commerce, Bureau of the Census, *Volume I: Population, Fifteenth Census, 1930*. Table 2: Color, Nativity, and Sex for the State, Urban and Rural.

_____. Bureau of the Census, *Volume II: Characteristics of the Population, Sixteenth Census of the United States, 1940*. Table A-37: Potential Voting Population by Citizenship, Race, Nativity and Sex for the City of Seattle: 1940 and 1930.

_____. Bureau of the Census, *Volume I: Census of Population, Seventeenth Decennial Census of the US, 1950*. Table 14: Race by Sex, for the State, Urban and Rural.

_____. Bureau of the Census, *1970 Census of Population*. Table 17: Race by Sex. Table 23: Race by Sex for Areas and Places.

_____. Census Office, *Report of Vital and Social Statistics in the United States, Eleventh Census, 1890*. Table III: Population of Civil Divisions Less than Counties, Territory of Washington. Table 14: Chinese, Japanese, and Civilized Indian Population, By States and Territories: 1860–1890. Table 16: Chinese Population, By Counties: 1870 to 1890. Table 19: Population by Sex, General Nativity, and Color of Places Having 2,500 Inhabitants or More.

_____. Census Office, *Population—Part I, Twelfth Census, 1900*. Table 17: Population, Race by Sex. Table 23: Population by Sex, General Nativity, and color for Places Having 2,500 Inhabitants or More.

US Congress. House of Representatives. Japanese Immigration. *Hearings before the Committee on Immigration and Naturalization*. 66th Cong., 1st sess., 12–14, 18–20 June and 25 Sept 1919.

_____. Japanese Immigration. *Hearings before the Committee on Immigration and Naturalization*. 66th Cong., 2nd sess., Part 1, 12–14 July 1920.

_____. Japanese Immigration. *Hearings before the Committee on Immigration and Naturalization*. 66th Cong., 2nd sess., Part 3, 19–21 July, 1920.

US Department of Housing and Urban Development. Section 441 of the McKinney-Vento Homeless Assistance Act (42 U.S.C. 11401) Regulations at 24CFR, Part 882, Subpart H. http://portal.hud.gov/hudportal/HUD?src=/program_offices/comm_planning/homeless/programs/sro.

_____. Stuart B. McKinney Homeless Programs. http://www.huduser.org/publications/homeless/mckin/sro.html.

_____. *A Study of the Problems of Abandoned Housing*. November 1971.

_____. *Methods of Urban Impact Analysis: HUD's Section 312 Program*. September 1978.

_____. Office of Community Planning and Development. *Housing Homeless Individuals Through HUD's Section 8 Moderate Rehabilitation Single Room Occupancy (SRO) Program*, March 2001.

US Department of the Interior. Census Office, *Statistics of the Population of the United States, Tenth Census, 1880*. Table XIX: Sex of the Colored, Chinese and Japanese, and Civilized Indian Population, with General Nativity.

US Senate. Report to the Chairman, Subcommittee on Housing and Urban Affairs, Committee on Banking, Housing and Urban Affairs. *Homelessness: McKinney Act Programs provide Assistance but are Note Designed to be the Solution*, May 1994.

US Supreme Court. Takuji Yamashita v. Hinkle, 260 U.S. 199 (1922).

University of Washington, Special Collections, Williard Jue Papers, 1880–1905, Accession 5191-001, Boxes 1, 2, 3.

Women's Social Hygiene Department of the Washington State Board of Health. *Survey of Seattle and Bremerton District,* 1 April 1919.

Maps

Baist's Real Estate Atlas of Survey of Seattle, Washington. Philadelphia: G.Wm. Baist, 1912.

Kroll Atlas of Seattle, 1920. Seattle, Washington: Kroll Map Company.

Sanborn Fire Insurance Company. Sanborn Maps: 1884, 1888, 1893, 1901, 1904, 1916.

Microfilm and Microfiche

1879 King County Census (filed May 5, 1879). Washington Territorial Census Rolls. Olympia, Washington State Archives, reel 4.

1880 King County Census. Washington Territorial Census Rolls. Olympia, Washington State Archives, reel 4.

1881 King County Census. Washington Territorial Census Rolls. Olympia, Washington State Archives, reel 4.

1887 King County Census. Washington Territorial Census Rolls. Olympia, Washington State Archives, reel 5.

King County Assessor Data, 1951. N-S Freeway (James to Plummer), Microfiche 2615.02, 2/1613, #1 and #2.

Newspapers and Magazines

Argus (Seattle), 1900–1936.

Bellingham Herald, 1905–1920.

Cosmopolitan Courier, 1936.

Cosmopolitan Weekly, 1937.

Daily Pacific Tribune (Seattle), 1877.

International Examiner, 1974–2010.

The New York Times, 1994.

North American Post (also published under *The North American Times*, 1902–1942), 1946–2010.

Northwest Asian Weekly, 1987–2007.

Olympia Record, 1920.

Oregonian, 1908–1911.

Patriarch, 1910.

Philippine Advocate, 1935.

The Philippine American Advocate, 1935.

The Philippine-American Chronicle, 1934–36.

The Philippine Monthly, 1934.

The Philippine Review, 1931.

Seattle Mail & Herald, 1902–1906.

The Seattle Star, 1919–1943.

Seattle Times (under various titles including *Seattle Daily Times, The Seattle Daily Times, The Seattle Times, Seattle Sunday Times, The Seattle Sunday Times, Seattle Times Seattle Post Intelligencer*), 1889–2008.

Seattle Post-Intelligencer (under various titles including *Seattle Gazette, Post-Intelligencer, Seattle Times Seattle Post-Intelligencer, Post Intelligencer, Weekly Intelligencer*), 1863–2009

Reference Works

Avakian, Monique. *Atlas of Asian-American History*. New York: Checkmark Books, 2002.

Choir's Pioneer Directory of the City of Seattle and King County. Pottsville, PA: Miners' Journal Book and Job Rooms, 1878, 23.

The Electronic Encyclopedia of Chicago, *Encyclopedia of Chicago* (Chicago History Society, 2005). Slayton, Robert A. Single Room Occupancy Hotels, 2005. http://www.encyclopedia.chicagohistory.org/pages/613.html

Niiya, Brian, ed. *Encyclopedia of Japanese American History: An A-to-Z Reference from 1868 to the Present*. New York: Facts on File, Inc., 2001.

Hanford, C.H., ed. *Seattle and Environs, 1852–1924*. Chicago and Seattle: Pioneer Historical Publishing Company, 1924, 164–167.

Seattle City Directory, Vols. 1889–1976. Seattle: R.L. Polk.

Ward, Kirk C. *Business Directory of Seattle for the Year 1876*. Seattle: B.L. Northup, Printer, 1876.

Unpublished Papers

Hamanaka, Joseph U. *Two Flags Over Main Street*. Self-published Newsletter, various years.

Lange, Greg. *Chinese Population in Seattle*. Seattle, 2010.

Websites

Crowley, Walt, "Seattle Neighborhoods: Chinatown-International District-Thumbnail History," HistoryLink. http://www.historylink.org/essays/output.cfm?-file_id=1058.

CIDBIA, "Celebrating the Diverse Cultures of Asia." http://internationaldistrict.org/history.asp

Dollar Steamship Line Travel Brochures, Historical Documents Archives. https://www.gjenvick.com/SteamshipLines/DollarSteamshipLine/index.html.

Federal Government Aid for the Homeless—The McKinney-Vento Homeless Assistance Act. http://www.libraryindex.com/pages/2307/Federal-Government-Aid-Homeless-McKinney-Vento-homelessassistance-act.htm

Gregory, James N., Director. Seattle Civil Rights and Labor History Project. http://www.civilrights.washington.edu

Housing and Urban Development, "Stuart B. McKinney Homeless Programs." http://www.huduser.org/publications/homeless/mckin/sro.html.

Pierce, J. Kingston, "Panic of 1893: Seattle's First Great Depression" HistoryLink.org Essay 2030, 24 November 1999. http://www.historylink.org/index.cfm?DisplayPage=output.cfm&File_ID=2030.

INDEX

COLOPHON

This book was designed in Seattle, Washington during the winter of 2018 by Dan D Shafer, assisted by Kyle Leitch. Text is set in Sentinal and Trade Gothic, with headings in Rubic Mono One. Images are reproduced as duotones using Pantones 484 and 447. Printed and bound in Michigan by McNaughton & Gunn.

CPSIA information can be obtained
at www.ICGtesting.com
Printed in the USA
BVHW061652291219
568007BV00001B/1/P

9 781634 059671